BIRTHDAY SCRIPTURES

BY TRINA ANGELES

Published by Winn Publications
Texas, United States • www.winnpublications.com

This devotional book is intended to inspire readers through prayer and Scripture. It is not intended to replace personal, pastoral, or spiritual counseling where needed. Readers are encouraged to seek support from trained professionals if necessary.

Book Title: Birthday Scriptures

Author: Trina Angeles
Paperback ISBN: 979-8-9926780-2-4
Hardcover ISBN: 979-8-9926780-0-0

Formatted and published by Winn Publications, Texas

Printed in the United States of America

PREFACE

Has there ever been a defining moment in your life? A wake-up call that changed you forever? I've had a few and I chalk them all up to God's provision over my life. In 2023, I spoke to a small crowd in my hometown of Pittsburg, California. This was only my second time speaking at a church. Pastor Kim, the woman that I opened for, came and spoke a word of prophecy over me. That encouraging word is why this book is in your hands. It gave me that push, that extra confidence that God was asking me to write a book. I stepped forward and started my writing. I pray these birthday Scriptures and prayers spoken over you give you that same encouragement that the pastor and the Lord gave me. I pray it leads you to a sense of boldness to achieve what's next in your life. Search for the truth about yourself and it will set you free in life!

FOREWORD BY THE AUTHOR

As you begin this journey through these pages, I want to share something close to my heart. Traditionally, books often include a foreword written by someone who lends credibility or reflects on the author's work. But for this, my first book, I felt led to do things a little differently.

This book is rooted deeply in God's Word and His guidance in my life. My greatest source of credibility come not from a well-known individual, but from the Lord Himself. It is His Scripture, His truth, and His Spirit that have inspired every word you'll read here. My prayer is that this book will glorify Him and point you closer to the One who holds all wisdom and authority.

I humbly offer this work as a reflection of my journey with Him, trusting that His word is enough to give it the foundation it needs. Thank you for walking this road with me.

With gratitude,

Trina

INTRODUCTION
YOU BELONG TO HIS KINGDOM

There's an urgency in me to share God's sword with you. To share the love of Jesus in a practical way. I'm confident that these Scriptures are going to renew your mind. Replace old thoughts with new ones.

In this book you will find Scripture that matches the day you were born. Scripture is your weapon! Say it out loud! Yell it if you want. Own it! It was made for you! Memorize it, so you can call it out when in joy and in trouble. Jesus calls Scripture our sword. It must be used to not only define yourself but also defend yourself against the enemy. Memorize the Scripture!

It's easy when it's actually your own birthday or the birthday of a family member or loved one. Memorizing Scripture reminds you of what is true about God and His character.

His Word is our sword to fight with, this book is a compilation of different versions of the Bible. Some verses are taken from KJV, NKJV, NIV, NLT and many other versions. Red letter type is used to signify the words of Jesus Christ.

I encourage you to know the Scripture in and out so that you're able to speak it boldly when needed. Store it in your heart! Write it down! Hold on to it as though your life depends on it.

When reading your "I am" at the top of your birthday, take ownership of it! God wants a relationship with you despite anything you have ever done. His kindness leads us to our repentance. In the prayers of your Scripture find treasure! Read and see what can be cast off and what can be declared! Determine your core values through Scripture! Jesus did not come to condemn but to save! God's mercy triumphs over judgment. Ask the Holy Spirit to speak to you as you read these Scriptures. God is looking to heal the broken places of your heart and give you mercy and restoration.

May this book of compiled wisdom of the Scripture and prayers bring you peace and encouragement.

INSTRUCTIONS

- Start with your birthday. For example, if your birthday is March 23 memorize the Scriptures that are for that specific date. Speak them out loud! Own them, as if God placed them on your birthday to speak directly to you!

- Then, pick a loved one and memorize the Scripture for their birthday and share it with them so they, too, can have the Word of God in their heart.

- Share on birthday cards. Share in times of trouble, share it when you've just had victory, keep it in your heart. At the end of each day is a prayer. This prayer includes a name of God (its translation is in Hebrew or Greek). Use the name to call on God in a unique and special way.

JANUARY 1

Genesis 1:1 (ESV) : In the beginning, God created the heavens and the earth.

Psalm 1:1 (ESV): Blessed is the man who walks not in the counsel of the wicked, nor stands in the way of sinners, nor sits in the seat of scoffers.

John 1:1 (ESV): In the beginning was the Word, and the Word was with God. and the Word was God.

Ezekiel 1:1 (ESV): . . . the heavens were opened, and I saw visions of God.

Jude 1:1 (ESV): . . . To those who have been called, beloved in God the Father and kept for Jesus Christ.

–––––––––––––––––––––––– **PRAYER** ––––––––––––––––––––––––

Dear Heavenly Father, Logos (The Word),

I come before You with a heart full of reverence and awe. In Genesis 1:1, I am reminded of the unity and determination of humanity, yet also the dangers of pride. Help me to seek unity in Your name and for Your glory, not my own. Lord, Your throne is in heaven, as Psalm 1:1 declares, and Your eyes see all. You test the righteous and the wicked, and my desire is to be found righteous in Your sight. Strengthen my heart to trust in Your justice and love, especially when I see evil around me. As it is written in John 1:1, "In the beginning was the Word, and the Word was with God, and the Word was God." I thank You for the eternal presence of Your Word and its power in my life. Lord, help me to embrace Your Word with faith and reverence. May it shine on paths, guide my decisions, and fill my heart with Your truth and love. I ask for Your wisdom and understanding as I study and meditate on Your Word, that I may grow closer to You each day. In Ezekiel 1:1, just as You opened the heavens and revealed visions to Ezekiel by the river, I ask that You let the heavens be opened over my life and let me see visions as well. Grant me the wisdom to understand Your messages and the courage to act upon them. Thank You, Lord, for Your constant presence and the revelations. Finally, as Jude 1:1 warns me against the path of those who rebel against You, may I remain vigilant and steadfast in my faith. Keep me from falling into the enemies traps but instead guide me by Your truth and Spirit. I thank You, Yahweh for Your guidance, mercy, and love. Let my life reflect Your glory and honor.

In Jesus' name I pray, Amen

JANUARY 2

John 1:2 (ESV): He was in the beginning with God.

James 1:2 (ESV): Count it all joy, my brothers [and sisters], when you meet trials of various kinds.

Psalm 1:2 (ESV): But his delight is in the law of the LORD, and on His law he meditates day and night.

1 Peter 1:2 (ESV): . . . for obedience to Jesus Christ and for sprinkling with his blood: may grace and peace be multiplied to you.

PRAYER

Dear Lord, Elohim (Mighty Creator),

As You teach me in John 1:2, help me to follow Your example of humility and service. I'm willing to lay down my life for others, just as You laid down Your life for me. May I always seek to glorify Your name. In James 1:2, I am reminded that blessed is the one who perseveres under trial because, having stood the test, I will receive the crown of life that the Lord has promised to those who love Him. Father, give me the strength to endure challenges and remain steadfast in my faith, knowing that You have great rewards for those who remain faithful. From Psalm 1:2, I hear the cry for Your protection against deceitful and harmful words. Lord, guard my heart and mind from the lies of the enemy. Let Your truth be my shield. Purify my speech and make me an instrument of Your peace and righteousness in this world. As I read 1 Peter 1:2, I thank You for the privilege of understanding the gospel, for the blood of Your Son, Jesus, that multiplies grace and peace over my life. Fill me with Your Spirit, that I may walk in holiness and love, reflecting Your glory in all I do.

I lift up this prayer in the name of Jesus Christ, my Lord and Savior, Amen.

John 1:3 (ESV): All things were made through him, and without him was not any thing made that was made.

Psalm 1:3 (ESV): He is like a tree planted by streams of water that yields its fruit in its season, and its leaf does not wither. In all that he does, he prospers.

Philippians 1:3 (ESV): I thank my God in all my remembrance of you.

Ephesians 1:3 (ESV): . . . who has blessed us in Christ with every spiritual blessing in the heavenly places.

PRAYER

Lord hear my prayer, El Kanna (Jealous God),

I come before You with a grateful heart, reflecting on Your Word and its profound truths. John 1:3 says, "Through Him all things were made; without Him nothing was made that has been made" (NIV). Lord, I acknowledge that You are the Creator of all things. Every part of my life and the world around me is crafted by Your hand. I thank You for Your creation and for giving life and purpose to everything. In Psalm 1:3, Your Word tells me that those who delight in Your law "are like a tree planted by streams of water, which yields its fruit in season and whose leaf does not wither"—whatever I do prospers. Father, I pray that I may be like this tree, deeply rooted in Your love and fed by Your Spirit. Help me to stay steadfast in Your Word and to bear fruit in my life that brings glory to Your name. Philippians 1:3 expresses gratitude and joy: "I thank my God every time I remember you." Lord, I am thankful for the people You have placed in my life, for my family, friends, and community. Each one is a precious gift from You. May I always remember them with thankfulness and lift them up in prayer, staying steadfast in the fellowship we share in Christ. And as Ephesians 1:3 declares, "Praise be to the God and Father of our Lord Jesus Christ, who has blessed us in the heavenly realms with every spiritual blessing in Christ" (NIV). Lord, I praise You for the countless blessings You have showered upon me. You have blessed me with every spiritual blessing through Christ, and I am eternally grateful. Help me to live in the fullness of these blessings, walking in Your ways and shining Your light to those around me.

In Jesus' blessed name I pray, Amen

JANUARY 4

Genesis 1:4 (ESV): And God saw that the light was good. And God separated the light from the darkness.

James 1:4 (NIV): Let perseverance finish its work so that you may be mature and complete, not lacking anything.

Ephesians 1:4 (ESV): For he chose us in him before the foundation of the world, to be holy and blameless in his presence.

--- **PRAYER** ---

Dear Heavenly Father, Yahweh Yireh (The LORD Who Provides),

In Genesis 1:4, You saw the light, and it was good. Lord, shine Your light on my path, guiding me through the challenges of this world. You separated light from darkness so make darkness light before me. I turn to James 1:4 and pray that You help me persevere in faith, so that I may be mature and complete, lacking nothing. Let patience have its perfect work within me, refining me through every trial and tribulation, so that I may grow stronger in my trust and reliance on You. I thank You for choosing me before the foundation of the world, to be holy and blameless in Your sight, as Ephesians 1:4 teaches us. Help me to walk in this truth daily, knowing that I am loved and called according to Your purpose. May Your light, patience, and calling be ever present in my life, shaping me into the person You have created me to be.

In the mighty name of Christ Jesus I pray these Scriptures over my life, Amen

JANUARY 5

James 1:5 (ESV): If any of you lacks wisdom, let him ask God, who gives generously to all without reproach, and it will be given to him.

Habakkuk 1:5 (BSB): Look at the nations and observe, be utterly astounded! For I am doing a work in your days that you would never believe even if someone told you.

Joshua 1:5 (ESV): I will not leave you, nor forsake you.

―――――――――――――― PRAYER ――――――――――――――

Abba Father,

I come before You with a heart seeking Your wisdom and guidance. Your Word tells me in James 1:5 that if anyone lacks wisdom, they should ask You, who gives generously to all without finding fault, and it will be given to them. Lord, I ask for Your wisdom now. Fill my mind with clarity and understanding, that I may walk in the path You have set before me. I also hold on to the promise in Habakkuk 1:5, where You declare that You are doing something in my days that I would not believe, even if I were told. Help me to trust in Your plans, even when I do not fully comprehend them. Open my eyes to see Your wonders and to recognize the miraculous work You are doing in my life. And as You assured Joshua in Joshua 1:5 that no one would be able to stand against him all the days of his life, and that You would be with him as You were with Moses, not leaving him nor forsaking him, I pray for the same assurance in my life. Lord, let me be confident in Your presence with me. Strengthen me with the knowledge that You are always by my side, guiding, protecting, and leading me. I trust in Your wisdom, Your plans, and Your unfailing presence. Help me to live out my days in faith, knowing that You are with me every step of the way.

In Jesus' seeking name I pray, Amen

Proverbs 1:6 (KJV): To understand a proverb, and the interpretation; the words of the wise, and their dark sayings.

Philippians 1:6 (NIV): Being confident of this, that he who began a good work in you will carry it on to completion until the day of Christ Jesus.

James 1:6 (NIV): But when you ask, you must believe and not doubt, because then, one who doubts is like a wave of the sea, blown and tossed by the wind.

1 Peter 1:6 (TLB): So be truly glad! There is wonderful joy ahead . . .

Romans 1:6 (ESV): . . . you who are called to belong to Jesus Christ.

PRAYER

Heavenly Father, Atik Yomin (Ancient of Days),

I come before You today, seeking Your wisdom, strength, and guidance. Your Word tells me that the fear of the Lord is the beginning of knowledge, and that wisdom will guard and protect me. As I meditate on Proverbs 1:6, help me to discern the meaning of parables and the sayings of the wise, so that I may walk in understanding and apply Your truths in my life. Lord, I am confident in the work You have begun in me, as Philippians 1:6 reminds me that You, who began a good work in me, will carry it on to completion until the day of Christ Jesus. I trust that You are shaping me according to Your purpose, and I surrender myself to Your will. When doubts and fears arise, I remember James 1:6, which urges me to ask in faith without doubting. Let my faith be steadfast and unwavering, that I may receive Your wisdom and peace, trusting fully in Your provision and care. Even in trials, as 1 Peter 1:6 speaks of, I rejoice, knowing that these challenges are refining my faith like gold in the fire. Help me to embrace every moment, understanding that the testing of my faith produces perseverance, and that perseverance must finish its work so that I may be mature and complete, lacking nothing. Finally, Lord, I stand firm in the truth of Romans 1:6, knowing that I am called to belong to Jesus Christ. I am grateful to be counted among the saints, set apart for Your glory. Let my life reflect Your love and grace, and may I always be a beacon of Your light in this world.

In Jesus' complete name I pray, Amen.

JANUARY 7

2 Timothy 1:7 (NKJV): For God has not given us a spirit of fear, but of power and of love and of a sound mind.

Nahum 1:7 (CSB): The LORD is good, a stronghold in a day of distress; he cares for those who take refuge in him.

1 John 1:7 (ESV): Walk in the light, as he is in the light.

Ephesians 1:7 (NIV): In him, we have redemption through his blood, the forgiveness of sins, in accordance with the riches of God's grace.

Hebrews 1:7 (ESV): Of the angels he says, "He makes his angels winds, and his ministers a flame of fire."

PRAYER

Dear Heavenly Father, Jehovah Shalom (The LORD Is Peace),

Thank You for Your presence and unwavering love in my life. I am comforted by the words of 2 Timothy 1:7, knowing that You have not given me a spirit of fear, but of power, love, and a sound mind. When I feel uncertain or afraid, remind me of the strength You have placed within me. Lord, I take refuge in You, for You are good, a stronghold in times of trouble, and You know those who trust in You, as it is written in Nahum 1:7. Help me to lean on You and trust in Your goodness, no matter the circumstances. As I walk in the light, just as You are in the light, I thank You for the fellowship I have with others and the cleansing power of the blood of Jesus, as declared in 1 John 1:7. May Your light guide my steps and purify my heart. I rejoice in the redemption I have through Your blood, the forgiveness of sins, in accordance with the riches of Your grace, as stated in Ephesians 1:7. Let this grace be my constant reminder of Your love and mercy, drawing me closer to You. And, Father, I lift my praise to You, acknowledging the words of Hebrews 1:7, where You make Your angels spirits and Your ministers flames of fire. May Your Spirit fill me with holy fire, igniting my heart to serve You with passion.

In the holy name of Jesus I pray, Amen

JANUARY 8

I have power in the Holy Spirit

Joshua 1:8 (ESV): This book of the law must not depart from your mouth; meditate on it day and night, so that you may be careful to do everything written in it. For then, you will prosper and succeed in all you do.

Acts 1:8 (ESV): But you will receive power when the Holy Spirit has come upon you.

Hebrews 1:8 (ESV): The scepter of uprightness is the scepter of your kingdom.

1 Peter 1:8 (ESV): Whom having not seen you love. Though now you do not see Him, yet believing, you rejoice with joy inexpressible and full of glory.

1 John 1:8 (ESV): If we say that we have no sin, we deceive ourselves, and the truth is not in us.

 **PRAYER**

Heavenly Father, Shub Nephesh (Renewer of Life),

I come before You with a heart full of gratitude and reverence. Your Word is my guide, my strength, and my source of life. As in Joshua 1:8, help me to speak of God's laws always. Never letting the laws leave my mouth, day or night. I will not only speak them but will make them my actions. For then You will make my way prosperous, and then I will have good success. Empower me, Lord, as Your Spirit did the apostles in Acts 1:8. Holy Spirit, lead me in all areas of my life. As Your Word declares in Hebrews 1:8, I acknowledge that Your Son, Jesus Christ, reigns forever and ever. Lord, show me your justice is steady and unshakeable. Help me to trust that You are in control even when things around me seem uncertain. In 1 Peter 1:8, it is written that there is a reward for my trust. My salvation and soul are dependent on it. Remind me, as in 1 John 1:8, if I ever think I've got it all figured out, or start acting like I don't need You, Lord, that I still have so much to learn. Help me to be honest with myself and open to Your truth. I ask for Your forgiveness and for the cleansing power of Your blood to wash me clean from all unrighteousness. Let Your truth dwell richly in me, that I may walk in the light as You are in the light.

In Jesus' powerful name I pray, Amen

JANUARY 9

Ephesians 1:9 (ESV): Making known to us the mystery of his will.

Joshua 1:9 (ESV): Have I not commanded you? Be strong and courageous. Do not be frightened, and do not be dismayed, for the LORD your God is with you wherever you go.

1 John 1:9 (ESV): If we confess our sins, he is faithful and just to forgive us our sins and cleanse us from all wickedness.

—————————————— PRAYER ——————————————

Gracious Heavenly Father, El Haggadol (The Great God),

You have revealed to me the mystery of Your will according to Your good pleasure, which You purposed in Christ, as it says in Ephesians 1:9. Thank You for the gift of understanding Your divine plan, and for guiding me according to Your perfect will. Help me to align my desires and actions with Your purpose, so that I may walk in the path You have set before me. Lord, I take courage in Your command in Joshua 1:9, where You say, "Have I not commanded you? Be strong and of good courage; do not be afraid, nor be dismayed, for the LORD your God is with you wherever you go." Strengthen me, Father, to face every challenge with boldness and faith, knowing that You are always by my side. Let Your presence fill me with the confidence I need to overcome fear and discouragement. I also come before You with a heart seeking forgiveness, as 1 John 1:9 assures us, "If we confess our sins, He is faithful and just to forgive us our sins and to cleanse us from all unrighteousness." Lord, I confess my sins before You, trusting in Your faithfulness and justice. Cleanse me, Father, from all unrighteousness, and renew a right spirit within me. Let me walk in the light of Your truth, free from guilt and shame.

In the fulfilling name of Jesus I pray, Amen

Colossians 1:10 (ESV): So that you may walk in a manner worthy of the Lord, fully pleasing to him; bearing fruit in every good work an increasing in the knowledge of God.

Galatians 1:10 (ESV): Am I now seeking the approval of men, or of God? Or am I striving to please man? If I were still trying to please men, I would not be a servant of Christ.

Proverbs 1:10 (ESV): My child, if sinners entice you, do not give in to them.

Jeremiah 1:10 (ESV): See, I have set you this day over nations and over kingdoms, to pluck up and to break down, to destroy and to overthrow, to build and to plant.

PRAYER

Dear Elohim (Creator God),

I come before You with a heart full of gratitude and reverence, seeking to walk in a manner worthy of You, Lord, fully pleasing to You, bearing fruit in every good work and increasing in the knowledge of God, as Colossians 1:10 guides us. Lord, help me to not seek the approval of man, but rather to be a servant of Christ, as Galatians 1:10 teaches. Let my actions and decisions be a reflection of Your will, not influenced by the temptations of this world, as Proverbs 1:10 warns. Father, just as You appointed Jeremiah in Jeremiah 1:10 to uproot, tear down, build, and plant, I ask that You give me the strength and wisdom to discern when to break away from harmful influences and when to nurture and build what is good and righteous in Your sight. May Your Word be a lamp unto my feet and a light unto my path. Guide me in all that I do, and may my life be a testimony of Your love and grace.

In the light of Jesus' name I pray, Amen

JANUARY 11

God is pleased with me

Colossians 1:11 (ESV): Being strengthened with all power, according to his glorious might, for all endurance and patience with joy.

Mark 1:11 (NIV): And a voice came from heaven, "You are my Son, whom I love; with you I am well pleased."

3 John 1:11 (NIV): Dear friend, do not imitate what is evil but what is good.

Ephesians 1:11 (ESV): In him we have obtained an inheritance.

 PRAYER

Dear Yahweh Tsuri (The Lord Is My Rock),

As it is written in Colossians 1:11, I pray that You strengthen me with all power according to Your glorious might, so that I may have great endurance and patience in all that I do. Lord, I hold on to the words spoken in Mark 1:11, where You declared, "You are my Son, whom I love; with You I am well pleased." I pray that I may walk in Your love and always remember that I am Your heir. Let me live in a way that is pleasing to You, reflecting Your love and grace to others. In 3 John 1:11, You remind us, "Dear friend, do not imitate what is evil but what is good." Help me, Lord, to pursue what is good and to walk in Your truth. May my actions be a reflection of Your goodness, and may I always seek to do what is right in Your eyes. Father, as Ephesians 1:11 states, "In Him we were also chosen, having been predestined according to the plan of Him who works out everything in conformity with the purpose of His will" (NIV). I thank You for choosing me and for the plans You have for my life. I trust that You are working all things for my good, according to Your divine purpose. Guide my steps, Lord, and help me to walk in the path that You have laid out for me.

In Jesus' pleasing name I pray, Amen

JANUARY 12

Jeremiah 1:12 (ESV): The LORD said to me, "You have seen well, for I am watching over my word to perform it."

James 1:12 (ESV): Blessed is the [person] who perseveres under trial, for when he has stood the test he will receive the crown of life, which God has promised to those who love him.

John 1:12 (ESV): But to all who did receive him, who believed in his name, he gave the right to become children of God.

Philippians 1:12 (ESV): I want you to know, brothers, that what has happened to me has really served to advance the gospel.

PRAYER

Dear Heavenly Father, Yahweh Rohi (The LORD Is My Shepherd),

I come before You with a heart full of faith and hope. I thank You for watching over Your Word to fulfill it in my life, as You promised in Jeremiah 1:12. Help me to stand firm in the tests and trials that come my way, knowing that as I persevere, You will bless me with the crown of life just as You have said in James 1:12. Lord, I thank You that through my faith in Jesus, I have the right to be called Your child, as declared in John 1:12. Help me to live as Your beloved child, growing in the knowledge of Your love and grace. Finally, I ask that You help me see every situation in my life as an opportunity for Your purposes to be fulfilled. Just as Philippians 1:12 reminds me, even what seems difficult can serve to advance the gospel and bring glory to Your name.

In Jesus' mighty name I pray, Amen

JANUARY 13

WITH CHRIST I AM STONGER THAN THE ENEMY

Colossians 1:13 (ESV): He has delivered us from the domain of darkness and transferred us to the kingdom of his beloved Son.

James 1:13 (NIV): When tempted, no one should say, "God is tempting me." For God cannot be tempted by evil, nor does he tempt anyone.

1 Peter 1:13 (NIV): Therefore, with minds that are alert and fully sober, set your hope on the grace to be brought to you when Jesus Christ is revealed at his coming.

PRAYER

Dear Heavenly Father, Jehovah Nissi (The LORD Is My Banner),

I come to You today with a humble heart, seeking Your guidance and strength. Colossians 1:13 says, "For he has rescued us from the dominion of darkness and brought us into the kingdom of the Son he loves" (NIV). Thank You for rescuing me from darkness and bringing me into the light of Your Son, Jesus. Help me to live fully in the freedom and love that You provide. James 1:13 reminds us, "When tempted, no one should say, 'God is tempting me.' For God cannot be tempted by evil, nor does he tempt anyone." Help me to recognize that when I face temptation, it is not from You. Grant me strength to resist and to seek Your guidance in overcoming challenges. 1 Peter 1:13 says, "Therefore, with minds that are alert and fully sober, set your hope on the grace to be brought to you when Jesus Christ is revealed at his coming." Help me to stay focused and alert, setting my hope on the grace that You offer through Jesus Christ. Let this hope guide me and sustain me in my daily life. Thank You for Your protection, guidance, and grace. Help me to live in Your light, resist temptation, and remain hopeful in Your promises.

In the powerful name of Jesus I pray, Amen

JANUARY 14

John 1:14 (ESV): And the Word became flesh and dwelt among us.

Philippians 1:14 (NIV): And because of my chains, most of the brothers and sisters have become confident in the Lord, and dare all the more to reclaim the gospel without fear.

Haggai 1:14 (ESV): And the Lord stirred up the spirit of Zerubbabel the son of Shealtiel, governor of Judah, and the spirit of Joshua the son of Jehozadak, the high priest, and the spirit of all the remnant of the people. And they came and worked on the house of the Lord of hosts, their God.

PRAYER

Dear Heavenly Father, El Qadosh (The Holy One),

I come before You with a heart full of gratitude and hope, seeking Your guidance and strength. As John 1:14 says, "The Word became flesh and made his dwelling among us. We have seen his glory, the glory of the one and only Son, who came from the Father, full of grace and truth." Thank You for sending Your Son, Jesus, to dwell among us and show us Your grace and truth. Help me to reflect His grace and truth in my own life. Philippians 1:14 teaches, "And because of my chains, most of the brothers and sisters have become confident in the Lord and dare all the more to proclaim the gospel without fear." Lord, give me the courage and confidence to share Your message boldly, just as Paul did. Strengthen my faith and help me to overcome any fears or obstacles that stand in the way of spreading Your love. Haggai 1:14 says, "So the Lord stirred up the spirit of Zerubbabel son of Shealtiel, governor of Judah, and the spirit of Joshua son of Jozadak, the high priest, and the spirit of the whole remnant of the people. They came and began to work on the house of the Lord Almighty, their God" (NIV). Stir up my spirit, Lord, to be active in Your service and to work faithfully at the tasks You have set before me. May I serve You wholeheartedly and contribute to Your work with dedication. Thank You for Your presence in my life, for the strength You provide, and for the purpose You give. Help me to live with grace, courage, and a willing heart.

In Jesus' strong name I pray, Amen

I BELIEVE IN GOD'S KINGDOM

Mark 1:15 (NIV): "The time has come," he said. "The kingdom of God has come near. Repent and believe the good news."

Genesis 1:15 (ESV): "And let them be lights in the expanse of the heavens to give light upon the earth." And it was so.

1 Timothy 1:15 (ESV): Christ Jesus came into the world to save sinners.

—————————————— **PRAYER** ——————————————

Dear Heavenly Father, Elohay Selichot (The God Who Is Ready to Forgive),

I come to You with a heart open to Your guidance and grace, seeking Your presence in my life. Mark 1:15 says, "The time has come, . . . The kingdom of God has come near. Repent and believe the good news!" Lord, help me to recognize the nearness of Your kingdom and to live with a repentant heart. Fill me with faith in the good news of Your love and salvation. Genesis 1:15 reminds us, "And let them be lights in the expanse of the sky to give light upon the earth." Thank You for the light and guidance You provide in my life. Help me to be a light to others, reflecting Your love and truth in all that I do. 1 Timothy 1:15 says, "Here is a trustworthy saying that deserves full acceptance: Christ Jesus came into the world to save sinners—of whom I am the worst." I am grateful for the saving grace of Jesus, who came to save us all. Help me to live in the light of this grace and to extend forgiveness and love to others as You have done for me. Thank You for Your endless love, for the light You bring into my life, and for the gift of salvation through Jesus Christ. Guide me in living out these truths each day.

In Jesus' believable name I pray, Amen

JANUARY 16

Romans 1:16 (ESV): For I am not ashamed of the gospel, for it is the power of God for salvation to everyone who believes.

John 1:16 (ESV): For from his fullness we have all received, grace upon grace.

Ephesians 1:16 (NIV): I have not stopped giving thanks for you, remembering you in my prayers.

PRAYER

Dear Heavenly Father, Jehovah-Jireh (LORD My Provider),

I come before You with a heart full of gratitude and hope, seeking Your guidance and strength. Romans 1:16 says, "For I am not ashamed of the gospel, because it is the power of God that brings salvation to everyone who believes." Lord, give me the courage and boldness to stand firm in my faith and to share the good news of Your salvation with others. Help me to be unashamed and to live out the power of Your gospel each day. John 1:16 reminds us, "Out of his fullness we have all received grace in place of grace already given" (NIV). Thank You for the abundant grace You pour into our lives. Help me to embrace and extend this grace, recognizing that Your blessings are new each day and that Your love continually surrounds me. Ephesians 1:16 says, "I have not stopped giving thanks for you, remembering you in my prayers." Lord, I am grateful for Your ongoing presence in my life. I thank You for Your blessings, Your guidance, and the support of fellow believers. Help me to remain thankful and to lift up others in prayer as well. Thank You for Your power, grace, and the gift of community. Guide me in living out these truths and in showing Your love and grace to those around me.

In Jesus' truthful name I pray, Amen

JANUARY 17

Ephesians 1:17 (ESV): That the God of our Lord Jesus Christ, the Father of glory, may give you the Spirit of wisdom and of revelation in the knowledge of him.

James 1:17 (ESV): Every good and perfect gift is from above.

1 Timothy 1:17 (ESV): To the King of the ages, immortal, invisible, the only God, to be honored and glorified forever and ever. Amen.

PRAYER

Dear Heavenly Father, Basilei ton Aionon (King Eternal),

I come before You with a grateful heart, seeking Your wisdom and guidance. Ephesians 1:17 says, "I keep asking that the God of our Lord Jesus Christ, the glorious Father, may give you the Spirit of wisdom and revelation, so that you may know him better" (NIV). Lord, grant me a deeper understanding of You. Fill me with Your Spirit of wisdom and revelation so I can know You more intimately and follow Your will more closely. James 1:17 reminds us, "Every good and perfect gift is from above, coming down from the Father of the heavenly lights, who does not change like shifting shadows." Thank You for the many blessings You have given me. Help me to always remember that every good thing in my life comes from You, and may I never take Your gifts for granted. 1 Timothy 1:17 declares, "Now to the King eternal, immortal, invisible, the only God, be honor and glory for ever and ever. Amen" (NIV). Lord, I honor and praise You as the eternal King. You are immortal and invisible, yet so real and present in my life. I give You all the glory and honor, and I thank You for Your constant presence and love. Guide me to live with gratitude, wisdom, and a heart full of praise.

In Jesus' wise name I pray, Amen

JANUARY 18

Isaiah 1:18 (ESV): Though your sins be as scarlet, they shall be as white as snow.

Ephesians 1:18 (NIV): I pray that the eyes of your heart may be enlightened in order that you may know the hope to which he has called you, the riches of his glorious inheritance in his holy people.

John 1:18 (NIV): No one has ever seen God, but the one and only Son, who is himself God and is in closest relationship with the Father, has made him known.

PRAYER

Dear Heavenly Father, Elohim Shama (The God Who Hears),

Thank You for Your love and the promise of renewal. Isaiah 1:18 says, "Come now, let us reason together,' says the LORD. 'Though your sins are like scarlet, they shall be as white as snow; though they are red like crimson, they shall become like wool." Lord, I come before You seeking Your forgiveness and transformation. Cleanse my heart and mind, and make me pure in Your sight. Help me to experience the joy of a fresh start in You. Ephesians 1:18 prays, ". . . that the eyes of your heart may be enlightened in order that you may know the hope to which He has called you, the riches of His glorious inheritance in His holy people." Father, open the eyes of my heart to understand the hope and the incredible blessings You have prepared for me. Help me to fully grasp the depth of Your love and the richness of Your grace. John 1:18 tells us, "No one has ever seen God, but the one and only Son, who is himself God and is in closest relationship with the Father, has made Him known." Thank You, Jesus, for revealing the Father to us. I am grateful for Your presence and the way You show us who God is. Help me to grow closer to You and to reflect Your love and truth in my life. Guide me in this journey of understanding and renewal. May Your light shine brightly in my life.

In the washed-clean name of Jesus I pray, Amen

JANUARY 19

James 1:19 (NIV): Everyone should be quick to listen, slow to speak and slow to become angry.

Jeremiah 1:19 (ESV): They will fight against you, but they shall not prevail against you, for I am with you, declares the LORD, to deliver you.

1 Timothy 1:19 (ESV): Holding *faith*, and a good conscience. By rejecting this, some have made shipwreck of their faith.

PRAYER

Dear Heavenly Father, El Sela (God My Rock),

Thank You for Your guidance and wisdom. James 1:19 tells us, "Everyone should be quick to listen, slow to speak and slow to become angry." Lord, help me to be patient and wise in my interactions with others. Grant me a listening heart, and teach me to respond with kindness and understanding, avoiding unnecessary anger. Jeremiah 1:19 says, "'They will fight against you but will not overcome you, for I am with you and will rescue you,' declares the LORD" (NIV). Father, I trust in Your protection and strength. Even when challenges come my way, remind me that You are with me and will help me overcome any obstacles. 1 Timothy 1:19 encourages us to "Hold on to faith and a good conscience, which some have rejected and so have suffered shipwreck with regard to the faith" (NIV). Lord, strengthen my faith and help me to maintain a clear conscience. Guide me to hold firmly to my beliefs and to live in a way that honors You. Thank You for Your constant presence and support. Help me to live wisely, to trust in Your protection, and to hold fast to my faith.

In Jesus' listening name I pray, Amen

JANUARY 20

I HAVE THE HOLY SPIRIT IN ME

Colossians 1:20 (NLT): Through him God reconciled everything to himself. He made peace with everything in heaven and on earth by means of Christ's blood on the cross.

Ephesians 1:20 (ESV): [God put this power to work] in Christ when he raised him from the dead and seated him at his right hand in the heavenly places.

Jude 1:20 (ESV): But you, beloved, by building yourselves up in your most holy faith and praying in the Holy Spirit.

Romans 1:20 (NKJV): For since the creation of the world His invisible attributes are clearly seen, being understood by the things that are made, even His eternal power and Godhead, so that they are without excuse.

Philippians 1:20 (NKJV): According to my earnest expectation and hope that in nothing I shall be ashamed, but with all boldness, as always, so now also Christ will be magnified in my body, whether by life or by death.

PRAYER

Dear Heavenly Father, El Roi (The God Who Sees Me),

Thank You for Your grace and the work You are doing in my life. Colossians 1:20 encourages me to rebuke all the spirits of torment and fear because I have peace through the blood of Jesus. Lord, help me to hold that understanding deep inside my heart. Ephesians 1:20 reminds me that our heavenly Father displayed His power in raising Jesus from the dead. Lord, I ask for Your strength and power to be evident in my life as I face challenges and seek to follow You. Jude 1:20 encourages me to build my faith through prayer and trust in the Holy Spirit. Lord, I want a deeper relationship with You in my spiritual understanding in all areas of my life. According to Romans 1:20, I recognize God's power and divine nature in the worked around me. Lord, let Your creation remind me of Your greatness and inspire me to live with and for You. Philippians 1:20 teaches me to live unashamed in boldness because of Christ Jesus. I will honor Christ and reflect His love and grace in all I do. Thank You, God, for Your guidance and support. May Your peace, power, and purpose fill me every day of my life.

In Jesus' powerful name I pray, Amen

Matthew 1:21 (NIV): She will give birth to a son, and you are to give him the name Jesus, because he will save his people from their sins.

Deuteronomy 1:21 (KJV): As the LORD God of thy fathers hath said unto thee; fear not, neither be discouraged.

James 1:21 (BSB): Therefore, get rid of all moral filth and every expression of evil, and humbly accept the word planted in you, which can save your souls.

——————————————— PRAYER ———————————————

Dear Heavenly Father, El Shaddai (The All-Sufficient One, God Almighty),

Thank You for Your wonderful promises and guidance. Matthew 1:21 tells us, "She will give birth to a son, and you are to give him the name Jesus, because he will save his people from their sins." Lord, I am grateful for Jesus and the salvation He brings. Help me to live in a way that honors this incredible gift and to reflect His love and grace in my daily life. Deuteronomy 1:21 encourages us, "See, the LORD your God has given you the land. Go up and take possession of it as the LORD, the God of your ancestors, told you. Do not be afraid; do not be discouraged" (NIV). Father, give me the courage to step into the opportunities You have prepared for me. Help me to trust in Your promises and to act boldly without fear or discouragement. James 1:21 advises, "Therefore, get rid of all moral filth and the evil that is so prevalent and humbly accept the word planted in you, which can save you" (NIV). Lord, purify my heart and mind. Help me to remove anything that is not pleasing to You and to embrace Your Word with humility. Let Your truth guide and transform me. Thank You for Your guidance, courage, and the gift of salvation. May Your Word be a light to my path and strength for my journey.

In Jesus' safe name I pray, Amen

James 1:22 (NIV): Do not merely listen to the word, and so deceive yourselves. Do what it says.

Ephesians 1:22 (NLT): God has put all things under the authority of Christ and has made him head over all things for the benefit of the church.

1 Peter 1:22 (BSB): Since you have purified your souls by obedience to the truth so that you have a genuine love for your brothers, love one another deeply, from a pure heart.

PRAYER

Dear Heavenly Father, El Yeshuati (The God of My Salvation),

Thank You for Your guidance and the powerful truths found in Your Word. James 1:22 reminds us, "Do not merely listen to the word, and so deceive yourselves. Do what it says." Lord, help me to not only hear Your Word but to put it into practice. May my actions reflect the teachings of the Bible and demonstrate my faith in You. Ephesians 1:22 tells us, "And God placed all things under his feet and appointed him to be head over everything for . . . the church." Father, thank You for placing all things under the authority of Jesus. Help me to acknowledge His lordship in every aspect of my life and to trust in His sovereign control. 1 Peter 1:22 says, "Now that you have purified yourselves by obeying the truth so that you have sincere love for each other, love one another deeply, from the heart" (NIV). Lord, purify my heart and mind through obedience to Your truth. Fill me with sincere love for others and help me to love deeply and genuinely. Guide me to live according to Your Word, embrace Jesus' authority, and show sincere love to those around me. Thank You for Your constant presence and for shaping me into a reflection of Your love.

In Jesus' pure name I pray, Amen

John 1:23 (NIV): "I am the voice of one calling in the wilderness, 'Make straight the way for the Lord.'"

Proverbs 1:23 (NIV): Repent at my rebuke! Then I will pour out my thoughts to you, I will make known to you my teachings.

1 Peter 1:23 (ESV): You have been born anew, not of perishable but of imperishable seed, through the living and abiding word of God.

PRAYER

Dear Heavenly Father, El HaNe'eman (The God Who Is Faithful),

Thank You for Your Word and the guidance it provides. John 1:23 says, "John replied in the words of Isaiah the prophet, 'I am the voice of one calling in the wilderness, "Make straight the way for the Lord."'" Lord, help me to prepare my heart and life for You. Teach me to clear away any obstacles and to make Your path straight in my daily walk. Proverbs 1:23 encourages us, "Repent at my rebuke! Then I will pour out my thoughts to you, I will make known to you my teachings." Father, I seek Your wisdom and correction. Open my heart to Your teachings and guide me to align my life with Your truth. Help me to respond to Your guidance with repentance and humility. 1 Peter 1:23 reminds us, "For you have been born again, not of perishable seed, but of imperishable, through the living and enduring word of God" (NIV). Thank You for the new life You have given me through Your Word. Help me to live in the fullness of this new birth, reflecting Your enduring truth and love. Guide me as I seek to make way for You, embrace Your teachings, and live out the new life You have given me. May Your Word continually shape and renew me.

In Jesus' guiding name I pray, Amen

Jude 1:24 (ESV): Now to him who is able to keep you from stumbling and to present you blameless before the presence of his glory with great joy.

1 Corinthians 1:24 (ESV): But to those who are called, both Jews and Greeks, Christ the power of God and the wisdom of God.

1 Peter 1:24 (NKJV): Because "All flesh is as grass, and all the glory of a man as the flower of the grass. The grass withers, and its flower falls away."

—————————————————— **PRAYER** ——————————————————

Dear Heavenly Father, Jehovah-Sabaoth (The LORD of Hosts),

Thank You for Your incredible promises and for the guidance You provide in Your Word. Jude 1:24 says, "To Him who is able to keep you from stumbling and to present you before His glorious presence without fault and with great joy." Lord, I trust in Your power to keep me steady and to guide me through life's challenges. Help me to rely on You completely, knowing You will protect me and present me faultless before You. 1 Corinthians 1:24 states, "But to those whom God has called, both Jews and Greeks, Christ the power of God and the wisdom of God." Father, thank You for calling me to be part of Your family. Help me to recognize the power and wisdom of Christ in my life, and to seek His guidance in all things. 1 Peter 1:24 tells us, "For, 'All people are like grass, and all their glory is like the flowers of the field; the grass withers and the flowers fall'" (NIV). Lord, remind me of the temporary nature of worldly things and help me to focus on what is eternal and unchanging in You. Guide me to stay steadfast in Your truth, to trust in Christ's power and wisdom, and to value what truly lasts. Thank You for Your constant presence and the assurance of Your care.

In Jesus' incredible name I pray, Amen

JANUARY 25

1 Peter 1:25 (ESV): "But the word of the Lord remains forever." And this word is the good news that was preached to you.

Philemon 1:25 (ESV): The grace of the Lord Jesus Christ will be with your spirit.

Mark 1:25 (BSB): But Jesus rebuked the spirit. "Be silent!" He said. "Come out of him!"

PRAYER

Dear Heavenly Father, Elohim Ahavah (The God Who Loves),

Thank You for Your Word, which brings comfort and strength to our lives. 1 Peter 1:25 reminds us, "But the word of the Lord stands forever." Lord, I am grateful that Your Word is eternal and unchanging. Help me to rely on Your promises and find comfort in Your everlasting truth, especially in times of uncertainty. Philemon 1:25 says, "The grace of the Lord Jesus Christ be with your spirit." Father, I ask for Your grace to fill my spirit. Please surround me with Your grace and peace, guiding me through each day with Your love and support. Mark 1:25 tells us, "'Be quiet!' said Jesus sternly. 'Come out of him!'" (NIV). Lord, help me to recognize Your authority and power in my life. Quiet the voices of doubt and fear, and give me the strength to follow Your commands with confidence. Guide me, fill me with Your grace, and let Your Word be my source of hope and strength. Thank You for Your unchanging promises and Your presence in my life.

In Jesus' great name I pray, Amen

JANUARY 26

I am made in God's image

Genesis 1:26 (ESV): Then God said, "Let us make mankind in our image, in our likeness, so that they may rule over the fish in the sea and the birds in the sky, over the livestock and all the wild animals, and over all the creatures that move along the ground."

James 1:26 (KJV): If anyone, among you seems to be religious, and bridleth not his tongue, but deceiveth his own heart, this man's religion is vain.

Romans 1:26 (BSB): For this reason, God gave them over to dishonorable passions. Even their women exchanged natural relations for unnatural ones.

 **PRAYER**

Dear Heavenly Father, Georgos (The Gardener),

Thank You for creating me in Your image and for guiding me through Your Word. Genesis 1:26 says, "Then God said, 'Let us make mankind in our image, in our likeness . . .'" Lord, I am grateful for being made in Your image. Help me to reflect Your love, compassion, and wisdom in all that I do. James 1:26 warns us, "Those who consider themselves religious and yet do not keep a tight rein on their tongues deceive themselves, and their religion is worthless" (NIV). Father, give me the wisdom to use my words wisely. Help me to speak with kindness and truth, and to let my actions reflect Your teachings. Romans 1:26 tells us, "Because of this, God gave them over to shameful lusts. Even their women exchanged natural sexual relations for unnatural ones" (NIV). Lord, help me to live according to Your design and to seek Your guidance in all areas of my life. Protect me from falling into ways that are contrary to Your will. Guide me in Your truth, help me to live in a way that honors You, and renew my spirit daily. Thank You for Your creation and for the guidance You provide.

In Jesus' honorable name I pray, Amen

Genesis 1:27 (ESV): So God created man in his own image; in the image of God he created him; male and female he created them.

Colossians 1:27 (ESV): Christ in you, the hope of glory.

James 1:27 (NKJV): Pure and undefiled religion before God and the father is this; to visit orphans and widows in their trouble, and to keep oneself unspotted from the world.

Philippians 1:27 (NKJV): Only let your conduct be worthy of the gospel of Christ, so that whether I come and see you or am absent, I may hear of your affairs, that you stand fast in one spirit, with one mind striving together for the faith of the gospel.

 **PRAYER**

Dear Heavenly Father, Akal Esh (Consuming Fire),

Thank You for the profound truths in Your Word that guide and uplift us. Genesis 1:27 tells us, "So God created mankind in his own image, in the image of God he created them; male and female he created them." Lord, thank You for creating me in Your image. Help me to live in a way that reflects Your love and character. Colossians 1:27 says, "To them God has chosen to make known among the Gentiles the glorious riches of this mystery, which is Christ in you, the hope of glory" (NIV). Father, I am grateful for the hope and glory of Christ in my life. Help me to live with the confidence and joy that come from knowing You are in me. James 1:27 instructs us, "Religion that God our Father accepts as pure and faultless is this: to look after orphans and widows in their distress and to keep oneself from being polluted by the world" (NIV). Lord, guide me to live out my faith by serving others and keeping myself pure in Your sight. Show me how to care for those in need and to avoid the ways of the world that lead away from You. Philippians 1:27 encourages us, "Whatever happens, conduct yourselves in a manner worthy of the gospel of Christ" (NIV). Help me to conduct myself in a manner worthy of Your gospel. Let my actions and words reflect Your grace and truth, no matter what challenges I face. Guide me to live fully in Your image, empowered by the hope of Christ, and to act with integrity and compassion in all that I do.

In Jesus' witnessing name I pray, Amen

Luke 1:28 (NIV): "Greetings, you who are highly favored! The Lord is with you."

Genesis 1:28 (ESV): And God blessed them. And God said to them, "Be fruitful, and multiply and fill the earth and subdue it, and have dominion . . ."

Isaiah 1:28 (ESV): But rebels and sinners shall be broken together, and those who forsake the LORD shall be consumed.

PRAYER

Dear Heavenly Father, Jehovah Uzzi (The LORD My Strength),

I come to You with gratitude and hope, reflecting on Your Word and the promises it holds. Luke 1:28 says, "The angel went to her and said, 'Greetings, you who are highly favored! The Lord is with you.'" Thank You, Lord, for Your favor and presence in my life. Help me to recognize Your blessings and guidance in all I do. In Genesis 1:28, You blessed Adam and Eve, saying, "Be fruitful and increase in number; fill the earth and subdue it." Father, I ask for Your help in living out the purpose You have set for me. May I bear fruit in my life and use the gifts and opportunities You have given me to make a positive impact. Isaiah 1:28 reminds us, "But rebels and sinners will both be broken, and those who forsake the LORD will perish" (NIV). Lord, keep me close to You and help me to follow Your ways. Guide me away from sin and rebellion, and strengthen my faith in You. Thank You for Your blessings, for Your guidance, and for Your unwavering love. Help me to live in a way that honors You and reflects Your grace.

In Jesus' highly favored name, Amen

JANUARY 29

HE TOOK MY SIN

Philippians 1:29 (ESV): For it has been granted to you that for the sake of Christ, you should not only believe in him but also suffer for his sake.

John 1:29 (ESV): The next day he saw Jesus coming toward him, and said, "Behold, the Lamb of God, who takes away the sins of the world!"

Deuteronomy 1:29 (NIV): Then I said to you, "Do not be terrified; do not be afraid of them."

—————————————————— PRAYER ——————————————————

Dear Heavenly Father, Immanuel (God With Us),

Thank You for Your love and care in my life. I come to You today with a heart full of gratitude and hope. Philippians 1:29 reminds me that ". . . it has been granted to you on behalf of Christ not only to believe in Him, but also to suffer for Him" (NIV). Lord, I ask for the strength to endure any trials or challenges that come my way. Help me to remain steadfast in my faith and to trust in Your plan, even when things are difficult. In John 1:29, John the Baptist declares, "Look, the Lamb of God, who takes away the sin of the world!" (BSB). Thank You, Jesus, for Your sacrifice and for the forgiveness of my sins. Please help me to live in a way that reflects the grace You have given me. Deuteronomy 1:29 says, "Then I said to you, 'Do not be terrified; do not be afraid of them.'" Lord, grant me courage and peace as I face any fears or uncertainties in my life. Help me to trust in Your protection and guidance. Thank You for Your promises and for Your constant presence. Guide me, strengthen me, and help me to live according to Your will.

In Jesus' courageous name I pray, Amen

JANUARY 30

God fights for me before my very eyes

Luke 1:30 (NIV): But the angel said to her, "Do not be afraid, Mary; you have found favor with God."

Deuteronomy 1:30 (NIV): The Lord your God, who is going before you, will fight for you, as he did for you in Egypt, before your very eyes.

1 Corinthians 1:30 (ESV): It is because of him that you are in Christ Jesus, who has become for us wisdom from God—that is, our righteousness, holiness, and redemption.

PRAYER

Dear Heavenly Father, Baselei ton Aionon (King Eternal),

Thank You for Your steadfast love and grace. I come before You today with a heart full of trust and gratitude. In Luke 1:30, the angel said to Mary, "Do not be afraid, Mary; you have found favor with God." Lord, I ask for the same reassurance and courage in my life. Help me to trust in Your favor and to overcome any fears or worries I may have. Deuteronomy 1:30 reminds me, "The Lord your God, who is going before you, will fight for you, as he did for you in Egypt, before your very eyes." Father, please go before me and fight my battles. Help me to remember that You are always with me, guiding and protecting me. In 1 Corinthians 1:30, it says, "It is because of him that you are in Christ Jesus, who has become for us wisdom from God—that is, our righteousness, holiness, and redemption." Thank You for making Jesus our wisdom, righteousness, and redemption. Help me to live out these truths in my daily life, reflecting Your grace and wisdom in all I do. Guide me, strengthen me, and fill me with Your peace. Thank You for Your constant presence and for the assurance that I am never alone.

In Jesus' eternal name I pray, Amen

JANUARY 31

Luke 1:31 (NIV): "You will conceive, and give birth to a son, and you are to call him, Jesus."

Genesis 1:31 (ESV): And God saw everything that he had made, and behold, it was very good. And there was evening and there was morning, the sixth day.

1 Corinthians 1:31 (ESV): So that, as it is written, "Let the one who boasts, boast in the Lord."

─────────────────── **PRAYER** ───────────────────

Dear Heavenly Father, Migdal Oz (Strong Tower),

I come to You with a heart full of gratitude and hope. Your Word provides me with comfort and direction. In Luke 1:31, the angel told Mary, "You will conceive and give birth to a son, and you are to call him Jesus." Lord, just as Mary was given a special purpose, I ask You to reveal Your purpose for my life. Help me to embrace the path You have set before me with faith and obedience. Genesis 1:31 tells us, "God saw all that He had made, and it was very good." Thank You for creating everything with care and purpose, including me. Help me to see the goodness You have placed in my life and to live in a way that reflects Your perfect creation. In 1 Corinthians 1:31, it says, "Therefore, as it is written: 'Let the one who boasts boast in the Lord.'" Lord, may my life bring glory to You. Let me boast only in Your goodness and grace, acknowledging that all my achievements and blessings come from You. Guide me to live according to Your will and to use my gifts and talents to honor You. Fill me with Your peace and joy as I walk in the purpose You have for me.

In Jesus' strong high name I pray, Amen

FEBRUARY 1

TODAY I BREATHED MY FIRST BREATH

1 Samuel 2:1 (KJV): My mouth is enlarged over mine enemies.

1 Peter 2:1 (ESV): So put away all malice and all the deceit and hypocrisy and every and all slander.

1 John 2:1 (ESV): My little children, I am writing these things to you so that you may not sin. But if anyone does sin, we have an advocate with the Father, Jesus Christ the righteous.

PRAYER

Dear Lord, Parakletos (Advocate),

I come before You with a humble heart and a spirit of thanksgiving. In 1 Samuel 2:1, Hannah prayed, "My heart rejoices in the LORD; in the LORD my horn is lifted high. My mouth boasts over my enemies, for I delight in Your deliverance" (NIV). Lord, I rejoice in Your goodness and mercy. I am grateful for the strength and courage You give me each day. Help me to trust in Your deliverance and to find joy in Your presence. 1 Peter 2:1 instructs us, "Therefore, rid yourselves of all malice and all deceit, hypocrisy, envy, and slander of every kind " (NIV). Lord, help me to let go of anything that stands between me and Your will. Fill my heart with purity and sincerity, and guide me to live in truth and love. In 1 John 2:1, we are reminded, "My dear children, I write this to you so that you will not sin. But if anybody does sin, we have an advocate with the Father—Jesus Christ, the Righteous One" (NIV). Thank You for the grace and forgiveness that come through Jesus. When I stumble, remind me of Your endless mercy and the advocate I have in Christ. Guide me in Your ways, strengthen me with Your grace, and help me to live in a way that honors You.

In the image of Jesus' name I pray, Amen

FEBRUARY 2

Ephesians 2:2 (ESV): in which you once walked, following the course of this world, following the prince of the power of the air, the spirit that is now at work in the sons of disobedience.

Deuteronomy 2:2 (ESV): Then the LORD said to me.

Habakkuk 2:2 (ESV): And the LORD answered me: "Write the vision; make it a plain on tablets, so that he may run to whoever needs it."

Titus 2:2 (ESV): Older men are to be sober-minded, dignified, self controlled, sound in faith, in love, and in steadfastness.

--- **PRAYER** ---

Dear Heavenly Father, Shaphat (Judge),

I come to You with a grateful heart, seeking Your guidance and strength. Ephesians 2:2 reminds me that I once followed the ways of this world, but now I seek to walk in Your truth. Help me to resist the temptations of the world and to live according to Your will, reflecting the new life You have given me in Christ. Deuteronomy 2:2 recounts Your direction to move forward and possess the land You promised. Father, guide me and continue to speak to me as I move forward in life. Help me to trust in Your timing and to have faith that You will lead me to where You want me to be. Habakkuk 2:2 Tells us to write down the vision and make it plain, so that we can follow Your direction. Lord, give me clarity in understanding Your plans for me and the courage to follow them. Help me to see the vision You have for my life and to trust in Your promises. Titus 2:2 speaks of being sound in faith, love, and endurance. Lord, help me to live with integrity and faithfulness in all areas of my life. Strengthen my character and my commitment to live in a way that reflects Your love and truth. Guide me, strengthen me, and help me to follow Your path with confidence and joy.

In Jesus' spoken name I pray, Amen

FEBRUARY 3

I am God's servant

Philippians 2:3 (ESV): Do nothing from selfish ambition or conceit, but in humility count others more significant than yourselves.

Job 2:3 (ESV): And the Lord said to Satan, "Have you considered my servant Job, that there is none like him on the earth, a blameless and upright man, who fears God and turns away from evil? He still holds fast his integrity, although you incited me against him to destroy him without reason."

Romans 2:3 (ESV): Do you suppose, O man—you who judge those who practice such things and do them yourself—that you will escape the judgment of God?

1 Samuel 2:3 (ESV): Do not keep talking so proudly or let your mouth speak such arrogance, for the Lord is a God who knows, and by him deeds are weighed.

PRAYER

Dear Lord, El Deah (The God of Knowledge),

I come before You today seeking Your guidance and strength. Philippians 2:3 reminds me to do nothing out of selfish ambition or vain conceit but to value others above myself. Help me to embrace humility in my actions and attitudes, putting others' needs and interests before my own. Job 2:3 speaks of Job's integrity and faithfulness. Lord, I ask for the strength to remain steadfast and true in my own life, even when faced with challenges. Help me to maintain my integrity and to trust in Your plan for me. Romans 2:3 warns against judging others while ignoring our own faults. Father, help me to reflect on my own life and correct my shortcomings before I look at the faults of others. Give me wisdom to judge with fairness and grace, focusing on self-improvement rather than criticism. In 1 Samuel 2:3, Your Word reminds me not to speak proudly or let arrogance come from my mouth, for You, Lord, are the God of knowledge, and by You, actions are weighed. Guide me to live a life that honors You, full of humility, integrity, and genuine love for others.

In Jesus' humble name I pray, Amen

FEBRUARY 4

Galatians 2:4 (ESV): . . . the freedom we have in Christ Jesus.

1 Corinthians 2:4 (ESV): My speech and my message were not in plausible words of wisdom, but with in demonstration of the Spirit and of power.

2 Timothy 2:4 (NKJV): No one engaged in warfare entangles himself with the affairs of this life.

Psalm 2:4 (ESV): He who sits in the heavens laughs.

Philippians 2:4 (ESV): Let each of you look not only for his own interests, but also to the interests of others.

Romans 2:4 (NLT): Don't you see how wonderfully kind, tolerant, and patient God is with you? Does this mean nothing to you? Can't you see that his kindness is intended to turn you away from your sin?

--------------------------------- PRAYER ---------------------------------

Dear Heavenly Father, YAH (Self-Existent, "I AM"),

I come to You today seeking Your strength and guidance in my life. Galatians 2:4 reminds me that even when facing challenges, I should remain steadfast in my faith. Help me to stay true to Your Word, no matter the pressures or difficulties I encounter. 1 Corinthians 2:4 tells me that our faith should not rest on human wisdom but on Your power. Please fill me with Your wisdom and strength so that my faith is grounded in Your truth, not just my own understanding. 2 Timothy 2:4 encourages me to focus on pleasing You rather than being entangled by worldly concerns. Guide me to prioritize my relationship with You and to seek Your approval in all that I do. Psalm 2:4 speaks of Your sovereign power and authority. Remind me that You are in control of all things and that I can trust in Your perfect plan for my life. Philippians 2:4 urges me to look not only to my own interests but also to the interests of others. Help me to be considerate and compassionate, putting others' needs alongside my own. Romans 2:4 highlights Your kindness and patience toward us. May Your love and grace flow through me, helping me to show kindness and patience to others as You have shown to me. Thank You for Your constant presence and guidance. I trust in Your promises and seek to live according to Your will.

In Jesus' instructional name I pray, Amen

FEBRUARY 5

I HAVE THE MINDSET OF JESUS CHRIST

Ephesians 2:5 (ESV): "Even when we were dead in our trespasses, [He] made us alive together with Christ.

Philippians 2:5 (NIV): In your relationship with one another, have the same mindset as Christ Jesus.

James 2:5 (NIV): Listen, my brothers and sisters: Has not God chosen those who are poor in the eyes of the world to be rich in faith.

PRAYER

Dear Lord, Jehovah Gibbor Milchamah (The LORD Mighty in Battle),

Thank You for Your amazing grace and mercy in my life. Ephesians 2:5 reminds me that even when I was dead in my sins, You made me alive through Christ. I am grateful for the gift of new life and for the way You have transformed me by Your love. Philippians 2:5 encourages me to have the same mindset as Christ Jesus. Help me to embrace humility and compassion, just as Jesus did. Teach me to think and act with a heart of love and selflessness. James 2:5 speaks of Your choice to bless those who are poor in the eyes of the world, but rich in faith. I pray that I may always remember that true richness comes from a relationship with You and that I would be rich in faith and good deeds. Guide me, Lord, to live each day in a way that reflects Your love and grace. Help me to stay humble and to seek Your will in all I do. Thank You for Your ongoing presence and for the work You are doing in my life.

In Jesus' strong and mighty name I pray, Amen

FEBRUARY 6

I WAS RAISED FROM DEATH TO LIFE WITH JESUS CHRIST

Ephesians 2:6 (CEV): God raised us from death to life with Jesus Christ, and he has given us a place beside Christ in heaven.

Proverbs 2:6 (ESV): For the LORD gives wisdom; from his mouth comes knowledge and understanding.

Romans 2:6 (ESV): God "will repay each person according to what they have done."

Colossians 2:6 (NIV): So then, just as you received Christ Jesus as Lord, continue to live your lives in him.

—————————————————————— **PRAYER** ——————————————————————

Dear Heavenly Lord, Jehovah Go'el (Redeeming LORD),

Thank You for the many blessings You pour into my life. Ephesians 2:6 says that You have raised me up with Christ and seated me in the heavenly realms. I am grateful for the new life You have given me and for the position of honor and grace You have placed me in. Proverbs 2:6 teaches that wisdom comes from You, and that understanding and knowledge are gifts from Your hand. Please guide me with Your wisdom and help me to seek Your understanding in all aspects of my life. Colossians 2:6 reminds me to continue to live in Christ Jesus, rooted and built up in Him. Help me to remain steadfast in my faith, growing deeper in my relationship with You, and living according to Your ways. May Your wisdom lead me, Your grace sustain me, and Your love fill me each day. Thank You for being my guide and my source of strength.

In the freedom of Jesus' name I pray, Amen

FEBRUARY 7

I LISTEN AND RECEIVE GOD'S HIDDEN WISDOM

1 Corinthians 2:7 (ESV): But we impart a secret and hidden wisdom of God.

Ezekiel 2:7 (ESV): You must speak my words to them, whether they listen or fail to listen, for they are rebellions.

Genesis 2:7 (NIV): The LORD God formed a man from the dust of the ground and breathed into his nostrils the breath of life, and the man became a living being.

Ephesians 2:7 (NKJV): That in the ages to come, he might show the exceeding riches of His grace and His kindness toward us in Christ Jesus.

 PRAYER

Dear Heavenly Father, Jehovah Gibbor Milchamah (The LORD Mighty in Battle),

Thank You for Your guidance and grace in my life. 1 Corinthians 2:7 tells me that You have revealed Your wisdom to us through the Spirit, a wisdom that is hidden from the world. I ask that You continue to reveal Your deep truths to me, helping me to understand and embrace Your perfect plan. Ezekiel 2:7 reminds me to speak Your words faithfully, even in challenging times. Help me to be courageous and faithful in sharing Your message, trusting in Your strength and wisdom. Genesis 2:7 says that You breathed life into me, forming me from the dust. I am grateful for the life and breath You have given me. Renew my spirit each day and help me to live in a way that honors You. Ephesians 2:7 speaks of the immeasurable riches of Your grace that You have shown me in Christ Jesus. I am thankful for the grace and kindness You have poured into my life. May Your grace continue to transform me and guide me. Help me to live in Your truth, speak Your words, and reflect Your grace in all I do.

In Jesus' truthful name I pray, Amen

FEBRUARY 8

Ephesians 2:8 (NIV): For it is by grace you have been saved, through faith—and this is not from yourselves, it is the gift of God.

Psalm 2:8 (KJV): Ask of me, and I shall give thee the heathen for thine inheritance, and the uttermost parts of the earth for thy possession.

2 Kings 2:8 (NLT): Then Elijah folded his cloak together and struck the water with it. The river divided, and the two of them went across on dry ground!

PRAYER

Dear Heavenly Father, Sar Shalom (Prince of Peace),

I come before You with a heart full of gratitude for Your incredible blessings. Ephesians 2:8 reminds me that it is by Your grace I am saved, through faith. Thank You for this precious gift that I could not earn on my own. Help me to trust in Your grace daily and to live in a way that reflects my gratitude. Psalm 2:8 assures me that You will give us the nations as our inheritance. I trust in Your promises and pray for Your guidance in all areas of my life. Lead me in Your will and help me to seek Your kingdom above all else. 2 Kings 2:8 shows me the power of Your guidance and protection. Just as Elijah struck the Jordan and it parted, I ask for Your help to overcome the obstacles in my path. Strengthen me, Lord, and make a way where there seems to be none. Thank You for Your grace, Your promises, and Your guidance. I place my trust in You, knowing that You are with me every step of the way.

In Jesus' brotherly name I pray, Amen

I AM FAITHFUL AND CHOSEN

Ephesians 2:9 (NIV): Not by works, so that no one can boast.

Luke 2:9 (NIV): An angel of the Lord appeared to them, and the glory of the Lord shone around them, and they were terrified.

Mark 2:9 (NIV): "Which is easier: to say to this paralyzed man 'your sins are forgiven, or to say, get up, take your mat and walk?'"

1 Peter 2:9 (ESV): But you are a chosen people, a royal priesthood, . . .

1 Samuel 2:9 (NLT): He will protect his faithful ones, but the wicked will disappear in darkness. No one will succeed by strength alone.

PRAYER

Dear Heavenly Father, Jehovah Nissi (The LORD Is My Banner),

I come before You with gratitude and humility. Your Word reminds me of Your incredible grace and promises. In Ephesians 2:9, You tell me that my salvation is not of my own doing, but a gift from You. Help me to remember this truth daily and to live with a heart full of thankfulness for Your unmerited favor. Luke 2:9 speaks of the angel of the Lord shining with Your glory, bringing great joy. I pray that Your light continues to shine brightly in my life, guiding me and filling my heart with Your joy and peace. As Mark 2:9 reminds me, it is easier to heal the soul than to heal the body. I ask for Your healing touch, not just in my physical needs but in my spirit and mind as well. Grant me the strength to live a life that reflects Your love and grace. 1 Peter 2:9 calls me a chosen people, a royal priesthood. Help me to live according to this high calling, to proclaim Your excellencies, and to be a witness of Your transformative power in my life. Lastly, 1 Samuel 2:9 says that You will guard the feet of Your faithful servants. I ask for Your protection and guidance as I walk through each day. Keep me steady in Your ways and safe from harm. Thank You, Lord, for Your promises and Your love. I trust in Your guidance and rely on Your strength.

In Jesus' faithful name I pray, Amen

FEBRUARY 10

1 Corinthians 2:10 (NIV): These are the things God has revealed to us by his Spirit. The Spirit searches all things, even the deep things of God.

Ephesians 2:10 (KJV): For we are his workmanship, created in Christ Jesus unto good works.

Jonah 2:10 (NIV): And the LORD commanded the fish, and it vomited Jonah onto dry land.

Philippians 2:10 (ESV): That at the name of Jesus every knee should bow, in heaven and on earth and under the earth.

Proverbs 2:10 (ESV): For wisdom will come into your heart, and knowledge will be pleasant to your soul.

Revelation 2:10 (ESV): "Be faithful unto death, and I will give you the crown of life."

PRAYER

Dear Heavenly Father, Jehovah Raah (The LORD Is My Shepherd),

I come before You with a grateful heart, reflecting on the truths of Your Word. In 1 Corinthians 2:10, Your Word tells me that You reveal wisdom and understanding through Your Spirit. Help me to be open to Your guidance and revelation in my life. Ephesians 2:10 reminds me that "We are God's handiwork, created in Christ Jesus to do good works, which God prepared in advance for us to do" (NIV). I am grateful for the purpose You have given me. Help me to walk in the good works You have prepared for me, reflecting Your love and grace in all I do. Just as in Jonah 2:10 You commanded the fish, and it vomited Jonah onto dry land, I trust in Your power to work miracles in my life. When I feel overwhelmed or lost, remind me of Your mighty hand and Your ability to bring me through any situation. In Philippians 2:10, Your Word tells us that one day, every knee will bow to Jesus. I acknowledge Your authority and lordship over my life. Help me to honor You in all that I do, knowing that You are sovereign over all things. In keeping with Proverbs 2:10, grant me wisdom and understanding, Lord, that Your knowledge may bring joy and guidance to my life. Finally, in Revelation 2:10, You promise, that if I am faithful unto death, You will give me the heavenly crown of life. Strengthen my faith, Lord, so that I may remain steadfast and true to You, no matter the challenges I face. Thank You for Your promises and Your love. I trust in Your guidance and strength.

In Jesus' heavenly name I pray, Amen

FEBRUARY 11

2 Corinthians 2:11 (NKJV): Lest Satan should take advantage of us; for we are not ignorant of his devices.

Luke 2:11 (NIV): "Today in the town of David a Savior has been born to you; he is the Messiah, the Lord."

Proverbs 2:11 (NIV): Discretion will protect you, and understanding will guard you.

Romans 2:11 (NIV): For God does not show favoritism.

PRAYER

Dear Heavenly Father, Jehovah Rapha (The LORD Who Heals),

I come to You today with a heart full of gratitude and faith. Your Word guides and strengthens me, and I want to reflect on its promises. In 2 Corinthians 2:11, it says, "In order that Satan might not outwit us. For we are not unaware of his schemes" (NIV). Lord, help me to be vigilant and aware of the challenges I face. Give me the wisdom to recognize and overcome any temptation or deceit. As Luke 2:11 tells us, "In the town of David a Savior has been born to you; he is the Messiah, the Lord." Thank You for the gift of Your Son, Jesus, who came into the world humbly and for our salvation. Help me to remember the humility and grace with which He came. Proverbs 2:11 says, "Discretion will protect you, and understanding will guard you." Lord, grant me wisdom and discernment in all my decisions. Protect me from making choices that lead me away from Your path and guide me with Your understanding. In Romans 2:11, it states, "For God does not show favoritism." Thank You for treating everyone with equal love and fairness. Help me to reflect Your impartial love in my own life, treating others with kindness and respect. Thank You for Your guidance, protection, and unwavering love. I trust in Your wisdom and grace each day.

In Jesus' healing name I pray, Amen

FEBRUARY 12

Luke 2:12 (ESV): And this will be the sign to you: you will find a babe wrapped in swaddling clothes, lying in a manger.

Zechariah 2:12 (NKJV): And the Lord will take possession of Judah and his inheritance in the Holy Land, and will again choose Jerusalem.

Joel 2:12 (NKJV): "Now, therefore," says the Lord, "Turn to Me with all your heart, with fasting, with weeping, and with mourning."

2 Timothy 2:12 (ESV): If we endure, we shall also reign with Him; if we deny Him, He will also deny us.

PRAYER

Dear Heavenly Father, Jehovah Shammah (The Lord Is There),

I come before You with a heart full of gratitude and faith, seeking Your guidance and strength. Luke 2:12 reminds me that the angel said, "This will be a sign to you: You will find a baby wrapped in cloth and lying in a manger." Thank You for the humble and precious gift of Jesus. Help me to always remember the significance of His coming and to live in a way that honors Him. In Zechariah 2:12, Your Word says, "The Lord will inherit Judah as His portion in the holy land and will again choose Jerusalem." I am grateful that You choose us and dwell with us. Please guide me in making choices that align with Your will and bring honor to Your name. Joel 2:12 encourages us, "Even now, declares the Lord, return to me with all your heart, with fasting and weeping and mourning." Lord, help me to return to You wholeheartedly, seeking Your presence and renewal in every area of my life. Finally, 2 Timothy 2:12 says, "If we endure, we will also reign with Him. If we disown Him, He will also disown us" (NIV). Grant me the strength to endure in faith, remaining steadfast and true to You through all circumstances. Let my life reflect Your love and faithfulness. I will not deny You, Father. Thank You for Your promises and for being with me in every step of my journey. I trust in Your guidance and grace.

In Jesus' enduring name I pray, Amen

Micah 2:13 (NIV): The One who breaks open the way will go up before them; they will break through the gate and go out.

Revelation 2:13 (NIV): I know where you live—where Satan has his throne. Yet you remain true to my name.

Ruth 2:13 (NKJV): Then she said, "Let me find favor in your site, my lord; for you have comforted me, and have spoken kindly to your maidservant, though I am not like one of your maidservants."

──────────────── **PRAYER** ────────────────

Dear Heavenly Father, Maqowr Chay Mayim (Fountain of Living Waters),

I come to You with a heart open to Your guidance and grace. I'm thankful for the wisdom and promises in Your Word. In Micah 2:13, it says, "The One who breaks open the way will go up before them; they will break through the gate and go out. Their King will pass through before them, the LORD at their head." Thank You for going before me, opening the way, and leading me through any obstacles I face. Help me to trust in Your guidance and follow You with confidence. Revelation 2:13 reminds me of Your presence even in challenging times: "I know where you live—where Satan has his throne. Yet you remain true to my name; you did not renounce your faith in me, not even in the days of Antipas, my faithful witness, who was put to death in your city where Satan lives." Lord, strengthen my faith to remain true to You, no matter the difficulties or temptations around me. In Ruth 2:13, Ruth says, "May I continue to find favor in your eyes, my lord . . . You have put me at ease by speaking kindly to your servant." I ask for Your favor and kindness in my life. Help me to see Your blessings and to extend kindness to others, reflecting Your love and grace. Thank You, Lord, for Your constant presence, guidance, and favor. I trust in Your promises and seek to live faithfully in Your light.

In Jesus' trusting name I pray, Amen

FEBRUARY 14

Habakkuk 2:14 (ESV): For the earth shall be filled with the knowledge of the glory of the LORD as the waters cover the sea.

2 Corinthians 2:14 (NKJV): Now thanks be to God who always leads us in triumph in Christ.

Luke 2:14 (NKJV): "Glory to God in the highest, and on earth peace, goodwill toward men!"

James 2:14 (NKJV): What does it profit, my brethren, if someone says he has faith but does not have works? Can faith save him?

Philippians 2:14 (ESV): Do all things without grumbling or disputing.

PRAYER

Dear Heavenly Father, Jehovah Sabaoth (The LORD of Hosts),

I come before You with a grateful heart, reflecting on the truths of Your Word. In Habakkuk 2:14, it says, "For the earth will be filled with the knowledge of the glory of the LORD as the waters cover the sea." I pray that Your glory and knowledge fill my life and the world around me. Help me to recognize Your presence and reflect Your glory in all that I do. 2 Corinthians 2:14 assures us, "But thanks be to God, who always leads us as captives in Christ's triumphal procession and uses us to spread the aroma of the knowledge of Him everywhere" (NIV). Thank You for leading me in victory through Christ and using me to share Your love and truth. Help me to be a beacon of Your light and to spread Your message of hope. In Luke 2:14, the angels proclaimed, "Glory to God in the highest heaven, and on earth peace to those on whom His favor rests" (NIV). Lord, I praise You for Your peace and favor. Let Your peace fill my heart and guide my actions, and help me to live in a way that honors You. James 2:14 reminds me, "What good is it, my brothers and sisters, if someone claims to have faith but has no deeds? Can such faith save them?" (NIV). Help me to live out my faith through my actions, showing love and kindness to others. Let my life be a testimony of Your grace and truth. Finally, in Philippians 2:14, it says, "Do everything without grumbling or arguing." Lord, help me to approach each day with a positive spirit and to handle challenges with grace and patience. Thank You for Your guidance and for the blessings You provide. I trust in Your promises and seek to live faithfully in Your light.

In Jesus' almighty name I pray, Amen

FEBRUARY 15

Colossians 2:15 (ESV): And when he had disarmed the rulers and the authorities, he made a public spectacle of them, triumphing over them in the cross.

Malachi 2:15 (NIV): Has not the one God made you? You belong to Him in body and spirit. And what does the one God seek? Godly offspring.

Titus 2:15 (NKJV): Speak these things, exhort, and rebuke with all authority. Let no one despise you.

1 Timothy 2:15 (NIV): But women will be saved through childbearing—if they continue in faith, love and holiness with propriety.

PRAYER

Dear Heavenly Father, Jehovah Tzidkenu (The LORD Our Righteousness),

I come before You with a heart full of gratitude and trust in Your Word. In Colossians 2:15, it says, "And having disarmed the powers and authorities, He made a public spectacle of them, triumphing over them by the cross" (NIV). Thank You for the victory that Jesus achieved on the cross, overcoming all forces of evil. Help me to live in the confidence of this victory and to stand firm in Your strength. Malachi 2:15 speaks of the covenant You made: "Has not the one God made you? You belong to Him in body and spirit. And what does the one God seek? Godly offspring." Lord, guide me to honor the covenant we have with You, living a life that reflects Your love and pursuing godliness in all I do. In Titus 2:15, it says, "These, then, are the things you should teach. Encourage and rebuke with all authority. Do not let anyone despise you" (NIV). Give me the wisdom and courage to live by Your teachings and to share Your truth with others, doing so with authority and love. 1 Timothy 2:15 reminds us, "But women will be saved through childbearing—if they continue in faith, love, and holiness with propriety." Lord, help me to live a life marked by faith, love, and holiness, reflecting Your grace in all aspects of my life. Thank You for Your guidance and the strength You provide. Help me to live in a way that honors You and to share Your love with those around me.

In Jesus' righteous name I pray, Amen

FEBRUARY 16

I HAVE THE MIND OF CHRIST

1 Corinthians 2:16 (ESV): But we have the mind of Christ.

Judges 2:16 (NKJV): Nevertheless, the LORD raised up judges who delivered them out of the hand of those who plundered them.

Song of Solomon 2:16 (KJV): My beloved is mine, and I am His. He feeds his flock among the lilies.

PRAYER

Dear Heavenly Father, Hode (Majesty),

I come to You with a grateful heart, seeking Your guidance and wisdom through Your Word. 1 Corinthians 2:16 says, "For who has known the mind of the Lord so as to instruct him? But we have the mind of Christ." Thank You for giving me the mind of Christ through Your Spirit. Help me to think and act with Your wisdom and understanding, aligning my thoughts with Your will. In Judges 2:16, it tells us, "Then the LORD raised up judges, who saved them out of the hands of these raiders" (NIV). Lord, I ask for Your deliverance from any troubles or challenges I face. Just as You raised up judges to save Your people, please provide me with the help and guidance I need. Song of Solomon 2:16 reminds us, "My beloved is mine and I am his; he browses among the lilies" (NIV). Thank You for the intimate relationship You offer us. Help me to cherish and nurture my relationship with You, knowing that I am Yours and You are mine. Thank You, Lord, for Your guidance, wisdom, and the deep relationship You offer. Help me to trust in Your plans and to live each day with Your love and grace.

In Jesus' majestic name I pray, Amen

I WILL DO THE WILL OF GOD

James 2:17 (NKJV): Thus also faith by itself, if it does not have works, is dead.

Mark 2:17 (ESV): When Jesus heard it, he said to them, "Those who are well have no need of a physician, but those who are sick. I did not come to call the righteous, but sinners, to repentance."

1 John 2:17 (NKJV): And the world is passing away, and the lust of it; but he who does the will of God abides forever.

PRAYER

Dear Heavenly Father, Ner (Lamp),

I come before You with a humble heart, seeking Your guidance and strength. James 2:17 reminds me that "Faith by itself, if it is not accompanied by action, is dead" (NIV). Lord, help me to live out my faith through my actions. Let my life be a reflection of Your love and grace, demonstrating my faith through the way I treat others and the choices I make. In Mark 2:17, Jesus said, "It is not the healthy who need a doctor, but the sick. I have not come to call the righteous, but sinners" (NIV). Thank You for Your grace and for coming to save us when we are in need. Help me to recognize my need for Your forgiveness and to extend that same grace to those around me. 1 John 2:17 tells us, "The world and its desires pass away, but whoever does the will of God lives forever" (NIV). Lord, guide me to focus on Your will and to live according to Your purposes. Help me to keep my eyes on eternal things rather than temporary desires, finding my hope and fulfillment in You. Thank You for Your guidance and for the promises in Your Word. Strengthen me to live out my faith and to seek Your will each day.

In Jesus' faithful name I pray, Amen

FEBRUARY 18

1 Thessalonians 2:18 (NIV): For we wanted to come to you—certainly I, Paul, did, again and again—but Satan blocked our way.

Hebrews 2:18 (NKJV): For in that He Himself has suffered, being tempted, He is able to aid those who are tempted.

Genesis 2:18 (NKJV): And the Lord God said, "It is not good that man should be alone; I will make him a helper comparable to him."

——————————————— **PRAYER** ———————————————

Dear Heavenly Father, Maon (Dwelling Place),

I come before You with a grateful heart, seeking Your comfort and guidance. 1 Thessalonians 2:18 says, "For we wanted to come to you—certainly I, Paul, did, again and again—but Satan blocked our way" (NIV). Lord, I ask for Your protection and help in overcoming any obstacles that may come my way. Strengthen me to persevere and trust in Your plan even when I face challenges. In Hebrews 2:18, it tells us, "Because He Himself suffered when He was tempted, He is able to help those who are being tempted" (NIV). Thank You for understanding our struggles and for being a source of comfort and help. Help me to turn to You in times of temptation and difficulty, knowing that You offer support and strength. Genesis 2:18 reminds us, "The Lord God said, 'It is not good for the man to be alone. I will make a helper suitable for him.'" I am grateful for the relationships and support You provide in my life. Help me to appreciate and nurture these connections, and guide me to be a source of encouragement and help to others. Thank You for Your love, support, and for always being with me. I trust in Your guidance and seek to honor You in all that I do.

In Jesus' secure name I pray, Amen

I WILL RECIEVE THE HEAVENLY CROWN OF REJOICING

Colossians 2:19 (NLT): And they are not connected to Christ, the head of the body. For he holds the whole body together with its joints and ligaments, and it grows as God nourishes it.

Luke 2:19 (NKJV): But Mary kept all these things and pondered them in her heart.

John 2:19 (NKJV): Jesus answered and said to them, "Destroy this temple, and in three days I will raise it up."

1 Thessalonians 2:19 (NIV): For what is our hope, our joy, or the crown in which we will glory in the presence of our Lord Jesus when he comes? Is it not you?

PRAYER

Dear Heavenly Father, Di Ou Ta Panta (My Everything),

I come to You with a humble heart, seeking Your wisdom and strength. Colossians 2:19 says, "They have lost connection with the Head, from whom the whole body, supported and held together by its ligaments and sinews, grows as God causes it to grow" (NIV). Lord, help me stay closely connected to You, the Head of the Church. Strengthen my faith and keep me rooted in Your truth, so I may grow spiritually and be supported by Your love. In Luke 2:19, it tells us, "But Mary treasured up all these things and pondered them in her heart" (NIV). Help me to reflect deeply on the blessings and lessons You provide. Like Mary, may I treasure Your work in my life and ponder Your guidance with a grateful heart. John 2:19 says, "Jesus answered them, 'Destroy this temple, and I will raise it again in three days'" (NIV). Thank You for the promise of Jesus' resurrection and the hope it brings. Help me to live in the power of His resurrection, knowing that You can bring new life and transformation in my own life. 1 Thessalonians 2:19 reminds us, "For what is our hope, our joy, or the crown in which we will glory in the presence of our Lord Jesus when He comes? Is it not you?" Lord, I find joy in the relationships and community You've blessed me with. Help me to be a source of encouragement and support to others, reflecting Your love in all my interactions. I will stay the course and receive the heavenly crown of rejoicing. Thank You for Your presence and guidance in my life. I trust in Your promises and seek to live faithfully in Your light.

In Jesus' all-fulfilling name I pray, Amen

FEBRUARY 20

My sin died with Christ and I am reborn

Galatians 2:20 (KJV): I am crucified with Christ.

Colossians 2:20 (NLT): You have died with Christ and he has set you free from the spiritual powers of this world.

Daniel 2:20 (NKJV): Daniel answered and said: "Blessed be the name of God forever and ever, for wisdom and might be His."

PRAYER

Dear Heavenly Father, Gabahh (Transcendent),

I come before You with a heart full of gratitude and trust in Your Word. Galatians 2:20 says, "I have been crucified with Christ and I no longer live, but Christ lives in me. The life I now live in the body, I live by faith in the Son of God, who loved me and gave Himself for me" (NIV). Lord, thank You for the new life I have in Christ. Help me to live each day reflecting His love and grace, with my faith firmly anchored in Him. In Colossians 2:20, it tells us, "Since you died with Christ to the elemental spiritual forces of this world, why, as though you still belonged to the world, do you submit to its rules?" (NIV). Lord, guide me to live in the freedom and victory You've given me through Christ, avoiding the pitfalls of worldly distractions and staying focused on Your truth. Daniel 2:20 says, "Praise be to the name of God forever and ever; wisdom and power are His" (NIV). Thank You for Your infinite wisdom and power. Help me to seek Your wisdom in all areas of my life and to rely on Your strength to guide me through every challenge. Thank You for Your guidance, strength, and the new life You offer through Christ. I trust in Your promises and seek to live faithfully according to Your Word.

In Jesus' trusting name I pray, Amen

Romans 2:21 (ESV): You, therefore, who teach another, do you not teach yourself? You who preach that a man should not steal, do you steal?

Hosea 2:21 (ESV): "It shall come to pass in that day that I will answer," says the LORD; "I will answer the heavens, and they shall answer the earth."

Acts 2:21 (ESV): And it shall come to pass that whoever calls on the name of the Lord shall be saved.

PRAYER

Dear Heavenly Father, Miqweh Yisrael (Hope of Israel),

I come to You with a heart open to Your guidance and grace. Romans 2:21 says, "You, then, who teach others, do you not teach yourself? You who preach against stealing, do you steal?" (NIV). Lord, help me to live authentically and to practice what I preach. Guide me to be genuine in my faith and to act according to Your teachings in every area of my life. In Hosea 2:21, it says, "'In that day I will respond,' declares the LORD—'I will respond to the skies, and they will respond to the earth'" (NIV). Thank You for Your promise to respond to us and to our needs. Help me to trust in Your timing and to remain faithful, knowing that You hear my prayers and respond with Your perfect wisdom. Acts 2:21 tells us, "And everyone who calls on the name of the Lord will be saved" (NIV). I am grateful for the promise of salvation through calling on Your name. Help me to always turn to You in times of need and to share this hope with others. Thank You for Your faithfulness and for the promises in Your Word. I trust in Your guidance and seek to live in a way that reflects Your love and grace.

In Jesus' peaceful name I pray, Amen

FEBRUARY 22

I HAVE GOD'S SECRETS

Danielle 2:22 (ESV): He reveals deep and hidden things; He knows what lies in darkness, and light dwells with Him.

Haggai 2:22 (ESV): "I will overthrow the throne of kingdoms; I will destroy the strength of Gentile kingdoms."

Proverbs 2:22 (ESV): But the wicked will be cut off from the land, and the treacherous will be rooted out of it.

—————————————— **PRAYER** ——————————————

Dear Heavenly Father, Theos Monos Sophos (The Only Wise God),

I come to You with a heart full of gratitude and trust in Your guidance. Daniel 2:22 says, "He reveals deep and hidden things; He knows what lies in darkness, and light dwells with Him." Thank You for revealing Your wisdom and understanding to me. Help me to seek Your light in every area of my life and to trust that You know what is best. In Haggai 2:22, it tells us, "I will overturn royal thrones and shatter the power of foreign kingdoms" (NIV). Lord, I trust in Your sovereignty over all things. Help me to remember that You are in control and to rely on Your power to guide and protect me. Proverbs 2:22 says, "But the wicked will be cut off from the land, and the unfaithful will be torn from it" (NIV). Lord, guide me to live a life of faithfulness and integrity. Help me to follow Your path and to stay true to Your commands, avoiding the pitfalls of wickedness. Thank You for Your guidance, protection, and the wisdom You provide through Your Word. I trust in Your promises and seek to live according to Your will each day.

In Jesus' blessed name I pray, Amen

I AVOID FOOLISHNESS

Romans 2:23 (NKJV): You who make your boast in the law, do you dishonor God through breaking the law?

Genesis 2:23 (NKJV): And Adam said; "This is now bone of my bones and flesh of my flesh; she shall be called woman, because she was taken out of man."

2 Timothy 2:23 (NKJV): But avoid foolish and ignorant disputes, knowing that they generate strife.

—————————————— PRAYER ——————————————

Dear Heavenly Father, Theos Pas Paraklesis (The God of All Comfort),

I come to You with a heart open to Your guidance and wisdom. Romans 2:23 says, "You who boast in the law, do you dishonor God by breaking the law?" (NIV). Lord, help me to live consistently with Your teachings, avoiding hypocrisy and honoring You in both my words and actions. Guide me to be genuine in my faith and to uphold Your standards in all areas of my life. In Genesis 2:23, it tells us, "The man said, 'This is now bone of my bones and flesh of my flesh; she shall be called "woman," for she was taken out of man'" (NIV). Thank You for the gift of relationships and the way You created us to be in community with one another. Help me to appreciate and nurture the relationships in my life, reflecting Your love and unity. 2 Timothy 2:23 says, "Don't have anything to do with foolish and stupid arguments, because you know they produce quarrels" (NIV). Lord, grant me the wisdom to avoid unnecessary conflicts and to approach disagreements with grace and understanding. Help me to focus on building peace and fostering good relationships. Thank You for Your guidance and the wisdom found in Your Word. Help me to live according to Your truth and to reflect Your love in all that I do.

In Jesus' comforting name I pray, Amen

FEBRUARY 24

Genesis 2:24 (NKJV): Therefore a man shall leave his father and mother and be joined to his wife, and they shall become one flesh.

James 2:24 (NKJV): You see then that a man is justified by works, and not by faith only.

2 Timothy 2:24 (NKJV): And a servant of the Lord must not quarrel but be gentle to all, able to teach, patient.

PRAYER

Dear Heavenly Father, Elohim Shama (The God Who Hears),

I come before You with a heart seeking Your wisdom and guidance. Genesis 2:24 says, "That is why a man leaves his father and mother and is united to his wife, and they become one flesh" (NIV). Thank You for the beautiful design of relationships and unity that You have established. Help me to cherish and honor the relationships in my life, reflecting Your love and commitment in all that I do. James 2:24 tells us, "You see that a person is considered righteous by what they do and not by faith alone" (NIV). Lord, guide me to live out my faith through my actions. Let my life be a testament to Your grace, showing love and kindness in all my interactions. 2 Timothy 2:24 reminds us, "And the Lord's servant must not be quarrelsome but must be kind to everyone, able to teach, not resentful" (NIV). Help me to approach others with kindness and patience, avoiding unnecessary arguments and fostering peace. Grant me the ability to teach and guide with a loving and gentle spirit. Thank You for Your guidance and the strength You provide through Your Word. Help me to live in a way that honors You and reflects Your love to those around me.

In Jesus' justified name I pray, Amen

FEBRUARY 25

Genesis 2:25 (NKJV): And they were both naked, the man and his wife, and were not ashamed.

Exodus 2:25 (NKJV): And God looked up upon the children of Israel, and God acknowledged them.

Revelation 2:25 (NKJV): "But hold fast what you have till I come."

PRAYER

Dear Heavenly Father, Melekh HaGoyim (King of Nations),

I come before You with a heart open to Your guidance and grace. Genesis 2:25 says, "Adam and his wife were both naked, and they felt no shame" (NIV). Lord, thank You for the purity and innocence You created in the beginning. Help me to live with transparency and integrity, free from shame, and to embrace the life You have called me to live. Exodus 2:25 tells us, "So God looked on the Israelites and was concerned about them" (NIV). Thank You for Your deep concern and care for us. I am grateful that You see my struggles and joys and that You are always attentive to my needs. Help me to trust in Your care and to lean on Your strength in times of difficulty. Revelation 2:25 says, "Except hold on to what you have until I come" (NIV). Lord, help me to remain steadfast in my faith and to hold on to Your promises and truths. Give me the strength to persevere and stay true to You, even as I wait for Your return. Thank You for Your unwavering love, concern, and the guidance found in Your Word. Help me to live faithfully and to trust in Your promises each day.

In Jesus' appointed name I pray, Amen

Ecclesiastes 2:26 (ESV): For God gives wisdom and knowledge and joy to a man who is good in His sight; but to the sinner He gives the work of gathering, and collecting, that he may give to him who is good before God. This also is vanity and grasping for the wind.

2 Timothy 2:26 (NLT): Then they will come to their senses and escape from the devil's trap.

Acts 2:26 (NKJV): Therefore my heart rejoiced, and my tongue was glad; moreover my flesh also will rest in hope.

PRAYER

Dear Heavenly Father, Pneuma (Spirit),

I come before You with a heart seeking Your wisdom and guidance. Ecclesiastes 2:26 says, "To the one who pleases Him, God gives wisdom, knowledge, and happiness, but to the sinner, He gives the task of gathering and storing up wealth to hand it over to the one who pleases God" (NIV). Lord, thank You for offering wisdom, knowledge, and joy to those who seek to please You. Help me to live in a way that honors You, so that I may receive the blessings You promise and experience true contentment. 2 Timothy 2:26 tells us, "And that they will come to their senses and escape from the trap of the devil, who has taken them captive to do his will" (NIV). Lord, I ask for Your help in escaping any traps or deceptions that may come my way. Grant me clarity and strength to resist temptation and to follow Your path with discernment. Acts 2:26 says, "Therefore my heart is glad and my tongue rejoices; my body also will rest in hope" (NIV). Thank You for the joy and security that come from knowing You. Help me to rest in Your peace and to rejoice in the security of Your presence, finding comfort and strength in Your promises. Thank You for Your guidance and the wisdom You provide through Your Word. Help me to live faithfully and to experience the fullness of joy and peace that comes from You.

In Jesus' hopeful name I pray, Amen

I REMAIN IN GOD

Jeremiah 2:27 (NKJV): Saying to a tree, "You are my father," and to a stone "You gave birth to me." For they have turned their back to Me, and not their face. But in the time of their trouble they will say, "Arise and save us."

Mark 2:27 (NKJV): And He said to them, "The Sabbath was made for man, and not man for the Sabbath."

1 John 2:27 (NIV): As for you, the anointing you received from Him remains in you, and you do not need anyone to teach you. But as His anointing teaches you about all things and as that anointing is real, not counterfeit—just as it has taught you, remain in Him.

PRAYER

Dear Heavenly Father, Yahweh Channun (LORD of Grace),

I come before You with a heart open to Your guidance and love. Jeremiah 2:27 says, "They say to wood, 'You are my father,' and to stone, 'You gave me birth.' They have turned their backs to me and not their faces; yet when they are in trouble, they say, 'Come and save us!'" (NIV). Lord, help me to always turn to You first and not rely on anything or anyone else for guidance and support. Teach me to seek Your help in every circumstance and to keep my focus on You. Mark 2:27 tells us, "Then He said to them, 'The Sabbath was made for man, not man for the Sabbath'" (NIV). Thank You for creating rest and renewal for us. Help me to use this time wisely, finding rest in Your presence and allowing it to rejuvenate my spirit, so I can live fully in Your purpose. 1 John 2:27 says, "As for you, the anointing you received from Him remains in you, and you do not need anyone to teach you. But as His anointing teaches you about all things and as that anointing is real, not counterfeit—just as it has taught you, remain in Him." Lord, thank You for the anointing of Your Spirit that teaches and guides me. Help me to remain in You, trusting in Your guidance and wisdom, and to be faithful to Your calling. Thank You for Your presence, guidance, and the strength You provide through Your Word. Help me to stay focused on You and to find rest and renewal in Your love.

In Jesus' restful name I pray, Amen

FEBRUARY 28

Daniel 2:28 (ESV): "There is a God in heaven who reveals mysteries."

Acts 2:28 (NIV): You have made known to me the paths of life; you will feel me with joy in your presence.

Joel 2:28 (NKJV): And it shall come to pass afterward that I will pour out My Spirit on all flesh; your sons and your daughters shall prophesy, your old man shall dream dreams, your young men shall see visions.

PRAYER

Dear Heavenly Father, Gelah Raz (Revealer of Mysteries),

I come to You with a heart open to Your guidance and blessings. Daniel 2:28 says, "But there is a God in heaven who reveals mysteries; He has shown King Nebuchadnezzar what will happen in days to come" (NIV). Lord, I am grateful that You are a God who reveals and guides us through the mysteries of life. Help me to trust in Your wisdom and to seek Your guidance in all areas of my life. In Acts 2:28, it tells us, "You have made known to me the paths of life; You will fill me with joy in Your presence." Thank You for revealing the path to life and for the joy that comes from being in Your presence. Help me to walk in the way You have set before me and to find true joy and fulfillment in knowing You. Joel 2:28 promises, "And afterward, I will pour out my Spirit on all people. Your sons and daughters will prophesy, your old men will dream dreams, your young men will see visions" (NIV). Lord, thank You for the gift of Your Spirit and the ways You speak to us. Fill me with Your Spirit, and guide me with Your visions and dreams. Help me to be attentive to Your voice and to use the gifts You have given me to serve others. Thank You for Your guidance, joy, and the outpouring of Your Spirit. I trust in Your promises and seek to live faithfully in Your light.

In Jesus' revealing name I pray, Amen

I HAVE EARS TO HEAR

Joel 2:29 (NKJV): And also on My menservants and on My maidservants I will pour out My Spirit in those days.

Revelation 2:29 (ESV): "He who has an ear, let him hear what the Spirit says to the churches."

1 John 2:29 (NKJV): If you know that He is righteous, you know that everyone who practices righteousness is born of Him.

PRAYER

Dear Heavenly Father, Alpha and Omega (The First and the Last),

Hear my prayer, pour Your Spirit on to me, give me ears to hear what the Holy Spirit speaks. I will walk in righteousness. Joel 2:29 says, "Even on my servants, both men and women, I will pour out My Spirit in those days" (NIV). Lord, I thank You for the outpouring of Your Spirit on all Your people. Fill me with Your Spirit and guide me in all that I do, so that I can serve You faithfully and reflect Your love to those around me. In Revelation 2:29, it tells us, "Whoever has ears, let them hear what the Spirit says to the churches" (NIV). Lord, help me to listen carefully to Your Spirit's guidance. Open my ears and my heart to receive Your wisdom and direction, so that I can follow Your will and live according to Your plan. 1 John 2:29 says, "If you know that He is righteous, you know that everyone who does what is right has been born of Him." Thank You for Your righteousness and for the example of living a righteous life that You set for us. Help me to live according to Your standards and to act justly in all my interactions, reflecting Your character in my daily life. Thank You for Your Spirit, Your guidance, and Your call to righteousness. I trust in Your promises and seek to live faithfully according to Your Word.

In Jesus' almighty name I pray, Amen

MARCH 1

Colossians 3:1 (ESV): If then you have been raised with Christ, seek the things that are above.

Galatians 3:1 (ESV): O foolish Galatians! Who has bewitched you?

1 John 3:1 (NIV): See what great love the Father has lavished on us, that we should be called children of God! And that is what we are! The reason the world does not know us is that it did not know Him.

Proverbs 3:1 (NIV): My son, do not forget my teaching, but keep my commands in your heart.

PRAYER

Dear Heavenly Father, El Shaddai (God Almighty),

I will not forget my Father in heaven. All His teachings I will place in my heart. I am risen as is Christ. I bind and rebuke any bewitchment that would keep me from obeying the truth of God. Colossians 3:1 says, "Since, then, you have been raised with Christ, set your hearts on things that are above, where Christ is, seated at the right hand of God" (NIV). Lord, help me to focus on heavenly things and to keep my heart and mind set on You, where Christ reigns. Guide me to live each day with a focus on Your eternal promises and not on temporary concerns. In Galatians 3:1, it says, "You foolish Galatians! Who has bewitched you? Before your very eyes Jesus Christ was clearly portrayed as crucified" (NIV). Lord, keep me grounded in the truth of the Gospel. Help me to stay focused on the sacrifice of Jesus and not be swayed by anything that leads me away from the core of Your message. 1 John 3:1 tells us, "See what great love the Father has lavished on us, that we should be called children of God! And that is what we are!" Thank You for Your incredible love and for adopting me as Your child. Help me to live in the confidence of Your love and to reflect Your kindness and grace to others. Proverbs 3:1 says, "My son, do not forget my teaching, but keep my commands in your heart." Lord, remind me daily of Your teachings and help me to keep Your commands close to my heart. Guide me to live according to Your wisdom and to follow Your guidance in all I do. Thank You for Your love, guidance, and the promise of new life in Christ. Help me to stay focused on You and to live out Your teachings faithfully.

In Jesus' intimate name I pray, Amen

MARCH 2

Malachi 3:2 (ESV): Who can endure the day of his coming, and who can stand when he appears? For he is like a refiner's fire and like fullers' soap.

2 Thessalonians 3:2 (NIV): And pray that we may be delivered from wicked and evil people, for not everyone has faith.

Zechariah 3:2 (KJV): The LORD rebuke thee, O Satan!

1 John 3:2 (NIV): But we know that when Christ appears, we shall be like him, for we shall see him as he is.

PRAYER

Dear Heavenly Father, El Yeshurun (The God of Jeshurun),

My life is purified by the Lord's fire as in Malachi 3:2. No wicked or unreasonable people will overcome me. My God reigns over all, and I will be more like Jesus. Lord, I recognize Your holiness and the refining work You do in our lives. Help me to prepare my heart to stand before You, trusting that Your refining process will make me more like Christ. According to 2 Thessalonians 3:2, it tells us to ask for Your protection from those who seek to lead us astray. Strengthen my faith and help me to discern truth from deception, relying on Your guidance in all situations. Zechariah 3:2 says, "The LORD said to Satan, 'The LORD rebuke you, Satan! The LORD, who has chosen Jerusalem, rebukes you! Is not this man a burning stick snatched from the fire?'" (NIV). Thank You for rebuking the enemy on our behalf. I trust in Your power to protect and deliver me from the attacks of the enemy. Help me to stand firm in Your strength and to trust in Your deliverance. 1 John 3:2 tells us, "Dear friends, now we are children of God, and what we will be has not yet been made known. But we know that when Christ appears, we shall be like Him, for we shall see Him as He is." Lord, I am grateful for the promise of being transformed to be like Christ. Help me to live each day with the hope of Your return, growing in Your likeness and reflecting Your love. Thank You for Your protection, refining, and the promise of transformation. Help me to remain steadfast in faith and to live according to Your will.

In Jesus' safe name I pray, Amen

HE LIFTS MY HEAD ON HIGH

Proverbs 3:3 (NIV): Let love and faithfulness, never leave you; bind them around your neck, write them on the tablet of your heart.

Psalm 3:3 (NIV): But you, LORD, are a shield around me, my glory, the One who lifts my head high.

Philippians 3:3 (NKJV): Rejoice in Christ Jesus, and have no confidence in the flesh.

Colossians 3:3 (NIV): For you died, and your life is now hidden with Christ in God.

John 3:3 (NIV): Jesus replied, "Very truly I tell you, no one can see the kingdom of God unless they are born again."

––––––––––––––––––– **PRAYER** –––––––––––––––––––

Dear Heavenly Father, Rum Rosh (The One Who Lifts My Head),

My body is filled with love and faithfulness, the love and faithfulness only God can provide. He keeps me safe and lifts my head up high. I will sing of Christ's protection. Thank You for showing me Your kingdom, Lord. I am born again because of my belief in Christ. As in Proverbs 3:3, Lord, help me to embrace love and faithfulness in all aspects of my life. May these qualities be evident in my actions and relationships, reflecting Your character in everything I do. Lord, thank You for being my protector and source of honor. I trust in Your protection and strength to lift me up through any challenges I face. Help me to remain steadfast in You and find comfort in Your presence as I'm reminded in Psalm 3:3. Philippians 3:3 tells me to place my confidence in You alone, rather than in my own abilities or achievements. Help me to boast only in Christ and to rely on Your Holy Spirit for strength and direction. Colossians 3:3 says, "For you died, and your life is now hidden with Christ in God." Thank You for the new life I have in Christ. Help me to live each day with the understanding that my true identity is found in Jesus. Guide me to live in a way that reflects this new life and remains focused on Your will. John 3:3 tells us, "Jesus replied, 'Very truly I tell you, no one can see the kingdom of God unless they are born again.'" Lord, I am grateful for the new birth and transformation that comes through Christ. Help me to live out the change You have made in my life and to share the hope of being born again with others. Thank You for Your love, protection, and the new life I have in Christ. Guide me to live faithfully and to reflect Your grace in all I do.

In Jesus' affectionate name I pray, Amen

MARCH 4

Colossians 3:4 (NIV): When Christ, who is your life, appears, then you also will appear with him in glory.

Habakkuk 3:4 (NIV): His splendor was like the sunrise; rays flashed from his hand, where his power was hidden.

James 3:4 (NIV): Or take ships as an example. Although they are so large and are driven by strong winds, they are steered by a very small rudder wherever the pilot wants to go.

Galatians 3:4 (NIV): Have you experienced so much in vain—if it really was in vain?

Hebrews 3:4 (NIV): For every house is built by someone, but God is the builder of everything.

PRAYER

Dear Heavenly Father, El Gibbor (Mighty God),

I come to You with a heart open to Your guidance and grace. Colossians 3:4 says, "When Christ, who is your life, appears, then you also will appear with Him in glory." Lord, I am thankful that Christ is my life and my hope. Help me to live each day with a focus on His return, and to let His presence shine through me as I await the day of His glory. In Habakkuk 3:4, it tells us, "His splendor was like the sunrise; rays flashed from His hand, where His power was hidden." Thank You for the power and splendor of Your presence. Help me to recognize and trust in Your hidden power and to be encouraged by Your mighty works in my life. James 3:4 says, "Or take ships as an example. Although they are so large and are driven by strong winds, they are steered by a very small rudder wherever the pilot wants to go." Lord, guide my thoughts and actions as the rudder steers a ship. Help me to direct my life according to Your will and to let Your guidance shape my path. In Galatians 3:4, it says, "Have you experienced so much in vain—if it really was in vain?" Lord, help me to stay focused on the purpose of my faith and not to let my efforts be in vain. Strengthen me to continue in Your ways and to see the value in the journey of faith. Hebrews 3:4 tells us, "For every house is built by someone, but God is the builder of everything." Thank You for being the ultimate Builder of my life and all creation. Help me to trust in Your plan and to build my life on the foundation of Your truth and guidance. Thank You for Your presence, guidance, and the strength You provide. Help me to live faithfully and to see Your hand at work in every part of my life.

In Jesus' everlasting name I pray, Amen

MARCH 5

I DO NOT LEAN ON MY OWN UNDERSTANDING

Proverbs 3:5 (ESV): Trust in the LORD with all your heart, and do not lean on your own understanding.

Psalm 3:5 (NIV): I lie down and sleep; I wake again, because the LORD sustains me.

Genesis 3:5 (ESV): For God knows that when you eat of it, your eyes will be opened, and you will be like God, knowing good and evil.

Colossians 3:5 (NIV): Put to death, therefore, whatever belongs to your earthly nature; sexual immorality, impurity, lust, evil desires, and greed, which is idolatry.

 **PRAYER**

Dear Heavenly Father, Bara' (Creator),

I come before You seeking Your guidance and wisdom. Proverbs 3:5 says, "Trust in the LORD with all your heart and lean not on your own understanding" (NIV). Lord, help me to fully trust in You and not rely solely on my own thoughts and plans. Guide me with Your wisdom and help me to trust Your direction in every aspect of my life. In Psalm 3:5, it says, "I lie down and sleep; I wake again, because the LORD sustains me." Thank You for the peace and security You provide each day. Help me to rest in Your care, knowing that You sustain me through all circumstances and that I can find comfort in Your presence. Genesis 3:5 tells us, "For God knows that when you eat from it your eyes will be opened, and you will be like God, knowing good and evil" (NIV). Lord, give me discernment to understand the difference between good and evil and to make choices that honor You. Help me to seek Your guidance rather than relying on my own judgment. I will not listen to the voice of the enemy. Colossians 3:5 says, "Put to death, therefore, whatever belongs to your earthly nature: sexual immorality, impurity, lust, evil desires and greed, which is idolatry." Lord, help me to overcome the desires and behaviors that do not align with Your will. Strengthen me to live according to Your standards and to focus on what is pure and pleasing to You. Thank You for Your guidance, protection, and the strength You provide to live according to Your will. Help me to trust You fully, rest in Your care, and seek Your wisdom in all I do.

In Jesus' pure name I pray, Amen

MARCH 6

1 Timothy 3:6 (ESV): He must not be a recent convert, or he may become puffed up with conceit and fall into the condemnation of the devil.

Malachi 3:6 (NKJV): For I am the LORD, I do not change; therefore, you are not consumed, O sons of Jacob.

Proverbs 3:6 (NKJV): In all your ways acknowledge Him, and He shall direct your paths.

Exodus 3:6 (NIV): Then he said, "I am the God of your father, the God of Abraham, the God of Isaac and the God of Jacob." At this Moses hid his face, because he was afraid to look at God.

——————————————————  **PRAYER** ——————————————————

Dear Heavenly Father, Lo Shanah (Unchanging God),

I come to You with a heart open to Your guidance and wisdom. 1 Timothy 3:6 says, "He must not be a recent convert, or he may become conceited and fall under the same judgment as the devil" (NIV). Lord, help me to grow in my faith with humility and wisdom. Protect me from pride and guide me to remain grounded in Your truth as I mature spiritually. Malachi 3:6 tells us, "I the LORD do not change. So you, the descendants of Jacob, are not destroyed" (NIV). Thank You for Your unchanging nature and for the assurance that Your promises are steadfast. Help me to trust in Your constant love and faithfulness, knowing that You are always with me. Proverbs 3:6 says, "In all your ways submit to Him, and He will make your paths straight" (NIV). Lord, guide me to submit every aspect of my life to You. Help me to follow Your path and trust that You will lead me in the right direction. Exodus 3:6 says, "Then He said, 'I am the God of your father, the God of Abraham, the God of Isaac and the God of Jacob.' At this, Moses hid his face, because he was afraid to look at God." Lord, I am in awe of Your majesty and power. Help me to approach You with reverence and respect, recognizing Your greatness and the sacredness of Your presence. Thank You for Your guidance, unchanging nature, and the direction You provide. Help me to live in submission to Your will and to honor You in all that I do.

In Jesus' steadfast name I pray, Amen

MARCH 7

I FEAR THE LORD

1 Samuel 3:7 (ESV): Now Samuel did not yet know the LORD, and the word of the LORD had not yet been revealed to him.

Zechariah 3:7 (NIV): This is what the LORD Almighty says; "If you will walk in obedience to me and keep my requirements, then you will govern my house and have charge of my courts, and I will give you a place among these standing here."

Ecclesiastes 3:7 (NIV): A time to tear and a time to mend, a time to be silent and a time to speak.

Proverbs 3:7 (NIV): Do not be wise in your own eyes; fear the LORD and shun evil.

Psalm 3:7 (NIV): Arise, LORD! Deliver me, my God! Strike all my enemies on the jaw; break the teeth of the wicked.

PRAYER

Dear Heavenly Father, Maqowr Chay Mayim (Fountain of Living Water),

I come to You seeking Your guidance and wisdom for my life. In 1 Samuel 3:7 the word of the Lord had not yet been revealed. Lord, I ask for Your revelation and understanding in my life. Help me to grow in my knowledge of You and to hear Your voice clearly, just as You revealed Yourself to Samuel. Lord, as in Zechariah 3:7, help me to walk in obedience to Your commands. Guide me to fulfill the responsibilities You have entrusted to me and to live in accordance with Your will. Ecclesiastes 3:7 tells me there's a time to mend, be silent, and speak. Lord, grant me the wisdom to recognize the right time for every action in my life. Help me to know when to speak and when to remain silent, and to navigate the different seasons with grace and discernment. Proverbs 3:7 shows me to stay humble and reminds me not to rely on my own understanding. Help me to honor You with reverence and to turn away from anything that is not pleasing to You. Psalm 3:7 reminds me to seek Your protection and deliverance from any challenges or adversities I may face. Please strengthen me and guide me through difficult times, knowing that You are my ultimate defender.

In Jesus' living name I pray, Amen

Psalm 3:8 (MSG): Real help comes from God. Your blessing clothes your people.

Colossians 3:8 (NIV): But now you must also rid yourselves of all such things as these; anger, rage, malice, slander, and filthy language from your lips.

Ecclesiastes 3:8 (ESV): A time to love and a time to hate, a time for war and a time for peace.

Philippians 3:8 (NLT): Yes, everything else is worthless when compared with the infinite value of knowing Christ Jesus, my Lord. For his sake, I have discarded everything else, counting it all as garbage, so that I could gain Christ.

2 Peter 3:8 (NLT): But you must not forget this one thing, dear friends; a day is like a thousand years to the Lord, and a thousand years is like a day.

 **PRAYER**

Dear Heavenly Father, Jehovah-Jireh (The LORD My Provider),

I come to You with a humble heart, seeking Your guidance and grace. As in Psalm 3:8, Lord, I trust that deliverance comes from You alone. Please bless me and guide me through any challenges I face. In Colossians 3:8, it tells me to let go of negative behaviors and to cultivate a heart that reflects God's love and purity. Cleanse me from anything that does not honor You and guide me to live in a way that pleases You. Ecclesiastes 3:8 says, "A time to love and a time to hate, a time for war and a time for peace." Lord, give me wisdom to understand and navigate the different seasons in my life. Help me to respond with love and peace, even when facing difficult times. Philippians 3:8 teaches me to value knowing God above all else. May I see everything else in my life as secondary to the relationship I have with You. Strengthen my commitment to You and help me to live with the passion of knowing Christ. 2 Peter 3:8 reminds me to remember that Your timing is perfect and different from ours. Teach me to trust in Your timing and to be patient as I wait for Your promises to unfold. Thank You for Your deliverance, guidance, and the incredible worth of knowing You. Help me to live with a heart that reflects Your love, patience, and wisdom.

In Jesus' divine name I pray, Amen

MARCH 9

I honor the Lord

Revelation 3:9 (ESV): Behold, I will make those of the synagogue of Satan who say that they are Jews and are not, but lie—behold, I will make them come and bow down before your feet, and they will learn that I have loved you.

Proverbs 3:9 (NKJV): Honor the Lord with your possessions, and with the first fruits of all your increase.

Colossians 3:9 (NIV): Do not lie to each other, since you have taken off your old self with its practices.

James 3:9 (NIV): With the tongue we praise our Lord and Father, and with it we curse human beings, who have been made in God's likeness.

Genesis 3:9 (ESV): Then the Lord God called the man, "Where are you?"

PRAYER

Dear Heavenly Father, Malak Haggoel (Redeeming Angel),

I come to You with a heart open to Your guidance and grace. Revelation 3:9 shows me to trust in Your justice and Your love for Your people. Help me to remain steadfast in my faith and to trust that You will uphold Your promises. Proverbs 3:9 teaches me to honor You with all that I have, including my resources and the firstfruits of my labor. Teach me to give generously and to use my blessings in ways that bring glory to Your name. Colossians 3:9 says, "Do not lie to each other, since you have taken off your old self with its practices." Lord, guide me to live with honesty and integrity in all my relationships. Help me to shed any deceit and to embrace the new self that reflects Your truth and righteousness. James 3:9 says, "With the tongue we praise our Lord and Father, and with it we curse human beings, who have been made in God's likeness." Lord, help me to use my words to build others up and to praise You, rather than tearing others down. Teach me to be mindful of how I speak and to reflect Your love and respect in my communication. Genesis 3:9 tells us, "But the Lord God called to the man, 'Where are you?'" Lord, I am grateful that You seek us and call us back to You, even when we stray. Help me to respond to Your call and to seek Your presence in my daily life. Thank You for Your justice, guidance, and the reminder to live honestly and with integrity. Help me to honor You with my resources, my words, and my actions, and to always seek Your presence.

In Jesus' honorable name I pray, Amen

MARCH 10

Malachi 3:10 (NIV): "Bring the whole tithe into the storehouse, that there may be food in my house. Test me in this," says the LORD Almighty, "and see if I will not throw open the floodgates of heaven and pour out so much blessing that there will not be room enough to store it."

Ephesians 3:10 (NIV): His intent was that now, through the church, the manifold wisdom of God should be made known to the rulers and authorities in the heavenly realms.

Habakkuk 3:10 (NIV): The mountains saw You and writhed; torrents of water swept by. The deep roared and lifted its waves on high.

Isaiah 3:10 (NIV): Tell the righteous it will be well with them, for they will enjoy the fruit of their deeds.

———————————————— **PRAYER** ————————————————

Dear Heavenly Father, Yated Aman Maqom (Nail in a Firm Place),

I come before You with gratitude and a heart seeking Your guidance. Malachi 3:10 says, to bring my tithe fully to the Lord. I thank You for Your promise of abundance when we are faithful in our giving. Help me to be generous with my resources and to trust in Your provision as the floodgates of heaven open over my life. In Ephesians 3:10, it tells us, "His intent was that now, through the church, the manifold wisdom of God should be made known to the rulers and authorities in the heavenly realms." Lord, guide me to be a part of Your work through the church, sharing Your wisdom and love with others. Help me to contribute to the mission of spreading Your truth and grace. Habakkuk 3:10 says, "The mountains saw You and writhed; torrents of water swept by. The deep roared and lifted its waves on high." Lord, You are powerful and sovereign over all creation. Help me to recognize Your majesty and to trust in Your power, even when facing overwhelming challenges. Isaiah 3:10 tells us, "Tell the righteous it will be well with them, for they will enjoy the fruit of their deeds." Lord, I thank You for the promise that it will be well with those who live righteously. Help me to live in a way that pleases You and to find comfort in the knowledge that my actions have eternal significance. Thank You for Your promises of provision, wisdom, power, and blessings. Help me to live faithfully, generously, and with trust in Your plans.

In Jesus' stable name I pray, Amen

Habakkuk 3:11 (NIV): "The sun and moon stood still in the heavens at the glint of Your flying arrows, at the lightning of Your flashing spear."

Amos 3:11 (ESV): Therefore this is what the Sovereign LORD says: "An enemy will overrun your land, pull down your strongholds and plunder your fortresses."

Luke 3:11 (NIV): Anyone who has two shirts should share with the one who has none, and anyone who has food should do the same.

Ecclesiastes 3:11 (NIV): He has made everything beautiful in its time. He has also set eternity in the human heart; yet no one can fathom what God has done from beginning to end.

PRAYER

Dear Heavenly Father, 'Or Yisraẹl (Light of Israel),

I come to You with a heart open to Your wisdom and guidance. Lord, I am in awe of Your power and majesty as in Habakkuk 3:11. Help me to trust in Your mighty works and to find peace knowing that You are in control of all things even the sun and the moon. In Amos 3:11, it says, "Therefore this is what the Sovereign LORD says: 'An enemy will overrun your land, pull down your strongholds and plunder your fortresses.'" Lord my God, let the palaces and headquarters of darkness be spoiled in the name of Jesus. Luke 3:11 tells us, "John answered, 'Anyone who has two shirts should share with the one who has none, and anyone who has food should do the same.'" Lord, help me to live generously and to share my blessings with others. Teach me to be compassionate and to use what I have to help those in need. Ecclesiastes 3:11 says, "He has made everything beautiful in its time. He has also set eternity in the human heart; yet no one can fathom what God has done from beginning to end." Lord, I trust that You make everything beautiful in Your timing. Help me to have patience and to find hope in Your eternal plan, even when I don't understand the full picture. Thank You for Your power, provision, and the beauty of Your timing. Help me to listen to Your Word, live generously, and trust in Your perfect plan.

In Jesus' illuminating name I pray, Amen

MARCH 12

Malachi 3:12 (NIV): "Then all the nations will call you blessed, for yours will be a delightful land," says the Lord Almighty.

John 3:12 (NIV): "I have spoken to you of earthly things and you do not believe; how then will you believe if I speak of heavenly things?"

1 Thessalonians 3:12 (NIV): May the Lord make your love increase and overflow for each other and for everyone else, just as ours does for you.

Ephesians 3:12 (NIV): In Him and through faith in Him we may approach God with freedom and confidence.

Colossians 3:12 (NIV): Therefore, as God's chosen people, holy and dearly loved, clothe yourselves with compassion, kindness, humility, gentleness and patience.

PRAYER

Dear Heavenly Father, El Chaiyai (God of My Life),

I come before You with a heart full of gratitude and faith. Malachi 3:12 says all nations will call me blessed. Lord, I pray that Your blessings will be evident in my life and that others will see Your goodness and favor through me. Help me to live in a way that reflects Your blessings and draws others to You. John 3:12 reminds me to increase my faith and understanding. Help me to trust in Your Word and believe in the greater heavenly truths You reveal, even when they are beyond my earthly understanding. As in 1 Thessalonians 3:12, I ask that You fill my heart with Your love and enable it to overflow to others. Teach me to love those around me with the same compassion and grace that You have shown me. Ephesians 3:12 tells me I can come to You with a bold confidence. Help me to approach You with a heart full of faith and to seek Your guidance in all areas of my life. Colossians 3:12 says, "Therefore, as God's chosen people, holy and dearly loved, clothe yourselves with compassion, kindness, humility, gentleness and patience." Lord, help me to embody these qualities in my daily life. Let me be a reflection of Your love and grace to everyone I encounter. Thank You for Your blessings, love, and the ability to approach You with confidence. Guide me to live with compassion, faith, and trust in Your presence.

In Jesus' everlasting name I pray, Amen

MARCH 13

I am redeemed

Galatians 3:13 (NIV): Christ redeemed us from the curse of the law by becoming a curse for us, for it is written: "Cursed is everyone who is hung on a pole."

James 3:13 (ESV): Who is wise and understanding among you? Let them show it by their good life, by deeds done in the humility that comes from wisdom.

Colossians 3:13 (NLT): Make allowance for each other's faults, and forgive anyone who offends you. Remember the Lord forgave you, so you must forgive others.

Genesis 3:13 (NIV): Then the Lord God said to the woman, "What is this you have done?" The woman said, "The serpent deceived me, and I ate it."

PRAYER

Dear Heavenly Father, Elohim Qarob (God Is Near),

I come to You seeking Your guidance and grace for my life. Galatians 3:13 says, I am redeemed from the curse of the law. I am redeemed from poverty. I am redeemed from sickness. I am redeemed from spiritual death. Lord, thank You for the incredible sacrifice of Jesus that redeems me from curses. Help me to live in the freedom and grace that Christ has provided, and to reflect His love and redemption in my daily life. In James 3:13, it tells us that if we are wise and understand God's way, we are to prove it by living an honorable life, doing good works with the humility that comes from wisdom. Help me to live a life that reflects Your wisdom through my actions and to approach others with humility. Colossians 3:13 says, "Bear with each other and forgive one another if any of you has a grievance against someone. Forgive as the Lord forgave you" (NIV). Lord, help me to extend forgiveness to others as You have forgiven me. Teach me to bear with others and to let go of any offenses. According to Genesis 3:13, I'm to be honest with God about my shortcomings and mistakes. Guide me to seek Your help and wisdom to overcome temptation and to make choices that honor You. Thank You for Your redemption, wisdom, forgiveness, and guidance. Help me to live a life that honors You and reflects Your love and grace in all I do.

In Jesus' loyal name I pray, Amen

Colossians 3:14 (ESV): And above all these put on love, which binds everything together in perfect harmony.

Philippians 3:14 (KJV): I press toward the mark of the high calling of God in Christ Jesus.

Hebrews 3:14 (NIV): We have come to share in Christ, if indeed we hold our original conviction firmly to the very end.

Galatians 3:14 (NIV): He redeemed us in order that the blessing given to Abraham might come to the Gentiles through Christ Jesus, so that by faith we might receive the promise of the Spirit.

Exodus 3:14 (NLT): God replied to Moses, "I AM WHO I AM" say this to the people of Israel; "I AM has sent me to you."

PRAYER

Dear Lord, YHWH (I AM),

I come before You with a heart seeking Your guidance and strength. Colossians 3:14 reminds me to embrace love in all that I do. May Your love guide my actions and thoughts, bringing unity and harmony in my relationships and in my life. Philippians 3:14 gives me the strength and determination to press on toward the goals You have set for me. Help me to stay focused on the prize of eternal life with You and to pursue it with unwavering commitment. Hebrews 3:14 says, I am a partaker in Christ Jesus. Lord, help me to hold firm to my faith and conviction in Christ. Strengthen me to stay steadfast in my belief and to remain true to You until the very end. Galatians 3:14 shows us we are the seed of Abraham, and His blessings are mine. Lord, thank You for the blessings and promises given to us through Jesus. Help me to live in faith, receiving and embracing the promise of the Holy Spirit and the blessings You have in store. Exodus 3:14 says, "God said to Moses, 'I AM WHO I AM.' This is what you are to say to the Israelites: 'I AM has sent me to you'" (NIV). Lord, I am grateful for Your eternal and unchanging nature. Help me to trust in who You are and to find confidence in Your identity as the great "I AM" who is always present and powerful in my life. Thank You for Your love, guidance, and the strength You provide. Help me to live faithfully, pursue Your goals for my life, and hold firmly to my convictions.

In Jesus' victorious name I pray, Amen

James 3:15 (NIV): Such "wisdom" does not come down from heaven but is earthly, unspiritual, demonic.

Revelation 3:15 (NIV): "I know your deeds, that you are neither cold nor hot. I wish you were either one or the other."

Colossians 3:15 (NLT): And let the peace that comes from Christ rule in your hearts. For as members of one body you are called to live in peace. And always be thankful.

Proverbs 3:15 (NLT): Wisdom is more precious than rubies; nothing you desire can compare with her.

1 Peter 3:15 (ESV): But in your hearts revere Christ as Lord. Always be prepared to give an answer to everyone who asks you to give the reason for the hope that you have. But do this with gentleness and respect.

PRAYER

Dear Heavenly Father, Qeren Yesha (Horn of My Salvation),

I come to You with a heart open to Your guidance and wisdom. James 3:15 says I can renounce all earthly, sensual, and demonic wisdom in the powerful name of Jesus. Lord, help me to seek Your true wisdom that comes from above. Protect me from earthly and unspiritual wisdom, and guide me to discern and embrace the wisdom that is pure, peace-loving, and from You. Revelation 3:15 tells us to be fully committed and passionate in our faith. Help me to be zealous in my relationship with You and to live in a way that reflects Your love and truth consistently. Colossians 3:15 says to fill my heart with the peace of Christ and help it to rule over all my anxieties and fears. Teach me to live in peace with others and to always be thankful for Your presence and blessings in my life. Proverbs 3:15 tells us, "She is more precious than rubies; nothing you desire can compare with her" (NIV). Lord, help me to value wisdom and understanding as precious gifts from You. May I seek Your wisdom above all else and recognize its worth in my life. 1 Peter 3:15 says, to honor Christ as Lord in my heart and to be ready to share the hope I have in You with others. Give me the words to speak with gentleness and respect, reflecting Your love in all I do. Thank You for Your guidance, peace, and the wisdom You offer. Help me to remain committed to You, to value wisdom, and to share my faith with others in a respectful and loving manner.

In Jesus' great name I pray, Amen

MARCH 16

John 3:16 (NIV): "For God so loved the world that he gave his one and only Son, that whoever believes in him should not perish, but have eternal [everlasting] life."

Luke 3:16 (ESV): John answered them all, "I baptize you with water. But one who is more powerful than I will come, the straps of whose sandals I am not worthy to untie. He will baptize you with the Holy Spirit and fire."

Ephesians 3:16 (ESV): I pray that out of His glorious riches He may strengthen you with power through His Spirit in your inner being.

2 Thessalonians 3:16 (NIV): May the Lord of peace himself give you peace at all times and in every way. The Lord will be with all of you.

PRAYER

Dear Heavenly Father, El (God),

I come to You with a grateful heart, seeking Your guidance and grace. John 3:16 says, "For God so loved the world that He gave His one and only Son, that whoever believes in Him shall not perish but have eternal life." Lord, thank You for the incredible gift of Jesus and for Your profound love for me. Help me to fully grasp the depth of Your love and to live in the light of the eternal life You offer through faith in Your Son. Luke 3:16 shows me to be grateful for the promise of the Holy Spirit. Baptize and fill me with Your Holy Spirit and ignite my heart with the fire of Your love and power. Guide me to live a life empowered by Your Spirit and to bear fruit in Your name. Ephesians 3:16 strenghtens my inner being through the Holy Spirit, so that I may live with courage, hope, and faith in all circumstances. 1 Thessalonians 3:16 tells us, "Now may our Lord Jesus Christ Himself and God our Father, who loved us and gave us eternal comfort and good hope through grace" (ESV). Lord, I thank You for the eternal comfort and hope You provide through Your grace. Help me to remain steadfast in Your promises and to find comfort and hope in Your presence. Thank You for Your love, strength, and the comfort You offer. Help me to live according to Your will, empowered by Your Spirit, and to share the hope of eternal life with others.

In Jesus' faithful name I pray, Amen

MARCH 17

Ephesians 3:17 (ESV): So that Christ may dwell in your hearts through faith. And I pray that you, being rooted and established in love.

2 Timothy 3:17 (NKJV): That the man of God may be complete, thoroughly equipped for every good work.

Matthew 3:17 (NLT): And a voice from heaven said, "This is my dearly loved Son, who brings me great joy."

Zephaniah 3:17 (ESV): The Lord your God is with you, the Mighty Warrior who saves. He will take great delight in you; in His love He will no longer rebuke you, but will rejoice over you with singing.

2 Corinthians 3:17(ESV): Now the Lord is the Spirit, and where the Spirit of the Lord is, there is freedom.

PRAYER

Dear Heavenly Father, El Elohe Yisrael (God of Israel),

I come before You with a heart seeking Your presence and guidance. Ephesians 3:17 says I am rooted and grounded in love. Lord, I ask that You make Your home in my heart. Strengthen my faith and help me to be deeply rooted and established in Your love, so that Your love guides and sustains me in all things. 2 Timothy 3:17 tells us we are throughly equipped. Lord, I pray that You equip me with everything I need to do the good work You have planned for me. Matthew 3:17 speaks of Jesus being Your deeply loved Son. Lord, I am grateful for Your deep love for Jesus and for Your affirmation of Him. Help me to live in a way that brings You joy and to seek Your approval above all else. Zephaniah 3:17 tells me that You are with me as my Mighty Warrior who saves. Help me to find comfort in Your delight and to remember that Your love for me is everlasting. 2 Corinthians 3:17 tells us we have freedom that comes from the Holy Spirit. Help me to live in the freedom You provide, free from fear and burden, and to walk confidently in Your guidance and truth.

In Jesus' supernatural name I pray, Amen

MARCH 18

Ephesians 3:18 (NIV): May have power, together with all the Lord's holy people, to grasp how wide and long and high and deep is the love of Christ.

2 Peter 3:18 (ESV): But grow in the grace and knowledge of our Lord and Savior Jesus Christ. To Him be glory both now and forever! Amen.

1 Corinthians 3:18 (ESV): Let no one deceive himself. If anyone among you thinks that he is wise in this age, let him become a fool that he may become wise.

Proverbs 3:18 (NLT): Wisdom is a tree of life to those who embrace her; happy are those who hold her tightly.

John 3:18 (NIV): Whoever believes in Him is not condemned, but whoever does not believe stands condemned already because they have not believed in the name of God's one and only Son.

PRAYER

Dear Heavenly Father, Jehovah Qadash (The LORD Who Sanctifies),

I come before You with a heart seeking Your wisdom and guidance. According to Ephesians 3:18, Lord, help me to fully understand and experience the vastness of Your love for me together with all the saints. Let me grasp the depth and breadth of Your love and let it be the foundation of my life. Lord, I pray that I continually grow in Your grace and in the knowledge of Jesus Christ in accordance with 2 Peter 3:18. Help me to seek Your wisdom daily and to reflect Your glory in all aspects of my life. 1 Corinthians 3:18 says, "Let no one deceive himself." I bind and cast out any spirits of self-deception in the name of Jesus. Help me not to become wise by the standards of this age, but to see my need for your wisdom. Lord, as Proverbs 3:18 tells us, I desire to hold fast to Your wisdom and guidance. Help me to cling to Your truth and to be a source of life and blessing to others through Your Word. John 3:18 says that whoever believes in Christ is not condemned. Lord, thank You for the gift of salvation through Jesus. Help me to live in the freedom and assurance of my faith and to share this hope with others. Thank You for Your profound love, grace, and guidance. Help me to grow spiritually, to hold fast to Your wisdom, and to live confidently in the salvation You provide.

In Jesus' assured name I pray, Amen

Habakkuk 3:19 (NIV): The Sovereign LORD is my strength; he makes my feet like the feet of a deer, he enables me to tread on the heights.

Proverbs 3:19 (NLT): By wisdom, the LORD founded the earth; by understanding he created the heavens.

Colossians 3:19 (NLT): Husbands, love your wives and never treat them harshly.

Hebrews 3:19 (NLT): So we see that because of their unbelief they were not able to enter his rest.

Acts of the Apostles 3:19 (NLT): Now repent of your sins and turn to God, so that your sins may be wiped away.

PRAYER

Dear Heavenly Father, Tsur Yisrael (Rock of Israel),

I come to You with a heart open to Your guidance and wisdom. Lord, Habakkuk 3:19 reminds me to rely on You as my strength. Help me to navigate life's challenges with grace and stability, trusting that You will enable me to rise above any obstacles I face. Proverbs 3:19 tells us that by wisdom and understanding, You created the earth and the heavens. Lord, You are the source of all wisdom and understanding. Guide me to seek Your wisdom in all I do and to trust in Your perfect plan for my life. Colossians 3:19 tells husbands to love their wives and not be harsh. Lord, help me to show love and kindness in all my relationships. Whether in marriage or in other connections, teach me to act with compassion and understanding, avoiding harshness and reflecting Your love in all my interactions. Hebrews 3:19 tells us of those who were not able to enter Your rest, because of their unbelief. Lord, help me to overcome any unbelief or doubt in my heart. Strengthen my faith so that I can fully enter into the promises and blessings You have for me. Acts 3:19 says that if we repent and turn to God, our sins will be wiped out. Lord, I repent of my sins and turn to You with a humble heart. Cleanse me from all unrighteousness and bring refreshing and renewal to my life through Your grace. Thank You for being my strength, for providing wisdom, and for guiding me in love and faith. Help me to turn to You in repentance and to experience the refreshing renewal that comes from Your presence.

In Jesus' promising name I pray, Amen.

MARCH 20

Ephesians 3:20 (ESV): Now to him who is able to do immeasurably more than all we ask or imagine, according to his power that is at work within us.

Revelation 3:20 (NLT): "Look! I stand at the door and knock. If you hear my voice and open the door, I will come in, and we will share a meal together as friends."

Romans 3:20 (NLT): For no one can ever be made right with God by doing what the law commands. The law simply shows us how sinful we are.

Philippians 3:20 (NLT): But we are citizens of heaven, where the Lord Jesus Christ lives. And we are eagerly waiting for him to return as our savior.

PRAYER

Dear Heavenly Father, Abir Jacob (The Mighty One of Jacob),

I come to You with a heart full of gratitude and hope. Ephesians 3:20 says that it is Your power at work in us. Lord, thank You for Your incredible power and ability to exceed our greatest expectations. Help me to trust in Your limitless possibilities and to rely on Your strength in all areas of my life. Revelation 3:20 tells us that Jesus is waiting to be invited into our lives. Lord, I invite You into my life. Open my heart to Your presence, and let me experience the closeness of fellowship with You. I desire to welcome You fully into my daily life and to enjoy the intimacy of our relationship. Romans 3:20 says that no one will be declared righteous in God's sight by the works of the law. Lord, help me to understand that righteousness comes through faith in You, not by my own efforts. Teach me to rely on Your grace and to seek Your forgiveness and guidance in my life. Philippians 3:20 tells us that our citizenship is in heaven. Lord, remind me that my true home is with You in heaven. Help me to live with a perspective focused on eternal things, eagerly awaiting the return of Jesus and living in a way that reflects my heavenly citizenship. Thank You for Your power, for Your invitation into my life, and for the grace and hope You offer. Help me to live with a heart of faith and anticipation, trusting in Your promises and relying on Your strength.

In Jesus' immeasurable name I pray, Amen

MARCH 21

Lamentations 3:21 (KJV): This I recall to my mind, therefore I have hope.

Ephesians 3:21 (NKJV): To Him be glory in the church by Christ Jesus to all generations, forever and ever. Amen.

John 3:21 (ESV): "But whoever does what is true comes to the light, so that it may be clearly seen that his works have been carried out in God."

Luke 3:21 (ESV): Now when all the people were baptized, and when Jesus also had been baptized and was praying, the heavens were opened.

Colossians 3:21 (ESV): Fathers, do not provoke your children, lest they become discouraged.

PRAYER

Dear Heavenly Father, Abba (Father),

I come to You with a heart full of hope and trust in Your promises. Lamentations 3:21 says we can have hope as we call to mind what you have done. Lord, help me to remember Your faithfulness and to keep my hope anchored in You, even in difficult times. Remind me of Your promises and Your unchanging love. Ephesians 3:21 tells us that all glory belongs to You, in the church and in Christ Jesus throughout all generations. Lord, I give You all the glory and honor. Help me to live in a way that brings glory to You and to be a reflection of Your love and grace in all that I do. John 3:21 says that whoever lives by the truth comes into the light. Lord, guide me to live by Your truth and to walk in the light of Your presence. Let my actions and decisions reflect Your truth and be pleasing to You. Luke 3:21 tells us that when all the people were being baptized, Jesus was baptized too. Lord, thank You for the example of Jesus' baptism and His commitment to righteousness. Help me to follow His example and to seek Your presence in prayer, opening my heart to Your will and guidance. Colossians 3:21 warns fathers not to provoke their children. Lord, help me to nurture and encourage those around me with kindness and love. Teach me to build others up and to be a source of encouragement and support in their lives. Thank You for Your hope, for Your glory, and for the guidance You provide. Help me to live in Your truth, to seek Your presence, and to encourage others in Your love.

In Jesus' hopeful name I pray, Amen

Lamentations 3:22 (NLT): The faithful love of the LORD never ends! His mercies never cease.

Romans 3:22 (ESV): The righteousness of God through faith in Jesus Christ for all who believe. For there is no distinction.

Luke 3:22 (ESV): And the Holy Spirit descended on him in bodily form, like a dove; and a voice came from heaven, "You are my beloved Son; with you I am well pleased."

PRAYER

Dear Heavenly Father, Adonai (Lord),

I come before You with a heart full of gratitude and trust. Lamentations 3:22 says, "Because of the LORD's great love we are not consumed, for his compassions never fail" (NIV). Lord, I thank You for Your unending love and compassion. Even when I face challenges, I know that Your love sustains me and Your mercies are new every morning. Help me to trust in Your enduring faithfulness. Romans 3:22 tells us, "This righteousness is given through faith in Jesus Christ to all who believe. There is no difference between Jew and Gentile." Lord, I am grateful that righteousness comes through faith in Jesus Christ and is available to all who believe. Help me to fully embrace this gift and to live out my faith with gratitude and humility. Luke 3:22 says, "And the Holy Spirit descended on him in bodily form like a dove. And a voice came from heaven: 'You are my Son, whom I love; with you I am well pleased.'" Lord, I am comforted by the affirmation You gave to Jesus. Help me to feel Your love and approval in my life and to know that You are pleased with me as I seek to follow Your will. Thank You for Your great love, for the righteousness we have through faith, and for the reassurance of Your presence and approval. Guide me to live in a way that honors You and reflects Your love to those around me.

In Jesus' honorable name I pray, Amen

MARCH 23

Colossians 3:23 (NIV): Whatever you do, work at it with all your heart, as working for the Lord, not for human masters.

Romans 3:23 (ESV): For all have sinned and fall short of the glory of God.

Proverbs 3:23 (ESV): Then you will walk on your way securely, and your foot will not stumble.

Lamentations 3:23 (ESV): [Your compassions] are new every morning; great is Your faithfulness.

These are my birthday Scriptures and it gives me great peace to live by them each day!

———————————— PRAYER ————————————

Dear Heavenly Father, Adonai Tov (The Lord Is Good),

I come before You seeking Your guidance and grace. Colossians 3:23 says, "Whatever you do, work at it with all your heart, as working for the Lord, not for human masters." Lord, help me to approach all my tasks and responsibilities with a heart dedicated to You. May I work diligently and with integrity, knowing that my efforts are ultimately for Your glory. Romans 3:23 tells us, "For all have sinned and fall short of the glory of God." Lord, I acknowledge my imperfections and my need for Your forgiveness. Thank You for the grace You offer, despite my shortcomings. Help me to seek Your forgiveness and to strive to live in a way that honors You. Proverbs 3:23 says, "Then you will go on your way in safety, and your foot will not stumble" (NIV). Lord, guide me along the right path and keep me safe from harm. Help me to follow Your guidance so that I may walk securely and confidently in Your will. Lamentations 3:23 tells us, "They are new every morning; great is Your faithfulness." Lord, I am grateful for Your mercies that are new each day. Thank You for Your unwavering faithfulness and for the fresh start You offer each morning. Help me to embrace Your grace and to live each day with a heart full of gratitude. Thank You for Your guidance, forgiveness, and faithfulness. Help me to work with all my heart for You, to trust in Your protection, and to live each day with a renewed spirit.

In Jesus' secure name I pray, Amen

My sleep is sweet

Romans 3:24 (ESV): And all are justified freely by his grace through the redemption that came by Christ Jesus.

Lamentations 3:24 (ESV): "The LORD is my portion," says my soul, "Therefore I hope in Him."

Proverbs 3:24 (ESV): When you lie down, you will not be afraid; when you lie down, your sleep will be sweet.

Galatians 3:24 (NLT): The law was our guardian until Christ came; it protected us until we could be made right with God through faith.

Colossians 3:24 (NIV): Since you know that you will receive an inheritance from the Lord as a reward. It is the Lord Christ you are serving.

PRAYER

Dear Heavenly Father, El Tsuri (The Rock),

I come to You with a heart full of gratitude and trust in Your promises. Romans 3:24 reminds me to thank You for the gift of Your grace and the redemption we have through Jesus Christ. Help me to fully embrace this gift and to live in the freedom it provides. Lamentations 3:24 tells me, Lord, You are my portion and my hope. Help me to find my fulfillment and security in You alone, and to place my hope firmly in Your promises. Proverbs 3:24 grants me peace and comfort in Your presence. Help me to rest without fear and to experience Your peace and sweetness in my sleep. Galatians 3:24 tells us to be grateful that through faith in Christ, we are justified and no longer bound by the law. Help me to live in the freedom and grace that comes through faith in Jesus. Colossians 3:24 says my inheritance and reward come from serving You. Help me to serve You with a joyful heart, knowing that my labor is not in vain but is rewarded by You. Thank You for Your grace, for being my portion and hope, and for the peace You provide. Help me to live by faith, to rest in Your promises, and to serve You with all my heart.

In Jesus' restful name I pray, Amen

Lamentations 3:25 (ESV): The LORD is good to those whose hope is in Him, to the one who seeks Him.

Romans 3:25 (NLT): For God presented Jesus as the sacrifice for sin. People are made right with God when they believe that Jesus sacrificed his life, shedding his blood. This sacrifice shows that God was being fair when he held back and did not punish those who sinned in times past.

Proverbs 3:25 (NKJV): Do not be afraid of sudden terror, nor of trouble from the wicked when it comes.

PRAYER

Dear Heavenly Father, El Chai (The Living God),

I come before You with a heart full of hope and trust in Your promises. Lamentations 3:25 says, "The LORD is good to those whose hope is in him, to the one who seeks him." Lord, I place my hope in You and seek Your presence. Thank You for Your goodness and faithfulness. Help me to remain steadfast in my hope and to trust that You are always good. Romans 3:25 tells us, "God presented Christ as a sacrifice of atonement, through the shedding of his blood—to be received by faith. He did this to demonstrate his righteousness, because in his forbearance he had left the sins committed beforehand unpunished" (NIV). Lord, I am grateful for the sacrifice of Jesus and the atonement we have through His blood. Thank You for Your grace and for demonstrating Your righteousness through His sacrifice. Proverbs 3:25 says, "Have no fear of sudden disaster or of the ruin that overtakes the wicked" (NIV). Lord, help me to trust in You and not be afraid of sudden challenges or uncertainties. Strengthen my faith so that I can face difficulties with confidence, knowing that You are my protector and guide. Thank You for Your goodness, for the sacrifice of Jesus, and for Your protection in times of trouble. Help me to trust in Your promises and to live with a heart full of faith and courage.

In Jesus' protective name I pray, Amen

MARCH 26

Proverbs 3:26 (ESV): For the LORD will be your confidence, and will keep your foot from being caught.

Galatians 3:26 (NKJV): For you are all sons of God through faith in Jesus Christ.

Mark 3:26 (NIV): And if Satan opposes himself and is divided, he cannot stand; his end has come.

Lamentations 3:26 (NKJV): It is good that one should hope and wait quietly for the salvation of the LORD.

PRAYER

Dear Heavenly Father, Metzudah (Fortress),

Lord, help me to trust in Your protection and to find confidence in Your presence as in Proverbs 3:26. When fear and challenges arise, remind me that You are my shield and my defender acording to Galations 3:26. Thank You, Father, for adopting me into Your family through faith in Jesus Christ. Let my identity as Your child be the foundation of my life, giving me strength and purpose each day. As in Mark 3:26 Lord, grant me the wisdom to seek unity and peace in all my relationships. Help me to be an instrument of Your love, fostering harmony and understanding in my community and beyond. Teach me, O God, to wait patiently for Your salvation as we are told in Lamentations 3:26, knowing that Your timing is perfect. Fill my heart with hope and peace as I trust in Your promises and Your faithful love.

In Jesus' secure name I pray, Amen

MARCH 27

Galatians 3:27 (NIV): For all of you who were baptized into Christ have clothed yourselves with Christ.

Proverbs 3:27 (NKJV): Do not withhold good from those to whom it is due, when it is in the power of your hand to do so.

John 3:27 (NKJV): John answered and said, "A man can receive nothing unless it has been given to him from heaven."

Lamentations 3:27 (NLT): And it is good for people to submit at an early age to the yolk of his discipline.

PRAYER

Dear Heavenly Father, El Yalad (The God Who Gave You Birth),

I come before You with a heart full of gratitude and trust in Your Word. Galatians 3:27 says, "For all of you who were baptized into Christ have clothed yourselves with Christ." Lord, thank You for the new identity we have in Jesus. Help me to live each day with the understanding that I am clothed with Christ, reflecting His love and grace in all I do. Proverbs 3:27 tells us, "Do not withhold good from those to whom it is due, when it is in your power to act." Lord, guide me to be generous and kind to others. Help me to act with compassion and to offer help whenever I have the opportunity to do so. John 3:27 says, "To this John replied, 'A person can receive only what is given them from heaven'" (NIV). Lord, I acknowledge that all I have comes from You. Help me to be content and thankful for the blessings You have provided, and to use them wisely for Your purposes. Lamentations 3:27 tells us, "It is good for a man to bear the yoke while he is young" (NIV). Lord, help me to embrace the responsibilities and challenges in my life with a willing and obedient heart. Teach me to grow through these experiences and to rely on Your strength. Thank You for the new life we have in Christ, for the guidance to be generous and kind, and for Your provision in all things. Help me to embrace life's challenges with faith and to act in accordance with Your will.

In Jesus' saving name I pray, Amen

I AM ONE IN CHRIST JESUS

Galatians 3:28 (NKJV): There is neither Jew nor gentile, neither slave nor free, nor is there male or female, for you are all one in Christ Jesus.

Proverbs 3:28 (NLT): If you can help your neighbor now, don't say ,"Come back tomorrow, and then I'll help you."

Romans 3:28 (NLT): So we are made right with God through faith and not by obeying the law.

PRAYER

Dear Heavenly Father, El Deah (The God of Knowledge),

I come to You with a heart full of gratitude and a desire to follow Your will. Galatians 3:28 says, "There is neither Jew nor Gentile, neither slave nor free, neither male nor female, for you are all one in Christ Jesus." Lord, thank You for the unity we have in Christ. Help me to embrace this truth in my relationships with others, treating everyone with equal respect and love, and recognizing that we are all one in Your sight. Proverbs 3:28 tells us, "Do not say to your neighbor, 'Come back tomorrow and I'll give it to you'—when you already have it with you" (NIV). Lord, teach me to act with generosity and kindness. When I have the means to help others, guide me to do so immediately, reflecting Your love and compassion in my actions. Romans 3:28 says, "For we maintain that a person is justified by faith apart from the works of the law" (NIV). Lord, I am grateful that our justification comes through faith in Jesus, not by our own efforts. Help me to rely on Your grace and to live out my faith with confidence in Your saving power. Thank You for the unity we have in Christ, for teaching me to act with immediate generosity, and for the gift of justification through faith. Help me to live each day reflecting Your love and grace

In Jesus' steadfast name I pray, Amen

Proverbs 3:29 (NLT): Don't plot harm against your neighbor, for those who live nearby trust you.

Galatians 3:29 (NLT): And now that you belong to Christ, you are the true children of Abraham. You are his heirs, and God's promise to Abraham belongs to you.

Daniel 3:29 (NIV): "Therefore I decree that the people of any nation or language who say anything against the God of Shadrach, Meshach and Abednego be cast into pieces and their houses be turned into piles of rubble, for no other god can save in this way."

PRAYER

Dear Heavenly Father, El Elyon (God Most High),

I come to You with a humble heart, seeking Your guidance and blessings. Proverbs 3:29 says, "Do not plot harm against your neighbor, who lives trustfully near you" (NIV). Lord, help me to live peacefully with those around me. Guide me to act with integrity and kindness, and to avoid any thoughts or actions that could harm others. Teach me to build trust and foster positive relationships. Galatians 3:29 tells us, "If you belong to Christ, then you are Abraham's seed, and heirs according to the promise" (NIV). Lord, I am grateful to be an heir to the promises You made to Abraham. Help me to live in the full assurance of this promise, knowing that I am part of Your family and that You have a purpose and plan for my life. Daniel 3:29 shows the reverence and awe we must keep for the Lord our God. No one in all the nations of this world should speak against the Lord God Almighty. Thank You for Your guidance, for making me an heir to Your promises, and for knowing and loving me personally. Help me to live in harmony with others and to trust in Your plans for my life.

In Jesus' trustful name I pray, Amen

LESS OF ME AND MORE OF HIM

John 3:30 (NLT): [Jesus] must increase, but I must decrease.

Proverbs 3:30 (NIV): Do not accuse anyone for no reason—when they have done you no harm.

Lamentations 3:30 (NLT): Let them turn the other cheek to those who strike them and accept the insults of their enemies.

——————————————— PRAYER ———————————————

Dear Heavenly Father, El Hakkavod (The God of Glory),

I come before You with a grateful heart, seeking Your guidance and strength. John 3:30 says, "He must become greater; I must become less" (NIV). Lord, help me to live with a heart that seeks to magnify You in all things. Teach me to put aside my own desires and to make You the center of my life, reflecting Your greatness and love to those around me. Show me how to be selfless in this selfish world. Proverbs 3:30 tells us, "Do not accuse anyone for no reason—when they have done you no harm." Lord, guide me to act with fairness and kindness. Help me to avoid unjust judgments and to address conflicts with a spirit of grace and understanding. Lamentations 3:30 says, "Let him offer his cheek to one who would strike him, and let him be filled with disgrace" (NIV). Lord, give me the strength to endure challenges and mistreatment with patience and humility. Help me to respond to difficulties with a spirit of grace, trusting in Your justice and mercy. Thank You for Your guidance and strength. Help me to magnify You in my life, to act with fairness, and to endure challenges with grace.

In Jesus' loving name I pray, Amen

MARCH 31

Proverbs 3:31 (NLT): Don't envy violent people or copy their ways.

John 3:31 (NLT): "He has come from above and is greater than anyone else. We are of the earth, and we speak of earthly things, but he has come from heaven and is greater than anyone else."

Romans 3:31 (NLT): Well then, if we emphasize *faith*, does this mean that we can forget about the law? Of course, not! In fact, only when we have faith, do we truly fulfill the law.

—————————————— **PRAYER** ——————————————

Dear Heavenly Father, El Nathan Neqamah (The God Who Avenges Me),

I come to You seeking Your wisdom and strength for my daily life. Proverbs 3:31 says, "Do not envy the violent or choose any of their ways." Lord, help me to stay away from those who act unjustly or with violence. Guide me to follow Your ways of peace and righteousness, avoiding paths that lead to harm or conflict. I will not be envious or a copycat. John 3:31 tells us, "The one who comes from above is above all; the one who is from the earth belongs to the earth and speaks as one from the earth. The one who comes from heaven is above all" (NIV). Lord, I recognize that Jesus, who came from above, is above all. Help me to focus on His teachings and to live according to His example, knowing that He holds ultimate authority and wisdom. Romans 3:31 says, "Do we, then, nullify the law by this faith? Not at all! Rather, we uphold the law" (NIV). Lord, thank You for the faith we have in Jesus. Help me to understand that this faith does not nullify Your commands but rather upholds and fulfills them. Teach me to live by faith while honoring Your laws and commands. Thank You for Your guidance in avoiding wrong paths, for the authority of Jesus in my life, and for the way faith upholds Your commands. Help me to walk in Your ways with integrity and trust.

In Jesus' authoritative name I pray, Amen

APRIL 1

God hears my prayers

1 Corinthians 4:1 (NIV): This, then, is how you ought to regard us: as servants of Christ and as those entrusted with the mysteries God has revealed.

1 Timothy 4:1 (NIV): The Spirit clearly says that in later times some will abandon the faith and follow deceiving spirits and things taught by demons.

Psalm 4:1 (NIV): Answer me when I call to you, my righteous God. Give me relief for my distress; have mercy on me and hear my prayer.

1 John 4:1 (NIV): Dear friends, do not believe every spirit, but test the spirits to see whether they are from God, because many false prophets have gone out into the world.

 **PRAYER**

Dear Heavenly Father, El Olam (The Everlasting God, The Eternal God),

I come to You with a heart open to Your guidance and strength. 1 Corinthians 4:1 helps me to see myself and others as Your servants, entrusted with the important work of sharing Your truth and revelations. Guide me to be faithful in my role and to handle Your mysteries with care and humility. 1 Timothy 4:1 reveals that in later times there will be false teachings and deceptive influences. Strengthen my faith and keep me grounded in Your Word so that I may recognize and avoid anything that is not of You. Psalm 4:1 says, "Answer me when I call to You, my righteous God. Give me relief from my distress; have mercy on me and hear my prayer." Lord, I come to You with my concerns and troubles. Please provide relief and comfort in times of distress. Show Your mercy and listen to my prayers, giving me peace and assurance. 1 John 4:1 tells us, "Dear friends, do not believe every spirit, but test the spirits to see whether they are from God, because many false prophets have gone out into the world." Lord, help me to discern the truth from falsehood. Guide me in testing the spirits and teachings around me, ensuring that I remain aligned with Your truth and teachings. Thank You for entrusting me with Your truth, for protecting me from deception, for providing relief in times of trouble, and for guiding me in discernment. Help me to remain faithful and true to Your Word.

In Jesus' magnified name I pray, Amen

APRIL 2

Ephesians 4:2 (NIV): Be completely humble and gentle; be patient; bearing with one another in love.

1 John 4:2 (NIV): This is how you can recognize the spirit of God: Every spirit that acknowledges that Jesus Christ has come in the flesh is from God.

Colossians 4:2 (NIV): Devote yourselves to prayer, being watchful and thankful.

PRAYER

Dear Heavenly Father, El Racham (The Compassionate God),

I come to You seeking Your guidance and grace in my daily life. Ephesians 4:2 says, "Be completely humble and gentle; be patient, bearing with one another in love." Lord, help me to embrace humility and gentleness in all my interactions. Teach me to be patient with others and to show love in everything I do, reflecting Your character in my relationships. 1 John 4:2 tells us, "This is how you can recognize the Spirit of God: Every spirit that acknowledges that Jesus Christ has come in the flesh is from God." Lord, guide me to discern Your truth in all things. Help me to recognize and uphold the truth that Jesus Christ came in the flesh and is our Savior, and to remain steadfast in this fundamental truth. Colossians 4:2 says, "Devote yourselves to prayer, being watchful and thankful." Lord, teach me to be devoted to prayer, staying alert and grateful in my conversations with You. Help me to make prayer a central part of my life, seeking Your guidance and giving thanks for Your blessings. Thank You for the call to humility, for the truth of Jesus Christ, and for the gift of prayer. Help me to live out these truths daily, with a heart full of love, discernment, and gratitude.

In Jesus' merciful name I pray, Amen

APRIL 3

Colossians 4:3 (NIV): And pray for us, too, that God may open a door for our message, so that we may proclaim the mystery of Christ, for which I am in chains.

Malachi 4:3 (ESV): "Then you will trample down the wicked; they will be ashes under the soles of your feet on the day when I do these things," says the Lord Almighty.

Leviticus 4:3 (ESV): If the anointed priest sins, bringing guilt on the people, he must bring to the Lord a young bull without defect as a sin offering for the sin he has committed.

Psalm 4:3 (ESV): Know that the Lord has set apart his faithful servant for himself; the Lord hears when I call to him. Look at this; look who got picked by God! He listens the split second I called to him.

PRAYER

Dear Heavenly Father, Elohim Yare (God Most Awesome),

I come before You with a heart open to Your guidance and grace. Colossians 4:3 reminds me to speak the mysteries of God and share His message with others. Open doors for me to speak about Your love and grace, and help me to be bold and faithful in proclaiming the mystery of Christ. Malachi 4:3 tells us to trust in Your promise of justice and victory over evil. I will tread down the wicked: they are ashes under my feet. Help me to stay strong in faith, knowing that You will bring justice and that evil will not prevail. Leviticus 4:3 says, "If the anointed priest sins, bringing guilt on the people, he must offer to the Lord a young bull without defect as a sin offering for the sin he has committed." Lord, I thank You for the forgiveness we receive through Jesus Christ. Help me to acknowledge my sins and seek Your forgiveness, trusting in the sacrifice of Jesus as the ultimate atonement for sin. Psalm 4:3 reminds me to be grateful that You set apart those who are faithful to You. Thank You for hearing my prayers and for being present in my life. Help me to remain faithful and to trust that You are always listening and answering according to Your will. Thank You for the opportunities to share Your message, for Your promise of justice, for the forgiveness through Jesus, and for Your attentive care. Help me to live faithfully and to trust in Your guidance and grace.

In Jesus' victorious name I pray, Amen

I REJOICE IN THE LORD

1 John 4:4 (NIV): You, dear children, are from God and have overcome them, because the one who is in you is greater than the one who is in the world.

Philippians 4:4 (NKJV): Rejoice in the Lord always; again I will say, rejoice!

Matthew 4:4 (ESV): But he answered, "It is written, 'Man shall not live by bread alone, but by every word that comes from the mouth of God.'"

PRAYER

Dear Heavenly Father, Gelah Raz (Revealer of Mysteries),

I come to You with a heart full of trust and gratitude. 1 John 4:4 says, "You, dear children, are from God and have overcome them, because the one who is in you is greater than the one who is in the world." Lord, thank You for the assurance that You are greater than any challenge or opposition I may face. Help me to remember Your strength within me and to overcome difficulties with confidence in Your power. Philippians 4:4 tells us, "Rejoice in the Lord always. I will say it again: Rejoice!" (NIV). Lord, help me to maintain a joyful heart, regardless of my circumstances. Teach me to find joy in You every day and to celebrate Your presence and goodness in my life. Matthew 4:4 says, "Jesus answered, 'It is written: "Man shall not live on bread alone, but on every word that comes from the mouth of God."'" Lord, help me to rely not only on physical sustenance but also on Your Word for spiritual nourishment. Guide me to seek Your wisdom and to find strength and guidance through Your Scriptures. Thank You for Your power within me, for the call to rejoice in You, and for the importance of living on Your Word. Help me to embody these truths in my daily life and to grow closer to You each day.

In Jesus' meaningful name I pray, Amen

APRIL 5

Isaiah 4:5 (ESV): Then the LORD will create over all of Mount Zion and over those who assemble there a cloud of smoke by day and a glow of flaming fire by night; over all the glory will be a canopy.

Proverbs 4:5 (NKJV): Get wisdom! Get understanding! Do not forget, nor turn away from the words of my mouth.

Philippians 4:5 (NKJV): Let your gentleness be known to all men. the Lord is at hand.

PRAYER

Dear Heavenly Father, Rum Rosh (The One Who Lifts My Head),

I come to You with a heart full of gratitude and a desire for Your guidance. Isaiah 4:5 says, "Then the LORD will create over all of Mount Zion and over those who assemble there a cloud of smoke by day and a glow of flaming fire by night; over all the glory will be a canopy." Lord, thank You for Your presence and protection over Your people. Help me to recognize Your guiding hand in my life and to find comfort in Your constant presence and care. Proverbs 4:5 tells us, "Get wisdom, get understanding; do not forget my words or turn away from them" (NIV). Lord, I ask for Your wisdom and understanding. Help me to seek Your guidance diligently and to keep Your teachings close to my heart, living according to Your wisdom in every aspect of my life. Philippians 4:5 says, "Let your gentleness be evident to all. The Lord is near" (NIV). Lord, help me to show gentleness and kindness to everyone I encounter. Remind me that You are near and that my actions should reflect Your love and compassion. Thank You for Your protective presence, for the gift of wisdom, and for the call to live with gentleness. Help me to embrace these truths daily and to live in a way that honors You.

In Jesus' powerful name I pray, Amen

APRIL 6

Isaiah 4:6 (NIV): "[He] will be a shelter and shade from the heat of the day, and a refuge and hiding place from the storm and rain.

1 John 4:6 (NIV): We are from God, and whoever knows God hears us; but whoever is not from God does not listen to us. This is how we recognize the Spirit of truth and the spirit of falsehood.

Malachi 4:6 (NIV): He will turn the hearts of the parents to their children, and the hearts of the children to their parents.

Philippians 4:6 (NLT): Don't worry about anything; instead, pray about everything.

Hebrews 4:6 (NLT): So God's rest is there for people to enter, but those who first heard this good news failed to enter because they disobeyed God.

PRAYER

Dear Abba (Father),

I come before You with a heart full of trust and a desire to align my life with Your will. As Isaiah 4:6 says, God will be my shelter and refuge, my cover from any storms. I seek Your protection and comfort in times of trouble and need. Help me to find safety and peace in Your presence. 1 John 4:6 tells us to loose ourselves from every spirit of error, in the name of Jesus. Lord, guide me to discern Your truth and to recognize the voice of the Holy Spirit. Help me to stay connected to Your Word and to remain faithful to the truth You reveal. Malachi 4:6 reveals that we can pray for harmony and reconciliation in relationships, especially within families. Turn our hearts toward each other with love and understanding, and bring healing where there is division. Philippians 4:6 tells me to bring my worries and concerns before You. Help me to replace anxiety with prayer, trusting You with all my needs and being thankful for Your provision and care. Hebrews 4:6 reminds me to seek the Lord's help and to enter into His rest by being obedient to Your Word. Teach me to trust in Your promises and to live in a way that honors You. Thank You for being my shelter, for guiding me in Your truth, for healing relationships, for relieving my anxieties, and for offering rest through obedience. Help me to live in accordance with these truths every day.

In Jesus' hopeful name I pray, Amen

APRIL 7

James 4:7 (NIV): Submit yourselves, then, to God. Resist the devil, and he will flee from you.

Romans 4:7 (NIV): Blessed are those whose transgressions are forgiven, whose sins are covered.

1 John 4:7 (ESV): Beloved, let us love one another, for Love is from God, and whoever loves has been born of God and knows God.

Galatians 4:7 (NIV): So you are no longer a slave, but God's child; and since you are His child, God has made you also an heir.

Zechariah 4:7 (NIV): What are you, mighty mountain? Before Zerubbabel you will become level ground. Then he will bring out the capstone to shouts of "God bless it! God bless it!"

Philippians 4:7 (NIV): The peace of God, which transcends all understanding, will guard your hearts, and your minds in Christ Jesus.

PRAYER

Dear Heavenly Father, Elohim Qarob (God Is Near),

I come before You with a heart full of hope and a desire to align my life with Your will. James 4:7 tells me to submit fully to Your will and to resist any temptation or evil that comes my way. Romans 4:7 reminds me my sins are forgiven, and I am blessed. I am grateful for the forgiveness You offer through Jesus. Thank You for covering my sins and granting me grace. Help me to live in the freedom of Your forgiveness and to extend grace to others. As in 1 John 4:7, Lord, teach me to love others as You have loved me. Let Your love flow through me and help me to show genuine care and kindness to those around me. Galatians 4:7 tells me I am an heir of God through Christ. Help me to live with the confidence and joy of being Your child and to embrace the inheritance of Your promises. Zechariah 4:7 shows me my authority to ask the Lord to remove any obstacles or challenges in my life that seem insurmountable. Help me to see Your power at work, leveling the mountains before me, and to rejoice in Your blessings and victories. Philippians 4:7 shows how we can ask the Lord to grant us His peace that surpasses all understanding. Guard my heart and mind with Your calm and assurance, even in difficult times.

In Jesus' understanding name I pray, Amen

APRIL 8

1 Peter 4:8 (ESV): Above all, keep loving one another earnestly, since love covers a multitude of sins.

Psalm 4:8 (NIV): In peace I will lie down and sleep, for you alone, LORD, make me dwell in safety.

Luke 4:8 (NIV): Jesus answered, "It is written: 'Worship the Lord your God and serve him only.'"

2 Timothy 4:8 (NIV): Now there is in store for me the crown of righteousness, which the Lord, the righteous Judge, will award to me on that day—and not only to me, but also to all who have longed for his appearance.

James 4:8 (NLT): Come close to God, and God will come close to you. Wash your hands, you sinners; purifier your hearts, for your loyalty is divided between God and the world.

PRAYER

Dear Heavenly Father, El Nahsah (Forgiving God),

I come to You with a heart seeking Your guidance and strength. 1 Peter 4:8 shows me to love others deeply and sincerely. May Your love in me cover faults and extend grace to those around me, reflecting Your mercy and kindness. According to Psalm 4:8 Lord, grant me Your peace and rest, knowing that You are my protector. Help me to trust in Your safety and to rest securely in Your care. Luke 4:8 says to focus my worship and service solely on God. I will speak out loud to the enemy, "Get behind me Satan." 2 Timothy 4:8 reminds me to look forward to the crown of righteousness as a reward in heaven. You promised this crown to those who are faithful and waiting for the return of Jesus. Help me to remain steadfast in my faith, eagerly anticipating Your return and the righteousness You will bestow. James 4:8 teaches me to come closer to You. Help me to cleanse my heart and mind, seeking purity and sincerity in my relationship with You. Teach me to live with a single focus on You. Thank You for Your call to love deeply, for the gift of peace, for guiding my worship, for the promise of righteousness, and for the invitation to draw near to You. Help me to embody these truths in my daily life and to grow closer to You each day.

In Jesus' forgiving name I pray, Amen

Proverbs 4:9 (NKJV): She will place on your head an ornament of grace; a crown of glory she will deliver to you.

1 John 4:9 (ESV): In this, the love of God was made manifest among us, God sent out his only Son into the world, so that we might live through him.

Ecclesiastes 4:9 (AMP): Two are better than one because they have a more satisfying return for their labor.

PRAYER

Dear Heavenly Father, Jehovah Shalom (The LORD Is Peace),

I come to You with a heart full of gratitude and a desire for Your wisdom and love. Proverbs 4:9 says, "She will give you a garland to grace your head and present you with a glorious crown" (NIV). Lord, thank You for the wisdom and understanding that You offer. Help me to seek Your wisdom diligently so that I may receive the blessings and honor You promise to those who value Your guidance. 1 John 4:9 tells us, "This is how God showed his love among us: He sent his one and only Son into the world that we might live through him" (NIV). Lord, I am deeply grateful for the incredible love You demonstrated by sending Jesus to be our Savior. Help me to live fully in the light of Your love and to share that love with others. Ecclesiastes 4:9 says, "Two are better than one, because they have a good return for their labor" (NIV). Lord, I thank You for the relationships and partnerships in my life. Help me to build strong, supportive connections with others, working together to achieve Your purposes and to encourage and uplift each other. Thank You for Your wisdom and the promise of honor, for Your immense love shown through Jesus, and for the value of supportive relationships. Help me to embrace these truths in my life and to reflect Your love and wisdom in all that I do.

In Jesus' peaceful name I pray, Amen

APRIL 10

1 Chronicles 4:10 (NKJV): Bless me indeed, and enlarge my [coast], that Your hand be with me, and keep me from evil.

Matthew 4:10 (KJV): Get thee hence, Satan, for it is written, . . .

James 4:10 (NLT): Humble yourselves before the Lord, and he will lift you up in honor.

Ecclesiastes 4:10 (NASB): If either of them falls, the one will lift up his companion. But woe to him who is alone when he falls and does not have another to lift him up.

PRAYER

Dear Heavenly Father, Logos (The Word),

I come to You with a heart open to Your guidance and strength. 1 Chronicles 4:10 says, "Jabez cried out to the God of Israel, 'Oh, that You would bless me and enlarge my territory! Let Your hand be with me, and keep me from harm so that I will be free from pain.' And God granted his request" (NIV). Lord, like Jabez, I ask for Your blessings in my life. Please guide me, protect me from harm, and help me to grow in Your grace and purpose. Matthew 4:10 tells us, "Jesus said to him, 'Away from me, Satan! For it is written: Worship the Lord your God, and serve him only'" (NIV). Lord, help me to worship and serve You alone. Strengthen me to resist temptation and to remain focused on You in every area of my life. James 4:10 says, "Humble yourselves before the Lord, and He will lift you up" (NIV). Lord, teach me to walk in humility, recognizing my dependence on You. As I humble myself before You, I trust that You will lift me up and guide me according to Your will. Ecclesiastes 4:10 tells us, "If either of them falls down, one can help the other up. But pity anyone who falls and has no one to help them up" (NIV). Lord, I thank You for the people You have placed in my life who support and uplift me. Help me to be a source of encouragement and support to others as well, reflecting Your love through my actions. Thank You for Your blessings, for guiding me to worship You alone, for lifting me up as I walk in humility, and for the supportive relationships You provide. Help me to live out these truths in my daily life and to grow closer to You.

In Jesus' divine name I pray, Amen

APRIL 11

Mark 4:11: Let me know and understand the mysteries of the kingdom.

1 John 4:11: Beloved, if God still loved us, we also ought to love one another.

Hebrews 4:11: So let us do our best to enter rest. But if we disobey God, as the people of Israel did, we will fall.

PRAYER

Dear Heavenly Father, El Sela (God My Rock),

Thank You for the privilege of knowing You and walking in Your truth. As Jesus said in Mark 4:11, You have given me the mystery of Your kingdom—not because of my worth, but because of Your grace. Open my heart to understand more of Your ways, and let Your Word take deep root in my life, bearing fruit that glorifies You. Lord, as 1 John 4:11 reminds me, You have shown me unfathomable love through Jesus. Because You first loved me, help me to love others with the same selfless, sacrificial love. May my walk with You be marked by a heart that overflows with compassion, grace, and forgiveness. And Father, Hebrews 4:11 calls me to be diligent, to strive to enter into Your rest. Teach me to surrender my striving and trust fully in Your finished work. Keep me from unbelief and distractions that would pull me away from Your peace. May my faith be active, yet my soul be at rest in You. Lord, I desire to walk with You more closely, to love as You love, and to remain steadfast in faith. Keep my heart pure, my steps firm, and my spirit willing to follow wherever You lead.

In Jesus' understanding name I pray, Amen

APRIL 12

Colossians 4:12 (NIV): Epaphras, who is one of you and a servant of Christ Jesus, sends greetings. He is always wrestling in prayer for you, that you may stand firm in all the will of God, mature and fully assured.

Hosea 4:12 (NIV): My people consult a wooden idol, and a diviner's rod speaks to them. A spirit of prostitution leads them astray; they are unfaithful to their God.

Acts 4:12 (NIV): Salvation is found in no one else, for there is no other name under heaven given to mankind by which we must be saved.

Hebrews 4:12 (NLT): For the word of God is alive and powerful. It is sharper than the sharpest two edged sword, cutting between soul and spirit, between joint and marrow. It exposes our innermost thoughts and desires.

PRAYER

Dear Heavenly Father, Jehovah-Palat (The LORD My Deliverer),

I come to You with a heart seeking Your guidance and strength. In Colossians 4:12, "Epaphras wrestles in prayer." Lord, like Epaphras, I ask for Your help to stand firm in Your will. Guide me to grow in maturity and assurance in my faith, and help me to support others in prayer and encouragement. Hosea 4:12 tells us to not be lead astray by sexual distractions or false teachings. Keep my heart and mind focused on You alone, and help me remain faithful to Your truth. Acts 4:12 reminds me to thank You for the gift of salvation through Jesus. Help me to hold fast to this truth and to share the good news with others, knowing that Jesus is the only way to eternal life. As in Hebrews 4:12 Lord, help me to embrace Your Word as a living and powerful guide in my life. Let Your Scripture penetrate my heart, revealing truth and guiding me in all my thoughts and actions. Thank You for the encouragement of prayer, for the protection from being led astray, for the gift of salvation, and for the power of Your Word. Help me to live these truths daily and to grow closer to You.

In Jesus' capable name I pray, Amen

APRIL 13

Philippians 4:13 (ESV): I can do all things through Christ who strengthens me.

Micah 4:13 (NIV): Rise and thresh, Daughter Zion, for I will give you horns of iron; I will give you hooves of bronze, and you will [crush] many nations.

John 4:13 (NLT): Jesus replied, "Anyone who drinks this water will soon become thirsty again."

Hebrews 4:13 (NLT): Nothing in all creation is hidden from God. Everything is naked and exposed before his eyes, and he is the one to whom we are all accountable.

1 John 4:13 (ESV): By this we know that we abide in him and he in us, because he has given us his Spirit.

PRAYER

Dear Heavenly Father, Qadosh Yisrael (The Holy One of Israel),

I come to You with a heart full of trust and gratitude, seeking Your strength and guidance. Philippians 4:13 tells me I can do all things through Christ. Thank You, Lord, for the strength You provide me through Christ. Help me to rely on Your power in all aspects of my life, trusting that You are with me and will enable me to face any challenge. Micah 4:13 tells us, I can arise and thresh and beat the enemy into pieces. Lord, empower me to stand strong and overcome the enemy with Your strength. Help me to be bold and courageous in pursuing Your will and achieving the purposes You have set before me. In John 4:13 Jesus tells us the water from the well will only make us thirty again, but You have living water for us that truly satisfies our thirst. Lord, I seek Your living water, the true and lasting satisfaction that only You can provide. Help me to turn to You for my deepest needs and desires, finding fulfillment and peace in Your presence. Hebrews 4:13 tells us that absolutely nothing is hidden from God. Lord, I am grateful that You see and know everything about me. Help me to live with integrity and to seek Your guidance in all that I do, knowing that I am accountable to You. 1 John 4:13 tells us to abide in God because the Holy Spirit has been given to us as a gift. Lord, Help me to walk in the Spirit and to reflect Your love and truth in all my interactions. Help me to live out these truths and to grow closer to You each day.

In Jesus' Holy name I pray, Amen

I'VE BEEN GIVEN GIFTS

Esther 4:14 (NIV): "For if you remain silent at this time, relief and deliverance for the Jews will arise from another place, but you and your father's family will perish. And who knows but that you have come to your royal position for such a time as this?"

1 Timothy 4:14 (NKJV): Do not neglect the gift that is in you.

Proverbs 4:14 (ESV): Do not enter the path of the wicked, and do not walk in the way of evil.

John 4:14 (NIV): "But those who drink the water I give them will never be thirsty again. It becomes a fresh, bubbling spring within them, giving them eternal life."

Hebrews 4:14 (NIV): Therefore, since we have a great high priest who has ascended into heaven, Jesus the Son of God, let us hold firmly to the faith we profess.

PRAYER

Dear Heavenly Father, El Moshaah (The God Who Saves),

I come before You with a heart open to Your guidance and strength. Esther 4:14 proclaims I have received deliverance and enlargement over my life, help me to recognize the unique position and opportunities You have given me. Grant me the courage to step forward and fulfill the purpose You have set before me, knowing that You have placed me where I am for a reason. 1 Timothy 4:14 reminds me not to neglect the gifts and talents You have given me. Help me to use them wisely and faithfully, for Your glory and the benefit of others. Proverbs 4:14 guides my steps and keeps me away from paths that lead away from You. Help me to choose righteousness and to follow Your ways, avoiding temptation and staying true to Your guidance. John 4:14 tells us, of the bubbling fresh spring of water that will never leave us thirsty. Lord, thank You for the living water You provide through Jesus. Help me to find my satisfaction and fulfillment in You alone, and let Your Spirit flow through me, bringing life and hope to others. Hebrews 4:14 instructs me to hold firmly to faith. Lord, strengthen my faith in Jesus, my great High Priest. Help me to hold firmly to the truth of Your promises and to live with confidence and hope in Your salvation. Thank You for placing me in this moment, for the gifts You have given, for guiding my path, for the living water You provide, and for the confidence we have in Jesus.

In Jesus' eternal name I pray, Amen

APRIL 15

HOLY SPIRIT ABIDES IN ME

Ephesians 4:15 (NIV): Instead, speaking the truth in love, we will grow to become in very respect the mature body of him who is the head, that is, Christ.

Proverbs 4:15 (NIV): Avoid [evil], do not travel on it; turn from it and go on your way.

Hebrews 4:15 (NIV): For we do not have a high priest who is unable to empathize with our weaknesses, but we have one who has been tempted in every way, just as we are—yet he did not sin.

1 John 4:15 (ESV): Whoever confesses that Jesus is the Son of God, God abides in Him and he in God.

PRAYER

My Adonai (Lord),

Thank You for Your love and truth that guide my life. Help me to speak the truth in love as Your Word instructs us in Ephesians 4:15, that my words may build others up and reflect the heart of Christ. According to Proverbs 4:15, I ask You to give me wisdom and discernment to avoid the path of the wicked, that I may walk in righteousness and holiness before You. Lord Jesus, I am comforted in knowing that You are my High Priest. As Hebrews 4:15 tells us, You understand my weaknesses and were tempted in every way, yet without sin. Strengthen me to stand firm in faith and draw near to Your throne of grace in my time of need. I boldly confess that Jesus is the Son of God, and I thank You for abiding in me, as 1 John 4:15 says, as I abide in You. May my life be a testimony of Your love, grace, and truth.

In Jesus' truthful name I pray, Amen.

I ABIDE IN LOVE

Hebrews 4:16 (NIV): Let us then approach God's throne of grace with confidence, so that we may receive mercy and find Grace to help us with our time of need.

2 Corinthians 4:16 (NKJV): Therefore we do not lose heart. Even though our outward man is perishing, yet our inward man is being renewed day by day.

1 John 4:16 (NKJV): And we have known and believed the love that God has for us. God is love, and he who abides in love abides in God, and God in him.

PRAYER

Dear Heavenly Father, Shub Nephesh (Renewer of Life),

I come to You with a heart full of trust and hope, seeking Your presence and guidance. Hebrews 4:16 says, "Let us then approach God's throne of grace with confidence, so that we may receive mercy and find grace to help us in our time of need." Lord, thank You for inviting us to come to You with confidence. Help me to approach Your throne of grace boldly, knowing that You will provide the mercy and help I need in every situation. 2 Corinthians 4:16 tells us, "Therefore we do not lose heart. Though outwardly we are wasting away, yet inwardly we are being renewed day by day" (NIV). Lord, even when I face difficulties and challenges, remind me that You are renewing my spirit each day. Help me to stay strong and hopeful, trusting in Your ongoing work in my life. 1 John 4:16 says, "So we have come to know and to believe the love that God has for us. God is love. Whoever lives in love lives in God, and God in them." Lord, thank You for Your incredible love. Help me to live in Your love and to reflect it in my relationships with others. May Your love flow through me and bring me closer to You. Thank You for the confidence to approach You, for the renewal You provide each day, and for the love that You pour into my life. Help me to live out these truths and to grow closer to You every day.

In Jesus' incredible name I pray, Amen

APRIL 17

1 John 4:17 (NKJV): Love has been perfected among us in this: that we may have boldness in the day of judgment; because as He is, so are we in this world.

2 Corinthians 4:17 (NLT): For our present troubles are small and won't last very long. Yet they produce for us a glory that vastly outweighs them and will last forever!

Colossians 4:17 (NLT): "Be sure to carry out the ministry the Lord gave you."

──────────── **PRAYER** ────────────

Dear Heavenly Father, El Shamayim (The God of Heaven),

I come before You with a heart open to Your love and guidance. 1 John 4:17 says, "This is how love is made complete among us so that we will have confidence on the day of judgment: In this world we are like Jesus" (NIV). Lord, thank You for the complete love You offer us through Jesus. Help me to grow in Your love and to reflect Your character in my daily life, so that I can stand confidently before You on the day of judgment. 2 Corinthians 4:17 tells us, "For our light and momentary troubles are achieving for us an eternal glory that far outweighs them all" (NIV). Lord, when I face challenges and difficulties, remind me of the eternal glory that You are preparing for me. Help me to keep my focus on the hope and promise of Your eternal blessings, rather than being overwhelmed by temporary struggles. Colossians 4:17 says, "Tell Archippus: 'See to it that you complete the ministry you have received in the Lord'" (NIV). Lord, I want to be faithful in the calling and tasks You have given me. Help me to be diligent and committed to completing the work You have set before me, using the gifts and opportunities You have provided. Thank You for Your complete love, for the promise of eternal glory, and for guiding me in fulfilling the ministry You have entrusted to me. Help me to live these truths each day and to grow closer to You in all that I do.

In Jesus' glorious name I pray, Amen

APRIL 18

2 Timothy 4:18 (NIV): The Lord will rescue me from every evil attack and will bring me safely to His heavenly kingdom. To Him be glory forever and ever. Amen.

1 John 4:18 (NKJV): There is no fear in love; but perfect love casts out fear, because fear involves torment. But he who fears has not been made perfect in love.

2 Corinthians 4:18 (NLT): So we don't look at the troubles we can see now; rather, we fix our gaze on the things that cannot be seen. For the things we see now will soon be gone, but the things we cannot see will last forever.

PRAYER

Dear Heavenly Father, Jehovah Machsi (The LORD Is My Refuge),

I come to You with a heart full of trust and gratitude, seeking Your guidance and strength. 2 Timothy 4:18 says, "The Lord will rescue me from every evil attack and will bring me safely to His heavenly kingdom. To Him be glory forever and ever. Amen." Lord, I am grateful for Your promise to rescue me from all harm and to bring me safely to Your heavenly kingdom. I trust in Your protection and look forward to Your glorious presence forever. 1 John 4:18 tells us, "There is no fear in love. But perfect love drives out fear, because fear has to do with punishment. The one who fears is not made perfect in love" (NIV). Lord, help me to embrace Your perfect love that casts out fear. Replace any anxieties or worries in my heart with the assurance of Your unconditional love and the peace that comes from knowing You. 2 Corinthians 4:18 says, "So we fix our eyes not on what is seen, but on what is unseen, since what is seen is temporary, but what is unseen is eternal" (NIV). Lord, help me to focus on the eternal and unseen realities of Your kingdom rather than being consumed by temporary concerns. Strengthen my faith and keep my eyes set on the hope and promises You provide. Thank You for Your protection, for casting out fear with Your perfect love, and for guiding me to focus on the eternal. Help me to live in the assurance of Your promises and to grow closer to You each day.

In Jesus' safe name I pray, Amen

APRIL 19

1 John 4:19 (NIV): We love because he loved us first.

Philippians 4:19 (NIV): And my God will meet all your needs according to the riches of His glory in Christ Jesus.

1 Peter 4:19 (AMP): Therefore, those who are ill treated and suffer in accordance with the will of God, must [continue to] do right and commit their souls [for safe-keeping] to the faithful creator.

 PRAYER

Dear Heavenly Father, Jehovah Magen (The LORD, My Shield),

I come before You with a heart full of gratitude and trust in Your provision. 1 John 4:19 says, "We love because He first loved us." Lord, I am grateful for Your unconditional love that empowers me to love others. Help me to reflect Your love in all that I do and to share Your love with those around me. Philippians 4:19 tells us, "And my God will meet all your needs according to the riches of His glory in Christ Jesus." Lord, thank You for the promise that You will provide for all my needs. I trust in Your abundance and grace, knowing that You will supply everything I require for a fulfilling and purposeful life. 1 Peter 4:19 says, "So then, those who suffer according to God's will should commit themselves to their faithful Creator and continue to do good" (NIV). Lord, in times of difficulty, help me to commit myself fully to You. Strengthen my faith and guide me to continue doing good, even when it's challenging. Thank You for Your perfect love, for meeting all my needs, and for guiding me through difficulties. Help me to trust in Your care and to live out these truths every day.

In Jesus' guiding name I pray, Amen

1 John 4:20 (ESV): If someone says, "I love God," and hates his brother, he is a liar; for he who does not love his brother whom he has seen, how can he love God whom he has not seen?

Proverbs 4:20 (NLT): My child, pay attention to what I say. Listen carefully to my words.

Philippians 4:20 (NLT): Now all glory to God our father forever and ever! Amen.

PRAYER

Dear Heavenly Father, YHWH (I AM),

I come before You with a heart seeking Your guidance and strength. 1 John 4:20 says, "Whoever claims to love God yet hates a brother or sister is a liar. For whoever does not love their brother and sister, whom they have seen, cannot love God, whom they have not seen" (NIV). Lord, help me to truly love those around me. Let Your love flow through me so that my actions reflect Your love for everyone, not just in words but in my heart and deeds. Proverbs 4:20 tells us, "My son, pay attention to what I say; turn your ear to my words" (NIV). Lord, open my ears to hear Your guidance and wisdom. Help me to pay close attention to Your words and to apply them in my life. Let Your truth shape my thoughts, actions, and decisions. Philippians 4:20 says, "To our God and Father be glory forever and ever. Amen" (NIV). Lord, I give You all the glory and praise. Thank You for Your constant presence and provision in my life. I honor You with my life and seek to reflect Your glory in all that I do. Thank You for teaching me to love deeply, for guiding me with Your wisdom, and for the glory You deserve. Help me to live out these truths and to grow closer to You each day.

In Jesus' powerful name I pray, Amen

APRIL 21

1 John 4:21 (NKJV): And this commandment we have from Him; that he who loves God must love his brother also.

Proverbs 4:21 (NLT): Don't lose sight of my words. Let them penetrate deep into your heart.

Ephesians 4:21 (ESV): Since you have heard about Jesus and have learned the truth that comes from him.

Mark 4:21 (NLT): Then Jesus asked them, "Would anyone light a lamp and then put it under a basket or under a bed? Of course, not! A lamp is placed in a stand, where its light will shine."

PRAYER

Dear Heavenly Father, Entunchano (The God Who Intercedes),

I come before You with a heart open to Your wisdom and love. 1 John 4:21 says, "And this commandment we have from Him: whoever loves God must also love his brother" (ESV). Lord, help me to live out this commandment by loving others as You have loved me. Teach me to show genuine love and kindness to everyone around me, reflecting Your love in all my relationships. Proverbs 4:21 tells us, "Do not let them out of your sight, keep them within your heart" (NIV). Lord, help me to keep Your wisdom and truth close to my heart. Guide me to meditate on Your Word daily and let Your teachings influence my thoughts and actions. Ephesians 4:21 says, "Surely you heard of Him and were taught in Him in accordance with the truth that is in Jesus" (BSB). Lord, thank You for teaching me through Your Son, Jesus. Help me to live according to the truth I've learned from Him and to embody His teachings in my life. Mark 4:21 asks, "Do you bring in a lamp to put it under a bowl or a bed? Instead, don't you put it on its stand?" (NIV). Lord, let Your light shine through me in everything I do. Help me to be a beacon of Your love and truth in the world, not hiding Your light but letting it shine brightly for others to see. Thank You for guiding me with Your wisdom, for teaching me through Your Son, and for calling me to be a light in the world. Help me to live out these truths and to grow closer to You each day.

In Jesus' heavenly name I pray, Amen

APRIL 22

Proverbs 4:22 (NLT): [My words] bring life to those who find them, and healing to their whole body.

Mark 4:22 (NLT): For everything that is hidden will eventually be brought into the open, and every secret will be brought to light.

Ephesians 4:22 (NLT): Throw off your old sinful nature and your former ways of life, which is corrupted by lust and deception.

PRAYER

Dear Heavenly Father, Sane (The God Who Hates Sin),

I come before You with a heart full of gratitude and trust in Your guidance. Proverbs 4:22 says, "They are life to those who find them and health to one's whole body" (NIV). Lord, I am thankful for Your wisdom and truth, which bring life and healing to my spirit and body. Help me to seek and treasure Your words, allowing them to nourish and guide me each day. Mark 4:22 tells us, "For whatever is hidden is meant to be disclosed, and whatever is concealed is meant to be brought out into the open" (NIV). Lord, I ask for Your light to reveal any areas in my life that need Your touch. Help me to be open and honest before You, knowing that Your truth will bring clarity and growth. Ephesians 4:22 says, "You were taught, with regard to your former way of life, to put off your old self, which is being corrupted by its deceitful desires" (NIV). Lord, help me to let go of my old ways and to embrace the new life You have called me to. Strengthen me to overcome any deceitful desires and to live according to Your will. Thank You for Your life-giving words, for revealing truth in my life, and for transforming me to be more like You. Guide me each day to live in Your light and to walk in the newness You provide.

In Jesus' merciful name I pray, Amen

Matthew 4:23 (NIV): Jesus went throughout Galilee, teaching in their synagogues, proclaiming the good news of the kingdom, and healing every disease and sickness among the people.

Proverbs 4:23 (NASB): Watch over your heart with all diligence, for from it flows the springs of life.

Mark 4:23 (NLT): "Anyone with ears to hear should listen and understand."

PRAYER

Dear Heavenly Father, Akal Esh (Consuming Fire),

I come to You with a heart seeking Your guidance and healing. Matthew 4:23 says, "Jesus went throughout Galilee, teaching in their synagogues, proclaiming the good news of the kingdom, and healing every disease and sickness among the people." Lord, I thank You for Jesus' ministry of teaching and healing. Please bring Your healing touch to my life, whether in body, mind, or spirit, and help me to understand and embrace the good news of Your kingdom. Proverbs 4:23 tells us, "Above all else, guard your heart, for everything you do flows from it" (NIV). Lord, help me to protect my heart from negative influences and to keep it focused on You. Guide me to fill my heart with Your truth and love so that everything I do flows from Your goodness and wisdom. Mark 4:23 says, "If anyone has ears to hear, let them hear" (NIV). Lord, give me ears to hear Your voice clearly. Help me to listen attentively to Your guidance and to apply Your teachings in my daily life. Thank You for Your healing power, for guiding me to guard my heart, and for helping me to hear and follow Your voice. I trust in Your care and seek to live according to Your will each day.

In Jesus' healing name I pray, Amen

Proverbs 4:24 (NLT): Avoid all perverse talk; stay away from corrupt speech.

Mark 4:24 (NLT): Then [Jesus] added, "Pay close attention to what you hear. The closer you listen, the more understanding you will be given—and then you will receive even more."

Romans 4:24 (NIV): But also for us, to whom God will credit righteousness—for us who believe in him who raised Jesus our Lord from the dead.

John 4:24 (NIV): "God is spirit, so those who worship him must worship in Spirit and in truth."

Deuteronomy 4:24 (NIV): The LORD your God is devouring fires; he is a jealous God.

PRAYER

Dear Heavenly Father, Pneuma (Spirit),

I come to You seeking Your guidance and wisdom for my life. Proverbs 4:24 says, "Keep your mouth free of perversity; keep corrupt talk far from your lips" (NIV). Lord, help me to be mindful of my words. Guide me to speak with kindness, honesty, and integrity, avoiding any harmful or misleading talk. In Mark 4:24, Jesus tells us, "Consider carefully what you hear, . . . With the measure you use, it will be measured to you—and even more" (NIV). Lord, help me to be discerning about what I listen to and how I use Your teachings. Let me apply Your wisdom generously and accurately in my life, so that Your truth can deeply impact me and those around me. Romans 4:24 says, "But also for us, to whom God will credit righteousness—for us who believe in Him who raised Jesus our Lord from the dead." Lord, I thank You for the righteousness You offer through faith in Jesus. Help me to live in the light of this truth, trusting in Your promises and reflecting Your love. Jesus tells us in John 4:24, "God is spirit, and his worshipers must worship in Spirit and in truth." Lord, guide me to worship You with sincerity and truth, fully engaging in Your Spirit. Let my worship be genuine and from the heart, honoring You in all I do. Deuteronomy 4:24 shows me to acknowledge Your mighty presence and Your passionate love for me. Help me to understand and respect Your holiness and to align my life with Your will.

In Jesus' truthful name I pray, Amen

Romans 4:25 (NKJV): Who was delivered up because of our offenses, and was raised because of our justification.

Ephesians 4:25 (NKJV): Therefore, putting away lying, "Let each one of you speak truth with his neighbor," for we are members of one another.

Proverbs 4:25 (NLT): Look straight ahead, and fix your eyes on what lies before you.

Mark 4:25 (NLT): "To those who listen to my teaching, more understanding will be given. But for those who are not listening, even what little understanding they have will be taken away from them."

PRAYER

Dear Heavenly Father, Ori (My Light),

I come to You with a heart open to Your guidance and grace. Romans 4:25 says, "He was delivered over to death for our sins and was raised to life for our justification" (NIV). Lord, thank You for the sacrifice of Jesus, who died for our sins and was raised to give us new life. Help me to live in the freedom and righteousness that His resurrection provides. Ephesians 4:25 tells us, "Therefore each of you must put off falsehood and speak truthfully to your neighbor, for we are all members of one body" (NIV). Lord, guide me to be honest and truthful in all my interactions. Help me to build trust and unity with others by speaking with integrity and love. Proverbs 4:25 says, "Let your eyes look straight ahead; fix your gaze directly before you" (NIV). Lord, help me to stay focused on Your path and purpose for my life. Keep me from distractions and guide me to follow Your direction with unwavering commitment. Mark 4:25 tells us, "Whoever has will be given more; whoever does not have, even what they have will be taken from them" (NIV). Lord, help me to be faithful with the blessings and responsibilities You have given me. Teach me to use my resources wisely and to seek more of Your guidance and grace in my life. Thank You for the gift of Jesus' sacrifice, for the call to speak truth, for guidance to stay focused, and for the wisdom to manage Your blessings.

In Jesus' honest name I pray, Amen

Proverbs 4:26 (NLT): Mark out a straight path for your feet; stay on the safe path.

Ephesians 4:26 (NLT): "Don't sin by letting anger control you." And don't let the sun go down while you are still angry.

John 4:26 (NLT): Then Jesus told her, "I Am the Messiah!"

--------------------------------- PRAYER ---------------------------------

Dear Heavenly Father, Tsaddik (Righteous),

I come to You seeking Your guidance and strength for my life. Proverbs 4:26 says, "Give careful thought to the paths for your feet and be steadfast in all your ways" (NIV). Lord, help me to carefully consider the choices I make and the paths I follow. Guide my steps and keep me steadfast in Your ways, making decisions that honor You. Ephesians 4:26 tells us, "'In your anger do not sin': Do not let the sun go down while you are still angry" (NIV). Lord, help me to manage my emotions wisely. When I am angry or upset, give me the grace to address it in a way that is loving and constructive, and to resolve conflicts before they fester. John 4:26 says, "Then Jesus declared, 'I, the one speaking to you—I am He'" (NIV). Lord, thank You for revealing Yourself through Jesus. Help me to recognize and embrace Your presence in my life and to respond to Your call with faith and trust. Thank You for guiding my choices, helping me handle my emotions, and revealing Yourself to me. I seek to walk in Your ways, resolve conflicts peacefully, and grow closer to You each day.

In Jesus' peaceful name I pray, Amen

I WILL NOT BE SIDETRACKED BY EVIL

Ephesians 4:27 (NIV): And do not give the devil a foothold.

Proverbs 4:27 (NLT): Don't get sidetracked; keep your feet from following evil.

Mark 4:27 (NIV): "Night and day, whether he sleeps or gets up, the seeds sprouts and grows, though he does not know how."

PRAYER

Dear Heavenly Father, Or Goyim (Light of the Nations),

I come to You seeking Your wisdom and protection for my life. Ephesians 4:27 says, "And do not give the devil a foothold" (NIV). Lord, help me to guard my heart and mind against any temptation or deceit. Protect me from giving the enemy any opportunity to influence my thoughts or actions. Strengthen me to stand firm in Your truth, I renounce ant ungodly anger that gives the enemy a foothold. Proverbs 4:27 tells us, "Do not turn to the right or the left; keep your foot from evil" (NIV). Lord, guide me to stay on the path of righteousness and avoid distractions that lead me away from Your will. Help me to keep my focus on You and to walk in Your ways. Mark 4:27 says, "Night and day, whether he sleeps or gets up, the seed sprouts and grows, though he does not know how" (NIV). Lord, thank You for Your work in my life, even when I don't see it. Help me to trust in Your timing and to be patient as You nurture the growth and transformation You are working in me. Thank You for Your protection, guidance, and for the unseen work You do in my life. Help me to remain steadfast in You, avoiding evil, and trusting in Your faithful work within me.

In Jesus' protecting name I pray, Amen

APRIL 28

Ephesians 4:28 (NLT): If you are a thief, quit stealing. Instead, use your hands for good hard work, and then give generously to those in need.

Galatians 4:28 (NLT): And you, dear brothers and sisters, our children of the promise, just like Isaac.

Acts of the Apostles 4:28 (NLT): But everything they did was determined beforehand according to your will.

PRAYER

Dear Heavenly Father, Parakletos (Advocate),

I come to You with a heart full of gratitude and a desire for Your guidance. Ephesians 4:28 says, "Anyone who has been stealing must steal no longer, but must work, doing something useful with their own hands, that they may have something to share with those in need" (NIV). Lord, help me to use my abilities and resources to work honestly and to contribute positively to others. Teach me to share generously and support those in need. Galatians 4:28 tells us, "Now you, brothers and sisters, like Isaac, are children of promise" (NIV). Lord, thank You for making me a part of Your promises through faith. Help me to live in the light of Your promises, knowing that I am Your beloved child and inheritor of Your grace. Acts 4:28 says, "They did what your power and will had decided beforehand should happen" (NIV). Lord, I trust that Your plans and purposes are at work in my life, even when I don't fully understand them. Help me to trust in Your sovereign will and to remain faithful to Your guidance. Thank You for teaching me to work with integrity, for making me a child of Your promise, and for guiding my steps according to Your will. I trust in Your plan for my life and seek to follow You with a grateful and faithful heart.

In Jesus' defending name I pray, Amen

I seek God with all my heart

Ephesians 4:29 (NLT): Don't use foul or abusive language. Let everything you say, be good and helpful, so that your words will be an encouragement to those who hear them.

Deuteronomy 4:29 (BSB): Seek the Lord your God, and you will find him if you seek him with all your heart and with all your soul.

Jeremiah 4:29 (NIV): At the sound of horsemen and archers every town takes to flight; some go into the thickets; some climb up the rocks; all the towns are deserted; no one lives in them.

PRAYER

Dear Heavenly Father, Alethinos Theos (True God),

I come to You today seeking Your guidance and grace. Ephesians 4:29 says, "Do not let any unwholesome talk come out of your mouths, but only what is helpful for building others up according to their needs, that it may benefit those who listen" (NIV). Lord, help me to speak words that are encouraging and uplifting. Guard my tongue so that my words build others up and reflect Your love and truth. Deuteronomy 4:29 tells us, "But if from there you seek the Lord your God, you will find Him if you seek Him with all your heart and with all your soul" (NIV). Lord, I want to seek You wholeheartedly. Help me to pursue You with all my heart and soul, trusting that I will find You in every aspect of my life. Jeremiah 4:29 says, "At the sound of horsemen and archers every town takes to flight; some go into the thickets; some climb up the rocks; all the towns are deserted; no one lives in them." Lord, when I face challenges and difficulties, help me not to retreat in fear or uncertainty. Instead, give me the courage to face them with Your strength and to remain steadfast in Your presence. Thank You for guiding my speech, drawing me closer to You, and strengthening me in times of trouble. Help me to live according to Your will and to trust in Your unwavering support.

In Jesus' true name I pray, Amen

APRIL 30

Ephesians 4:30 (NLT): And do not bring sorrow to God's Holy Spirit by the way you live. Remember, he has identified you as his own, guaranteeing that you will be saved on the day of redemption.

Deuteronomy 4:30 (NLT): In the distant future, when you are suffering all these things, you will finally return to the LORD your God and listen to what he tells you.

Acts 4:30 (NLT): Stretch out your hand with healing power; may miraculous signs and wonders be done through the name of your holy servant Jesus.

PRAYER

Dear Heavenly Father, Yotzerenu (Potter),

I come before You seeking Your guidance and protection in my life. Ephesians 4:30 says, "And do not grieve the Holy Spirit of God, with whom you were sealed for the day of redemption" (NIV). Lord, help me to live in a way that honors You and does not grieve Your Holy Spirit. Teach me to be aware of Your presence in my life and to act in a way that reflects Your love and grace. Deuteronomy 4:30 tells us, "When you are in distress and all these things have happened to you, then in later days you will return to the LORD your God and obey Him" (NIV). Lord, when I face difficult times and challenges, help me to turn to You with a humble heart and to trust in Your guidance and care. Let these times draw me closer to You and strengthen my obedience to Your will. Acts 4:30 says, "Stretch out your hand to heal and perform signs and wonders through the name of your holy servant Jesus" (NIV). Lord, I ask for Your healing and guidance in my life. Use me as an instrument of Your work, whether through acts of kindness, healing, or sharing Your love with others. Empower me to live out Your mission with boldness and faith. Thank You for Your Spirit's guidance, for drawing me back to You in times of distress, and for empowering me to be a vessel of Your work in the world. Help me to remain faithful and to trust in Your plans for my life.

In Jesus' miraculous name I pray, Amen

I have freedom in Christ

Ephesians 5:1 (NLT): Imitate God, therefore, in everything you do, because you are his dear children.

1 John 5:1 (NIV): Everyone who believes that Jesus is the Christ is born of God, and everyone who loves the father loves his child as well.

Romans 5:1 (NLT): Therefore, since we have been made right in God's sight by faith, we have peace with God because of what Jesus Christ our Lord has done for us.

Galatians 5:1 (NKJV): Stand fast therefore in the liberty by which Christ has made us free, and do not be entangled again with a yoke of bondage.

PRAYER

Dear Heavenly Father, Basileus Basileon (King of Kings),

I come to You seeking Your guidance and strength. Ephesians 5:1 says, "Follow God's example, therefore, as dearly loved children" (NIV). Lord, help me to live in a way that reflects Your love and character. Teach me to follow Your example in all I do, showing compassion, kindness, and integrity in my daily life. 1 John 5:1 tells us, "Everyone who believes that Jesus is the Christ is born of God, and everyone who loves the father loves his child as well." Lord, thank You for the gift of faith in Jesus. Help me to grow in my love for You and to express that love by caring for others, just as You have loved me. Romans 5:1 says, "Therefore, since we have been justified through faith, we have peace with God through our Lord Jesus Christ" (NIV). Lord, I am grateful for the peace You have given me through Jesus. Help me to live in this peace, knowing that I am justified and reconciled with You. Galatians 5:1 tells us, "It is for freedom that Christ has set us free. Stand firm, then, and do not let yourselves be burdened again by a yoke of slavery" (NIV). Lord, thank You for the freedom we have in Christ. Help me to stand firm in this freedom and not be weighed down by worries or past burdens. Give me the strength to live freely and joyfully in Your grace. Thank You for Your example, for the peace You provide, and for the freedom we have in Christ. Guide me to live out these truths each day and to reflect Your love in all that I do.

In Jesus' praiseful name I pray, Amen

MAY 2

Ephesians 5:2 (NLT): Live life filled with love, following the example of Christ. He loved us and offered himself as a sacrifice for us, a pleasing aroma to God.

2 Corinthians 5:2 (NLT): We grow weary in our present bodies, and we long to put in our heavenly bodies like new clothing.

Psalm 5:2 (KJV): Hearken unto the voice of my cry, my King and my God: For unto thee will I pray.

Job 5:2 (KJV): For wrath killeth the foolish man, and envy slayeth the silly one.

PRAYER

Dear Heavenly Father, Hashem (The Name),

I come before You seeking Your guidance and grace for my life. Ephesians 5:2 says, "And walk in the way of love, just as Christ loved us and gave himself up for us as a fragrant offering and sacrifice to God" (NIV). Lord, help me to walk in love every day, following the example of Christ. Teach me to love others selflessly and to offer my life as a reflection of Your love. 2 Corinthians 5:2 tells us, "Meanwhile we groan, longing to be clothed instead with our heavenly dwelling" (NIV). Lord, I look forward to the hope of being with You in Your heavenly kingdom. Help me to remain hopeful and focused on Your promises, even as I face challenges in this life. Psalm 5:2 says, "Hear my cry for help, my King and my God, for to You I pray" (NIV). Lord, I come to You with my needs and concerns, asking You to hear my prayers and to respond with Your grace and wisdom. You are my King and my God, and I trust You to guide and support me. Job 5:2 tells us, "Resentment kills a fool, and envy slays the simple" (NIV). Lord, protect me from feelings of resentment and envy. Help me to cultivate a heart of contentment and gratitude, focusing on Your blessings rather than what I lack. Thank You for teaching me to walk in love, for the hope of Your heavenly promises, for hearing my prayers, and for helping me overcome negative feelings. Guide me to live in a way that honors You and reflects Your love.

In Jesus' teaching name I pray, Amen

I PRAY AND GIVE THE LORD MY REQUESTS IN THE MORNING

Matthew 5:3 (NIV): "Blessed are the poor in spirit, for there is the kingdom of heaven."

Psalm 5:3 (NIV): In the morning, LORD, you hear my voice; in the morning I lay my requests before you and wait expectantly.

Romans 5:3 (NLT): We can rejoice, too, when we run into problems and trails, for we know that they help us develop endurance.

Ecclesiastes 5:3 (NLT): Too much activity gives you restless dreams; too many words make you a fool.

PRAYER

Dear Heavenly Father, Lo Shanah (Unchanging),

I come before You with a heart open to Your guidance and grace. Matthew 5:3 says, "Blessed are the poor in spirit, for theirs is the kingdom of heaven." Lord, I recognize my need for You and come before You with humility. Help me to remain dependent on Your grace and to trust in the blessings of Your kingdom. Psalm 5:3 tells us, "In the morning, LORD, You hear my voice; in the morning I lay my requests before You and wait expectantly." Lord, I bring my prayers and requests to You each day. Help me to wait with patience and faith, trusting that You hear me and will respond according to Your will. Romans 5:3 says, "Not only so, but we also glory in our sufferings, because we know that suffering produces perseverance" (NIV). Lord, help me to face challenges with a hopeful spirit, knowing that You use our difficulties to build our character and strengthen our faith. Ecclesiastes 5:3 tells us, "A dream comes when there are many cares, and many words mark the speech of a fool" (NIV). Lord, guide my thoughts and words. Help me to manage my worries and to speak wisely, reflecting Your wisdom and peace. Thank You for blessing those who are humble, for hearing my morning prayers, for using my struggles to build perseverance, and for guiding my thoughts and speech. May my life reflect Your love and wisdom each day.

In Jesus' unchanging name I pray, Amen

MAY 4

1 Peter 5:4 (NIV): And when the Chief Shepherd appears, you will receive the crown of glory that will never fade away.

Matthew 5:4 (NIV): "Blessed are those who mourn, for they will be comforted."

Psalm 5:4 (NIV): For you are not a God who is pleased with wickedness; with you, evil people are not welcome.

Amos 5:4 (NIV): This is what the LORD says to Israel: "Seek me and live."

Ecclesiastes 5:4 (NIV): When you make a vow to God, do not delay to fulfill it. He has no pleasure in fools; fulfill your vow.

PRAYER

Dear Heavenly Father, Parakletos (Advocate),

I come before You with a heart full of gratitude and trust in Your guidance. 1 Peter 5:4 shows me that I will be given a crown of glory when I stay faithful in the minisrty God has given me. Lord, I look forward to the eternal rewards You promise to those who faithfully follow You. Help me to remain steadfast in my faith, knowing that my efforts and struggles are not in vain. Matthew 5:4 tells us that when we mourn, the Lord will be our comforter. Lord, I bring before You any pain or sorrow in my heart. Comfort me with Your presence and peace, and help me to find solace in Your promises. Psalm 5:4 says God does not like wickedness. Lord, guide me to live a life that is pleasing to You. Help me to turn away from anything that is contrary to Your will and to seek righteousness in all I do. Amos 5:4 tells us to seek Him and live. Lord, I desire to seek You with all my heart. Draw me closer to You and fill my life with Your presence and guidance. Ecclesiastes 5:4 says, "When you make a vow to God, do not delay to fulfill it. He has no pleasure in fools; fulfill your vow." Lord, help me to keep my commitments and promises to You. Give me the strength and integrity to follow through on my commitments and to honor You in all my actions. Thank You for Your eternal promises and for comforting me. May my life reflect Your love and faithfulness each day.

In Jesus' glorious name I pray, Amen

MAY 5

I AM MEEK IN CHRIST JESUS

1 Peter 5:5 (NIV): In the same way, you who are younger, submit yourselves to your elders. All of you, clothe yourselves with humility toward one another, because "God opposes the proud but shows favor to the humble."

Judges 5:5 (NIV): The mountains quaked before the LORD, the One of Sinai, before the LORD, the God of Israel.

Matthew 5:5 (NIV): "Blessed are the meek, for they will inherit the Earth."

Psalm 5:5 (NIV): The arrogant cannot stand in your presence. You hate all who do wrong.

PRAYER

Dear Heavenly Father, Sane (The God Who Hates Sin),

I come before You with a humble and open heart, seeking Your guidance and grace. 1 Peter 5:5 says, "In the same way, you who are younger, submit yourselves to your elders. All of you, clothe yourselves with humility toward one another, because 'God opposes the proud but shows favor to the humble.'" Lord, help me to embrace humility in all my relationships. Teach me to honor and respect others and to approach each day with a humble heart. Judges 5:5 tells us, "The mountains quaked before the LORD, the One of Sinai, before the LORD, the God of Israel." Lord, You are mighty and powerful, and the mountains melt at Your presence. Help me to remember Your greatness and to live in a way that reflects my awe of Your power and majesty. Matthew 5:5 says, "Blessed are the meek, for they will inherit the earth." Lord, guide me to live with meekness and gentleness. Help me to trust in Your plans and promises, knowing that in Your time and way, You will bless and guide me. Psalm 5:5 tells us, "The arrogant cannot stand in Your presence. You hate all who do wrong." Lord, I ask for Your help in turning away from arrogance and sin. Purify my heart and guide me in Your ways, so I can stand in Your presence with integrity and humility. Thank You for Your guidance in embracing humility, for reminding me of Your greatness, for blessing the meek, and for leading me away from arrogance. May my life reflect Your love, grace, and wisdom each day.

In Jesus' purifying name I pray, Amen

MAY 6

Jeremiah 5:6 (NIV): Therefore a lion from the forest will attack them, a wolf from the desert will ravage them, a leopard will lie in wait near their towns to tear to pieces any who venture out, for their rebellion is great and their backslidings many.

Matthew 5:6 (NIV): "Blessed are those who hunger and thirst for righteousness, for they will be filled."

Psalm 5:6 (NIV): You destroy those who tell lies. The bloodthirsty and deceitful you, LORD, detest.

PRAYER

Dear Heavenly Father, El Shaddai (The All-Sufficient One, God Almighty),

I come before You with a heart full of trust and hope in Your promises. Jeremiah 5:6 says, "Therefore a lion from the forest will attack them, a wolf from the desert will ravage them, a leopard will lie in wait near their towns to tear to pieces any who venture out, for their rebellion is great and their backslidings many." Lord, this verse reminds me of the dangers and challenges in life. Please protect me from harm and guide me safely through difficult times. I rebuke every lion of the forest that comes to slay. Matthew 5:6 tells us, "Blessed are those who hunger and thirst for righteousness, for they will be filled." Lord, I desire to seek You and pursue righteousness. Fill my heart with Your truth and guide me in living a life that honors You. Psalm 5:6 says, "You destroy those who tell lies; bloodthirsty and deceitful men the LORD abhors." Lord, help me to be truthful and honest in all my dealings. Keep me away from deceit and guide me to live with integrity and sincerity. Thank You for protecting me from harm, for filling me with a desire for righteousness, and for guiding me in truth. Help me to live a life that reflects Your love and grace each day.

In Jesus' safe name I pray, Amen

I WALK BY FAITH

2 Corinthians 5:7 (ESV): For we walk by faith, not by sight.

1 Corinthians 5:7 (NIV): Get rid of the old yeast, so that you may be a new unleavened batch—as you really are. For Christ, our Passover lamb, has been sacrificed.

Matthew 5:7 (NIV): "Blessed are the merciful, for they will be shown mercy."

PRAYER

Dear Heavenly Father, Elohim (Mighty Creator),

I come before You with a heart full of faith and trust in Your promises. 2 Corinthians 5:7 says, "For we live by faith, not by sight" (NIV). Lord, help me to trust You fully even when I can't see the outcome. Strengthen my faith and remind me to rely on Your guidance and wisdom in all circumstances. 1 Corinthians 5:7 tells us, "Get rid of the old yeast, so that you may be a new unleavened batch—as you really are. For Christ, our Passover lamb, has been sacrificed." Lord, cleanse me from any old habits or sins that keep me from fully living in Your grace. For our Messiah the Passover lamb, has been sacrificed. Help me to embrace the new life You offer through Jesus. Matthew 5:7 says, "Blessed are the merciful, for they will be shown mercy." Lord, teach me to be merciful and compassionate toward others. May my actions reflect Your kindness and love, and may I also receive Your mercy in my own life. Thank You for guiding me to live by faith, for renewing me through Your grace, and for teaching me to be merciful. Help me to walk in Your light and reflect Your love each day.

In Jesus' compassionate name I pray, Amen

1 Peter 5:8 (NLT): Stay alert! Watch out for your great enemy, the devil. He prowls around like a roaring lion, looking for someone to devour.

1 John 5:8 (NIV): The Spirit, the water and the blood; and the three are in agreement.

1 Corinthians 5:8 (NIV): Therefore let us keep the Festival, not with the old bread leavened with malice and wickedness, but with the unleavened bread of sincerity and truth.

Psalm 5:8 (NIV): Lead me, Lord, in Your righteousness because of my enemies—make Your way straight before me.

Matthew 5:8 (NIV): "Blessed are the pure in heart, for they will see God."

PRAYER

Dear Heavenly Father, El Kanna (Jealous God),

I come to You with a heart seeking Your guidance and protection. 1 Peter 5:8 reminds me to stay vigilant and aware of the spiritual battles around me. Protect me from the schemes of the enemy and keep me grounded in Your truth. 1 John 5:8 speaks for the powerful testimony of Your Spirit, the water of baptism, and the blood of Christ. The blood of Jesus bears witness to my deliverance and salvation. Help me to live in the truth of this testimony and to find strength and assurance in Your promises. 1 Corinthians 5:8 tells us to live with sincerity and truth. I remove all leaven of malice and wickedness from my life. Help me to remove any deceit or bitterness from my life and to embrace a heart that is pure and genuine. Psalm 5:8 proclaims that I can I ask for Your guidance in every step I take. Lead me in Your righteousness and make Your path clear, so I may walk according to Your will. In Matthew 5:8, Jesus says, "Blessed are the pure in heart, for they will see God." Lord, purify my heart and mind. Help me to live with integrity and purity so that I may experience Your presence in my life and see Your work clearly. Thank You for protecting me from the enemy, for the testimony of Your Spirit, for guiding me to live in sincerity and truth, for leading me in righteousness, and for honoring my prayers. May my heart be pure and my life reflect Your love and grace.

In Jesus' truthful, promising name I pray, Amen

MAY 9

I AM A PEACEMAKER

James 5:9 (MSG): Friends, don't complain about each other. A far greater complaint could be lodged against you, you know. The judge is standing just around the corner.

Matthew 5:9 (NIV): "Blessed are the peacemakers, for they will be called children of God."

Romans 5:9 (NIV): Since we have now been justified by [Jesus'] blood, how much more shall we be saved from God's wrath through him!

Job 5:9 (NIV): He performs wonders that cannot be fathomed, miracles that cannot be counted.

PRAYER

Dear Heavenly Father, Atik Yomin (Ancient of Days),

I come before You with a heart open to Your guidance and grace. James 5:9 says, "Don't grumble against one another, brothers and sisters, or you will be judged. The Judge is standing at the door!" (NIV). Lord, help me to avoid grumbling and complaining. Teach me to build others up with my words and actions, reflecting Your love and patience. Matthew 5:9 tells us, "Blessed are the peacemakers, for they will be called children of God." Lord, guide me to be a peacemaker in all my relationships. Not just a peace keeper but a peace maker. Help me to seek peace and reconciliation, and let my actions reflect Your peace and harmony. Romans 5:9 reminds us, "Since we have now been justified by His blood, how much more shall we be saved from God's wrath through Him!" Lord, thank You for the sacrifice of Jesus that justifies and saves us. Help me to live in the confidence of this salvation and to share Your grace with others. Job 5:9 says, "He performs wonders that cannot be fathomed, miracles that cannot be counted." Lord, I am amazed by Your greatness and the wonders You do. Help me to trust in Your power and to recognize the miracles You work in my life, even when I cannot fully understand them. Thank You for guiding me to avoid grumbling, for calling me to be a peacemaker, for the salvation provided through Jesus, and for Your wondrous deeds. May I live each day reflecting Your love, grace, and peace.

In Jesus' unchanging name I pray, Amen

I WANT TO KNOW WHAT PLEASES THE LORD

Matthew 5:10 (NIV): "Blessed are those who are persecuted because of righteousness, for there is the kingdom of heaven."

Deuteronomy 5:10 (NLT): But I lavish unfailing love for a thousand generations on those who love me and obey my commands.

Ephesians 5:10 (NIV): Find out what pleases the Lord.

PRAYER

Dear Heavenly Father, Shub Nephesh (Renewer of Life),

I come before You with a heart full of faith and trust in Your Word. Matthew 5:10 says, "Blessed are those who are persecuted because of righteousness, for theirs is the kingdom of heaven." Lord, when I face challenges or opposition for living according to Your will, help me to remain steadfast and courageous. May I find comfort in knowing that Your kingdom belongs to those who endure for righteousness. Deuteronomy 5:10 reminds us, "Showing love to a thousand generations of those who love me and keep my commandments" (NIV). Lord, thank You for Your steadfast love and faithfulness. Help me to love You wholeheartedly and to keep Your commandments, so that Your blessings may extend to many generations after me. Ephesians 5:10 says, "Find out what pleases the Lord." Lord, guide me to seek Your will in all that I do. Help me to understand what truly pleases You and to align my actions and thoughts with Your desires. Thank You for Your promise of blessing to those who are faithful, for Your enduring love, and for guiding me to understand and follow Your will. May my life reflect Your righteousness, love, and pleasure.

In Jesus' faithful name I pray, Amen

MAY 11

1 Thessalonians 5:11 (NIV): Therefore encourage one another and build one another up, just as in fact you are doing.

Matthew 5:11 (NIV): "Blessed are you when people insult you, persecute you and falsely say all kinds of evil against you because of [Jesus]."

Psalm 5:11 (NIV): But let all who take refuge in God be glad; let them ever sing for joy.

Spread your protection over them, that those who love your name may rejoice in you.

Deuteronomy 5:11 (NIV): You shall not misuse the name of the LORD your God, for the LORD will not hold anyone guiltless who misuses his name.

PRAYER

Dear Heavenly Father, El Sela (God My Rock),

I come before You with gratitude and a desire to grow in Your grace. 1 Thessalonians 5:11 says, "Therefore encourage one another and build each other up, just as in fact you are doing." Lord, help me to be a source of encouragement and support to those around me. Let my words and actions uplift others and reflect Your love and kindness. In Matthew 5:11, Jesus reminds us, "Blessed are you when people insult you, persecute you, and falsely say all kinds of evil against you because of me." Lord, when I face trials or opposition for my faith, give me strength and courage. Help me to remain steadfast and joyful, knowing that I am blessed in Your eyes. Psalm 5:11 says, "But let all who take refuge in You be glad; let them ever sing for joy. Spread Your protection over them, that those who love Your name may rejoice in You." Lord, I seek refuge in You and ask for Your protection. Fill my heart with joy and help me to rejoice in Your presence, trusting in Your care and guidance. Deuteronomy 5:11 states, "You shall not misuse the name of the LORD your God, for the LORD will not hold anyone guiltless who misuses His name." Lord, help me to honor Your name in all that I say and do. May I always speak and act in ways that respect and glorify You. Thank You for Your encouragement, for blessing me through trials, for Your protection and joy, and for the call to honor Your name.

In Jesus' safe name I pray, Amen

I HAVE A GREAT REWARD IN HEAVEN

Psalm 5:12 (NIV): Surely, LORD, you bless the righteous; you surround them with your favor as with a shield.

Matthew 5:12 (NIV): "Rejoice and be glad, because great is your reward in heaven, for in the same way they persecuted the prophets who were before you."

Deuteronomy 5:12 (NIV): Observe the Sabbath day, to keep it holy, as the LORD your God has commanded you.

Micah 5:12 (NIV): I will destroy your witchcraft and you will no longer cast spells.

PRAYER

Dear Heavenly Father, El Haggadol (The Great God),

I come to You with a heart full of faith and gratitude. Psalm 5:12 says, "Surely, LORD, you bless the righteous; you surround them with your favor as with a shield." Lord, thank You for Your blessings and favor. Surround me with Your shield of protection and grace, and help me to live righteously in Your sight. Matthew 5:12 reminds us, "Rejoice and be glad, because great is your reward in heaven, for in the same way they persecuted the prophets who were before you." Lord, when I face difficulties or opposition for my faith, help me to rejoice and remain glad. Remind me of the great reward You have prepared for those who stand firm in their faith. Deuteronomy 5:12 says, "Observe the Sabbath day by keeping it holy, as the LORD your God has commanded you." Lord, help me to honor the Sabbath and keep it holy. May I find rest and renewal in Your presence and use this day to draw closer to You. Micah 5:12 states, "I will destroy your witchcraft and you will no longer cast spells." Lord, cleanse my life of anything that is not of You. Help me to turn away from any harmful practices and to seek only Your truth and guidance. Thank You for Your blessings and favor, for the strength to rejoice through trials, for the gift of rest on the Sabbath, and for cleansing my life of anything contrary to Your will. May I live in a way that honors and glorifies You.

In Jesus' favorable name I pray, Amen

MAY 13

Matthew 5:13 (NIV): "You are the salt of the Earth. But if the salt loses its saltiness, how can it be made salty again? It is no longer good for anything, except to be thrown out and trampled underfoot."

Luke 5:13 (NIV): Jesus reached out his hand and touched the man. "I am willing," he said. "Be clean!" And immediately the leprosy left him.

Job 5:13 (NLT): He traps the wise in their own cleverness so their cunning schemes are thwarted.

Ephesians 5:13 (NIV): But everything exposed by the light becomes visible—and everything that is illuminated becomes a light.

PRAYER

Dear Heavenly Father, El Qadosh (The Holy One),

I come to You with a grateful heart and seek Your guidance and strength. Jesus says in Matthew 5:13, "You are the salt of the earth. But if the salt loses its saltiness, how can it be made salty again?" Lord, help me to be a positive influence in the world around me. Let my actions and words reflect Your love and truth, so that I may bring out the best in others and honor You in all that I do. Luke 5:13 tells us, "Jesus reached out His hand and touched the man. 'I am willing,' He said. 'Be clean!' And immediately the leprosy left him." Lord, I ask for Your healing touch in my life. Cleanse me from any spiritual or emotional burdens and restore me to wholeness. Help me to trust in Your willingness and power to heal and renew. Job 5:13 says, "He catches the wise in their own craftiness, and the schemes of the wily are swept away" (NIV). Lord, protect me from deceit and foolish schemes. Grant me wisdom and discernment to navigate life's challenges and to stay true to Your path. Ephesians 5:13 reminds us, "But everything exposed by the light becomes visible—and everything that is illuminated becomes a light." Lord, shine Your light upon me and in me. Help me to reveal and live out Your truth, so that others may see Your light through me and be drawn to Your love. Thank You for making me a vessel of Your influence.

In Jesus' holy name I pray, Amen

God hears me

1 John 5:14 (NKJV): Now this is the confidence that we have in Him, that if we ask anything according to Him will, He hear us.

Matthew 5:14 (NIV): "You are the light of the world. A town built on a hill cannot be hidden."

Hebrew 5:14 (NIV): But solid food is for the mature, who by constant use have trained themselves to distinguish good from evil.

Galatians 5:14 (NIV): For the entire law is fulfilled in keeping this one command: "Love your neighbor as yourself."

PRAYER

Dear Heavenly Father, Jehovah-Jireh (The Lord My Provider),

I come to You with a heart full of faith and hope. 1 John 5:14 says, "This is the confidence we have in approaching God: that if we ask anything according to His will, He hears us" (NIV). Lord, I place my trust in You, knowing that You hear my prayers and will answer according to Your perfect will. Help me to seek Your will in all things and trust in Your timing. Matthew 5:14 reminds me, "You are the light of the world. A town built on a hill cannot be hidden." Lord, let Your light shine brightly through me. Help me to be a source of light and hope to those around me, reflecting Your love and truth in all that I do. Hebrews 5:14 states, "But solid food is for the mature, who by constant use have trained themselves to distinguish good from evil." Lord, help me to grow in spiritual maturity. Give me the wisdom and discernment to understand and choose what is right, and to deepen my relationship with You through consistent study and prayer. Galatians 5:14 says, "For the entire law is fulfilled in keeping this one command: 'Love your neighbor as yourself.'" Lord, fill my heart with Your love and teach me to love others as You love me. Help me to live out this command daily and to treat everyone with kindness and compassion. Thank You for hearing my prayers, for guiding me to be a light in the world, for helping me grow in maturity and discernment, and for teaching me to love others. May my life reflect Your love and grace in all that I do.

In Jesus' attentive name I pray, Amen

MAY 15

Ephesians 5:15 (NIV): Be very careful, then, how you live—not as unwise but as wise,

Amos 5:15 (NIV): Hate evil, love good; maintain justice in the courts. Perhaps the LORD God Almighty will have mercy on the remnant of Joseph.

Galatians 5:15 (NIV): If you bite and devour each other, watch out or you will be destroyed by each other.

Micah 5:15 (NIV): I will take vengeance in anger and wrath on the nations that have not obeyed me.

PRAYER

Dear Heavenly Father, Elohim Shama (The God Who Hears),

I honor and seek You today, seeking Your wisdom and guidance. Ephesians 5:15 reminds us, "Be very careful, then, how you live—not as unwise but as wise." Lord, help me to live my life with wisdom and discernment. Guide my decisions and actions so that they reflect Your will and bring honor to You. Amos 5:15 says, "Hate evil, love good; maintain justice in the courts." Father, teach me to stand firm against what is wrong and to actively pursue what is good. Help me to uphold justice in my interactions with others and to act with integrity and fairness. Galatians 5:15 warns, "If you bite and devour each other, watch out or you will be destroyed by each other." Lord, protect me from conflict and division. Help me to build others up with my words and actions rather than tearing them down. Fill my heart with love and peace, and help me to foster harmony in my relationships. Micah 5:15 declares, "I will take vengeance in anger and wrath on the nations that have not obeyed me." Lord, I trust in Your justice and righteousness. Help me to rely on Your timing and judgment rather than seeking revenge. Teach me to trust in Your sovereignty and to leave all matters of justice in Your hands. Thank You for guiding me with wisdom, teaching me to pursue good and justice, protecting me from division, and reminding me to trust in Your justice. May my life reflect Your love and truth in all that I do.

In Jesus' teaching name I pray, Amen

I GLORIFY GOD IN ALL I DO

James 5:16 (NKJV): The effectual fervent prayer of a righteous man avails much.

1 Thessalonians 5:16 (NIV): Rejoice always!

Matthew 5:16 (NKJV): "Let your light so shine before men, that they may see your good works and glorify your Father in heaven."

Galatians 5:16 (NKJV): I say then: walk in the Spirit, and you shall not fulfill the lust of the flesh.

PRAYER

Dear Heavenly Father, El Sela (God My Rock),

I come to You with a heart open to Your guidance and grace. James 5:16 says, "The prayer of a righteous person is powerful and effective" (NIV). Lord, I lift up my prayers to You, trusting in Your power and effectiveness. Help me to pray with sincerity and faith, knowing that You listen and act according to Your will. 1 Thessalonians 5:16 encourages us, "Rejoice always." Father, even in times of difficulty, teach me to find joy in Your presence and in the blessings You provide. Let my heart be filled with gratitude and praise, and help me to rejoice in every circumstance. Matthew 5:16 reminds us, "In the same way, let your light shine before others, that they may see your good deeds and glorify your Father in heaven" (NIV). Lord, guide me to live in a way that reflects Your love and goodness. Let my actions and words shine brightly, so that others may see Your light in me and give glory to You. Galatians 5:16 advises, "So I say, walk by the Spirit, and you will not gratify the desires of the flesh" (NIV). Father, help me to walk daily in Your Spirit. Guide me to live according to Your will and not be led by my own desires. Strengthen me to choose Your path and to seek Your guidance in all areas of my life. Thank You for the power of prayer, for the joy You give, for the opportunity to reflect Your light, and for guiding me to walk in Your Spirit. May my life honor You and bring others closer to Your love.

In Jesus' gloried name I pray, Amen

MAY 17

Ephesians 5:17 (NIV): Therefore do not be foolish, but understand what the Lord's will is.

1 Thessalonians 5:17 (ESV): Pray without ceasing.

2 Corinthians 5:17 (NIV): Therefore, if anyone is in Christ, the new creation has come: The old has gone, the new is here!

Luke 5:17 (NIV): One day Jesus was teaching, and Pharisees and teachers of the law were sitting there. They had come from every village of Galilee and from Judea and Jerusalem. And the power of the Lord was with Jesus to heal the sick.

Matthew 5:17 (NIV): "Do not think that I have come to abolish the law of the prophet; I have not come to abolish them but to fulfill them."

PRAYER

Dear Heavenly Father, El Roi (The God Who Sees Me),

I come before You today seeking Your guidance and wisdom. Ephesians 5:17 tells us to not be foolish. I ask You for Your wisdom and clarity to understand Your will for my life. Help me to make choices that align with Your plans and purpose. 1 Thessalonians 5:17 instructs us to pray continually. Father, help me to maintain a constant connection with You through prayer. Let my heart be devoted to seeking Your presence in every moment of my day. 2 Corinthians 5:17 declares that I am a new creation in Christ. Help me to embrace this new life and live in the transformation You have brought about in me. Luke 5:17 tells us the Lord will release His power in healing and deliverance. Lord, I pray that Your power will be present in my life, bringing healing and restoration. May Your power work through me to touch others with Your love and grace. Matthew 5:17 shows us that Jesus fulfilled the law. Father, Help me to understand and live out the fullness of Your commands and teachings in my life. Thank You for Your wisdom, Your constant presence, the new life You've given me, Your abundant grace, Your healing power, and the fulfillment of Your promises through Jesus. Guide me to live in accordance with Your will and to be a reflection of Your love.

In Jesus' truthful name I pray, Amen

I am filled with the Holy Spirit

1 Thessalonians 5:18 (NIV): Give thanks in all circumstances; For this is God's will for you and Jesus Christ.

Matthew 5:18 (NIV): "For truly I tell you, until heaven and earth disappear, not the smallest letter, not the least stroke of a pen, will by any means disappear from the Law until everything is accomplished."

Ephesians 5:18 (NIV): Do not get drunk on wine, which leads to debauchery. Instead, be filled with the Spirit.

PRAYER

Dear Heavenly Father, El Shaddai (The All-Sufficient One, God Almighty),

I come to You with a heart full of gratitude and trust. 1 Thessalonians 5:18 says, "Give thanks in all circumstances; for this is God's will for you in Christ Jesus." Lord, I thank You for the blessings and challenges in my life. Help me to maintain a thankful heart, no matter what I face. Teach me to see Your hand in every situation and to be grateful for Your presence and provision. Matthew 5:18 states, "For truly I tell you, until heaven and earth disappear, not the smallest letter, not the least stroke of a pen, will by any means disappear from the Law until everything is accomplished." Father, thank You for Your faithful promises and the completeness of Your Word. Help me to trust in Your promises and live according to Your teachings, knowing that Your Word is everlasting and true. Ephesians 5:18 encourages us, "Do not get drunk on wine, which leads to debauchery. Instead, be filled with the Spirit." Lord, I pray that You fill me with Your Holy Spirit. Guide me to live a life that is centered on You and not on earthly distractions. Help me to be filled with Your Spirit, so that I can live wisely and reflect Your love to others. Thank You for teaching me to be thankful, for Your unchanging Word, and for filling me with Your Spirit. May my life be a reflection of Your grace and wisdom.

In Jesus' almighty name I pray, Amen

Ephesians 5:19 (NIV): Speaking to one another with psalms, hymns, and songs from the Spirit. Sing and make music from your heart to the Lord.

Deuteronomy 5:19 (NIV): You shall not steal.

Lamentations 5:19 (NIV): You, LORD, reign forever; your throne endures from generation to generation.

1 Thessalonians 5:19 (NIV): Do not quench the Spirit.

PRAYER

Dear Heavenly Father, Jehovah Ezrah (The LORD My Helper),

I come to You with a heart open to Your guidance and wisdom. Ephesians 5:19 encourages us to "Speak to one another with psalms, hymns, and songs from the Spirit. Sing and make music from your heart to the Lord." Father, fill my heart with joy and gratitude. Let my words and songs be a source of encouragement and praise to You and to those around me. Help me to make music from my heart that honors You. Deuteronomy 5:19 says, "You shall not steal." Lord, guide me to live with integrity and honesty in all my dealings. Help me to respect what belongs to others and to act with fairness and trustworthiness. Lamentations 5:19 declares, "You, LORD, reign forever; your throne endures from generation to generation." Thank You, Lord, for Your eternal reign and unchanging nature. I find comfort in knowing that You are always in control and Your promises are steadfast through all generations. 1 Thessalonians 5:19 advises, "Do not quench the Spirit." Lord, I ask that You keep me open to the work of Your Holy Spirit in my life. Help me to respond to Your guidance and not hinder Your work in me. Thank You for Your Word that guides me, for the call to honor and sing to You, for Your eternal reign, and for the reminder to stay open to Your Spirit. May my life be a reflection of Your love, truth, and grace.

In Jesus' teaching name I pray, Amen

MAY 20

HE'S THE GOD OF MY BREAKTHROUGHS

Matthew 5:20 (NIV): "For I tell you that unless your righteousness surpasses that of the Pharisees and the teachers of the law, you will certainly not enter the kingdom of heaven."

Ephesians 5:20 (NIV): And give things to God the father of everything in the name of our Lord Jesus Christ.

Luke 5:20 (NIV): When Jesus saw their faith he said, "Friend, your sins are forgiven."

Isaiah 5:20 (NIV): Woe to those who call evil good and good evil, who put darkness for light and light for darkness, who put bitter for sweet and sweet for bitter.

PRAYER

Dear Heavenly Father, Alethinos Theos (True God),

I come to You with a heart full of trust and gratitude. Matthew 5:20 says we must get our righteousness from God to enter the kingdom of heaven. Lord, help me to live with a righteousness that comes from You, one that goes beyond mere outward appearances and reflects a true heart transformed by Your grace. Guide me to live in a way that honors You and fulfills Your commands. Ephesians 5:20 teaches me to be grateful in every situation. Help me to see Your hand in all things and to express my thanks to You for Your constant provision and love. Luke 5:20 recounts, "When Jesus saw their faith, he said, 'Friend, your sins are forgiven.'" Father, I am grateful for the forgiveness You offer through Jesus. Help me to trust in Your grace and to extend that same forgiveness to others. Let my faith be evident in how I live and interact with those around me. Isaiah 5:20 warns, "Woe to those who call evil good and good evil, who put darkness for light and light for darkness, who put bitter for sweet and sweet for bitter." Lord, guide me to discern truth from falsehood. Help me to stand firm in Your light and to recognize and reject the confusion and deception that can cloud my judgment. Thank You, Lord, for Your victories, Your call to true righteousness, Your constant love, Your forgiveness, and Your guidance in truth. May my life reflect Your goodness and grace in all things.

In Jesus' triumphant name I pray, Amen

I am righteous in Christ

2 Corinthians 5:21 (NIV): God made him who had no sin to be sin for us, so that in him we might become the righteousness of God.

Ephesians 5:21 (NKJV): Submitting to one another in the fear of God.

Isaiah 5:21 (NIV): Woe to those who are wise in their own eyes and clever in their own sight.

Jeremiah 5:21 (NIV): Hear this, you foolish and senseless people, who have eyes but do not see, who have ears but do not hear.

PRAYER

Dear Heavenly Father, El Yeshuati (The God of My Salvation),

I come before You with a humble heart, seeking Your guidance and grace. 2 Corinthians 5:21 says, "God made him who had no sin to be sin for us, so that in him we might become the righteousness of God." Lord, I thank You for the incredible gift of Jesus, who took on our sin so that we could be made righteous before You. Help me to live in the light of this truth, embracing the righteousness that You have provided through Christ. Ephesians 5:21 instructs us, "Submit to one another out of reverence for Christ" (NIV). Father, teach me to live in humility and mutual respect. Help me to honor others and serve them with love, reflecting the selflessness of Christ in all my relationships. Isaiah 5:21 warns, "Woe to those who are wise in their own eyes and clever in their own sight." Lord, keep me from relying solely on my own understanding and pride. Help me to seek Your wisdom and guidance in every aspect of my life, recognizing that true wisdom comes from You. Jeremiah 5:21 states, "Hear this, you foolish and senseless people, who have eyes but do not see, who have ears but do not hear." Father, open my eyes to see Your truth and my ears to hear Your voice clearly. Help me to be attentive to Your will and responsive to Your guidance. Thank You for Your righteousness, Your call to mutual respect, Your wisdom, and Your guidance. May my life be a reflection of Your grace and truth.

In Jesus' embracing name I pray, Amen

MAY 22

Galatians 5:22 (ESV): But the fruit of the Spirit is love, joy, peace, patience, kindness, goodness, faithfulness.

Ephesians 5:22 (NIV): Wives, submit yourselves to your own husbands as you do to the Lord.

Proverbs 5:22 (NIV): The evil deeds of the wicked ensnare them; the cords of their sins hold them fast.

Isaiah 5:22 (NLT): What sorrows for those who are heroes at drinking wine and boast about all the alcohol they can hold.

PRAYER

Dear Heavenly Father, El HaNe'eman (The God Who Is Faithful),

I come before You seeking Your presence and guidance. Galatians 5:22 reminds us of the fruits of the Spirit: "But the fruit of the Spirit is love, joy, peace, forbearance, kindness, goodness, faithfulness, [gentleness, and self-control]" (NIV). Lord, I ask You to cultivate these qualities in my life. Help me to reflect Your love and joy, and to live with peace, kindness, and self-control. Let these fruits of the Spirit guide my actions and interactions. Ephesians 5:22 instructs us, "Wives, submit yourselves to your own husbands as you do to the Lord." Father, I pray for wisdom and understanding in my relationships. Help me to honor and respect those around me, reflecting Your love and humility in all my interactions. Proverbs 5:22 warns, "The evil deeds of the wicked ensnare them; the cords of their sins hold them fast." Lord, protect me from the snares of sin and guide me away from temptation. Help me to walk in Your ways and to find freedom and strength in Your righteousness. Isaiah 5:22 says, "Woe to those who are heroes at drinking wine and champions at mixing drinks" (NIV). Father, keep me from indulgence and excess. Help me to live with moderation and to seek fulfillment in You rather than in the pleasures of this world. Thank You for Your guidance and wisdom. May Your Spirit lead me to live a life filled with the fruits of Your presence, free from the snares of sin, and grounded in Your truth.

In Jesus' kind name I pray, Amen

MAY 23

1 Thessalonians 5:23 (NIV): May God himself, the God of peace, sanctify you through and through. May your whole spirit, soul, and body be kept blameless at the coming of our Lord Jesus Christ.

Ephesians 5:23 (NIV): For the husband is the head of the wife as Christ is the head of the church, his body, of which he is the savior.

Proverbs 5:23 (NLT): He will die for lack of self-control; he will be lost because of his great foolishness.

PRAYER

Dear Heavenly Father, Elah Yerushalem (God of Jerusalem),

I come before You with a grateful heart, seeking Your presence and guidance in my life. 1 Thessalonians 5:23 says, "May God himself, the God of peace, sanctify you through and through. May your whole spirit, soul, and body be kept blameless at the coming of our Lord Jesus Christ." Lord, I ask that You sanctify every part of my being—my spirit, soul, and body. Help me to live a life that is pure and blameless, fully devoted to You. I pray my soul will be persevered blameless into the coming of the Lord. Ephesians 5:23 reminds us, "For the husband is the head of the wife as Christ is the head of the church, his body, of which he is the Savior." Father, I pray for wisdom and strength in all my relationships. May I honor and respect the roles and responsibilities You have set before me, and may I reflect Your love and leadership in all that I do. Proverbs 5:23 warns, "He will die for lack of discipline, led astray by his own great folly" (NIV). Lord, grant me the discipline to follow Your path and the wisdom to avoid the pitfalls of foolishness. Help me to stay true to Your ways and to seek Your guidance in every decision I make. Thank You for Your continued guidance and grace. May Your peace and sanctification fill my life, and may Your wisdom lead me in all things.

In Jesus' loving name I pray, Amen

Galatians 5:24 (NKJV): And those who are Christ's have crucified the flesh with its passions and desires.

Amos 5:24 (NIV): But let justice roll on like a river, righteousness like a never-failing stream!

Ephesians 5:24 (NIV): Now as the church submits to Christ, so also wives should submit to their husbands in everything.

PRAYER

Dear Heavenly Father, Elohay Selichot (The God Who Is Ready to Forgive),

I come before You with a humble heart, seeking Your presence and guidance in my life. Galatians 5:24 reminds us, "Those who belong to Christ Jesus have crucified the flesh with its passions and desires" (NIV). Lord, help me to live in the freedom You provide by crucifying my old self with its sinful desires. Let Your Spirit lead me to live a life that is pleasing to You. Amos 5:24 says, "But let justice roll on like a river, righteousness like a never-failing stream!" Father, I pray that Your justice and righteousness flow through me. Help me to act justly in all my dealings and to seek righteousness in every aspect of my life. Ephesians 5:24 teaches, "Now as the church submits to Christ, so also wives should submit to their husbands in everything." Lord, grant me the wisdom to honor and respect the roles You have established in my relationships. Help me to reflect Your love and humility in all my interactions. Thank You for Your guidance and grace. May Your justice, righteousness, and Spirit lead me daily, and may I live in a way that honors You.

In Jesus' helping name I pray, Amen

THE ARMIES OF HEAVEN DEFEND ME

Galatians 5:25 (NLT): Since we are living by the Spirit, let us follow the Spirit's leading in every part of our lives.

Ephesians 5:25 (NIV): Husbands, love your wives, just as Christ loved the church and gave himself up for her.

Jeremiah 5:25 (NLT): Your wickedness has deprived you of these wonderful blessings. Your sin has robbed you of all these good things.

PRAYER

Dear Heavenly Father, Elohim Ahavah (The God Who Loves),

I come before You seeking Your wisdom and guidance for my life. Galatians 5:25 says, "Since we live by the Spirit, let us keep in step with the Spirit" (NIV). Lord, help me to walk daily with Your Holy Spirit. Guide me in Your ways and empower me to live a life that reflects Your love and grace. Ephesians 5:25 teaches, "Husbands, love your wives, just as Christ loved the church and gave himself up for her." Father, I pray that You help me show love and care in all my relationships, reflecting the sacrificial love that Christ has for the Church. May Your love be evident in everything I do. Jeremiah 5:25 warns, "Your wrongdoings have kept these away; your sins have deprived you of good" (NIV). Lord, I confess my sins and seek Your forgiveness. Help me to turn from anything that separates me from Your blessings and grace, and to seek Your goodness and righteousness in my life. Thank You for Your endless mercy and guidance. Help me to stay close to You, love others deeply, and live a life that is pleasing to You.

In Jesus' protecting name I pray, Amen

Luke 5:26 (NLT): Everyone was gripped with great wonder and awe, and they praise God, exclaiming, "We have seen amazing things today!"

Galatians 5:26 (NLT): Let us not become conceited, or provoke one another, or be jealous of one another.

1 Thessalonians 5:26 (NLT): Greet all the brothers and sisters with a sacred kiss.

--- PRAYER ---

Dear Heavenly Father, Georgos (The Gardener),

I come before You with a heart full of gratitude and trust. Luke 5:26 tells us, "Everyone was amazed and gave praise to God. They were filled with awe and said, 'We have seen remarkable things today'" (NIV). Lord, I thank You for the incredible ways You work in our lives. Help me to recognize and celebrate Your miracles and blessings every day, and to live in awe of Your power and love. Galatians 5:26 advises, "Let us not become conceited, provoking and envying each other" (NIV). Father, keep me humble and guard me against pride. Help me to treat others with kindness and respect, avoiding any behavior that might cause conflict or division. 1 Thessalonians 5:26 says, "Greet all the brothers and sisters with a holy kiss" (NASB). Lord, help me to approach everyone with love and warmth. May my interactions be filled with genuine care and affection, reflecting Your love in all my relationships. Thank You for Your guidance and grace. Help me to live a life that honors You, full of humility, awe, and love.

In Jesus' trusting name I pray, Amen

Matthew 5:27 (NIV): "You have heard that it was said, 'You shall not commit adultery.'"

Deuteronomy 5:27 (NLT): "Go yourself and listen to what the LORD our God says. Then come and tell us everything he tells you, and we will listen and obey."

Job 5:27 (NLT): "We have studied life and found all this to be true. Listen to my counsel, and apply it to yourself."

PRAYER

Dear Heavenly Father, Akal Esh (Consuming Fire),

I come before You seeking Your guidance and wisdom for my life. Matthew 5:27 says, "You have heard that it was said, 'You shall not commit adultery.'" Lord, I ask for Your strength to uphold Your commandments and to live a life of purity and faithfulness. Help me to honor Your teachings in all my relationships and to stay true to Your ways. Deuteronomy 5:27 reminds us, "'Go near and listen to all that the LORD our God says. Then tell us whatever the LORD our God tells you. We will listen and obey'" (NIV). Father, I desire to hear Your voice and follow Your guidance. Help me to be attentive to Your Word and to live according to Your instructions. Job 5:27 tells us, "'We have examined this, and it is true. So hear it and apply it to yourself'" (NIV). Lord, I pray for discernment to understand and apply Your wisdom in my life. Help me to learn from Your Word and to make choices that align with Your will. Thank You for Your constant presence and guidance. Strengthen me to live according to Your commands and to seek Your truth in all things.

In Jesus' attentive name I pray, Amen

I SEEK AND UNDERSTAND THE LORD

John 5:28 (ESV): "Do not marvel at this; for the hour is coming in which all who are in the graves will hear His voice."

Matthew 5:28 (NIV): "I tell you that anyone who looks at a woman lustfully has already committed adultery with her in his heart."

Ephesians 5:28 (NIV): In this same way, husbands ought to love their wives as their own bodies. He who loves his wife loves himself.

Luke 5:28 (NIV): And Levi got up, left everything and followed [Jesus].

1 Thessalonians 5:28 (NIV): The grace of our Lord Jesus Christ be with you.

PRAYER

Dear Heavenly Father, Jehovah Uzzi (The LORD My Strength),

I come to You today seeking Your wisdom and guidance. In John 5:28, Jesus says, "Do not be amazed at this, for a time is coming when all who are in their graves will hear his voice" (NIV). Father, I am in awe of Your power and the promise of eternal life. Help me to live with the hope and assurance of Your resurrection and to keep my focus on Your eternal promises. In Matthew 5:28, Jesus teaches, "But I tell you that anyone who looks at a woman lustfully has already committed adultery with her in his heart." Lord, I ask for Your strength to guard my heart and mind. Help me to live with purity and to respect others as You command. Ephesians 5:28 states, "In this same way, husbands ought to love their wives as their own bodies. He who loves his wife loves himself." Father, guide me in loving others with the same care and respect that You show to us. Help me to build relationships grounded in love and understanding. Luke 5:28 tells us, "And Levi got up, left everything and followed him." Lord, I pray for the courage and faith to follow You wholeheartedly, leaving behind anything that distracts me from Your path. Help me to fully commit to Your call on my life. 1 Thessalonians 5:28 says, "The grace of our Lord Jesus Christ be with you." Thank You, Lord, for Your unending grace. I pray that Your grace continues to guide and sustain me in all that I do.

In Jesus' wise name I pray, Amen

MAY 29

Matthew 5:29 (NIV): "If your right eye causes you to stumble, gouge it out and throw it away. It is better for you to lose one part of your body than for your whole body to be thrown into hell."

Ephesians 5:29 (NIV): No one ever hated their own body, but they feed and care for their body, just as Christ does the church.

Mark 5:29 (NLT): Immediately her bleeding stopped and she could feel in her body that she had been healed of her terrible condition.

PRAYER

Dear Heavenly Father, Immanuel (God With Us),

I come before You with a humble heart, seeking Your guidance and strength. Matthew 5:29 says, "If your right eye causes you to stumble, gouge it out and throw it away. It is better for you to lose one part of your body than for your whole body to be thrown into hell." Lord, I ask for Your help in removing anything in my life that leads me away from You. Give me the courage to let go of things that hinder my relationship with You and to seek Your righteousness. Ephesians 5:29 reminds us, "After all, no one ever hated their own body, but they feed and care for their body, just as Christ does the church." Father, help me to care for myself and others with the love and compassion that You have shown us. Teach me to nurture my body and spirit in ways that honor You and reflect Your love. Mark 5:29 tells us, "Immediately her bleeding stopped and she felt in her body that she was freed from her suffering" (NIV). Lord, I pray for Your healing touch in my life. Whether it's physical, emotional, or spiritual healing that I need, I trust in Your power to restore and renew. Help me to feel Your presence and experience Your healing grace. Thank You for Your guidance and healing. I trust in Your promise to care for me and to help me overcome any struggles I face.

In Jesus' comforting name I pray, Amen

I am a member of Christ's body

Matthew 5:30 (NIV): "And if your right hand causes you to stumble, cut it off and throw it away. It is better for you to lose one part of your body than for your whole body to be thrown into hell."

Ephesians 5:30 (NIV): We are [all] members of His body.

John 5:30 (NLT): "I can do nothing on my own. I judge as God tells me. Therefore, my judgment is just, because I carry out the will of the one who sent me, not my own will."

PRAYER

Dear Heavenly Father, Basilei ton Aionon (King Eternal),

I come before You seeking Your wisdom and grace for my life. Matthew 5:30 says, "And if your right hand causes you to stumble, cut it off and throw it away. It is better for you to lose one part of your body than for your whole body to go into hell." Lord, help me to identify and remove anything in my life that leads me away from You. Give me the strength to let go of behaviors or habits that do not honor You. Ephesians 5:30 reminds us, "For we are members of his body." Father, I am grateful to be part of Your family and Your Church. Help me to live in unity with other believers, and to act in ways that reflect Your love and care for us. John 5:30 says, "By myself I can do nothing; I judge only as I hear, and my judgment is just, for I seek not to please myself but him who sent me." Lord, I pray that my actions and decisions align with Your will. Help me to seek Your guidance in all I do and to live in a way that pleases You, not myself. Thank You for Your continued guidance and support. I trust in Your wisdom and ask for Your strength to follow Your path.

In Jesus' strong name I pray, Amen

GOD WILL TESTIFY FOR ME

Ephesians 5:31 (NIV): For this reason a man will leave his father and mother and be united to his wife, and the two will become one flesh.

Luke 5:31 (NLT): Jesus answered them, "Healthy people don't need a doctor—sick people do."

John 5:31 (NLT): "If I were to testify on my own behalf, my testimony would not be valid."

--- PRAYER ---

Dear Heavenly Father, Migdal Oz (Strong Tower),

I come before You with a heart open to Your guidance and wisdom. Ephesians 5:31 says, "For this reason a man will leave his father and mother and be united to his wife, and the two will become one flesh." Lord, I pray for the strength and commitment to honor and nurture my relationships, especially in marriage. Help me to build strong, loving connections based on Your principles. Luke 5:31 reminds us, "Jesus answered them, 'It is not the healthy who need a doctor, but the sick'" (NIV). Father, I acknowledge my own need for Your healing and grace. I seek Your help in times of weakness and struggle, trusting in Your mercy and support to make me whole. John 5:31 states, "If I testify about myself, my testimony is not true" (NIV). Lord, teach me to seek truth and rely on Your Word rather than my own understanding. Help me to find truth in You and to live according to Your will. Thank You for Your guidance and for the strength You provide in all aspects of my life. I trust in Your wisdom and ask for Your continued help and support.

In Jesus' heartful name I pray, Amen

JUNE 1

I DO WHAT IS RIGHT IN THE EYES OF THE LORD

Micah 6:1 (NIV): Listen to what the LORD says: "Stand up, plead my case before the mountains; let the hills hear what you have to say."

Matthew 6:1 (NLT): "Watch out! Don't do your good deeds publicly, to be admired by others, for you will lose the reward from your Father in heaven."

Ephesians 6:1 (NLT): Children, obey your parents because you belong to the Lord, for this is the right thing to do.

―――――――――――――――――― PRAYER ――――――――――――――――――

Dear Heavenly Father, Shaphat (Judge),

I come to You today seeking Your guidance and wisdom. Micah 6:1 says, "Listen to what the LORD says: 'Stand up, plead my case before the mountains; let the hills hear what you have to say.'" Lord, I ask for the courage to stand firm in Your truth and to be a voice for justice and righteousness. Help me to speak boldly and live faithfully according to Your will. Matthew 6:1 reminds us, "Be careful not to practice your righteousness in front of others to be seen by them. If you do, you will have no reward from your Father in heaven" (NIV). Father, guide me to live my life with integrity and humility, seeking to please You rather than seeking approval from others. Let my actions be genuine and reflect Your love and grace. Ephesians 6:1 says, "Children, obey your parents in the Lord, for this is right" (NIV). Lord, I pray for the strength and wisdom to honor and respect those You have placed in authority over me. Help me to live in a way that honors You and upholds Your commands in all my relationships. Thank You for Your continuous guidance and support. I trust in Your wisdom and seek Your help to live according to Your Word.

In Jesus' faithful name I pray, Amen

JUNE 2

Micah 6:2 (NIV): "Hear, you mountains, the LORD's accusation; listen, you everlasting foundations of the earth. For the LORD has a case against his people; he is lodging a charge against Israel."

Galatians 6:2 (NIV): Carry each other's burdens, and in this way you will fulfill the law of Christ.

Romans 6:2 (NIV): By no means! We are those who have died to sin; how can we live in it any longer?

Ephesians 6:2 (NIV): "Honor your father and mother"—which is the first commandment with a promise.

PRAYER

Dear Heavenly Father, YAH (self-existent, "I AM"),

I come before You with a heart full of gratitude and a desire to follow Your guidance. Micah 6:2 says, "Hear, you mountains, the LORD's accusation; listen, you everlasting foundations of the earth. For the LORD has a case against his people; he is lodging a charge against Israel." Lord, help me to be attentive to Your voice and to understand Your will for my life. Teach me to respond to Your guidance with humility and obedience. Galatians 6:2 instructs us, "Carry each other's burdens, and in this way you will fulfill the law of Christ." Father, help me to be compassionate and supportive of others, sharing their burdens and showing Your love through my actions. Guide me in being a source of encouragement and strength to those around me. Romans 6:2 reminds us, "By no means! We are those who have died to sin; how can we live in it any longer?" Lord, give me the strength to live a life free from sin and to walk in Your righteousness. Help me to resist temptation and to grow in holiness and integrity. Ephesians 6:2 says, "'Honor your father and mother'—which is the first commandment with a promise." Lord, I pray for the grace to honor and respect my parents and all those in authority. Help me to show them love and gratitude as I follow Your commands. Thank You for Your constant presence and guidance. I trust in Your wisdom and seek to live according to Your will in all aspects of my life.

In Jesus' loving name I pray, Amen

JUNE 3

Hosea 6:3 (NIV): Let us acknowledge the LORD; let us press on to acknowledge him. As surely as the sun rises, he will appear; he will come to us like the winter rains, like the spring rains that water the earth.

Daniel 6:3 (ESV): Then this Daniel became distinguished above all the other high officials and satraps, because an excellent spirit was in him. And the king planned to set him over the whole kingdom.

Matthew 6:3 (ESV): "But when you give to the needy, do not let your left hand know what your right hand is doing."

Psalm 6:3 (NIV): My soul is in deep anguish. How long, LORD, how long?

PRAYER

Dear Heavenly Father, Jehovah Gibbor Milchamah (The LORD, Mighty in Battle),

I come before You with a heart open to Your guidance and filled with gratitude for Your love. Hosea 6:3 says, "Let us know; let us press on to know the LORD. His going out is sure as the dawn; he will come to us as the showers, as the spring rains that water the earth" (ESV). Lord, help me to press on and deepen my relationship with You. May I seek to know You more and experience the renewal and blessing that comes from Your presence in my life. Daniel 6:3 tells us, "Then this Daniel became distinguished above all the other high officials and satraps, because an excellent spirit was in him. And the king planned to set him over the whole kingdom." Father, grant me the spirit of excellence and integrity in all I do. May my work and actions reflect Your character and bring glory to Your name, so that others may see Your light shining through me. In Matthew 6:3, Jesus instructs us, "But when you give to the needy, do not let your left hand know what your right hand is doing." Lord, help me to give generously and with a humble heart. Teach me to serve others selflessly and to seek Your approval rather than recognition from people. Psalm 6:3 says, "My soul also is greatly troubled. But you, O LORD—how long?" Father, when I face times of trouble and distress, remind me of Your faithfulness and presence. Help me to trust in Your timing and to find comfort in Your promises. Thank You for Your guidance and love.

In Jesus' present name I pray, Amen

JUNE 4

Psalm 6:4 (ERV): Return, O LORD, deliver my soul: save me for thy lovingkindness' sake.

Deuteronomy 6:4 (NIV): Hear, O Israel: The LORD our God, the LORD is one.

Ephesians 6:4 (ESV): Fathers, do not provoke your children to anger, but bring them up in the discipline and instructions of the Lord.

Galatians 6:4 (NIV): Each one should test their own actions. Then they can take pride in themselves alone, without comparing themselves to someone else.

PRAYER

Dear Heavenly Father, Jehovah-Go'el (Redeeming LORD),

I come before You today with a heart full of gratitude and a desire for Your guidance and strength. Psalm 6:4 says, "Turn, O LORD, deliver my life; save me for the sake of Your steadfast love" (ESV). Father, I ask for Your deliverance in times of trouble. Please rescue me from difficulties and challenges, and let Your steadfast love be my source of hope and comfort. Deuteronomy 6:4 declares, "Hear, O Israel: The LORD our God, the LORD is one." Lord, I acknowledge Your sovereignty and unity. You are the one true God, and I place my trust in Your wisdom and guidance. Help me to remember Your oneness and to seek You with my whole heart. Ephesians 6:4 instructs, "Fathers, do not provoke your children to anger, but bring them up in the discipline and instruction of the Lord." Father, guide me in how I interact with those around me, especially in relationships that require patience and love. Help me to nurture others with kindness and to teach them Your ways with a gentle spirit. Galatians 6:4 advises, "But let each one test his own work, and then his reason to boast will be in himself alone and not in his neighbor" (ESV). Lord, help me to focus on my own actions and growth rather than comparing myself to others. Grant me the strength to examine my work and my heart, finding joy in Your approval and not in the praise of people. Thank You for Your guidance and love. May Your wisdom direct my steps and Your peace fill my heart.

In Jesus' gentle name I pray, Amen

JUNE 5

I LOVE THE LORD WITH ALL MY HEART

Joshua 6:5 (ESV): When you hear the sound of [a long blast on] the trumpet, then all the people shall shout with a great shout, and the wall of the city will fall down flat, and the people shall go up, every man straight before him.

Deuteronomy 6:5 (ESV): You shall love the LORD your God with all your heart and with all your soul and with all your strength.

Luke 6:5 (NIV): Then Jesus said to them, "The Son of Man is Lord of the Sabbath."

Matthew 6:5 (NLT): "When you pray, don't be like the hypocrites who love to pray publicly on street corners and in the Synagogues where everyone can see them. I tell you the truth, that is all the reward they will ever get."

 **PRAYER**

Dear Lord, Jehovah-Makkeh (The LORD Who Strikes/Disciplines You),

I come before You with a heart full of faith and gratitude, seeking Your presence and guidance. Joshua 6:5 says, "When you hear the sound of [a long blast on] the trumpet, then all the people shall shout with a great shout, and the wall of the city shall fall down flat, and the people shall go up, every man straight before him." Lord, just as You brought down the walls of Jericho, I ask You to break down any barriers in my life that are keeping me from Your will. Help me to trust in Your mighty power and to follow Your leading with courage. Deuteronomy 6:5 commands me to desire to love You completely, with every part of my being. Help me to grow in my love for You and to live in a way that reflects Your love in all that I do. Luke 6:5 tells us You are the Lord of all things, including the Sabbath. I ask You to be the Lord of my life, guiding me in rest and in all my daily activities. Help me to find peace and renewal in You. Jesus warns us Matthew 6:5, "And when you pray, do not be like the hypocrites, for they love to pray standing in the synagogues and on the street corners to be seen by others. Truly I tell you, they have received their reward in full" (NIV). Father, help me to approach You with sincerity in my prayers. Teach me to seek Your presence for Your sake and not for the approval of others. Thank You, Lord, for Your guidance and love.

In Jesus' powerful name I pray, Amen

JUNE 6

Exodus 6:6 (NIV): "I am the LORD, and I will bring you out from under the yoke of the Egyptians; I will free you from being slaves to them, and I will redeem you with an outstretched arm and with mighty acts of judgment."

Ezekiel 6:6 (NIV): Wherever you live, the towns will be laid waste and the high places will demolished, so that your altars will be laid waste and devastated, your idols smashed and ruined, . . .

Hosea 6:6 (NKJV): For I desire mercy and not sacrifice, and the knowledge of God more than burnt offerings.

Matthew 6:6 (NIV): "But when you pray, go into your room, close the door and pray to your Father, who is unseen. Then your Father, who sees what is done in secret, will reward you."

PRAYER

Dear Heavenly Father, Sar Shalom (Prince of Peace),

I come before You with a humble heart, seeking Your guidance and presence in my life. Exodus 6:6 reminds us of Your promise to free us from being slaves. Lord, just as You delivered the Israelites from slavery, I ask for Your help in freeing me from any burdens or struggles I face. Redeem me from anything that holds me back from fully living in Your grace. Ezekiel 6:6 speaks of Your desire for our hearts. Father, help me to remove anything in my life that takes the place of You. May my heart be fully devoted to You, and may I seek Your presence above all else. Hosea 6:6 teaches me to live a life of mercy and compassion. Help me to know You deeply and to show Your love to others through my actions, rather than just through rituals or outward appearances. Matthew 6:6 advises us to have a sincere, private, and personal relationship with You. Guide me in my prayers so that they come from a place of genuine devotion and trust. Thank You, Lord, for Your faithfulness and for guiding me through Your Word. May I always seek You with a pure heart and be transformed by Your love.

In Jesus' devoted name I pray, Amen

JUNE 7

I WORK FOR GOD, NOT FOR PEOPLE

Acts 6:7 (NIV): So the word of God spread. The number of disciples in Jerusalem increased rapidly, and a large number of priests became obedient to the faith.

Matthew 6:7 (NKJV): "And when you pray, do not use vain repetitions as the heathens do. For they think that they will be heard for their many words."

Galatians 6:7 (NIV): A man reaps what he sows.

Ecclesiastes 6:7 (KJV): All the labor of man is for his mouth, and yet the appetite is not filled.

Ephesians 6:7 (NLT): Work with enthusiasm, as though you were working for the Lord rather than for people.

Romans 6:7 (NLT): For when we died with Christ we were set free from the power of sin.

PRAYER

Dear Heavenly Father, Jehovah-Nissi (The LORD My Banner),

I come before You today, seeking Your guidance and wisdom. Acts 6:7 instructs me to let the word of God increase in my life. Lord, may Your Word continue to spread in my life and in the lives of those around me. Help me to grow in faith and to be a witness of Your love and grace. Matthew 6:7 reminds me to pray with sincerity and simplicity. Help me to communicate with You from my heart, knowing that You hear and understand my deepest thoughts. Galatians 6:7 says to live a life that honors You and reflects Your values. Guide me in sowing good deeds and righteousness, so that my actions may bear fruit in alignment with Your will. Ecclesiastes 6:7 states, "Everyone's toil is for their mouth, yet their appetite is never satisfied" (NIV). Father, I ask for Your help in finding contentment and satisfaction in You alone. May I seek fulfillment in Your presence and not in the fleeting things of this world. Ephesians 6:7 teaches, "Serve wholeheartedly, as if you were serving the Lord, not people" (NIV). Lord, give me a heart of service. Help me to work diligently and to serve others with a spirit of love, as if I am serving You directly. Romans 6:7 reminds me of the freedom You have given me through Christ. Help me to live in the freedom from sin and to walk in Your light each day. Thank You for Your guidance through these Scriptures.

In Jesus' sinless name I pray, Amen

JUNE 8

Galatians 6:8 (ESV): For the one who sows to his own flesh will from the flesh reap corruption, but the one who sows to the Spirit will from the Spirit reap everlasting life.

Psalm 6:8 (NLT): Go away, all you who do evil, for the LORD has heard my weeping.

Genesis 6:8 (NIV): But Noah found favor in the eyes of the LORD.

Isaiah 6:8 (ESV): Then I heard The Lord asking "Whom shall I send, and who will go for us?" Then I said, "Here I am! Send me."

Matthew 6:8 (NLT): "Don't be like them, for your Father knows exactly what you need even before you ask him!"

------------------------------ **PRAYER** ------------------------------

Dear Heavenly Father, Jehovah-Raah (The LORD Is My Shepherd),

I come to You with a heart full of gratitude and a desire for Your guidance. Galatians 6:8 reminds us, "Whoever sows to please their flesh, from the flesh will reap destruction; whoever sows to please the Spirit, from the Spirit will reap eternal life" (NIV). Lord, help me to sow in Your Spirit and live in a way that pleases You. Guide me to make choices that honor You and lead to eternal life. Psalm 6:8 says, "Away from me, all you who do evil, for the LORD has heard my weeping" (NIV). Father, I trust that You hear my cries and my prayers. Help me to turn away from anything that is not of You and to find comfort in Your presence. Genesis 6:8 tells us, "But Noah found favor in the eyes of the LORD." Lord, like Noah, I seek Your favor. May Your grace and favor be upon me as I strive to live righteously and follow Your will. Isaiah 6:8 declares, "Then I heard the voice of the Lord saying, 'Whom shall I send? And who will go for us?' And I said, 'Here am I. Send me!'" (NIV). Father, I am here, ready and willing to follow Your call. Use me according to Your purpose and guide me in serving others and spreading Your love. In Matthew 6:8, Jesus teaches us, "Do not be like them, for your Father knows what you need before you ask him" (NIV). Thank You, Lord, for knowing my needs even before I ask. I trust in Your provision and timing, and I ask for Your continued guidance and wisdom. Thank You for Your Word and for the comfort it brings.

In Jesus' saving name I pray, Amen

JUNE 9

The Lord hears me

Psalm 6:9 (NIV): The Lord has heard my cry for mercy; the Lord accepts my prayer.

Galatians 6:9 (NKJV): And let us not grow weary while doing good, for in due season we shall reap if we do not lose heart.

Matthew 6:9 (NLT): "Pray like this: Our Father in heaven, may your name be kept holy."

Proverbs 6:9 (NLT): But you, lazybones, how long will you sleep? When will you wake up?

 **PRAYER**

Dear Heavenly Father, Jehovah-Shammah (The Lord Is There),

I come before You with a grateful heart, seeking Your guidance and strength. Psalm 6:9 says, "The Lord has heard my cry for mercy; the Lord accepts my prayer." Thank You, Lord, for hearing my prayers and for accepting them. I trust in Your mercy and in Your willingness to listen and respond. Galatians 6:9 reminds us, "Let us not become weary in doing good, for at the proper time we will reap a harvest if we do not give up" (NIV). Father, give me the strength to continue doing good and to stay persistent in my efforts. Help me to remain patient and faithful, knowing that You will bring about the right outcomes in Your perfect timing. Matthew 6:9 teaches us to pray, "Our Father in heaven, hallowed be Your name" (NIV). I honor and revere Your name, Lord. I acknowledge You as my Father and the sovereign Lord of all. May Your name be glorified in my life and in all that I do. Proverbs 6:9 asks, "How long will you lie there, you sluggard? When will you get up from your sleep?" (NIV). Lord, help me to rise up with diligence and commitment. Guide me to overcome laziness and to be proactive in all aspects of my life, honoring You through my actions and decisions. Thank You for Your Word that guides and encourages me. Strengthen me to live according to Your will and to persevere in faith and good works.

In Jesus' redeeming name I pray, Amen

JUNE 10

Matthew 6:10 (NIV): "Your kingdom come: Your will be done, on earth as it is in heaven."

Ephesians 6:10 (NIV): Finally, be strong in the Lord and in His mighty power.

Galatians 6:10 (NKJV): Therefore, as we have opportunity, let us do good to all, especially to those who are of the household of faith.

Hebrews 6:10 (NKJV): God is not unjust to forget your work and labor of love which you have shown toward His name.

PRAYER

Dear Heavenly Father, Jehovah-Rapha (The LORD Who Heals),

I come before You with a heart full of gratitude and hope. I seek Your guidance and strength in my daily life. Matthew 6:10 teaches us to pray, "Your kingdom come, Your will be done, on earth as it is in heaven." Lord, I ask that Your kingdom and Your will be established in my life and in the world around me. Help me to align my actions and decisions with Your divine plan. Ephesians 6:10 says, "Finally, be strong in the Lord and in His mighty power." Father, I ask for Your strength and power to face the challenges of each day. Empower me to stand firm in faith and to rely on Your strength in all situations. Galatians 6:10 encourages us, "Therefore, as we have opportunity, let us do good to all people, especially to those who belong to the family of believers" (NIV). Lord, help me to take every opportunity to do good and to serve others with love, especially those within my Christian community. Hebrews 6:10 reminds us, "God is not unjust; He will not forget your work and the love you have shown Him as you have helped His people and continue to help them" (NIV). Thank You, Lord, for Your faithfulness and for acknowledging our efforts. Help me to continue serving others with a sincere heart, trusting that You see and reward our acts of love and kindness. Guide me in Your ways and strengthen me to live a life that honors You and reflects Your love to those around me.

In Jesus' helpful name I pray, Amen

JUNE 11

2 Samuel 6:11 (NIV): The ark of the LORD remained in the house of Obed-Edom the Gittite for three months, and the LORD blessed him and his entire household.

Romans 6:11 (NIV): In the same way, count yourselves dead to sin but alive to God in Christ Jesus.

Ephesians 6:11 (NIV): Put on the full armor of God, so that you can take your stand against the devil's schemes.

Matthew 6:11 (NLT): "Give us today the food we need."

PRAYER

Dear Heavenly Father, Jehovah-Sabaoth (The LORD of Hosts),

I come to You with a heart open to Your guidance and grace. I seek Your strength and presence in my life. 2 Samuel 6:11 tells us, "The ark of the LORD remained in the house of Obed-Edom the Gittite for three months, and the LORD blessed him and his entire household." Lord, just as You blessed Obed-Edom, I ask for Your blessings upon my life and home. May Your presence dwell with me, bringing Your peace and favor. Romans 6:11 says, "In the same way, count yourselves dead to sin but alive to God in Christ Jesus." Father, help me to live fully for You, turning away from sin and embracing the new life You offer through Jesus Christ. Empower me to live according to Your will and to reflect Your love in all I do. Ephesians 6:11 instructs us to "Put on the full armor of God, so that you can take your stand against the devil's schemes." Lord, equip me with Your armor—truth, righteousness, peace, faith, and salvation—to stand firm against any challenges or temptations I face. Protect me and guide me through every trial. Matthew 6:11 reminds us to pray, "Give us today our daily bread" (NIV). Thank You, Lord, for providing for my needs each day. Help me to trust in Your provision and to rely on You for everything I need—physically, emotionally, and spiritually. Guide me, protect me, and fill me with Your grace. Help me to live in a way that honors You and reflects Your love to others.

In Jesus Christ's holy name I pray, Amen

JUNE 12

Hebrews 6:12(NIV): We do not want you to become lazy, but to imitate those who through faith and patience inherit what has been promised.

Ephesians 6:12 (ESV): For we do not wrestle against flesh and blood, but against the rulers, against the authorities, against the cosmic powers over this present darkness, against the spiritual forces of evil in the heavenly places.

Matthew 6:12 (NLT): "And forgive us our sins, as we have forgiven those who sin against us."

1 Corinthians 6:12 (NIV): "I have the right to do anything," you say—but not everything is beneficial. "I have the right to do anything"—but I will not be mastered by anything.

PRAYER

Dear Heavenly Father, Jehovah-Tzidkenu (The Lord Our Righteousness),

I come to You today seeking Your guidance and strength in my life. I ask for Your help to follow Your Word and live according to Your will. Hebrews 6:12 reminds us to "imitate those who through faith and patience inherit what has been promised." Lord, help me to be patient and faithful, following the example of those who have trusted in Your promises. Strengthen my faith as I wait for Your guidance and blessings. Ephesians 6:12 says, "For our struggle is not against flesh and blood, but against the rulers, against the authorities, against the powers of this dark world and against the spiritual forces of evil in the heavenly realms" (NIV). Father, help me to recognize the true nature of my struggles. Equip me with Your strength and armor to face spiritual battles with courage and faith. In Matthew 6:12, Jesus teaches us to pray, "And forgive us our debts, as we also have forgiven our debtors" (NIV). Lord, grant me a heart of forgiveness. Help me to let go of grudges and to forgive those who have wronged me, just as You have forgiven me. 1 Corinthians 6:12 says, "'I have the right to do anything,' you say—but not everything is beneficial. 'I have the right to do anything'—but I will not be mastered by anything." Father, guide me in making choices that honor You. Help me to use my freedom wisely, seeking what is beneficial and not allowing anything to control me. Thank You for Your guidance and grace.

In Jesus, Son of the living God's name I pray, Amen.

JUNE 13

Matthew 6:13 (NIV): "And lead us not into temptation, but deliver us from the evil one."

Deuteronomy 6:13 (NLT): You must fear the LORD your God and serve Him. When you take an oath, you must use only His name.

Ephesians 6:13 (ESV): Therefore, take up the whole armor of God, that you may be able to withstand in the evil day, and having done all, to stand firm.

―――――――――――――――――――― **PRAYER** ――――――――――――――――――

Dear Heavenly Father, Hode (Majesty),

I come before You with a heart full of gratitude and trust in Your guidance. I seek Your protection and strength in my daily life. Matthew 6:13 reminds me to pray, "And lead us not into temptation, but deliver us from the evil one." Lord, please keep me from falling into temptation. Help me to recognize and avoid the snares of the evil one. Guide my steps and protect me from the forces that seek to lead me astray. Deuteronomy 6:13 says, "Fear the LORD your God, serve him only and take your oaths in his name" (NIV). Father, I commit to serving You alone. Help me to honor You with my life, to trust in Your power, and to follow Your commands faithfully. May my actions and words always reflect my reverence for You. Ephesians 6:13 instructs us, "Therefore put on the full armor of God, so that when the day of evil comes, you may be able to stand your ground, . . ." (NIV). Lord, I ask for Your protection as I face the challenges of each day. Equip me with Your armor—truth, righteousness, the gospel of peace, faith, salvation, and the sword of the Spirit—so that I can stand firm and strong in the face of adversity. Thank You, Lord, for Your unwavering presence and guidance. Help me to live each day with faith and courage, fully trusting in Your protection and provision.

In the only begotten Son, Jesus' name I pray, Amen

JUNE 14

Ephesians 6:14 (ESV): Stand therefore, having fastened on the belt of truth, and having put on the breastplate of righteousness.

Matthew 6:14 (NLT): "If you forgive those who sin against you, your heavenly Father will forgive you."

Romans 6:14 (ESV): For sin shall not have dominion over you, since you are not under law but under grace.

Galatians 6:14 (NLT): As for me, may I never boast about anything except the cross of our Lord Jesus Christ. Because of the cross, my interest in this world has been crucified, and the world's interest in me has also died.

PRAYER

Dear Heavenly Father, Ner (Lamp),

I come before You with a humble heart, seeking Your wisdom and grace in my life. Ephesians 6:14 reminds me to stand firm in God's truth and to wear the armor of righteousness each day. Strengthen me to remain steadfast in my faith, knowing that Your truth and righteousness protect and guide me. Matthew 6:14 teaches me to have grace to forgive others as You have forgiven me. Help me to release any grudges and embrace Your forgiving heart, reflecting Your mercy in my interactions with others. Romans 6:14 explains that I have been given grace that frees me from the power of sin. Help me to live in the freedom You have provided and to walk in righteousness, empowered by Your grace. Galatians 6:14 declares that I should always find my boast and glory in the cross of Jesus Christ. Let me be reminded that my identity and salvation come from Your sacrifice and not from my own achievements. Thank You, Lord, for Your love, grace, and the strength You provide each day.

In Jesus' beloved name I pray, Amen

Ephesians 6:15 (NLT): For shoes, put on the peace that comes from the Good News so that you will be fully prepared.

1 Corinthians 6:15 (NIV): "Do you not know that your bodies are members of Christ himself? Shall I then take the members of Christ and unite them with a prostitute? Never!"

Matthew 6:15 (NLT): "But if you refuse to forgive others, your Father will not forgive your sins."

PRAYER

Dear Heavenly Father, Maon (Dwelling Place),

I come before You with a heart full of gratitude and a desire to align my life with Your will. Ephesians 6:15 tells us, "And with your feet fitted with the readiness that comes from the gospel of peace" (NIV). Lord, help me to be ready to share the message of peace that comes from knowing You. May my actions and words reflect the peace of the Gospel and guide others toward Your love. 1 Corinthians 6:15 says, "Do you not know that your bodies are members of Christ himself? Shall I then take the members of Christ and unite them with a prostitute? Never!" Father, remind me daily of the sacredness of my body and the importance of honoring You in all I do. Help me to make choices that honor You and reflect Your holiness. Matthew 6:15 teaches, "But if you do not forgive others their sins, your Father will not forgive your sins" (NIV). Lord, grant me the strength and grace to forgive others as You have forgiven me. Help me to let go of any bitterness or resentment, and to embrace a spirit of forgiveness in all my relationships. Thank You for Your guidance, Your forgiveness, and Your grace. Help me to live in a way that brings glory to Your name and reflects Your love and peace.

In Jesus' peaceful name I pray, Amen

Ephesians 6:16 (ESV): In all circumstances take up the shield of faith, with which you can extinguish all the flaming darts of the evil one.

Matthew 6:16 (NKJV): "Moreover, when you fast, do not look gloomy like the hypocrites, for they disfigure their faces that their fasting may appear to men to be fasting. Assuredly, I say to you, they have received their reward."

Proverbs 6:16 (NLT): There are six things the LORD hates—no seven things he detests.

PRAYER

Dear Heavenly Father, Di Ou Ta Panta (My Everything),

I come before You with a heart full of gratitude and trust in Your guidance. Ephesians 6:16 reminds me to "take up the shield of faith, with which you can extinguish all the flaming arrows of the evil one." Lord, strengthen my faith so that I can stand firm against all the challenges and temptations that come my way. Help me to rely on Your strength and protection every day. Matthew 6:16 teaches us, "When you fast, do not look somber as the hypocrites do" (NIV). Father, help me to seek You earnestly and to practice humility in my spiritual journey. May my actions reflect a sincere heart, not seeking praise from others, but honoring You in all that I do. Proverbs 6:16 says, "There are six things the LORD hates, seven that are detestable to him." Lord, guide me away from anything that displeases You. Help me to live a life of integrity and righteousness, avoiding actions and attitudes that are contrary to Your will. Thank You for Your guidance and grace. Help me to walk in Your ways and to live a life that honors You.

In Jesus' wonderful name I pray, Amen

He saved me from my enemies

Ephesians 6:17 (NIV): Take the helmet of salvation and the sword of the Spirit, which is the word of God.

Matthew 6:17 (NASB): "But you, when you fast, anoint your head and wash your face."

Revelation 6:17 (NKJV): For the great day of His wrath has come, and who is able to stand?

Deuteronomy 6:17 (NLT): You must diligently obey the commands of the LORD your God—all the laws and decrees he has given you.

PRAYER

Dear Heavenly Father, Gabahh (Transcendent),

Thank You for Your guidance and protection. I seek Your help and wisdom as I face each day. Ephesians 6:17 tells me to "take the helmet of salvation and the sword of the Spirit, which is the word of God." Lord, equip me with the helmet of salvation to guard my mind and the sword of the Spirit to guide my actions. Help me to use Your Word wisely and to stand firm in faith. Matthew 6:17 reminds me that "when you fast, anoint your head and wash your face." Father, teach me to seek You earnestly and to approach my spiritual disciplines with sincerity and humility. May my relationship with You be genuine and free from pretense. Revelation 6:17 speaks of the great day of Your wrath, and it reminds me of the importance of living in reverence of Your power and justice. Help me to live in a way that honors You, mindful of the seriousness of Your judgment and the grace You offer. Deuteronomy 6:17 instructs me to "diligently keep the commandments of the LORD your God, and His testimonies and His statutes which He has commanded you" (NASB 1995). Lord, give me the strength to follow Your commands with diligence and to keep Your Word close to my heart. Guide me in all I do, and let my life reflect Your love and truth.

In Jesus' mighty name I pray, Amen

JUNE 18

Ephesians 6:18 (NLT): Pray in the Spirit at all times and on every occasion. Stay alert and be persistent in your prayers for all believers everywhere.

Matthew 6:18 (NKJV): Do not appear to [others] to be fasting, but to your Father who is in the secret place: and your father who sees you in secret will reward you openly.

2 Corinthians 6:18 (ESV): I will be a Father to you, and you shall be sons and daughters to me, says the LORD Almighty.

Romans 6:18 (NKJV): And having been set free from sin, you became slaves of righteousness.

PRAYER

Dear Heavenly Father, Miqweh Yisrael (Hope of Israel),

Thank You for Your unending love and grace. I come before You with a heart full of gratitude and a desire to grow closer to You. Ephesians 6:18 teaches me to "pray in the Spirit on all occasions with all kinds of prayers and requests" (NIV). Lord, help me to stay connected to You through constant prayer. May I seek Your guidance and support in every moment, bringing all my needs and praises before You. Matthew 6:18 says that when I fast, I should anoint my head and wash my face, so that my fasting will not be obvious to others but only to You, my Father. Lord, guide me in my spiritual disciplines. Let my acts of devotion be genuine and focused solely on You, free from the desire for human recognition. 2 Corinthians 6:18 promises, "I will be a Father to you, and you will be my sons and daughters, says the LORD Almighty" (NLT). I am grateful for Your promise to be a loving Father. Help me to live as Your child, embracing the identity and inheritance You have given me. Romans 6:18 declares, "You have been set free from sin and have become slaves to righteousness" (NIV). Lord, thank You for setting me free from sin. Help me to live a life that reflects Your righteousness and to honor You in all that I do. Guide my thoughts, actions, and prayers, and let me walk closely with You each day.

In Jesus' hopeful name I pray, Amen

JUNE 19

Ephesians 6:19 (NIV): Pray also for me, that whenever I speak, words may be given me so that I will fearlessly make known the mystery of the gospel.

Hebrews 6:19 (NIV): We have this hope as an anchor for the soul, firm and secure.

Matthew 6:19 (NLT): "Don't store up treasures here on earth, where moths eat them and rust destroys them, and where thieves break in and steal."

Luke 6:19 (NLT): Everyone tried to touch him, because healing power went out from him, and he healed everyone.

2 Chronicles 6:19 (NLT): Listen to my prayer and my plea, O Lord my God. Hear my cry and the prayer that your servant is making to you.

―――――――――――――――――― PRAYER ――――――――――――――――――

Dear Heavenly Father, Theos Monos Sophos (The Only Wise God),

I come to You with a heart full of gratitude and trust in Your promises. As I reflect on Your Word, I am reminded of Your guidance and blessings. Ephesians 6:19 encourages me to pray that You give me the words to fearlessly make known the mystery of the gospel. Lord, grant me courage and clarity to share Your truth with others, and let my life reflect Your love and grace. Hebrews 6:19 reminds me that we have this hope as an anchor for the soul, firm and secure. Thank You for being my anchor in every storm of life. Help me to hold on to this hope and find peace in Your steadfast promises. Matthew 6:19 advises me not to store up treasures on earth where they can be destroyed, but to store up treasures in heaven. Lord, help me to focus on eternal values rather than material things. Teach me to invest in things that truly matter, like love, kindness, and faith. Luke 6:19 tells me that people came to Jesus from all over to be healed and that power was coming from Him. Father, I seek Your healing power in my life and the lives of those I love. 2 Chronicles 6:19 speaks of Your willingness to hear the prayers of Your people and respond with Your mercy. I ask for Your guidance and answers to my prayers, trusting that You hear and understand my heart's deepest needs. Thank You for Your unfailing love and faithfulness.

In Jesus' High Priest name I pray, Amen

I WAS BOUGHT AT A PRICE

Matthew 6:20 (NLT): "Store your treasures in heaven, where moths and rust cannot destroy, and thieves do not break in and steal."

Proverbs 6:20 (NLT): Obey your father's commands, and don't neglect your mother's instruction.

John 6:20 (NLT): [Jesus] called out to them, "Don't be afraid. I am here."

1 Corinthians 6:20 (NKJV): For you were bought at a price; therefore glorify God in your body and in your spirit, which are God's.

PRAYER

Dear Heavenly Father, Theos Pas Paraklesis (The God of All Comfort),

I come before You with a heart full of gratitude and humility, seeking Your guidance and wisdom. Matthew 6:20 reminds me to store up treasures in heaven, where they will last forever, rather than on earth where they are temporary. Lord, help me to focus on eternal values and to invest my time and resources in things that honor You and make a difference in Your kingdom. Proverbs 6:20 teaches me to keep Your commands and teachings close to my heart. Please help me to remember Your Word and to let it guide my decisions and actions daily. May Your wisdom be my compass in all that I do. John 6:20 assures me that when I am troubled or afraid, Jesus is with me, saying, "It is I; do not be afraid" (ESV). Lord, in moments of fear or uncertainty, remind me of Your presence and comfort me with Your peace. Help me to trust in You and find courage in Your promises. 1 Corinthians 6:20 tells me that I am bought with a price and should honor You with my body. Father, help me to live in a way that reflects Your love and grace, respecting and valuing the life You've given me. May my actions and choices honor You in all areas of my life. Thank You for Your constant presence, Your guidance, and Your unending love. Help me to live according to Your Word and to find joy and strength in Your promises.

In Jesus' comforting name I pray, Amen

JUNE 21

Matthew 6:21 (NIV): "Where your treasure is, there your heart will be also."

Luke 6:21 (NKJV): "Blessed are you who hunger now, you shall be filled. Bless are you who weep now, for you shall laugh."

Romans 6:12 (NLT): And what was the result? You are now ashamed of the things you used to do, things that end in eternal doom?

PRAYER

Dear Heavenly Father, Melekh Hagoyim (King of Nations),

I come before You with a grateful heart, seeking Your guidance and strength for today. Matthew 6:21 tells me that where my treasure is, there my heart will be also. Lord, help me to place my treasure in You and Your kingdom. Teach me to value what truly matters—love, kindness, and righteousness—so that my heart is aligned with Your will. Luke 6:21 assures me that You bless those who hunger for righteousness and who are in need. Father, I ask for Your provision and comfort in areas where I feel lacking. Fill me with Your peace and joy, and help me to seek Your righteousness above all else. Romans 6:12 reminds me not to let sin reign in my body but to offer myself to You as an instrument of righteousness. Lord, strengthen me to resist temptation and live a life that reflects Your love and grace. Help me to use my life and my actions to serve You and bring glory to Your name. Thank You for Your guidance and for the strength You provide. Help me to live each day in a way that honors You and brings my heart closer to Yours.

In Jesus' pure name I pray, Amen

JUNE 22

Genesis 6:22 (NLT): So Noah did everything exactly as God had commanded him.

Proverbs 6:22 (NIV): When you walk, they will guide you; when you sleep, they will watch over you; when you awake, they will speak to you.

Romans 6:22 (NLT): But now you are free from the power of sin and have become slaves of God. Now you do those things that lead to holiness and result in eternal life.

Luke 6:22 (NLT): "What blessings await you when people hate you and exclude you and mock you and curse you as evil because you follow the Son of Man."

PRAYER

Dear Heavenly Father, Pneuma (Spirit),

Thank You for Your guidance and the promises found in Your Word. As I come before You today, I hold on to the wisdom and truth You provide. Genesis 6:22 reminds me that Noah did everything just as You commanded. Lord, I pray for the strength and obedience to follow Your commands and trust in Your guidance for my life. Help me to be faithful and diligent in all that You ask of me. Proverbs 6:22 speaks of how Your teachings guide us and keep us safe. Father, I ask that Your Word light my path and guide my steps. Help me to remember Your instructions in times of decision and difficulty, and to walk in the ways of wisdom and understanding. Romans 6:22 tells me that, being set free from sin, I have become a servant of righteousness. Lord, thank You for the freedom You have given me through Christ. Help me to live out this freedom by pursuing righteousness and making choices that honor You. Luke 6:22 assures me that I am blessed when I am persecuted for Your sake. Father, if I face challenges or opposition because of my faith, grant me the courage and strength to remain steadfast. Let my heart be filled with joy, knowing that I am living in alignment with Your will. Thank You for Your constant presence and support. Guide me in every aspect of my life and help me to reflect Your love and grace in all that I do.

In Jesus' powerful name I pray, Amen

I AM LOVE AND FAITHFULNESS

Romans 6:23 (NIV): For the wages of sin is death, but the gift of God is eternal life in Christ Jesus our Lord.

Judges 6:23 (NLT): "It is all right," the LORD replied. "Do not be afraid, You will not die."

Proverbs 6:23 (NLT): For their command is a lamp and their instruction a light;

their corrective discipline is the way to life.

Ephesians 6:23 (NLT): Peace be with you, dear brothers and sisters, and may God the Father and the Lord Jesus Christ give you love with Faithfulness.

— **PRAYER** —

Dear Heavenly Father, Yahweh-Channun (LORD of Grace),

Thank You for Your love and grace that guide my life. I come before You today, seeking Your wisdom and strength through the truths found in Your Word. Romans 6:23 reminds me that the gift of God is eternal life through Jesus Christ our Lord. Thank You, Lord, for this incredible gift. Help me to live in a way that honors You and reflects the eternal life You have promised. Judges 6:23 tells us not to be afraid, for You are with us. Lord, I ask for Your peace and courage in times of fear or uncertainty. Help me to remember that You are always by my side, guiding and protecting me. Proverbs 6:23 speaks of Your commands being a light and Your teaching a path to life. Lord, I pray for Your guidance and wisdom to follow Your ways. Let Your Word illuminate my path and keep me on the right track. Ephesians 6:23 offers peace and love from You, God, to all who love You. Father, I pray for Your peace to fill my heart and Your love to surround me. May Your presence bring me comfort and strength each day. Thank You for Your unending support and guidance. I trust in Your promises and look to You for all my needs.

In Jesus' graceful name I pray, Amen

JUNE 24

Matthew 6:24 (NLT): "No one can serve two masters. For you will hate one and love the other; you will be devoted to one and despise the other. You cannot serve God and be enslaved to money."

Numbers 6:24 (NLT): May the LORD bless you and protect you.

Ephesians 6:24 (NLT): May God's grace be eternally upon all who love our Lord Jesus Christ.

Luke 6:24 (NLT): "What sorrow awaits you who are rich, for you have your only happiness now."

PRAYER

Dear Heavenly Father, Jehovah Shalom (The LORD Is Peace),

I come before You with a heart full of gratitude and need. Your Word guides and sustains me, and I seek Your presence and blessings today. Matthew 6:24 tells us that no one can serve two masters. Lord, help me to commit my heart fully to You and not be divided by the things of this world. Strengthen me to choose You above all else and to serve You faithfully in every aspect of my life. Numbers 6:24 says, "The LORD bless you and keep you" (NIV). Father, I ask for Your blessings and protection over my life. Watch over me and my loved ones and keep us safe under Your care. May Your favor rest upon us each day. Ephesians 6:24 speaks of love with faith in You. Lord, I pray that Your love will fill my heart and that my faith in You will grow stronger. Help me to live out this love in my interactions with others and to trust You more deeply with each passing day. Luke 6:24 reminds us of the woes for those who are rich, full, and satisfied in this world. Keep me mindful of the true riches that come from You. Help me to seek contentment in Your presence rather than in worldly gains, and to remember those in need around me. Thank You, Lord, for Your guidance and provision. May Your Word continue to be a lamp to my feet and a light to my path.

In Jesus' truthful name I pray, Amen

JUNE 25

Job 6:25 (NKJV): How forceful are right words! But what does your arguing prove?

Deuteronomy 6:25 (NLT): For we will be counted as righteous when we obey all the commands the LORD our God has given us.

Numbers 6:25 (NIV): The LORD make his face shine upon you and be gracious to you.

Matthew 6:25 (NIV): "Do not worry about your life, what you will eat or drink; or about your body, what you will wear. Is not life more than food, and the body more than clothes?"

PRAYER

Dear Heavenly Father, Alpha and Omega (The First and the Last),

I come to You today with a humble heart, seeking Your guidance and comfort through Your Word. Job 6:25 reminds me that Your words are powerful and true. Lord, let Your truth penetrate my heart and mind, guiding me in all things. Help me to grasp the depth and beauty of Your teachings and apply them to my life. In Deuteronomy 6:25, we see the promise of righteousness through obedience. Father, grant me the strength to live according to Your commandments. May my actions and choices reflect Your righteousness, and may I honor You in all that I do. Numbers 6:25 speaks of Your blessing and protection. I ask for Your blessing to be upon me and my loved ones. Keep us safe and shield us from harm. Surround us with Your love and grace, and let Your favor rest upon us. Matthew 6:25 tells us not to worry about our lives, for You provide for us. Help me to trust in Your provision and not be anxious about the future. Teach me to rely on Your promises and to seek first Your kingdom and righteousness, knowing that You will take care of all my needs. Thank You, Lord, for Your unwavering faithfulness and care. I place my trust in You, confident that You are always with me, guiding and providing for me.

In Jesus' gracious name I pray, Amen

Numbers 6:26 (NIV): The Lord turn his face toward you and gave you peace.

Matthew 6:26 (ESV): "Look at the birds of the air: they neither sow nor reap nor gather into barns, and yet your heavenly Father feeds them. Are you not of more value than they?"

John 6:26 (NIV): Jesus answered, "Very truly I tell you, you are looking for me, not because you saw the signs I performed but because you ate the loaves and had your fill."

─────────────────── **PRAYER** ───────────────────

Dear Heavenly Father, El Shaddai (God Almighty),

I come before You with a grateful heart, seeking Your presence and peace in my life. Numbers 6:26 says, "The Lord lift up His countenance upon you and give you peace" (ESV). Lord, I ask for Your countenance to shine upon me today. Fill my heart with Your peace and serenity, knowing that Your presence is with me in every moment. Matthew 6:26 reminds me of Your care for all creation: "Look at the birds of the air; they do not sow or reap or store away in barns, and yet your heavenly Father feeds them. Are you not much more valuable than they?" (NIV). Father, thank You for providing for me just as You provide for the birds. Help me to trust in Your provision and to remember that I am precious in Your sight. In John 6:26, Jesus said, "Very truly I tell you, you are looking for me, not because you saw the signs I performed but because you ate the loaves and had your fill." Lord, help me to seek You not for the blessings You give but for Your presence and Your love. Teach me to pursue a deeper relationship with You, focusing on Your heart rather than just Your gifts. Thank You for Your unwavering love and provision. May Your peace and provision be evident in my life, and may I always seek Your presence above all else.

In Jesus' providing name I pray, Amen

I SEE SIGNS AND WONDERS OF GOD

Daniel 6:27 (NIV): "He rescues and he saves; he performs signs and wonders in the heavens and on the earth. He has rescued Daniel from the power of the lions."

Luke 6:27 (NIV): "But to you who are listening I say: Love your enemies, do good to those who hate you."

John 6:27 (NIV): "Do not work for food that spoils, but for food that endures to eternal life, which the Son of Man will give you. For on him God the Father has placed his seal of approval."

Matthew 6:27 (NIV): "Can any one of you by worrying add a single hour to your life?"

PRAYER

Dear Heavenly Father, El Yeshurun (The God of Jeshurun),

I come before You with a humble heart, seeking Your guidance and blessings in my life. Daniel 6:27 says, "He rescues and he saves; he performs signs and wonders in the heavens and on the earth." Lord, I thank You for being my rescuer and savior. I trust in Your power to perform miracles in my life and to guide me through every challenge. Luke 6:27 reminds me of Your call to love others: "But to you who are listening I say: Love your enemies, do good to those who hate you." Father, help me to love those who may be difficult to love and to show kindness to those who do not treat me well. Fill my heart with compassion and grace. In John 6:27, Jesus said, "Do not work for food that spoils, but for food that endures to eternal life, which the Son of Man will give you." Lord, help me to focus on what truly matters—pursuing a relationship with You and seeking Your eternal promises rather than just temporary gains. Matthew 6:27 asks, "Can any one of you by worrying add a single hour to your life?" Father, help me to release my worries and anxieties to You, trusting that You are in control of every aspect of my life. Teach me to find peace in Your presence and to rely on Your provision. Thank You for Your love, guidance, and the promises in Your Word. May I live each day in a way that honors You and reflects Your love to those around me.

In Jesus' miraculous name I pray, Amen

JUNE 28

Luke 6:28 (NIV): "Bless those who curse you. Pray for those who mistreat you."

John 6:28 (NIV): Then they asked him, "What must we do to do the works God requires?"

Job 6:28 (NLT): "Look at me! Would I lie to your face?"

PRAYER

Dear Heavenly Father, Bara (Creator),

I come to You today with a heart full of gratitude and trust. Luke 6:28 says, "Bless those who curse you, pray for those who mistreat you." Lord, help me to respond with love and forgiveness to those who hurt or oppose me. Fill my heart with Your grace so that I can bless others and pray for their well-being, even when it's difficult. In John 6:28, the people asked Jesus, "What must we do to do the works God requires?" Father, guide me to understand and follow Your will in my life. Help me to live according to Your teachings and to seek Your purpose in all that I do. Job 6:28 reminds me of Job's plea, "But now be so kind as to look at me. Would I lie to your face?" (NIV). Lord, I ask for Your help in being honest and transparent in all my dealings. Grant me the strength and integrity to live truthfully and to be a witness of Your love and truth. Thank You for Your guidance and strength. Help me to reflect Your love in my actions and to seek Your will with a sincere heart.

In Jesus' persecuted name I pray, Amen

JUNE 29

Luke 6:29 (NLT): "If someone slaps you on one cheek, offer the other cheek also. If someone demands your coat, take off your shirt also."

John 6:29 (NLT): Jesus told them, "This is the only work God wants from you: Believe in the one he has sent."

Job 6:29 (NLT): "Stop assuming my guilt, for I have done no wrong."

—————————————— **PRAYER** ——————————————

Dear Heavenly Father, Maqowr Chay Mayim (Fountain of Living Waters),

Thank You for Your boundless love and guidance in my life. In Luke 6:29, Jesus teaches us, "If someone strikes you on one cheek, turn to him the other also" (ESV). Help me to respond with patience and grace when faced with challenges or mistreatment. Teach me to turn the other cheek and show Your love and forgiveness, even when it is difficult. In John 6:29, Jesus said, "The work of God is this: to believe in the one he has sent" (NIV). Lord, strengthen my faith and trust in Jesus Christ. Help me to understand that believing in Him and following His teachings is the true work You require of me. Job 6:29 states, "Stop assuming my guilt, for I have done no wrong." Job is speaking to his friends as they make their assumptions about why he is suffering. Lord, guide me to live without judgment of others. Thank You for Your continuous support and presence in my life.

In Jesus' living name I pray, Amen

Matthew 6:30 (NLT): "And if God cares so wonderfully for wildflowers that are here today and thrown into the fire tomorrow, he will certainly care for you. Why do you have so little faith?"

Luke 6:30 (NLT): "Give to everyone who begs from you, and from one who takes away your goods do not demand them back."

Proverbs 6:30 (KJV): Men do not despise a thief, If he steals to satisfy his soul when he is hungry.

2 Chronicles 6:30 (NLT): [Lord], hear from heaven where you live, and forgive. Give your people what their actions deserve, for you alone know every human heart.

PRAYER

Dear Heavenly Father, Malak Haggoel (Redeeming Angel),

Thank You for Your constant care and love in my life. In Matthew 6:30, You remind us, "If that is how God clothes the grass of the field, which is here today and tomorrow is thrown into the fire, will he not much more clothe you—you of little faith?" (NIV). Help me to trust in Your provision and not worry about my needs. Strengthen my faith to believe that You will take care of me just as You do the flowers of the field. Luke 6:30 teaches us, "Give to everyone who asks you, and if anyone takes what belongs to you, do not demand it back" (NIV). Father, grant me a generous heart that is willing to give without expecting anything in return. Help me to embody Your love by showing kindness and forgiveness to others. In Proverbs 6:30, it says, "People do not despise a thief if he steals to satisfy his hunger when he is starving." Lord, help me to understand and empathize with the struggles of others. Let me approach those in need with compassion rather than judgment. 2 Chronicles 6:30 says, "Then hear from heaven, Your dwelling place; forgive, and deal with everyone according to all they do, since You know their hearts (for You alone know every human heart)" (NIV). Father, I ask for Your forgiveness and seek Your guidance in my own life. Help me to understand and forgive others as You have forgiven me. Guide me to live in faith, generosity, and compassion, reflecting Your love in all I do. Thank You for Your unending grace and support.

In Jesus' redeeming name I pray, Amen

JULY 1

Matthew 7:1 (NIV): Do not judge, or you too will be judged.

Psalm 7:1 (NKJV): O LORD my God, in you I put my trust: Save me from all those who persecute me; And deliver me.

Proverbs 7:1 (ESV): My son, keep my words and treasure my commandments within you.

Ecclesiastes 7:1 (ESV): A good name is better than precious ointment, and the day of death then the day of birth.

PRAYER

Heavenly Father, Yated Aman Maqom (Nail in a Firm Place),

Thank You for Your unending love and guidance in my life. Matthew 7:1 reminds us, "Do not judge, or you too will be judged" (NIV). Lord, help me to approach others with kindness and understanding rather than judgment. Grant me the wisdom to see others through Your eyes and to respond with compassion and grace. Revelation 7:1 teaches me to trust in Your control over all things. Even when I face challenges or uncertainties, remind me that You are sovereign and have a purpose for every situation. Psalm 7:1 instructs me to put my trust in Your refuge and protection. Deliver me from any fears, struggles, or threats that I face. Help me to find peace and security in Your presence. Proverbs 7:1 teaches me to cherish Your teachings and to keep Your commands close to my heart. Let Your wisdom guide my decisions and actions each day. In Ecclesiastes 7:1, it states, "A good name is better than fine perfume, and the day of death better than the day of birth" (NIV). Lord, help me to live a life that honors You, focusing on what truly matters. Teach me to value character and integrity over material things, and to live in a way that reflects Your love and truth. Guide me with Your wisdom, protect me with Your strength, and surround me with Your peace.

In Jesus' never-ending name I pray, Amen

JULY 2

Matthew 7:2 (NIV): "For in the same way you judge others, you will be judged, and with the measure you use, it will be measured to you."

Proverbs 7:2 (NKJV): Keep my commands and live, and my law as the apple of your eye.

Ecclesiastes 7:2 (NIV): It is better to go to a house of mourning than to go to a house of feasting, for death is the destiny for everyone; the living should take this to heart.

Micah 7:2 (NIV): The faithful have been swept from the land; not one upright person remains. Everyone lies in wait to shed blood; they hunt each other with nets.

PRAYER

Heavenly Father, 'Or Yisrael (Light of Israel),

I come before You with a heart full of gratitude and a desire for Your guidance. Matthew 7:2 tells us, "For in the same way you judge others, you will be judged, and with the measure you use, it will be measured to you." Lord, help me to be fair and compassionate in my judgments of others. Let me treat others with the same grace and understanding that I hope to receive from You. In Proverbs 7:2, it is written, "Keep my commands and you will live; guard my teachings as the apple of your eye" (NIV). Father, I ask for Your help in keeping Your commands close to my heart. Teach me to cherish and obey Your Word, so that I may live a life that is pleasing to You. Ecclesiastes 7:2 says, "It is better to go to a house of mourning than to go to a house of feasting, for death is the destiny of everyone; the living should take this to heart." Lord, help me to reflect on the reality of life and death. Give me wisdom to live with purpose and to value what truly matters, seeking to honor You in all that I do. Lastly, Micah 7:2 states "The faithful have been swept from the land; not one upright person remains. Everyone lies in wait to shed blood; they hunt each other with nets." Father, in a world that often feels unjust, I pray for Your protection and strength. Help me to stand firm in my faith and to live righteously, even when it seems difficult. Guide my steps and fill me with Your peace. Let Your Word be a lamp to my feet and a light to my path. Thank You for Your endless love and guidance.

In Jesus' instructional name I pray, Amen

JULY 3

Daniel 7:3 (NLT): Then four huge beasts came up out of the water, each different from the others.

Psalm 7:3 (NLT): O Lord my God, if I have done wrong or am guilty of injustice,

Matthew 7:3 (NLT): "And why worry about a speck in your friend's eye when you have a log in your own?"

Ecclesiastes 7:3 (NLT): Sorrow is better than laughter, for sadness has a refining influence on us.

--------------------------------- **PRAYER** ---------------------------------

Dear Heavenly Father, El Chaiyai (God of My Life),

I come before You with a humble heart, seeking Your wisdom and guidance. Daniel 7:3 tells us, "Four great beasts, each different from the others, came up out of the sea" (NIV). Lord, just as You revealed visions to Daniel, I ask that You give me clarity and understanding in the midst of life's challenges. Help me to discern Your will amidst the many voices and distractions I face. In Psalm 7:3, David prays, "Lord my God, if I have done this and there is guilt on my hands." Father, I ask for Your forgiveness for any wrongs I have committed. Examine my heart, cleanse me of my sins, and renew my spirit. Let me live in a way that is pleasing to You. Matthew 7:3 says, "Why do you look at the speck of sawdust in your brother's eye and pay no attention to the plank in your own eye?" (NIV). Lord, help me to be self-aware and to focus on my own shortcomings before criticizing others. Teach me to approach others with love and humility, recognizing my own need for grace. Ecclesiastes 7:3 states, "Sorrow is better than laughter, because a sad face is good for the heart" (NIV). Father, help me to understand that even in moments of sorrow, there can be growth and healing. Grant me the strength to endure and learn from life's trials, knowing that You are with me every step of the way. Guide me, O Lord, in my journey. Fill my heart with Your peace, wisdom, and love. Thank You for Your unwavering presence and grace in my life.

In Jesus' refining name I pray, Amen

JULY 4

Isaiah 7:4 (NIV): Say to him, "Be careful, keep calm and don't be afraid. Do not lose heart because of these two smoldering stubs of firewood—because of the fierce anger of Rezin and Aram and of the son of Remaliah.

Matthew 7:4 (NIV): "How can you say to your brother, 'Let me take the speck out of your eye,' when all the time there is a plank in your own eye?"

John 7:4 (NKJV): For no one does anything in secret while he himself seeks to be known openly. If you do these things, show yourself to the world.

Job 7:4 (NIV): When I lie down I think, "How long before I get up?" The night drags on, and I toss and turn until dawn.

PRAYER

Heavenly Father, Elohim Qarob (God Is Near),

I come to You with a heart open to Your guidance and wisdom. Isaiah 7:4 says, "Be careful, keep calm and don't be afraid." Lord, help me to remain calm and trust in You, even when facing difficulties or uncertainties. Grant me the peace that comes from knowing You are in control. In Matthew 7:4, Jesus asks, "How can you say to your brother, 'Let me take the speck out of your eye,' when all the time there is a plank in your own eye?" Father, teach me to address my own faults and weaknesses before pointing out the flaws in others. Help me to approach others with humility and grace. John 7:4 tells us, "No one who wants to become a public figure acts in secret" (NIV). Lord, I pray for authenticity in my life. Help me to live in a way that reflects Your truth and love openly, without pretense or deceit. Job 7:4 reflects Job's struggle, "When I lie down I think, 'How long before I get up?' The night drags on, and I toss and turn until dawn." Father, in times of restlessness and distress, grant me Your comfort and reassurance. Help me to find peace and rest in Your presence. Guide me in my daily life, Lord. Fill me with Your wisdom and strength, and help me to live in accordance with Your will.

In Jesus' close name I pray, Amen

JULY 5

Deuteronomy 7:5 (NIV): This is what you are to do to them: Break down their altars, smash their sacred stones, cut down their Asherah poles and burn their idols in the fire.

Psalm 7:5 (ESV): Let the enemy pursue my soul and overtake it, and let him trample my life to the ground and lay my glory in the dust. (See Psalm 7:4 for context)

Matthew 7:5 (NKJV): "[Don't be a] hypocrite! First remove the plank from your eye, And then you will see clearly to remove the speck from your brother's eye."

Luke 7:5 (NKJV): For he loves our nation, and has built us a synagogue.

Genesis 7:5 (NKJV): And Noah did according to all that the LORD commanded him.

PRANER

Heavenly Father, Qeren Yesha' (Horn of My Salvation),

I come before You with a heart seeking Your guidance and strength. Deuteronomy 7:5 reminds me to "Break down their altars, smash their sacred stones, and cut down their Asherah poles and burn their idols in the fire." Lord, help me to remove anything in my life that stands in the way of my relationship with You. Guide me to live a life fully devoted to You. In Psalm 7:5, David prays, "Let the enemy pursue my soul and overtake it, and let him trample my life to the ground and lay my glory in the dust." Father, search my heart and reveal any wrongs I need to address. Help me to seek reconciliation and live with integrity. In Matthew 7:5, Jesus teaches us, "You hypocrite, first take the plank out of your own eye, and then you will see clearly to remove the speck from your brother's eye" (NIV). Lord, show me my own faults and guide me to address them before I try to help others. Help me to act with humility and compassion. In Luke 7:5, we read about those who "loved our nation and has built our synagogue" (NIV). Father, I pray that You help me to love and serve others with the same dedication. Let my actions reflect Your love and kindness to those around me. Genesis 7:5 says, "And Noah did all that the LORD commanded him." Help me, Lord, to follow Your commands with the same obedience and faithfulness as Noah did. Strengthen my resolve to live according to Your will and to trust in Your plan.

In the Lamb of God, Jesus' name I pray, Amen

JULY 6

Matthew 7:6 (NLT): "Don't waste what is holy on people who are unholy. Don't throw your pearls to pigs! They will trample the pearls, then turn and attack you."

Psalm 7:6 (NIV): Arise, LORD, in your anger; rise up against the rage of my enemies. Awake, my God; decree justice.

Mark 7:6 (NKJV): He answered and said to them, "Well did Isaiah prophesy of you hypocrites, as it is written, 'This people honors me with their lips, but their heart is far from Me.'"

Micah 7:6 (NLT): For the son despises his father. The daughter defies her mother. The daughter-in-law defies her mother-in-law. Your enemies are right in your own household!

PRAYER

Dear Heavenly Father, El (God),

I come to You today with a heart full of gratitude and trust in Your wisdom. Jesus says in Matthew 7:6, "Do not give dogs what is sacred; do not throw your pearls to pigs" (NIV). Lord, grant me discernment to know when and how to share the precious truths You have given me. Help me to use Your wisdom in all my interactions, and guide me to share Your love in ways that are meaningful and respectful. In Psalm 7:6, David prays, "Arise, LORD, in Your anger; rise up against the rage of my enemies." Father, I ask for Your protection and justice in times when I feel overwhelmed or wronged. Stand with me against the challenges I face and provide me with strength and courage. Mark 7:6 reminds me to desire a sincere heart that truly honors You, not just in words but in actions. Help me to live out my faith genuinely and wholeheartedly. Micah 7:6 says, "For a son dishonors his father, a daughter rises up against her mother, a daughter-in-law against her mother-in-law—a man's enemies are the members of his own household" (NIV). Father, I pray for peace and understanding in my relationships. Heal any divisions and strengthen our bonds with love and forgiveness. Thank You for Your guidance and presence in my life. Help me to follow Your will and to be a reflection of Your love and grace in all that I do.

In Jesus' defending name I pray, Amen

JULY 7

1 Corinthians 7:7 (NIV): Each of you has your own gift from God; One has this gift and another has that.

Matthew 7:7 (NIV): "Ask and it will be given to you; seek and you will find; knock and the door will be opened to you."

John 7:7 (NIV): "The world cannot hate you, but it hates me because I testify of it that its works are evil."

Hebrews 7:7 (NLT): And without question, the person who has the power to give a blessing is greater than the one who is blessed.

PRAYER

Heavenly Father, El Elohe Yisrael (God, God of Israel),

I come before You with a heart open to Your wisdom and grace. 1 Corinthians 7:7 says, "I wish that all of you were as I am. But each of you has your own gift from God; one has this gift, another has that." Lord, thank You for the unique gifts and talents You have given me. Help me to use them wisely and for Your glory. Matthew 7:7 encourages us, "Ask and it will be given to you; seek and you will find; knock and the door will be opened to you." Father, I seek Your guidance and provision. Help me to trust in Your promises and to ask with faith, knowing that You will answer according to Your perfect will. John 7:7 reminds us, "The world cannot hate you, but it hates me because I testify that its works are evil." Lord, give me the strength to stand firm in my faith, even when it is difficult or when others may not understand. Help me to be a light in the world, reflecting Your truth and love. Hebrews 7:7 tells us, "And without doubt the lesser is blessed by the greater" (NIV). Thank You, Lord, for Your blessings and for the ways You continually provide for me. I acknowledge Your greatness and am grateful for Your continuous care and love. Guide me in using my gifts, strengthen my faith, and bless me with Your wisdom and peace. I trust in Your goodness and seek to live in a way that honors You.

In Jesus' promising name I pray, Amen

JULY 8

Matthew 7:8 (NLT): "For everyone who asks, receives. Everyone who seeks, finds. And to everyone who knocks, the door will be opened."

Psalm 7:8 (NIV): Let the LORD judge the people. Vindicate me, LORD, according to my righteousness, according to my integrity, O Most High.

Ecclesiastes 7:8 (NLT): Finishing is better than starting. Patience is better than pride.

Micah 7:8 (NLT): Do not gloat over me, my enemies! For though I fall, I will rise again. Though I sit in darkness, the LORD will be my light.

PRAYER

Heavenly Father, Jehovah Qadash (The LORD Who Sanctifies),

I come before You with a heart full of gratitude and trust. Matthew 7:8 reminds me, "For everyone who asks receives; the one who seeks finds; and to the one who knocks, the door will be opened" (NIV). Lord, I ask You to guide me in my journey and open doors that align with Your will. Help me to seek You earnestly and trust that You will provide for my needs. Psalm 7:8 says, "Let the LORD judge the peoples. Vindicate me, LORD, according to my righteousness, according to my integrity, O Most High." Father, I place my trust in Your justice and righteousness. Help me to live with integrity and seek Your guidance in all that I do. Ecclesiastes 7:8 tells us, "The end of a matter is better than its beginning, and patience is better than pride" (NIV). Lord, teach me to be patient and trust in Your timing. Help me to remain steadfast and confident that Your plans for me are good, even when things seem uncertain or challenging. Micah 7:8 offers encouragement: "Do not gloat over me, my enemy! Though I have fallen, I will rise. Though I sit in darkness, the LORD will be my light" (NIV). Father, thank You for being my light in times of darkness. Even when I face difficulties or setbacks, help me to find strength in You and rise above them with Your support. Guide me in Your ways, grant me patience, and be my light through every trial. I trust in Your promises and seek Your presence in my life.

In Jesus' true name I pray, Amen

Psalm 7:9 (NIV): Bring to an end the violence of the wicked and make the righteous secure—you, the righteous God who probes minds and hearts.

Ecclesiastes 7:9 (NLT): Control your temper, for anger labels you as a fool.

Mark 7:9 (NLT): Then he said, "You skillfully sidestep God's law in order to hold on to your own traditions."

1 Corinthians 7:9 (NLT): But if they can't control themselves, they should go ahead and marry. It's better to marry than to burn with lust.

PRAYER

Heavenly Father, Jehovah-Makkeh (The LORD Who Strikes/Disciplines You),

I come before You today seeking Your wisdom and guidance. Psalm 7:9 declares, "Bring to an end the violence of the wicked and make the righteous secure, you, the righteous God who probes minds and hearts." Father, You know our hearts and thoughts. I ask You to guide me in Your righteousness and to bring justice where there is wrong. Help me to live in a way that reflects Your goodness and to seek Your protection and justice. Ecclesiastes 7:9 tells us, "Do not be quickly provoked in your spirit, for anger resides in the lap of fools" (NIV). Lord, grant me patience and self-control. Help me to manage my emotions wisely and to respond to situations with grace and understanding rather than anger. Mark 7:9 says, "And He continued, "'You have a fine way of setting aside the commands of God in order to observe your own traditions!'" (NIV). Father, let me not fall into the trap of valuing human traditions over Your commands. Guide me to live according to Your Word and to follow Your ways above all else. 1 Corinthians 7:9 states, "But if they cannot control themselves, they should marry, for it is better to marry than to burn with passion" (NIV). Lord, I seek Your guidance in all aspects of my life, including my personal relationships. Help me to make decisions that honor You and align with Your will. Guide me in Your truth and keep my heart focused on You. Help me to seek Your wisdom in all things and to live a life that is pleasing to You.

In Jesus' kingly name I pray, Amen

Psalm 7:10 (NKJV): My defense is of God, who saves the upright in heart.

Ecclesiastes 7:10 (NLT): Don't long for "the good old days." This is not wise.

Hosea 7:10 (NLT): Their arrogance testifies against them, yet they don't return to the LORD their God or even try to find him.

2 Corinthians 7:10 (NLT): For the kind of sorrow God wants us to experience leads us away from sin and results in salvation. There's no regret for that kind of sorrow. But worldly sorrow, which lacks repentance, results in spiritual death.

PRAYER

Dear Heavenly Father, El HaNe'eman (The God Who Is Faithful),

I come before You today with a humble heart, seeking Your guidance and strength. Psalm 7:10 says, "My shield is God Most High, who saves the upright in heart" (NIV). Lord, I find comfort in knowing that You are my protector and shield. Please safeguard my heart and mind, and help me to remain upright and faithful in all that I do. Ecclesiastes 7:10 reminds us, "Do not say, 'Why were the old days better than these?' For it is not wise to ask such questions" (NIV). Father, help me to embrace the present and trust in Your plan for my life. Guard me against longing for the past and help me to focus on Your work in the here and now. Hosea 7:10 states, "Israel's arrogance testifies against them; yet they do not return to the LORD their God or seek him" (NIV). Lord, I pray for humility and a heart that seeks You earnestly. Help me to recognize any pride or arrogance in my life and lead me back to You with sincerity and repentance. 2 Corinthians 7:10 says, "Godly sorrow brings repentance that leads to salvation and leaves no regret, but worldly sorrow brings death" (NIV). Father, grant me a heart that experiences true godly sorrow when I fall short and leads me to genuine repentance. Help me to seek Your forgiveness and to embrace the salvation You offer, free from regret. Guide me with Your wisdom and surround me with Your grace. Help me to live in a way that reflects Your love and righteousness.

In my savior, Jesus', name I pray, Amen

JULY 11

Matthew 7:11 (ESV): "If you then, who are evil, know how to give good gifts to your children, how much more will your Father who is in heaven give good things to those who ask him!"

Psalm 7:11 (NKJV): God is a just judge, and God is angry with the wicked every day.

Ecclesiastes 7:11 (KJV): Wisdom is good with an inheritance, and profitable to those who see the sun.

Revelation 7:11 (NLT): And all the angels were standing around the throne and around the elders and the four living beings. And they fell before the throne with their faces to the ground and worshiped God.

PRAYER

Dear Heavenly Father, Tsur Yisrael (Rock of Israel),

I come to You today with a grateful heart, knowing that You are good and loving. Matthew 7:11 says, "If you, then, though you are evil, know how to give good gifts to your children, how much more will your Father in heaven give good gifts to those who ask him!" (NIV). Lord, I trust in Your generosity and kindness. Please grant me the wisdom to ask for the things that align with Your will and to recognize and be grateful for the blessings You give me. Psalm 7:11 declares, "God is a righteous judge, a God who displays his wrath every day" (NIV). Father, I acknowledge Your righteousness and justice. Help me to live in a way that reflects Your justice and to trust in Your perfect judgment in all things. Ecclesiastes 7:11 reminds us, "Wisdom, like an inheritance, is a good thing and benefits those who see the sun" (NIV). Lord, I seek Your wisdom in every aspect of my life. Grant me understanding and discernment that I may make decisions that honor You and benefit those around me. Revelation 7:11 speaks of all the angels standing around the throne and around the elders and the four living creatures. It says they fell down on their faces before the throne and worshiped God. Father, help me to cultivate a heart of worship and reverence for You. Let me remember that You are worthy of all honor and praise, both in the good times and the challenging ones.

In Jesus' praiseful name I pray, Amen

JULY 12

Matthew 7:12 (NKJV): "Therefore, whatever you want anyone to do to you, do also to them, for this is the Law and the Prophets."

Ecclesiastes 7:12 (NIV): Wisdom is a shelter as money is a shelter, but the advantage of knowledge is this; Wisdom preserves those who have it.

Isaiah 7:12 (NLT): But the king refused. "No," he said, "I will not test the LORD like that."

Deuteronomy 7:12 (NLT): If you listen to these regulations and faithfully obey them, the LORD your God will keep his covenant of unfailing love with you, as he promised with an oath to your ancestors.

PRAYER

Heavenly Father, Abir Jacob (The Mighty One of Jacob),

I come before You today, seeking Your guidance and wisdom. In Matthew 7:12, Jesus teaches us, "So in everything, do to others what you would have them do to you" (NIV). Lord, help me to live by this Golden Rule. Teach me to treat others with kindness and respect, just as I wish to be treated. Let my actions reflect Your love and compassion. Ecclesiastes 7:12 tells us, "Wisdom is a shelter as money is a shelter, but the advantage of knowledge is this: Wisdom preserves those who have it." Father, grant me wisdom and knowledge that I may navigate life's challenges with Your guidance. Help me to understand and apply Your truth in my daily decisions. Isaiah 7:12 says, "But Ahaz said, 'I will not ask; I will not put the LORD to the test'" (NIV). Lord, help me to trust in Your plans for me and not to test You out of doubt or fear. Teach me to rely on Your promises and to trust in Your ways even when I cannot see the outcome. Deuteronomy 7:12 promises, "If you pay attention to these laws and are careful to follow them, then the LORD your God will keep his covenant of love with you, as he swore to your ancestors" (NIV). Father, I commit to following Your guidance and living according to Your Word. I trust that You will keep Your promises and continue to show Your love and faithfulness in my life.

In Jesus' mighty name I pray, Amen

JULY 13

Psalm 7:13 (NIV): He has prepared his deadly weapons; he makes ready his flaming arrows.

Matthew 7:13 (NLT): "You can enter God's kingdom only through the narrow gate. The highway to hell is broad, and its gate is wide for the many who choose that way."

Ecclesiastes 7:13 (NLT): Accept the way God does things, for who can straighten what he has made crooked?

Jeremiah 7:13 (NLT): While you were doing these wicked things, says the LORD, I spoke to you about it repeatedly, but you would not listen. I called out to you, but you refused to answer.

Luke 7:13 (NLT): When the Lord saw her, his heart overflowed with compassion. "Don't cry!" he said.

PRAYER

Dear Heavenly Abba (Father),

I come before You with a heart open to Your guidance and grace. Psalm 7:13 reminds me that You prepare deadly weapon against the enemies of righteousness. Lord, I trust that You are my protector and that You will fight for me against any forces that seek to harm me. Help me to stand firm in Your strength and to rely on Your protection. In Matthew 7:13, Jesus instructs me to enter through the narrow gate, for the path to life is narrow and the way is hard. Father, help me to choose the narrow path that leads to life. Guide me in making choices that align with Your will, and give me the strength to stay on the right path despite the challenges. Ecclesiastes 7:13 shows me I need to accept and trust in Your sovereignty. When I encounter difficulties or things seem out of control, remind me to trust that You are working everything according to Your perfect plan. Jeremiah 7:13 states, "While you were doing all these things, . . . I spoke to you again and again, but you did not listen" (NIV). Father, open my ears to hear Your voice and my heart to respond to Your calls. Help me to be attentive to Your guidance and obedient to Your instructions. Luke 7:13 tells us that Jesus was moved with compassion for a widow who had lost her only son. Lord, I ask for Your compassion and comfort in times of loss or sorrow. May Your presence bring peace to my heart and reassurance that You are always with me.

In the special name of Jesus I pray, Amen

JULY 14

Daniel 7:14 (NIV): He was given authority, glory and sovereign power; all nations and peoples of every language worshiped him. His dominion is an everlasting dominion that will not pass away, and his kingdom is one that will never be destroyed.

2 Chronicles 7:14 (NLT): Then if my people who are called by my name will humble themselves and pray and seek my face and turn from their wicked ways, I will hear from heaven and will forgive their sins and restore their land.

Matthew 7:14 (NLT): "But the gateway to life is very narrow and the road is difficult, and only a few ever find it."

Psalm 7:14 (NIV): Whoever is pregnant with evil conceives trouble and gives birth to disillusionment.

PRAYER

Dear Heavenly Father, Immanuel (God With Us),

I come before You with a heart full of gratitude and trust in Your promises. Daniel 7:14 says to acknowledge Jesus as King and Savior, with authority over all things. Help me to recognize His sovereignty in every area of my life and to honor Him in all that I do. I also pray that my nation will submit to the rule and reign of Christ. 2 Chronicles 7:14 instructs us to humble ourselves and pray, seek Your face, and turn from our wicked ways, promising that You will hear from heaven and heal our land. Father, I come to You with a humble heart, seeking Your forgiveness and guidance. Lead me to turn away from anything that separates me from You, and renew me according to Your will. Matthew 7:14 tells us that the gate is narrow and the way is hard that leads to life. Lord, I know the journey of faith can be challenging. Strengthen me to walk this narrow path, and help me to remain steadfast in my commitment to follow You. Psalm 7:14 speaks of a person who is pregnant with trouble and gives birth to disillusionment. Father, in times of trouble and uncertainty, remind me to trust in Your plan and to look to You for hope and guidance. Let me find comfort in Your promises and peace in Your presence.

In Jesus' promising name I pray, Amen

JULY 15

Matthew 7:15 (NIV): "Watch out for false prophets. They come to you in sheep's clothing, but inwardly they are ferocious wolves."

Romans 7:15 (NKJV): For what I am doing, I do not understand. For what I will to do, that I do not practice; but what I hate, that I do.

Ecclesiastes 7:15 (NLT): I have seen everything in this meaningless life, including the death of good young people and the long life of wicked people.

Genesis 7:15 (NLT): Two by two they came into the boat, representing every living thing that breathes.

Mark 7:15 (NLT): "It's not what goes into your body that defiles you; you are defiled by what comes from your heart."

PRAYER

Dear Adonai (Lord),

I come to You with a heart open to Your wisdom and guidance. Matthew 7:15 warns us to watch out for false prophets, who come in sheep's clothing but are actually wolves. Lord, grant me discernment to recognize truth from deception and to stay true to Your Word. Romans 7:15 expresses the struggle with doing what we don't want to do and not doing what we know we should do. Father, help me overcome these inner conflicts and empower me to live according to Your commands and desires. Ecclesiastes 7:15 reminds us of the fleeting nature of life and the complexity of our experiences. Lord, help me navigate the ups and downs with grace and faith, trusting in Your plan for my life even when things seem uncertain. Genesis 7:15 recounts how every living thing came to Noah on the ark. Lord, as I face the challenges and responsibilities in my life, help me to remember Your provision and guidance. Just as You protected Noah, protect and guide me in Your care. Mark 7:15 tells us that nothing outside a person can defile them by going into them. Help me understand that true purity comes from within and that my actions and thoughts should reflect Your love and truth.

In Jesus' caring name I pray, Amen

JULY 16

Matthew 7:16 (NKJV): You will know them by their fruits. Do people gather grapes from thornbushes or figs from thistles?

Psalm 7:16 (NLT): The trouble they make for others backfires on them. The violence they plan falls on their own heads.

John 7:16 (NLT): So Jesus told them, "My message is not my own; it comes from God who sent me."

1 Corinthians 7:16 (NLT): Don't you wives realize that your husbands might be saved because of you? And don't you husbands realize that your wives might be saved because of you?

PRAYER

Dear Heavenly Father, Adonai Tov (The Lord Is Good),

I come to You with a heart open to Your guidance and wisdom. Matthew 7:16 teaches that by their fruit you will recognize them. Lord, help me to bear good fruit in my life, reflecting Your love and truth through my actions and words. May I be a light to others, showing them Your goodness. Psalm 7:16 says, "The trouble they cause recoils on them; their violence comes down on their own heads" (NIV). Father, I ask for Your protection from harm and negative influences. Help me to trust in Your justice and not to repay evil with evil, but to rely on Your righteous judgment. John 7:16 reminds us that Jesus' teachings come from You. Lord, guide me to understand and apply the wisdom of Your Word in my life. May I always seek Your truth and follow the example of Jesus. 1 Corinthians 7:16 speaks of how our actions can influence others, saying, "How do you know, wife, whether you will save your husband? Or how do you know, husband, whether you will save your wife?" (NIV). Father, help me to be a positive influence in my relationships, showing Your love and grace to those around me. Thank You for Your guidance and for helping me to grow in faith and character. May my life reflect Your love and truth, and may I be a beacon of hope and encouragement to others.

In Jesus' good guiding name I pray, Amen

JULY 17

Matthew 7:17 (NIV): "Every good tree bears good fruit, but a bad tree bears bad fruit."

Psalm 7:17 (NLT): I will thank the LORD because he is just; I will sing praise to the name of the LORD Most High.

Romans 7:17 (NKJV): But now, it is no longer I who do it, but sin that dwells in me.

Daniel 7:17 (NLT): These four huge beasts represent four kingdoms that will arise from the earth.

Micah 7:17 (NLT): Like snakes crawling from their holes, they will come out to meet the LORD our God. They will fear him greatly, trembling in terror at his presence.

PRAYER

Dear Heavenly Father, El Tsuri (God the Rock),

I come to You with gratitude and seek Your presence in my life. In Matthew 7:17, Jesus teaches us that every good tree bears good fruit, but a bad tree bears bad fruit. Lord, help me to be like a good tree, producing good fruit in all that I do. Guide my actions and decisions so they reflect Your goodness and love. In Psalm 7:17, the psalmist says, "I will give thanks to the LORD because of his righteousness; I will sing the praises of the name of the LORD Most High." Thank You, Lord, for Your righteousness and for all the blessings You've given me. I want to live a life of gratitude and praise, acknowledging Your greatness in every moment. Romans 7:17 reminds us that "It is no longer I myself who do it, but it is sin living in me" (NIV). Father, help me to overcome the sin within me and to live in a way that honors You. Strengthen me to resist temptation and to walk in Your ways. Daniel 7:17 speaks of how "four great beasts are four kings that will rise from the earth" (NIV). Lord, in the midst of life's challenges and uncertainties, help me to trust in Your sovereignty and wisdom. Guide me through any trials and show me Your path. In Micah 7:17, it says, "They will lick dust like a snake, like creatures that crawl on the ground" (NIV). Lord, let me find humility and surrender before You. Teach me to approach life with humility and a heart that seeks Your guidance. Thank You for Your unfailing love and for guiding me through every situation.

In Jesus' most high name I pray, Amen

Daniel 7:18 (NIV): But the saints of the Most High will receive the kingdom and will possess it forever—yes, for ever and ever.

Job 7:18 (NLT): For you examine us every morning and test us every moment.

Matthew 7:18 (NIV): "A good tree cannot bear bad fruit, nor can a bad tree bear good fruit."

Romans 7:18 (MSG): For if I know the law but still can't keep it, and if the power of sin within me keeps sabotaging my best intentions, I obviously need help! I realize that I don't have what it takes. I can will it, but I can't do it.

──────────────── PRAYER ────────────────

Dear Heavenly Father, El Chai (The Living God),

I come before You with a humble heart, seeking Your guidance and strength. Daniel 7:18 promises, "But the saints of the Most High will receive the kingdom and will possess it forever—yes, for ever and ever." Lord, help me to remember that my true inheritance is with You. Give me the courage and faith to live according to Your will and to hold on to the hope of eternal life. Job 7:18 tells us that You visit us every morning and test us every moment. Father, I know that You care deeply about each of us. Please remind me of Your compassionate nature and give me comfort in times of trial. In Matthew 7:18, Jesus says, "A good tree cannot bear bad fruit, and a bad tree cannot bear good fruit." Father, help me to be a good tree in Your eyes. Transform my heart so that I may produce good fruit in my actions, thoughts, and words. In Romans 7:18, Paul reflects, "I know that nothing good dwells in me, that is, in my flesh. For I have the desire to do what is right, but not the ability to carry it out" (ESV). Lord, I acknowledge my weaknesses and need for Your strength. Help me to rely on You to overcome my shortcomings and to live a life that is pleasing to You.

In the light of Jesus' name I pray, Amen

MY HOPE IS IN GOD

Matthew 7:19 (NIV): "Every tree that does not bear good fruit is cut down and thrown into the fire."

Jeremiah 7:19 (NIV): But am I the one they are provoking? declares the LORD. Are they not rather harming themselves, to their own shame?

Hebrews 7:19 (NIV): (for the law made nothing perfect), and a better hope is introduced, by which we draw near to God.

Romans 7:19 (NIV): For I do not do the good I want to do, but the evil I do not want to do—this I keep on doing.

PRAYER

Dear Heavenly Father, Elah Yerushalem (God of Jerusalem),

I come to You today with a heart full of gratitude and trust in Your guidance. Matthew 7:19 reminds me, "Every tree that does not bear good fruit is cut down and thrown into the fire." Lord, help me to bear good fruit in my life. Guide me to live in a way that honors You and reflects Your love and truth. In Jeremiah 7:19, it says, "But am I the one they are provoking? declares the LORD. Are they not rather harming themselves, to their own shame?" Father, I ask for Your help in understanding and correcting any ways in which I might be harming myself through my actions. Give me wisdom to walk in Your ways and avoid actions that lead me away from Your blessings. Hebrews 7:19 says, "(for the law made nothing perfect), and a better hope is introduced, by which we draw near to God." Thank You, Lord, for the better hope we have in Christ Jesus. I am grateful that through Him, I can draw near to You and experience Your grace and mercy. Romans 7:19 states, "For I do not do the good I want to do, but the evil I do not want to do—this I keep on doing." Father, I acknowledge my struggle with sin and the conflict within me. Please give me strength to overcome my weaknesses and to live according to Your will. Thank You for Your patience and love. Help me to grow in faith and to bear fruit that glorifies You. Guide my steps and fill me with Your peace.

In Jesus' hopeful name I pray, Amen

Matthew 7:20 (NLT): "Yes, just as you can identify a tree by its fruit, so you can identify people by their actions."

Ecclesiastes 7:20 (ESV): Surely there is not a righteous man on earth who does good and never sins.

Mark 7:20 (NLT): And then [Jesus] added, "It is what comes from inside that defiles you."

Exodus 7:20 (NIV): Moses and Aaron did just as the LORD commanded. He raised his staff in the presence of Pharaoh and his officials and struck the water of the Nile, and all the water was changed into blood.

PRAYER

Dear Heavenly Father, Metzudah (Fortress),

Thank You for Your guidance and the wisdom that come from Your Word. As I reflect on Your Scriptures, I ask for Your help in my life. In Matthew 7:20, Jesus says, "Thus, by their fruit you will recognize them" (NIV). Lord, help me to produce good fruit in my life, reflecting Your love and character to those around me. Guide me to live in a way that truly shows who You are. In Ecclesiastes 7:20, it is written, "Indeed, there is no one on earth who is righteous, no one who does what is right and never sins" (NIV). I acknowledge my shortcomings and ask for Your forgiveness and strength to overcome my faults. Help me to rely on Your grace daily. Mark 7:20 reminds us, "He went on: 'What comes out of a person is what defiles them'" (NIV). Father, purify my heart and mind, so that what comes out of me is pleasing in Your sight. Help me to guard my thoughts and words. Exodus 7:20 tells us, "Moses and Aaron did just as the LORD had commanded; he raised his staff in the presence of Pharaoh . . . and the waters of the Nile turned into blood." Lord, just as Moses and Aaron obeyed Your command, help me to trust and obey You in all aspects of my life. Give me the courage to follow Your guidance even when it is challenging.

In Jesus' strong name I pray, Amen

JULY 21

Matthew 7:21 (NIV): "Not everyone who calls out to me, 'Lord! Lord!' will enter the kingdom of heaven, but only the one who does the will of my Father who is in heaven."

Romans 7:21 (NIV): So I find this law at work: Although I want to do good, evil is right there with me.

Proverbs 7:21 (NIV): With persuasive words she led him astray: She seduced him with her smooth talk.

Mark 7:21 (NLT): "For from within, out of a person's heart, come evil thoughts, sexual immorality, theft, murder."

PRAYER

Dear Heavenly Father, El Yalad (The God Who Gave You Birth),

Thank You for Your Word that guides and strengthens me. I come before You with a humble heart, seeking Your help and wisdom. Jesus says in Matthew 7:21, "Not everyone who says to me, 'Lord, Lord,' will enter the kingdom of heaven, but only the one who does the will of my Father who is in heaven." Lord, I want to live according to Your will and not just in words but through my actions. Help me to truly follow You and to live a life that honors You. Romans 7:21 reminds me, "So I find this law at work: Although I want to do good, evil is right there with me." Father, I recognize the struggle between wanting to do what is right and the pull of sin. Please give me strength to overcome temptation and to live according to Your ways. Proverbs 7:21 teaches us, "With persuasive words she led him astray; she seduced him with her smooth talk." Lord, protect me from deceitful influences and guide me to make wise choices. Help me to stay true to Your path and not be swayed by empty promises or false allurements. Mark 7:21 says, "For it is from within, out of a person's heart, that evil thoughts come—sexual immorality, theft, murder" (NIV). Father, I ask You to purify my heart and mind. Remove any evil thoughts and desires, and fill me with Your Spirit so that my thoughts and actions reflect Your love and righteousness.

In the new creation of Jesus' name I pray, Amen

JULY 22

Matthew 7:22 (NLT): "On judgment day many will say to me, 'Lord! Lord! We prophesied in your name and cast out demons in your name and performed many miracles in your name.'"

Ecclesiastes 7:22 (NIV): For you know in your heart that many times you yourself have cursed others.

Romans 7:22 (NIV): For in my inner being I delight in God's law.

2 Samuel 7:22 (NIV): How great you are, Sovereign LORD! There is no one like you, and there is no God but you, as we have heard with our own ears.

 **PRAYER**

Dear Heavenly Father, El Deah (The God of Knowledge),

I come before You with a grateful heart, seeking Your guidance and strength through Your Word. In Matthew 7:22, Jesus warns us, "Many will say to me on that day, 'Lord, Lord, did we not prophesy in your name, and in your name drive out demons and in your name perform many miracles?'" (NIV). Father, I want to truly honor You with my life, not just in words but in genuine obedience. Guide me to live in a way that truly reflects Your will. Ecclesiastes 7:22 reminds me, "For you know in your heart that many times you yourself have cursed others." Lord, I acknowledge my shortcomings and the times I've fallen short. Help me to forgive others as You have forgiven me, and to seek reconciliation and peace in my relationships. Romans 7:22 states, "For in my inner being I delight in God's law." Father, I desire to delight in Your Word and to follow Your commands. Strengthen me to live out Your teachings and to seek Your righteousness in all that I do. 2 Samuel 7:22 declares, "How great you are, Sovereign LORD! There is no one like you, and there is no God but you, as we have heard with our own ears." Lord, I praise You for Your greatness and sovereignty. There is none like You, and I am grateful for Your presence and guidance in my life. Thank You for Your love and for hearing my prayer. Help me to live according to Your Word and to reflect Your character in all that I do.

In the name of wisdom, Jesus, I pray, Amen

Matthew 7:23 (NLT): "But I will reply, 'I never knew you. Get away from me, you who break God's laws.'"

Romans 7:23 (NIV): But I see another law at work in me, waging war against the law of my mind and making me a prisoner of the law of sin at work within me.

Jeremiah 7:23 (NIV): But I gave them this command: Obey me, and I will be your God and you will be my people. Walk in obedience to all I command you, that it may go well with you.

Luke 7:23 (NIV): "Blessed is anyone who does not stumble on account of me."

PRAYER

Dear Heavenly Father, El Elyon (God Most High),

I come before You today seeking Your guidance and grace. Matthew 7:23 reminds me that Jesus said, "Then I will tell them plainly, 'I never knew you. Away from me, you evildoers!'" (NIV). Lord, I want to have a genuine relationship with You, not just in appearance but in truth. Help me to live in a way that truly reflects Your love and righteousness. Romans 7:23 speaks about the struggle between our desires and Your law, "But I see another law at work in me, waging war against the law of my mind and making me a prisoner of the law of sin at work within me." Father, I acknowledge the battle within me and ask for Your strength to overcome sin and live according to Your will. Jeremiah 7:23 says, "But I gave them this command: Obey me, and I will be your God and you will be my people. Walk in obedience to all I command you, that it may go well with you." Lord, help me to obey Your commands and walk faithfully in Your ways, so that Your blessings may flow in my life. In Luke 7:23, Jesus tells us, "Blessed is anyone who does not stumble on account of me." Father, protect me from stumbling in my faith. Help me to remain steadfast and trust in Your plans for my life, even when things are difficult. Thank You for Your grace and for guiding me through Your Word. I trust in Your promise to lead and support me.

In Jesus' overcoming name I pray, Amen

JULY 24

Matthew 7:24 (NIV): "Therefore anyone who hears these words of mine and puts them into practice is like a wise man who built his house on the rock."

Genesis 7:24 (NIV): The waters flooded the earth for a hundred and fifty days.

Proverbs 7:24 (NIV): Now then, my sons, listen to me; pay attention to what I say.

Jeremiah 7:24 (NIV): But they did not listen or pay attention; instead they followed the stubborn inclinations of their evil hearts. They went backward and not forward.

 PRAYER

Dear Heavenly Father, El Hakkavod (The God of Glory),

I come to You today seeking Your guidance and wisdom. Matthew 7:24 reminds me of the importance of building my life on a solid foundation. Jesus said, "Therefore everyone who hears these words of mine and puts them into practice is like a wise man who built his house on the rock." Lord, help me to build my life on the solid rock of Your Word and teachings, so that I may stand strong in every trial. In Genesis 7:24, we read about the great flood, "The waters flooded the earth for a hundred and fifty days." Even amidst the flood, You provided a way of salvation. Father, I trust that You are with me through all challenges, and I seek Your protection and guidance in every circumstance. Proverbs 7:24 says, "Now then, my sons, listen to me; pay attention to what I say." Lord, open my heart to listen and heed Your wisdom. Help me to be attentive to Your guidance and to follow Your path with faithfulness and understanding. Jeremiah 7:24 warns us of the dangers of not following You: "But they did not listen or pay attention; they followed the stubborn inclinations of their evil hearts. They went backward and not forward." Father, I ask for Your help to avoid the pitfalls of stubbornness and to keep moving forward in Your ways. Guide me away from evil inclinations and help me stay on the path of righteousness. Thank You for Your faithfulness and for being my guide and protector. I trust in Your promises and seek to walk in Your ways every day.

In Jesus' wondrous name I pray, Amen

JULY 25

Matthew 7:25 (NIV): "The rain came down, the steams rose, and the wind blew and beat against that house; yet it did not fall, because it had its foundation on the rock."

Romans 7:25 (NLT): Thank God! The answer is in Jesus Christ our Lord. So you see how it is: In my mind I really want to obey God's law, but because of my sinful nature I am a slave to sin.

Acts 7:25 (NIV): Moses thought that his own people would realize that God was using him to rescue them, but they did not.

PRAYER

Dear God, Entunchano (The God Who Intercedes),

I come before You today seeking Your strength and guidance. Matthew 7:25 tells us, "The rain came down, the streams rose, and the winds blew and beat against that house; yet it did not fall, because it had its foundation on the rock." Lord, help me to build my life on the solid foundation of Your Word. When challenges come my way, may I stand firm and strong, rooted in Your truth. In Romans 7:25, Paul declares, "Thanks be to God, who delivers me through Jesus Christ our Lord!" (NIV). Father, I am grateful for the deliverance and freedom You provide through Jesus. Help me to live in the victory He has won for me and to continually seek Your help in every area of my life. Acts 7:25 says, "Moses thought that his own people would realize that God was using him to rescue them, but they did not." Lord, give me the wisdom and patience to understand Your plans and purposes for my life. Even when I may not see Your hand clearly, help me to trust in Your timing and to remain faithful. Thank You for being my rock, my deliverer, and my guide. Strengthen me in my journey and help me to trust You in all things.

In the freedom of Jesus' name I pray, Amen

JULY 26

Ecclesiastes 7:26 (ESV): And I find something more bitter than death: the woman who is a snare, whose heart is a trap and whose hands are chains. The man who pleases God will escape her, but the sinner she will ensure.

Matthew 7:26 (NIV): "But everyone who hears these words of mine and does not put them into practice is like a foolish man who built his house on sand."

2 Samuel 7:26 (NIV): So that your name will be great forever. Then people will say, 'The LORD Almighty is God over Israel! And the house of your servant David will be established in your sight."

PRAYER

Dear Heavenly Father, El Nathan Neqamah (The God Who Avenges Me),

I come before You today with a humble heart, seeking Your guidance and strength. Ecclesiastes 7:26 says, "I find more bitter than death the woman who is a snare, whose heart is a trap and whose hands are chains. The man who pleases God will escape her, but the sinner she will ensnare" (NIV). Lord, I ask for Your wisdom to avoid traps and snares that may lead me away from You. Help me to stay true to Your path and seek Your guidance in all things. Matthew 7:26 warns, "But everyone who hears these words of mine and does not put them into practice is like a foolish man who built his house on sand." Father, I pray that my life may be built on the firm foundation of Your Word. Help me to not only hear Your teachings but to live them out daily, so that my life may stand strong in Your truth. In 2 Samuel 7:26, it is written, "So that your name will be great forever. Then people will say, 'The LORD Almighty is God over Israel!' And the house of your servant David will be established before you." Lord, I ask that You establish me in Your ways and let my life be a testament to Your greatness. May Your name be honored in all that I do. Thank You for Your constant presence and guidance. Help me to walk in Your wisdom and build my life on the solid rock of Your Word.

In Jesus' defending name I pray, Amen

Daniel 7:27 (NIV): Then the sovereignty, power, and greatness of all the kingdoms under heaven will be handed over to the holy people of the Most High. His kingdom will be an everlasting kingdom, and all rulers will worship and obey him.

Matthew 7:27 (NIV): "The rain came down, the streams arose, and the winds blew and beat against that house, and it fell with a great crash."

Proverbs 7:27 (NKJV): Her house is the way to hell, descending to the chambers of death.

Luke 7:27 (ESV): "This is he of whom it is written, 'Behold, I send my messenger before your face, who will prepare your way before you.'"

PRAYER

Dear Heavenly Father, El Olam (The Everlasting God, the Eternal God),

I come before You with gratitude and seek Your guidance today. Daniel 7:27 says, "Then the sovereignty, power, and greatness of all the kingdoms under heaven will be handed over to the holy people of the Most High." Lord, I ask for Your guidance to live as one of Your holy people, reflecting Your power and greatness in my life. Help me to live in a way that honors You and shows Your sovereignty. Matthew 7:27 teaches us that "The rain came down, the streams rose, and the winds blew and beat against that house, and it fell with a great crash." Lord, help me to build my life on the solid foundation of Your Word, so when challenges come, I will stand firm and unshaken. Proverbs 7:27 warns of the dangers of the path of sin: "Her house is a highway to the grave, leading down to the chambers of death" (NIV). Father, guide me away from the paths of temptation and protect me from the pitfalls of sin. Help me to choose the path of righteousness and wisdom. Luke 7:27 speaks of the one who prepares the way: "This is the one about whom it is written: 'I will send my messenger ahead of you, who will prepare your way before you'" (NIV). Lord, I pray for Your preparation in my life, that I may be ready to follow Your path and fulfill Your purpose. Thank You for Your protection and guidance. Help me to stay true to Your Word and walk in Your ways every day.

In Jesus' everlasting name I pray, Amen

GOD SPEAKS TO ME

John 7:28 (NKJV): Then Jesus cried out, as He taught in the temple saying, "You both know Me, and you know where I am from; And I have not come of Myself, but He who sent Me is true, whom you do not know."

Jeremiah 7:28 (NIV): Therefore say to them, "This is the nation that has not obeyed the LORD its God or responded to correction. Truth has perished; it has vanished from their lips."

Leviticus 7:28 (ESV): Then the LORD spoke to Moses, saying, . . .

PRAYER

Dear Heavenly Father, El Racham (The Compassionate God),

I come before You today seeking Your wisdom and guidance. John 7:28 tells us that Jesus taught with authority: "Then Jesus, still teaching in the temple courts, cried out, 'Yes, you know me, and you know where I am from. I am not here on my own authority, but he who sent me is true. You do not know him'" (NIV) Lord, I ask for Your guidance and wisdom in my life. Help me to understand and embrace the truth that Jesus brings and to know You more deeply. Jeremiah 7:28 speaks of the people not listening to God's words: "Therefore say to them, 'This is a nation that has not obeyed the LORD its God or responded to correction. Truth has perished; it has vanished from their lips.'" Father, I pray for Your help to be attentive to Your voice and open to Your correction. Let Your truth dwell in my heart and guide my actions. Leviticus 7:28 gives instructions to Moses. "The LORD said to Moses, . . ." (NIV). Lord, help me to offer up my life as I listen as Moses did when You speak to me. Thank You for Your direction and for hearing my prayers. Help me to live according to Your will and stay close to You each day.

In Jesus' caring name I pray, Amen

I HAVE AUTHORITY OVER UNCLEAN SPIRITS THROUGH JESUS

Mark 7:29 (NIV): Then he told her, "For such a reply, you may go; the demon has left your daughter."

John 7:29 (NKJV): "But I know Him, for I am from Him , and He sent me."

Luke 7:29 (NLT): When they heard this, all the people—even the tax collectors—agreed that God's way was right for they have been baptized by John.

—————————————— **PRAYER** ——————————————

Dear Heavenly Father, Elohim Yare (God Most Awesome),

I come to You with a humble heart, seeking Your guidance and wisdom. Mark 7:29 tells us, "Then he told her, 'For such a reply, you may go; the demon has left your daughter.'" Lord, I trust in Your power and authority to bring healing and deliverance. I ask for Your intervention in my life and the lives of those I care about. Please remove any obstacles or difficulties and bring Your healing where it is needed. John 7:29 says, "But I know him because I am from him and he sent me" (NIV). Father, help me to deepen my relationship with You and to know You more intimately. Just as Jesus knew You and was sent by You, I seek to understand Your purpose for my life and to follow Your guidance each day. Luke 7:29 states, "All the people, even the tax collectors, when they heard Jesus' words, acknowledged that God's way was right, because they had been baptized by John" (NIV). Lord, I pray that I, too, may acknowledge and follow Your ways, recognizing Your truth and righteousness in all aspects of my life. Guide me, Lord, in Your truth and help me to live according to Your will. Thank You for Your constant presence and for hearing my prayers.

In Jesus' authoritative name I pray, Amen

JULY 30

Jesus is my Savior

John 7:30 (NLT): Then the leaders tried to arrest him; but no one laid a hand on him, because his time had not yet come.

Mark 7:30 (NKJV): And when she had come to her house, she found the demon gone out, and her daughter lying on the bed.

1 Corinthians 7:30 (NLT): Those who weep or who rejoice or who buy things should not be absorbed by their weeping or their joy or their possessions.

PRAYER

Dear Heavenly Father, Gelah Raz (Revealer of Mysteries),

Thank You for Your love and guidance in my life. John 7:30 says, "At this they tried to seize him, but no one laid a hand on him, because his hour had not yet come" (NIV). Lord, I pray for Your protection over me and my loved ones. Keep us safe from harm and guide us according to Your perfect timing and plan. Mark 7:30 tells us, "She went home and found her child lying on the bed, and the demon was gone" (NIV). Father, I ask for Your intervention in my life and the lives of those I care about. Heal and restore us, and remove any troubles or obstacles that we face. 1 Corinthians 7:30 states, "Those who mourn, as if they did not; those who are happy, as if they were not; those who buy something, as if it were not theirs to keep" (NIV). Lord, help me to find contentment and balance in every situation. Teach me to focus on You and Your purposes, rather than being overwhelmed by my circumstances. Guide me, Lord, in Your wisdom and peace. Thank You for hearing my prayer and for Your constant presence in my life.

In the saving name of Jesus I pray, Amen

I AM FOCUSED ON ETERNITY

Jeremiah 7:31 (NIV): They have built the high places of Topheth in the Valley of Ben Hinnom to burn their sons and daughters in the fire—something I did not command, nor did it enter my mind.

Luke 7:31 (NLT): "To what can I compare the people of this generation?" Jesus asked. "How can I describe them?"

1 Corinthians 7:31 (NLT): Those who use the things of the world should not become attracted to them. For this world as we know it will soon pass away.

PRAYER

Dear Heavenly Father, Rum Rosh (The One Who Lifts My Head),

Thank You for Your constant presence and guidance in my life. Jeremiah 7:31 says, "They have built the high places of Topheth in the Valley of Ben Hinnom to burn their sons and daughters in the fire—something I did not command, nor did it enter my mind." Lord, I ask for Your help in understanding and avoiding actions that go against Your will. Guide me to live in a way that honors You and aligns with Your commands. Luke 7:31 tells us, "To what, then, can I compare the people of this generation? What are they like?" (NIV). Father, help me to be discerning and wise in my interactions with others. Give me insight into how to live a life that reflects Your love and truth, even in a world that may not always understand or follow Your ways. 1 Corinthians 7:31 states, "Those who use the things of the world, as if not engrossed in them. For this world in its present form is passing away" (NIV). Lord, remind me to keep my focus on eternal things rather than getting too caught up in temporary concerns. Help me to live with a heart set on Your kingdom and Your purposes. Guide me in Your wisdom and fill me with Your peace. Thank You for hearing my prayer and for Your unending love.

In Jesus' lifting name I pray, Amen

AUGUST 1

Joshua 8:1 (ESV): Arise, go up to Ai, See I have given into your hand the king of Ai, his people, his city, and his land.

Romans 8:1 (ESV): There is therefore now no condemnation to those who are in Christ Jesus.

Psalm 8:1 (NLT): O Lord, our Lord, your majestic name fills the earth! Your glory is higher than the heavens.

PRAYER

Dear Lord, El Nahsah (Forgiving God),

Thank You for Your steadfast love and faithfulness in my life. Joshua 8:1 says, "Then the Lord said to Joshua, 'Do not be afraid; do not be discouraged. Take the whole army with you, and go up and attack Ai. For I have delivered into your hands the king of Ai, his people, his city, and his land'" (NIV). Lord, I ask for Your strength and courage in the challenges I face. Help me to trust in Your promises and to move forward with confidence, knowing that You are with me. Romans 8:1 assures us, "Therefore, there is now no condemnation for those who are in Christ Jesus" (NIV). Thank You for the forgiveness and freedom I have through Jesus. Help me to embrace this grace and live without the weight of past mistakes, knowing that You have set me free. Psalm 8:1 proclaims, "O Lord, our Lord, how majestic is your name in all the earth! You have set your glory above the heavens" (NIV). I am in awe of Your greatness and Your creation. May I always remember Your majesty and let it inspire me to live in a way that honors You. Guide me, Lord, in Your wisdom and grace. Fill me with Your peace and help me to reflect Your love in all that I do.

In Jesus' forgiving name I pray, Amen

AUGUST 2

Psalm 8:2 (NIV): Through the praise of children and infants you have established a stronghold against your enemies, to silence the foe and the avenger.

Romans 8:2 (NLT): And because you belong to him, the power of the life-giving Spirit has freed you from the power of sin that leads to death.

Deuteronomy 8:2 (NLT): Remember how the LORD your God led you through the wilderness for these forty years, humbling you and testing you to prove your character, and to find out whether or not you would obey his commands.

PRAYER

Dear Heavenly Father, Jehovah-Shalom (The LORD Is Peace),

I come before You with a grateful heart, thankful for Your guidance and love. Psalm 8:2 says, "Through the praise of children and infants you have established a stronghold against your enemies, to silence the foe and the avenger." Lord, I praise You for Your power and protection. Even in the midst of challenges, I trust that Your strength surrounds me and that You are my shield against any adversity. Romans 8:2 tells us, "Because through Christ Jesus the law of the Spirit who gives life has set you free from the law of sin and death" (NIV). Thank You, Jesus, for the freedom You have given me. Help me to live fully in the grace and new life that You offer, free from the burden of sin and guilt. Deuteronomy 8:2 reminds us, "Remember how the Lord your God led you all the way in the wilderness these forty years, to humble and test you in order to know what was in your heart, whether or not you would keep his commands" (NIV). Father, I ask for Your help in remembering Your faithfulness in my life. Teach me to trust You in every season, knowing that You are guiding me and growing me through every experience. Please guide my steps, fill my heart with Your peace, and help me to remain steadfast in Your commands.

In Jesus' peaceful name I pray, Amen

AUGUST 3

Psalm 8:3 (NLT): When I look at the night sky and see the work of your fingers—the moon and the stars you set in place.

Romans 8:3 (NLT): The law of Moses was unable to save us because of the weakness of our sinful nature. So God did what The law could not do. He sent his own Son in a body like the bodies we sinners have. And in that body God declared an end to sin's control over us by giving his Son as a sacrifice for our sins.

Numbers 8:3 (NLT): So Aaron did this. He set up the seven lamps so they reflected their light forward, just as the LORD had commanded Moses.

PRAYER

Dear Heavenly Father, Logos (The Word),

I come to You with a heart full of gratitude and trust in Your mighty power. Psalm 8:3 says, "When I consider your heavens, the work of your fingers, the moon and the stars, which you have set in place" (NIV). Lord, as I look at the beauty of Your creation, I am reminded of Your incredible power and the care You put into every detail. Help me to always see the wonder of Your work in my life and in the world around me. Romans 8:3 tells us, "For what the law was powerless to do because it was weakened by the flesh, God did by sending his own Son in the likeness of sinful flesh to be a sin offering" (NIV). Thank You, Jesus, for coming into the world to save us. I am grateful for the grace and forgiveness You offer, which sets me free from sin and helps me to live a new life in You. Numbers 8:3 says, "So Aaron did this. He set up the seven lamps so they reflected their light forward, just as the LORD had commanded Moses. " Father, like Aaron who followed Your commands, I seek to follow Your will in my own life. Guide me in all that I do, and help me to be obedient to Your instructions, reflecting Your light to others. Thank You for Your guidance, Your grace, and Your creation. May I always honor You with my life and find joy in Your presence.

In Jesus' ruling name I pray, Amen

I HAVE GREAT POWER THROUGH CHRIST

Ecclesiastes 8:4 (NLT): His command is backed by great power. No one can resist or question it.

Psalm 8:4 (NKJV): What is man that You are mindful of him, and the son of man that You visit him.

Jeremiah 8:4 (NLT): Jeremiah, say to the people, "This is what the LORD says: 'When people fall down, don't they get up again? When they discover they're on the wrong road, don't they turn back?'"

Romans 8:4 (NLT): He did this so that the just requirement of the law would be fully satisfied for us, who no longer follow our sinful nature but instead follow the Spirit.

Acts 8:4 (NLT): But the believers who were scattered preached the Good News about Jesus wherever they went.

_____   _____

PRAYER

Dear Lord, Jehovah-Palat (The LORD My Deliverer),

I come before You today with a heart open to Your wisdom and guidance. Ecclesiastes 8:4 says, Lord, You are the ultimate authority over all things. Help me to trust in Your supreme wisdom and to submit to Your plans for my life, knowing that Your ways are higher than mine. As I consider Psalm 8:4, I am humbled and grateful that You care for me so deeply. Despite my smallness in this vast universe, Your love and attention toward me are boundless. Thank You for Your constant presence and care. Jeremiah 8:4 tells us I must ask for Your help to stand firm when I fall and to return to You whenever I stray. Guide me back to Your path whenever I falter. Romans 8:4 instructs me to live by the Spirit, fulfilling the righteous requirements of Your law through Your strength and grace. Transform my heart and mind to align with Your will. Acts 8:4 inspires me to share Your love and truth with others, just as the early believers did. Empower me to be a light in my community, spreading Your message wherever I go. Thank You for Your guidance, Your love, and Your encouragement.

In Jesus' powerful name I pray, Amen

AUGUST 5

I am controlled by the Holy Spirit

Romans 8:5 (NLT): Those who are dominated by the sinful nature think about sinful things, but those who are controlled by the Holy Spirit think about things that please the Spirit.

Proverbs 8:5 (ESV): O Simple ones, learn prudence; O fools, learn sense.

Ecclesiastes 8:5 (NLT): Those who obey him will not be punished. Those who are wise will find a time and a way to do what is right.

Isaiah 8:5 (NLT): Then the LORD spoke to me again.

PRAYER

Dear Heavenly Father, Qadosh Yisrael (The Holy One of Israel),

I come to You today seeking Your guidance and wisdom. Romans 8:5 says, "Those who live according to the flesh have their minds set on what the flesh desires; but those who live in accordance with the Spirit have their minds set on what the Spirit desires" (NIV). Help me, Lord, to set my mind on what Your Spirit desires. Lead me to live according to Your Spirit, focusing on what pleases You and walking in Your ways. Proverbs 8:5 tells us, "You who are simple, gain prudence; you who are foolish, set your hearts on it" (NIV). Lord, grant me the wisdom to seek understanding and prudence in all that I do. Help me to grow in wisdom and to make choices that reflect Your will. Ecclesiastes 8:5 says, "Whoever obeys his command will come to no harm, and the wise heart will know the proper time and procedure" (NIV). Teach me to obey Your commands and to trust in Your timing. Give me a wise heart to recognize the right moments and the right steps to take in my life. Isaiah 8:5 reminds us, "The LORD spoke to me again:" Help me to embrace the gentle and guiding flow of Your Spirit rather than seeking after things that are fleeting. Teach me to rejoice in Your ways and to trust in Your guidance. Thank You for Your unending wisdom and grace. Guide me in every decision and lead me to follow Your path faithfully.

In Jesus' holy name I pray, Amen

AUGUST 6

Romans 8:6 (NLT): So letting your sinful nature control your mind leads to death. But letting the Spirit control your mind leads to life and peace.

Proverbs 8:6 (ESV): Hear, for I will speak noble things, and from my lips will come what is right.

John 8:6 (NLT): They were trying to trap him into saying something they could use against him, but Jesus stooped down and wrote in the dust with his finger.

Revelation 8:6 (NLT): Then the seven angels with the seven trumpets prepared to blow their mighty blasts.

Zechariah 8:6 (NLT): This is what the LORD of Heaven's Armies says: all this may seem impossible to you now, a small remnant of God's people. But is it impossible for me? Says the LORD of Heaven's Armies.

PRAYER

Dear Heavenly Father, Di Ou Ta Panta (My Everything),

I come before You today seeking Your guidance and wisdom. Romans 8:6 tells me to keep my mind focused on You and guided by Your Spirit. Grant me the peace and life that come from living according to Your will. Proverbs 8:6 says to open my ears to hear Your voice and my heart to receive Your truth. Speak to me through Your Word and guide me with Your wisdom. John 8:6 recounts how Jesus was asked a question to test Him. Lord, when I face trials and questions in my life, give me wisdom and clarity to respond in a way that honors You and reflects Your truth. Revelation 8:6 describes how the seven angels who had the seven trumpets prepared themselves to sound them. Help me, Lord, to be ready and prepared for the tasks and challenges You place before me. Equip me with Your strength and courage to face them with faith. Zechariah 8:6 reminds me to trust in Your power and majesty, Lord, and I pray that I will see Your marvelous works in my life and in the world around me. Help me to remain hopeful and expectant of Your miracles. Thank You for Your guidance and wisdom.

In Jesus' fulfilling name I pray, Amen

AUGUST 7

JESUS HEALS ME

Job 8:7 (NLT): And though you started with little, you will end with much.

Romans 8:7 (NLT): For the sinful nature is always hostile to God. It never did obey God's laws, and it never will.

Proverbs 8:7 (ESV): For my mouth will utter truth: wickedness is an abomination to my lips.

John 8:7 (NLT): They kept demanding an answer, so he stood up again and said, "All right, but let the one who has never sinned throw the first stone!"

Matthew 8:7 (NLT): Jesus said, "I will come and heal him."

PRAYER

Dear Heavenly Father, El Moshaah (The God Who Saves),

I come before You with a humble heart, seeking Your guidance and wisdom in my life. Job 8:7 reminds us, "Your beginnings will seem humble, so prosperous will your future be" (NIV). Lord, help me to trust You even when things seem small or difficult. I believe that You have great plans for me and will lead me to prosperity in Your time. Romans 8:7 tells us, "The mind governed by the flesh is hostile to God; it does not submit to God's law, nor can it do so" (NIV). Father, please help me to overcome any ways in which my mind is set on worldly things rather than on You. Transform my thoughts and actions so that they align with Your will. Proverbs 8:7 says, "My mouth speaks what is true, for my lips detest wickedness" (NIV). Lord, guide my speech and thoughts to be pure and truthful. Let my words reflect Your goodness and be a source of encouragement and truth to those around me. John 8:7 describes how Jesus said, "Let any one of you who is without sin be the first to throw a stone" (NIV). Father, teach me to show grace and understanding to others rather than judgment. Help me to recognize my own faults and to approach others with compassion. Matthew 8:7 records Jesus saying, "Shall I come and heal him?"(NIV). Lord, I ask for Your healing touch in my life. Whether it's physical, emotional, or spiritual healing that I need, I trust in Your power and love to restore and renew me.

In Jesus' healing name I pray, Amen

AUGUST 8

Romans 8:8 (NLT): That's why those who are still under the control of their sinful nature can never please God.

Proverbs 8:8 (ESV): All the words of my mouth are righteous, there is nothing twisted or crooked in them.

Luke 8:8 (NLT): "Still other seed fell on fertile soil. This seed grew and produced a crop that was a hundred times as much as had been planted!" When he had said this, he called out, "Anyone with ears to hear should listen and understand."

Ecclesiastes 8:8 (NLT): None of us can hold back our spirit from departing. None of us has the power to prevent the day of our death. There is no escaping that obligation, that dark battle. And in the face of death, wickedness will certainly not rescue the wicked!

PRAYER

Dear Heavenly Father, El Shamayim (The God of Heaven),

I come to You today, seeking Your presence and guidance in my life. Romans 8:8 says, "Those who are in the realm of the flesh cannot please God" (NIV). Lord, help me to live in a way that pleases You. Teach me to focus on Your Spirit rather than being led by my own desires or the ways of the world. Proverbs 8:8 declares, "All the words of my mouth are just; none of them is crooked or perverse" (NIV). Father, guide my words and thoughts so that they reflect Your truth and wisdom. Help me to speak with honesty and integrity, bringing light and encouragement to those around me. In Luke 8:8, Jesus states, "Still other seeds fell on good soil. It came up and yielded a crop, a hundred times more than was sow" (NIV). Lord, let my heart be good soil for Your Word. May Your teachings take root in my life and produce abundant fruit that honors You and benefits others. Ecclesiastes 8:8 says, "As no one has power over the wind to contain it, so no one has power over the time of their death" (NIV). Father, remind me that You are sovereign over all things. Help me to trust in Your perfect timing and to live each day with the assurance of Your control and care. Thank You for Your wisdom and Your love.

In Jesus' heavenly name I pray, Amen

AUGUST 9

The Spirit of God dwells within me

Romans 8:9 (NKJV): But you are not in the flesh but in the Spirit, if indeed the Spirit of God dwells in you. Now if anyone does not have the Spirit of Christ, he is not His.

Psalm 8:9 (NLT): O Lord, our Lord, your majestic name fills the earth!

Genesis 8:9 (NLT): But the dove could find no place to land because the water still covered the ground. So it returned to the boat, and Noah held out his hand and drew the dove back inside.

Jeremiah 8:9 (NLT): These wise teachers will fall into the trap of their own foolishness, for they have rejected the word of the Lord. Are they so wise after all?

Proverbs 8:9 (NLT): My words are plain to anyone with understanding, dear to these with knowledge.

PRAYER

Dear Heavenly Father, Jehovah-Machsi (The Lord My Refuge),

I come before You today with a heart full of gratitude and hope. Romans 8:9 tells us of Your Spirit dwelling in us. Help me to live in accordance with Your Spirit, to be guided by Your wisdom, and to reflect Your love in all I do. Psalm 8:9 shows us to praise You for Your greatness and majesty. May my life always honor You and bring glory to Your name. Genesis 8:9 mentions that Noah's dove found no place to rest until the waters receded. Lord, help me to find peace and rest in You. Guide me through times of uncertainty and fill me with Your comfort and assurance. Jeremiah 8:9 reminds me not to reject Your wisdom and fall into the trap of my own foolishness. Help me to always seek Your guidance and to value Your Word above all else. Proverbs 8:9 assures us, "They are all plain to the discerning, and upright to those who find knowledge" (BSB). Lord, grant me discernment and understanding. Help me to see things clearly and to follow Your path with wisdom and insight. Thank You, Lord, for Your guidance and presence in my life. May I always seek Your wisdom and find my rest and peace in You.

In Jesus' safe name I pray, Amen

AUGUST 10

I choose you, Lord

John 8:10 (NLT): Then Jesus stood up again and said to the woman, "Where are your accusers? Didn't even one of them condemn you?"

Ezekiel 8:10 (NIV): So I went in and looked, and I saw portrayed all over the walls all kinds of crawling things and unclean animals and all the idols of Israel.

Nehemiah 8:10 (NIV): Nehemiah said, "Go and enjoy choice food and sweet drinks, and send some to those who have nothing prepared. This day is holy to our Lord. Do not grieve, for the joy of the LORD is your strength."

Isaiah 8:10 (NLT): Call your councils of war, but they will be worthless. Develop your strategies, but they will not succeed. For God is with us!

Proverbs 8:10 (NLT): Choose my instruction rather than silver, and knowledge rather than pure gold.

PRAYER

Dear Heavenly Father, Jehovah-Magen (The LORD My Shield),

I come to You with a heart open to Your guidance and grace. John 8:10 reminds us of Your compassion and forgiveness. Help me to reflect Your mercy to others, and to always find hope in Your forgiveness. Ezekiel 8:10 describes the visions that Ezekiel saw: "So I went in and looked, and I saw portrayed all over the walls all kinds of crawling things and unclean animals and all the idols of Israel." Father, help me to turn away from anything that might lead me away from You. Cleanse my heart and mind from anything that doesn't honor You. Nehemiah 8:10 reminds me to ask for Your joy to fill my heart. I will enjoy food and drink on the Lord's Holy days. May I find strength and comfort in Your presence and share Your blessings with others. Isaiah 8:10 tells me to place my plans and worries in Your hands. May Your will be done in my life, and may I trust that Your guidance will lead me to the right path. Proverbs 8:10 advises me to value Your wisdom and guidance above all earthly treasures. May Your teachings be my greatest pursuit and guide.

In Jesus' protecting name I pray, Amen

AUGUST 11

Romans 8:11 (NKJV): But if the Spirit of Him who raised Jesus from the dead dwells in you, He who raised Christ from the dead will also give life to your mortal bodies through His Spirit who dwells in you.

Luke 8:11 (NIV): "This is the meaning of the parable: The seed is the word of God."

John 8:11 (ESV): She said, "No one, Lord." And Jesus said, "Neither do I condemn you; go, and from now on sin no more."

Proverbs 8:11 (NLT): For wisdom is far more valuable than rubies.. Nothing you desire can compare with it.

 **PRAYER**

Dear Heavenly Father, YHWH (I AM),

I come before You today, seeking Your presence and guidance in my life. Romans 8:11 tells me Holy Spirit dwells within me, bringing new life and strength to every part of my being. Fill me with Your Spirit and guide me in Your ways. Luke 8:11 explains, "This is the meaning of the parable: The seed is the word of God." Lord, let Your Word take root in my heart. Help me to understand and apply Your teachings so that I may bear fruit in my life, reflecting Your love and grace to those around me. John 8:11 reveals Jesus saying, "Then neither do I condemn you. . . . Go now and leave your life of sin" (NIV). Thank You for Your forgiveness and grace. Help me to turn away from anything that separates me from You and to live a life that honors You in all I do. Proverbs 8:11 says, "For wisdom is more precious than rubies, and nothing you desire can compare with her" (NIV). Lord, grant me the wisdom to navigate life's challenges and decisions. May I seek Your wisdom above all else, valuing it more than any material wealth. Help me to trust in Your timing and justice, knowing that Your plans are always perfect. Guard my heart and mind from desiring anything outside of Your will.

In Jesus' cherished name I pray, Amen

AUGUST 12

Romans 8:12 (NKJV): Therefore, brethren, we are debtors—not to the flesh, to live according to the flesh.

John 8:12 (NIV): When Jesus spoke again to the people, he said, "I am the light of the world. Whoever follows me will never walk in darkness, but will have the light of life."

Mark 8:12 (NKJV): But He sighed deeply in His spirit, and said, "Why does this generation seek a sign? Assuredly, I say to you, no sign shall be given to this generation."

Ecclesiastes 8:12 (NKJV): Through a sinner does evil a hundred times, and his days are prolonged, yet I purely know that it will be well with those who fear God, who fear before Him.

PRAYER

Dear Heavenly Father, Entunchano (The God Who Intercedes),

Thank You for Your incredible love and guidance in my life. I come before You with a heart full of gratitude and a desire to seek Your presence. Romans 8:12 reminds us to live according to Your Spirit and not be swayed by my own desires. Empower me to follow Your ways and live a life that reflects Your love and truth. In John 8:12, Jesus says, "I am the light of the world. Whoever follows me will never walk in darkness, but will have the light of life." I thank You for being the light that guides my path. Please illuminate my way, so that I may walk in Your light and avoid the darkness that seeks to lead me astray. Mark 8:12 speaks of Jesus sighing deeply and saying, "Why does this generation ask for a sign? Truly I tell you, no sign will be given to it" (NIV). Lord, I pray for faith in Your promises even when I don't see immediate signs. Help me trust in Your plan and purpose, knowing that You are always at work in my life. Ecclesiastes 8:12 tells us, "Although a wicked person commits evil a hundred times and still lives a long time, I know that it will go better with those who fear God, who are reverent before Him" (NIV). Lord, help me to live in reverence and awe of You. May I always seek to honor You with my actions and decisions, trusting that Your ways are best. Guide me with Your wisdom and grace as I navigate each day. Strengthen my faith and keep me close to You.

In the light of Jesus' name I pray, Amen

Proverbs 8:13 (NKJV): The fear of the LORD is to hate evil; pride and arrogance and the evil way and the perverse mouth I hate.

Romans 8:13 (ESV): For if you live according to the flesh you will die; but if by the Spirit you put to death the deeds of the body, you will live.

Matthew 8:13 (NLT): Then Jesus said to the Roman officer, "Go back home. Because you believed it happened." And the young servant was healed that same hour.

Job 8:13(NLT): The same happens to all who forget God. The hopes of the godless evaporate.

PRAYER

Dear Heavenly Father, Sane (The God Who Hates Sin),

Thank You for Your constant presence and guidance in my life. I come to You today with a humble heart, seeking Your wisdom and strength. Proverbs 8:13 tells us, "To fear the LORD is to hate evil; I hate pride and arrogance, evil behavior and perverse speech." Lord, help me to live in a way that honors You. Guide me away from pride and arrogance, and teach me to speak and act with integrity. In Romans 8:13, Your Word says, "For if you live according to the flesh, you will die; but if by the Spirit you put to death the misdeeds of the body, you will live" (NIV). Father, give me the strength to overcome my weaknesses and live according to Your Spirit. Help me to make choices that reflect Your will and bring life to my soul. Matthew 8:13 shows us Jesus saying, "Go! Let it be done just as you believed it would." I pray that You grant me faith like this, trusting in Your power and promises. Help me believe deeply in Your ability to work miracles in my life, just as You have done in the lives of others. Job 8:13 says, "Such is the destiny of all who forget God; so perishes the hope of the godless" (NIV). Lord, keep my heart steadfast in You, and never let me forget Your goodness. May my hope and trust remain firmly rooted in Your promises. Guide me in Your wisdom, strengthen my faith, and help me to live in a way that brings glory to Your name.

In Jesus' loving name I pray, Amen

AUGUST 14

Romans 8:14 (ESV): For all who are led by the Spirit of God are sons of God.

Proverbs 8:14 (NKJV): Council is mine, and sound wisdom; I am understanding, I have strength.

Deuteronomy 8:14 (NLT): Do not become proud at that time and forget the LORD your God, who rescued you from slavery in the land of Egypt.

───────────────── **PRAYER** ─────────────────

Dear Heavenly Father, Ori (My Light),

I come before You with a grateful heart, seeking Your guidance and strength. Romans 8:14 reminds me, "For those who are led by the Spirit of God are the children of God" (NIV). Lord, I ask that Your Spirit would lead me each day. Help me to follow Your guidance and grow closer to You, embracing my identity as Your child. In Proverbs 8:14, it is written, "Counsel and sound judgment are mine; I have insight, I have power" (NIV). Father, grant me Your wisdom and insight in all that I do. Help me to make decisions that reflect Your counsel and to act with the strength and understanding that come from You. Deuteronomy 8:14 warns us, "Then your heart will become proud and you will forget the Lord your God, who brought you out of Egypt, out of the land of slavery" (NIV). Lord, keep my heart humble and always mindful of Your incredible blessings and deliverance. Help me never to forget Your faithfulness and provision. Guide me with Your Spirit, fill me with Your wisdom, and keep my heart focused on You. Thank You for Your constant presence and love.

In the saving name of Jesus I pray, Amen

I AM AN HEIR OF GOD

Romans 8:15 (NKJV): For you did not receive the spirit of bondage again to fear, but you received the Spirit of adoption by whom we cry out, " Abba, father."

Luke 8:15 (NLT): "and the seeds that fell on the good soil represent honest, good-hearted people who hear God's word, cling to it, and patiently produce a huge harvest."

Matthew 8:15 (NLT): But when Jesus touched her hand, the fever left her. Then she got up and prepared a meal for him.

John 8:15 (NLT): "You judge me by human standards, but I do not judge anyone."

Ecclesiastes 8:15 (ESV): And I commend joy, for man has nothing better under the sun but to eat and drink and be joyful, for this will go with him in his toil through the days of his life that God has given him under the sun.

PRAYER

Dear Heavenly Father, Tsaddik (Righteous),

I come to You with a heart full of gratitude and hope. Romans 8:15 tells us we are not to be in fear but instead adopted as a child of Abba our Father. Help me to live confidently and fearlessly, knowing that I am loved and accepted by You. In Luke 8:15, Your Word says, "But the seed on good soil stands for those with a noble and good heart, who hear the word, retain it, and by persevering produce a crop" (NIV). Father, prepare my heart to be good soil for Your Word. May I hear, retain, and live out Your teachings, producing fruit that honors You. Matthew 8:15 recounts, "He touched her hand, and the fever left her; and she got up and began to wait on him" (NIV). Lord, just as Jesus healed, I ask for Your healing touch in my life. Heal me where I am hurting and give me the strength to serve and honor You with my whole being. In John 8:15 Jesus says, "You judge by human standards; I pass judgment on no one" (NIV). Jesus, help me to see others through Your eyes, not judging by human standards but showing grace and understanding as You do. Finally, Ecclesiastes 8:15 commands enjoyment, eat and be merry. Lord, help me to find joy in the simple blessings of life, enjoying each moment with a thankful heart.

In Jesus' healing name I pray, Amen

AUGUST 16

I am God's light

Matthew 8:16 (NIV): When evening came, many who were demon-possessed were brought to him, and he drove out the spirits with a word and healed all the sick.

Romans 8:16 (ESV): The Spirit himself bears witness with our spirit that we are children of God.

John 8:16 (NIV): "But if I do judge, my decisions are true, because I am not alone. I stand with the Father, who sent me."

Luke 8:16 (NKJV): "No one, when he has lit a lamp, covers it with a vessel or puts it under a bed, but sets it on a lampstand, that those who enter may see the light."

 **PRAYER**

Dear Heavenly Father, Or Goyim (Light of the Nations),

I come before You with a heart full of trust and faith. Matthew 8:16 tells us, "When evening came, many who were demon-possessed were brought to him, and he drove out the spirits with a word and healed all the sick." Lord, just as Jesus healed and set people free, I ask for Your healing and deliverance in my life. Help me to find peace and restoration in Your presence. In Romans 8:16, it says, "The Spirit himself testifies with our spirit that we are God's children" (NIV). Father, thank You for Your Holy Spirit who assures me of my identity as Your child. Help me to live confidently as Your beloved son or daughter, knowing that You are always with me. John 8:16 reminds us, "But if I do judge, my decisions are true, because I am not alone. I stand with the Father, who sent me." Jesus, guide me in making decisions that align with Your will. Let Your wisdom and truth guide my choices, knowing that You are always by my side. Finally, Luke 8:16 says, "No one lights a lamp and hides it in a clay jar or puts it under a bed. Instead, they put it on a stand, so that those who come in can see the light" (NIV). Lord, help me to let my light shine brightly for You. May my actions and words reflect Your love and truth, bringing light to those around me. Thank You for Your guidance, healing, and for making me Your child.

In the light of Jesus' name I pray, Amen

AUGUST 17

Romans 8:17 (NIV): Now if we are children, then we are heirs—heirs of God and co-heirs with Christ, if indeed we share in his sufferings in order that we may also share in his glory.

Ecclesiastes 8:17 (NIV): Then I saw all that God has done. No one can comprehend what goes on under the sun. Despite all their efforts to search it out, no one can discover its meaning. Even if the wise claim they know, they cannot really comprehend it.

Acts 8:17 (ESV): Then [Peter and John] laid their hands on them and they received the Holy Spirit.

Luke 8:17 (NKJV): "For nothing is secret that will not be revealed, nor anything hidden that will not be known and come to light."

Zechariah 8:17 (NIV): "Do not plot evil against each other, and do not love to swear falsely. I hate all this," declares the LORD.

PREYER

Dear Heavenly Father, Parakletos (Advocate),

I come before You with a grateful heart, seeking Your guidance and blessings. In Romans 8:17, Your Word tells me that as Your child, I am an heir to Your promises. I trust in Your plan for my life and believe that You will guide me in all things. Lord, I ask for wisdom and understanding in all situations. Just as Ecclesiastes 8:17 reminds us that Your works are beyond our full comprehension, help me to trust in Your wisdom even when I don't understand everything. In Acts 8:17, Your Word shows how Your Spirit was given to those who believed. I pray for Your Spirit to fill me with strength and clarity, so that I may live according to Your will and bear witness to Your grace. In Luke 8:17, Jesus tells us that nothing hidden will remain so, and that everything will be revealed in Your perfect timing. Help me to be patient and to trust in Your timing for revealing Your plans and purposes in my life. Finally, Zechariah 8:17 calls us to speak truth and justice. I ask that You guide my words and actions, that they may reflect Your love and truth in all that I do. Thank You, Lord, for Your presence and guidance.

In Jesus' present name I pray, Amen

Romans 8:18 (NLT): Yet what we suffer now is nothing compared to the glory he will reveal to us later.

Deuteronomy 8:18 (KJV): And you shall remember the LORD your God, for it is He who gives you power to get wealth, and He may establish His covenant which He swore to your father, as it is this day.

Luke 8:18 (NLT): "So pay attention to how you hear. To those who listen to my teaching, more understanding will be given. But for those who are not listening, even what they think they understand will be taken away from them."

Mark 8:18 (NIV): "Do you have eyes but fail to see, and ears but fail to hear? And don't you remember?"

PRAYER

Dear Heavenly Father, Alethinos Theos (True God),

I come to You today with a humble heart, seeking Your presence and guidance. Your Word reminds me in Romans 8:18 that the sufferings of this present time are nothing compared to the glory You have prepared for us. Help me to keep this eternal perspective and find comfort and hope in Your promises, even when life is challenging. Lord, Deuteronomy 8:18 tells me that You are the One who gives me the ability to produce wealth and blessings. I thank You for the resources and opportunities You provide. Please guide me to use these blessings wisely and for Your glory. In Luke 8:18, Jesus says that whoever has, more will be given. I pray that You help me to be a good steward of the gifts and opportunities You have entrusted to me. May I continue to grow in faith and understanding, using what You give me to make a positive impact in the world. In Mark 8:18, Jesus warns us not to have eyes that do not see or ears that do not hear. Open my eyes and ears to Your truth and to the needs around me. Help me to be attentive to Your guidance and to live a life that reflects Your love and wisdom. Thank You, Lord, for Your constant care and for the hope we have in You.

In Jesus' true name I pray, Amen

Isaiah 8:19 (NIV): When someone tells you to consult mediums and spiritists, who whisper and mutter, should not a people inquire of their God? Why consult the dead on behalf of the living?

John 8:19 (NIV): Then they asked him, "Where is your father?" "You do not know me or my Father," Jesus replied. "If you knew me, you would know my Father also."

Matthew 8:19 (NLT): Then one of the teachers of religious law said to him, "Teacher, I will follow you wherever you go."

Deuteronomy 8:19 (NLT): "But I assure you of this: If you ever forget the LORD your God and follow other gods, worshiping and bowing down to them, you will certainly be destroyed.

PRAYER

Dear Heavenly Father, Basileus Basileon (King of Kings),

I come before You today seeking Your wisdom and guidance. In Isaiah 8:19, Your Word warns us against turning to other sources for guidance and reminds us to seek You alone. Help me to turn to You in all things, trusting in Your direction and not in the ways of the world. In John 8:19, Jesus tells us that if we know Him, we know the Father. I ask for a deeper understanding of You, Lord, and for a closer relationship with Jesus, so that I may know and experience Your love more fully. Matthew 8:19 speaks of the cost of following Jesus. Help me to understand and embrace the sacrifices involved in following You, and grant me the strength and courage to remain steadfast in my faith. Deuteronomy 8:19 warns us not to forget You when we prosper. I thank You for the blessings in my life and ask for Your help in keeping You at the center of my heart and mind. May I never forget to give You thanks and to remain humble and grateful. Thank You, Lord, for Your guidance, love, and the blessings You provide. I trust in Your promises and seek to walk closely with You each day.

In King Jesus' name I pray, Amen

AUGUST 20

Daniel 8:20 (NLT): The two-horned ram represents the kings of Media and Persia.

Proverbs 8:20 (NLT): I walk in righteousness, in paths of justice.

Isaiah 8:20 (NLT): Look to God's instructions and teachings! People who contradict His word are completely in the dark.

Job 8:20 (KJV): Behold, God will not cast away a perfect man, neither will he help the evil doers.

PRAYER

Dear Heavenly Father, Hashem (The Name),

I come to You today with a heart full of gratitude and a desire for Your guidance. Your Word in Daniel 8:20 speaks of the vision and its meaning. Help me to understand the insights You provide and to trust in Your divine wisdom as You reveal Your plans for my life. Proverbs 8:20 says that wisdom walks in the way of righteousness. I pray for Your wisdom to guide me in making choices that align with Your will and reflect Your righteousness. Teach me to walk in Your ways and to live a life that honors You. Isaiah 8:20 reminds me that if we do not speak according to Your Word, there is no light in us. Help me to always turn to Your Scriptures for truth and to let Your Word be a guiding light in my life. Job 8:20 tells us that You do not reject a person of integrity. I ask for Your help in living with integrity and in following Your commands faithfully. Strengthen my character and keep me steadfast in my commitment to You. Thank You, Lord, for Your constant guidance and for the wisdom You provide. I trust in Your Word and seek to live according to Your truth each day.

In Jesus' instructional name I pray, Amen

AUGUST 21

I HEAR GOD'S WORD

John 8:21 (NIV): Once more Jesus said to them, "I am going away, and you will look for me, and you will die in your sin. Where I go, you cannot come."

Luke 8:21 (NLT): Jesus replied, "My mother and my brothers are all those who hear God's word and obey it."

Proverbs 8:21 (KJV): That I may cause those that love me to inherit substance; and I will fill their treasures.

Genesis 8:21 (NLT): And the LORD was pleased with the aroma of the sacrifice and said to himself, "I will never again curse the ground because of the human race, even though everything they think or imagine is bent toward evil from childhood. I will never again destroy all living things."

PRAYER

Dear Heavenly Father, Lo Shanah (Unchanging),

I come before You with a heart open to Your guidance and grace. Your Word in John 8:21 reminds us that without You, we are lost. Help me to stay close to You, knowing that true direction and understanding come from Your presence. In Luke 8:21, Jesus says that those who hear and do Your Word are truly His family. I pray that You help me to not only hear Your Word but to live it out each day. Guide me in actions that reflect Your love and teachings. Proverbs 8:21 speaks of wisdom bringing prosperity to those who love it. I ask for Your wisdom in my life, that it may lead to good decisions and blessings. Help me to cherish and seek Your wisdom in every aspect of my life. Genesis 8:21 shows Your promise to never again curse the ground because of humanity. I am grateful for Your promises and mercy. Help me to trust in Your faithfulness and to live in a way that honors Your grace and goodness. Thank You, Lord, for Your guidance and for the promises in Your Word. Strengthen my faith and help me to live according to Your truth each day.

In Jesus' unchanging name I pray, Amen

The Lord formed me

Genesis 8:22 (NIV): As long as the earth endures, seedtime and harvest, cold and heat, summer and winter, day and night will never crease.

Mark 8:22 (NLT): When they arrived at Bethsaida, some people brought a blind man to Jesus, and they begged him to touch the man and heal him.

Proverbs 8:22 (NLT): The Lord formed me from the beginning, before He created anything else.

Acts 8:22 (NIV): Repent of this wickedness and pray to the Lord in the hope that he may forgive you for having such a thought in your heart.

PRAYER

Dear Heavenly Father, Yotzerenu (Potter),

I come to You with a thankful heart, seeking Your guidance and blessings. Your Word in Genesis 8:22 reminds me of Your promise to provide the seasons of life and to keep the world in order. Thank You for Your faithful provision and for the stability You bring to my life. In Mark 8:22, Jesus heals a blind man in Bethsaida. I ask for Your healing touch in my life, whether it's physical, emotional, or spiritual. Open my eyes to Your truth and help me to see Your hand at work in my life. Proverbs 8:22 speaks of wisdom being with You from the beginning. I pray for Your wisdom to guide me in all that I do. Help me to seek Your understanding and to make decisions that align with Your will. Acts 8:22 speaks of repentance and prayer for forgiveness. I ask for Your forgiveness for any wrongs I've committed and for strength to turn away from anything that separates me from You. Help me to grow in faith and to live a life that's pleasing to You. Thank You, Lord, for Your constant care and guidance. I trust in Your promises and seek to follow You more closely each day.

In Jesus' crucified name I pray, Amen

AUGUST 23

John 8:23 (NIV): But He continued, "You are from below; I am from above. You are of this world; I am not of this world."

Judges 8:23 (NLT): But Gideon replied, "I will not rule over you, nor will my son. The Lᴏʀᴅ will rule over you!"

Ezra 8:23 (NLT): So we fasted and earnestly prayed that our God would take care of us, and He heard our prayers.

Proverbs 8:23 (NKJV): I have been established from everlasting, from the beginning, before there was ever an earth.

1 King 8:23 (NLT): And he prayed, "O Lᴏʀᴅ God of Israel, there is no God like you in all of heaven above or on the earth below. You keep your covenant and show unfailing love to all who walk before you in wholehearted devotion."

PRAYER

Dear Heavenly Father, Elohim (Mighty Creator),

I come before You with a heart full of gratitude and a desire for Your guidance. Your Word in John 8:23 reminds me that You are above all things and that I need to see my life from Your perspective. Help me to recognize the greater truths and to follow Your ways. In Judges 8:23, Gideon declares that he will not rule over Israel, but that You, Lord, will be their ruler. I surrender my plans and desires to You, trusting that Your leadership and wisdom are far greater than my own. Ezra 8:23 shows how Ezra sought Your help through fasting and prayer. I turn to You now, asking for Your assistance in my own needs and challenges. Guide me and provide for me as I trust in Your power and grace. Proverbs 8:23 speaks of wisdom being established from the beginning. I seek Your wisdom to guide my decisions and actions. Help me to walk in Your truth and to make choices that honor You. 1 Kings 8:23 reminds us that You alone are God in heaven and on earth, keeping Your covenant of love. Thank You for Your faithfulness and for the promises You have made. Help me to remain faithful to You and to trust in Your love.

In Jesus' mighty name I pray, Amen

AUGUST 24

John 8:24 (NIV): "I told you that you would die in your sins; if you do not believe that I am he, you will indeed die in your sins."

Luke 8:24 (NKJV): And they came to [Jesus] and awoke Him, Saying, "Master, Master, we are perishing!" Then He arose and rebuked the wind and the raging of the water. And they ceased, and there was a calm.

Proverbs 8:24 (NLT): I was born before the oceans were created, before the springs babbled forth their waters.

Romans 8:24 (NIV): For in this hope we were saved. But hope that is seen is no hope at all. Who hopes for what they already have?

PRAYER

Dear Heavenly Father, El Kanna (Jealous God),

I come before You with a humble heart, seeking Your guidance and comfort. Your Word in John 8:24 reminds me that without believing in Jesus, I am lost in my sins. I place my faith in Him, trusting in His sacrifice and salvation. In Luke 8:24, the disciples called on Jesus when they were in danger, and He calmed the storm. I ask for Your peace and calm in the midst of the storms in my life. Please bring Your calm to my fears and anxieties, and help me trust in Your presence and power. Proverbs 8:24 speaks of wisdom being present before creation. I seek Your wisdom to guide me in my decisions and daily life. Help me to understand and apply Your wisdom, and to walk in Your ways. Romans 8:24 talks about our hope in salvation and how we wait patiently for it. I trust in Your promises and ask for patience as I wait for Your guidance and answers in my life. Strengthen my faith and help me to remain hopeful. Thank You, Lord, for Your unfailing love and for the guidance You provide. I trust in Your plans and seek to follow You faithfully each day.

In Jesus' calming name I pray, Amen

AUGUST 25

I HAVE FAITH

Romans 8:25 (NIV): But if we hope for what we do not yet have, we wait for it patiently.

Mark 8:25 (ESV): Then Jesus placed his hands on the man's eyes again, and his eyes were opened. His sight was completely restored, and he could see everything clearly.

Luke 8:25 (NIV): "Where is your faith?" he asked his disciples. In fear and amazement they asked one another, "Who is this? He commands even the winds and the water, and they obey him."

Matthew 8:25 (NIV): The disciples went and woke him, saying, "Lord, save us! We're going to drown!"

PRAYER

Dear Heavenly Father, Atik Yomin (Ancient of Days),

I come before You with a heart full of faith and trust. Your Word in Romans 8:25 reminds me that even when I hope for things not yet seen, I should wait patiently and trust in Your timing. Help me to remain hopeful and to trust in Your perfect plan for my life. In Mark 8:25, Jesus healed a man's sight in stages, showing that Your work is sometimes gradual. I pray for patience as I wait for Your full work in my life. Help me to trust that You are working, even when I don't see immediate results. Luke 8:25 tells of Jesus calming the storm and asking His disciples where their faith was. In times of trouble and uncertainty, help me to remember that You are with me. Strengthen my faith and give me peace in the midst of life's storms. Matthew 8:25 shows the disciples crying out to Jesus in their fear during a storm. I ask for Your comfort and assurance during my own trials. When I feel overwhelmed, help me to turn to You for peace and calm. Thank You, Lord, for Your steadfast love and for being with me through every challenge. I place my trust in You and look to You for strength and guidance.

In Jesus' forever trusting name I pray, Amen

I AM NOT WEAK

Romans 8:26 (NKJV): Likewise the spirit also helps in our weaknesses. For we do not know what we should pray for as we ought, but the spirit Himself makes intercession for us with groanings which cannot be uttered.

Matthew 8:26 (NIV): Jesus replied, "You of little faith, why are you so afraid?" Then he got up and rebuked the winds and the waves, and it was completely calm.

John 8:26 (KJV): "I have many things to say and to judge of you; but he that sent me is true; and I speak to the world those things which I have heard of him."

––––––––––––––––––––––––––– **PRAYER** –––––––––––––––––––––––––––

Dear Heavenly Father, Shub Nephesh (Renewer of Life),

I come before You with a trusting heart, seeking Your presence and support. Romans 8:26 reminds me that Your Spirit helps us in our weakness and intercedes for us with groans that words cannot express. I ask for Your Spirit to guide and strengthen me, especially when I don't know how to pray or what to ask for. In Matthew 8:26, Jesus calms the storm and asks why we are afraid. When I face challenges and uncertainties, help me to trust in Your power and presence. Please calm my fears and remind me that You are always with me, guiding and protecting me. John 8:26 tells me that Jesus speaks only what He has heard from You. I pray for clarity and understanding of Your will and for the wisdom to follow Your guidance. Help me to listen closely to Your voice and to act according to Your truth. Thank You, Lord, for Your constant care and the assurance that You are with me in every situation. Strengthen my faith and help me to rely on Your Spirit, Your guidance, and Your peace.

In Jesus' renewing name I pray, Amen

AUGUST 27

John 8:27 (NIV): But they still didn't understand that [Jesus] was talking about his Father.

Romans 8:27 (NIV): And he who searches our hearts knows the mind of the Spirit, because the Spirit intercedes for God's people in accordance with the will of God.

Matthew 8:27 (ESV): The men marveled and asked, "What kind of man is this? Even the winds and waves obey him!"

PRAYER

Dear Heavenly Father, El Haggadol (The Great God),

I come to You with a heart full of trust and gratitude. Your Word in John 8:27 shows that Jesus spoke about You, but the people didn't understand what He meant. Help me to have clarity and understanding of Your Word and Your will for my life. Open my heart to Your truth and guide me in my journey of faith. Romans 8:27 reminds me that Your Spirit searches our hearts and intercedes for us according to Your will. I ask for Your Spirit to help me in my prayers and to align my desires with Your purposes. Guide me in understanding and following Your plan for me. Matthew 8:27 tells of how the disciples were amazed when Jesus calmed the storm, recognizing His authority. I pray that I will continually be amazed by Your power and presence in my life. Help me to trust in Your authority and to remain calm and confident knowing that You have control over all things. Thank You, Lord, for Your guidance, understanding, and the peace You bring. I trust in Your promises and seek to follow You faithfully each day.

In Jesus' protecting name I pray, Amen

AUGUST 28

I LOVE GOD

Matthew 8:28 (NIV): When he arrived at the other side in the region of the Gadarenes, two demon-possessed men coming from the tombs met him. They were so violent that no one could pass that way.

Romans 8:28 (KJV): And we know that all things work together for good to them that love God, to them who are called according to His purpose.

John 8:28 (NKJV): Then Jesus said to them, "When you lift up the Son of Man, then you will know that I am He, and that I do nothing of Myself; but as My Father taught me, I speak these things."

1 Kings 8:28 (NKJV): Yet regard the prayer of Your servant and his supplication, O LORD my God, and listen to the cry and prayers which Your servant is praying before You today.

PRAYER

Dear Heavenly Father, El Qadosh (The Holy God),

I come before You with a heart full of faith and trust. Your Word in Matthew 8:28 shows that Jesus has authority over evil and darkness. I ask for Your protection and strength against any challenges or fears that come my way. Help me to trust in Your power and to find peace in Your presence. Romans 8:28 reminds me that You work all things together for the good of those who love You and are called according to Your purpose. I trust that You are working in every situation of my life, even when I can't see the outcome. Help me to stay hopeful and to rely on Your promises. John 8:28 speaks of Jesus doing only what He sees from You. I pray for Your guidance to help me align my actions with Your will. Teach me to follow Christ's example and to seek Your direction in all that I do. 1 Kings 8:28 shows the prayer of Solomon asking You to hear from heaven and to act on behalf of Your people. I also ask for Your guidance and answers to my prayers. Please listen to my requests and provide me with Your wisdom and support. Thank You, Lord, for Your constant presence, guidance, and the assurance that You are working for my good. I place my trust in You and seek to follow Your will each day.

In Jesus' holy name I pray, Amen

John 8:29 (NIV): "The one who sent me is with me; He has not left me alone, for I always do what pleases him."

Proverbs 8:29 (KJV): When he gave to the sea his decree, that the water should not pass his commandment: when he appointed the foundation of the earth.

Mark 8:29 (NIV): "But what about you?" Jesus asked. "Who do you say I am?" Peter answered, "You are the Messiah."

Romans 8:29 (NLT): For God knew his people in advance, and he chose them to become like his Son, so that his Son would be the firstborn among many brothers and sisters.

PRAYER

Dear Heavenly Father, Jehovah-Jireh (The LORD My Provider),

I come before You with a heart full of trust and gratitude. Your Word in John 8:29 reminds me that Jesus always does what pleases You because He is never alone. I ask for Your presence in my life, that everything I do may be pleasing to You and guided by Your wisdom. In Proverbs 8:29, wisdom is described as being present when You set the earth's foundations. I seek Your wisdom in all aspects of my life. Help me to make decisions that are aligned with Your will and to build my life on Your truth. Mark 8:29 shows Peter acknowledging Jesus as the Messiah. I acknowledge Jesus as my Savior and Lord. Help me to follow Him faithfully and to live out my faith in a way that reflects Your love and truth. Romans 8:29 says that You predestined us to be conformed to the image of Your Son. I pray that You transform me more into the likeness of Jesus. Help me to grow in character and in love, reflecting His grace and compassion in all that I do. Thank You, Lord, for Your guidance and for the transformation You bring to our lives. I trust in Your plans and seek to follow You more closely each day.

In Jesus' present name I pray, Amen

AUGUST 30

John 8:30 (NKJV): As [Jesus] spoke these things, many believed in him.

Proverbs 8:30 (NIV): Then I was constantly at his side, I was filled with delight day after day, rejoicing always in his presence.

Exodus 8:30 (NIV): Then Moses left Pharaoh and prayed to the LORD.

--- PRAYER ---

Dear Heavenly Father, Elohim Shama (The God Who Hears),

I come to You with a heart open to Your guidance and grace. Your Word in John 8:30 tells us that many believed in Jesus because of His words. I pray that Your Word will continue to strengthen my faith and lead me closer to You. Help me to believe deeply in Your promises and to live in a way that reflects that belief. Proverbs 8:30 speaks of wisdom being beside You as You created the world. I seek Your wisdom to guide my decisions and actions. Please help me to embrace Your wisdom and to apply it in my daily life, trusting in Your perfect understanding. Exodus 8:30 describes how You answered the prayers of Moses and delivered the Israelites. I ask for Your intervention and help in my own life. Please hear my prayers, guide me through challenges, and deliver me from difficulties. Thank You, Lord, for Your constant presence and for the wisdom and guidance You provide. I place my trust in You and seek to follow Your will with a heart full of faith.

In the listening name of Jesus I pray, Amen

AUGUST 31

Romans 8:31 (KJV): What shall we then say to these things? If God be for us, who can be against us?

Matthew 8:31 (NIV): The demons begged Jesus, "If you drive us out, send us into the herd of pigs."

Proverbs 8:31 (KJV): Rejoicing in the habitable part of his earth; and my delights were with the sons of men.

───────────────────── **PRAYER** ─────────────────────

Dear Heavenly Father, El Sela (God My Rock),

I come before You with a heart full of trust and gratitude. Romans 8:31 reminds me that if You are for us, no one can be against us. I place my trust in Your protection and support. Help me to remember that with You on my side, I can face any challenge with confidence. In Matthew 8:31, the demons begged Jesus not to send them away, showing their recognition of His authority. I recognize Your supreme authority over all things. Please help me to trust in Your control over every situation in my life and to seek Your guidance in all that I do. Proverbs 8:31 speaks of wisdom rejoicing in God's creation. I ask for Your wisdom to guide me in my decisions and actions. Help me to find joy in following Your wisdom and to live a life that reflects Your love and understanding. Thank You, Lord, for Your constant support, guidance, and the wisdom You provide. I trust in Your promises and seek to follow You faithfully each day.

In Jesus' trusting name I pray, Amen

SEPTEMBER 1

I speak of God's marvelous work

Psalm 9:1 (NLT): I will praise you, Lord, with all my heart; I will tell of all the marvelous things you have done.

Genesis 9:1 (NIV): Then God blessed Noah and his sons, saying to them, "Be fruitful and increase in number and fill the earth."

Romans 9:1 (NKJV): I tell the truth in Christ, I am not lying, my conscience also bearing me witness in the Holy Spirit.

Ecclesiastes 9:1 (ESV): This, too, I carefully explored: Even though the actions of godly and wise people are in God's hands, no one knows whether God will show them favor.

 **PRAYER**

Dear Heavenly Father, El Roi (The God Who Sees Me),

I come to You with a grateful heart, seeking Your presence and guidance. Psalm 9:1 reminds me to give thanks to You with all my heart and to tell of Your wonderful deeds. I thank You for Your many blessings and the ways You work in my life. Help me to always remember to praise You for Your goodness. In Genesis 9:1, You blessed Noah and his family and commanded them to be fruitful and multiply. I pray for Your blessings upon my life and the work I do. Help me to live in a way that honors You and to use the gifts and opportunities You have given me for Your glory. Romans 9:1 speaks of Paul's deep sincerity in his faith. I pray for a sincere and genuine faith in You, Lord. Help me to live out my faith with integrity and to be steadfast in my commitment to You. Ecclesiastes 9:1 tells us that we do not know what the future holds, but You are in control of all things. I trust in Your plan for my life, even when I cannot see the path ahead. Help me to rely on Your wisdom and to find peace in knowing that You are guiding me. Thank You, Lord, for Your constant presence, blessings, and guidance. I place my trust in You and seek to follow Your will each day.

In Jesus' miraculous name I pray, Amen

SEPTEMBER 2

Isaiah 9:2 (NIV): The people walking in darkness have seen a great light; on those living in the land of deep darkness a light has dawned.

Psalm 9:2 (NLT): I will be filled with joy because of you. I will sing praises to your name, O Most High.

2 Chronicles 9:2 (NLT): Solomon had answers for all of her questions; Nothing was too hard for him to explain to her.

Ecclesiastes 9:2 (NLT): The same destiny ultimately awaits everyone, whether righteous or wicked, good or bad, ceremonially clean or unclean, religious or irreligious. Good people receive the same treatment as sinners, and people who make promises to God are treated like people who don't.

PRAYER

Dear Heavenly Father, El Shaddai (The All-Sufficient One, God Almighty),

I come before You with a heart full of gratitude and hope. Isaiah 9:2 speaks of the light coming into darkness and bringing joy. I pray for Your light to shine brightly in my life, guiding me through any darkness and filling my heart with Your joy and peace. In Psalm 9:2, the psalmist declares that we can find joy and delight in You. I thank You for the joy You bring into my life and ask that You help me to find delight in Your presence each day. May Your joy strengthen me and help me to share Your love with others. 2 Chronicles 9:2 tells of the wisdom and understanding that came to Solomon through You. I seek Your wisdom in all areas of my life. Please grant me understanding and discernment to make choices that honor You and reflect Your truth. Ecclesiastes 9:2 reminds us that everything is in Your hands, and that our future is under Your control. I trust in Your sovereignty over my life and ask for Your guidance as I navigate each day. Help me to trust in Your plan and to find peace in Your control. Thank You, Lord, for Your light, joy, wisdom, and guidance. I place my trust in You and seek to follow You faithfully.

In Jesus' joyful name I pray, Amen

SEPTEMBER 3

I GO TO THE LORD WITH CONFESSION AND PRAYER

Proverbs 9:3 (NLT): She has sent her servants to invite everyone to come. She calls out from the heights overlooking the city.

Psalm 9:3 (NLT): My enemies turned back; they stumble and perish before you.

Nehemiah 9:3 (NIV): They stood where they were and read from the Book of the Law of the LORD their God for a quarter of the day, and spent another quarter in confession and in worshiping the LORD their God.

Daniel 9:3 (NIV): So I turned to the Lord God and pleaded with him in prayer and petition, and fasting and in sackcloth and ashes.

 PRAYER

Dear Heavenly Father, Jehovah Ezrah (The LORD My Helper),

I come to You with a heart open to Your guidance and grace. Proverbs 9:3 tells us that wisdom calls out and invites us to seek understanding. I pray for Your wisdom to lead me in all that I do. Help me to hear Your call and to follow Your guidance with a willing heart. In Psalm 9:3, it says that when I seek You, my enemies will be put to flight, and I will find peace. I ask for Your protection from any difficulties or fears I may face. Surround me with Your strength and peace, and help me to trust in Your power. Nehemiah 9:3 shows how the people of Israel worshiped and confessed their sins before You. I come to You with a sincere heart, seeking Your forgiveness and guidance. Help me to worship You truly and to be transformed by Your presence. Daniel 9:3 speaks of Daniel seeking You earnestly in prayer and fasting. I pray for the same earnestness and commitment in my own prayers. Guide me in my times of prayer and help me to seek You with a full heart, trusting in Your answers and Your perfect timing. Thank You, Lord, for Your wisdom, protection, and the opportunity to come before You in prayer. I trust in Your promises and seek to follow You faithfully each day.

In Jesus' helping name I pray, Amen

SEPTEMBER 4

Psalm 9:4 (NLT): For you have judged in my favor; For your throne you have judged with fairness.

Ecclesiastes 9:4 (NIV): Anyone who is among the living has hope—even a live dog is better off than a dead lion!

Proverbs 9:4 (NLT): "Come in with me," she urges the simple. To those who lack good judgment.

Numbers 9:4 (NIV): So Moses told the Israelites to celebrate the Passover.

Daniel 9:4 (NLT): I prayed to the LORD my God and confessed; "O Lord, You are a great and awesome God! You always fulfill your covenant and keep your promises of unfailing love to those who love you and obey your commands.

PRAYER

Dear Heavenly Father, El Yeshuati (The God of My Salvation),

I come before You with a heart full of gratitude and trust. Psalm 9:4 reminds me that You uphold justice and have judged my enemies fairly. I thank You for Your righteous judgments and ask that You help me trust in Your justice and fairness in all aspects of my life. In Ecclesiastes 9:4, it speaks of hope being found in the living, for there is still a chance to live wisely. I pray for Your guidance to make wise choices and to live each day in a way that honors You. Help me to find hope and purpose in the life You've given me. Proverbs 9:4 describes wisdom calling out to those who are simple, inviting them to gain understanding. I seek Your wisdom and understanding in all areas of my life. Please open my heart to Your guidance and help me grow in wisdom. Numbers 9:4 tells of the Israelites observing the Passover as instructed by You. I ask for Your help in following Your commands and in staying true to Your Word. Help me to obey Your teachings and to remember the importance of Your guidance in my life. Daniel 9:4 shows Daniel's earnest prayer and confession before You. I come to You with a sincere heart, asking for Your forgiveness and guidance. Help me to pray earnestly and to seek Your presence in all things.

In Jesus' favorable name I pray, Amen

SEPTEMBER 5

I observe the Lord's festivals

Psalm 9:5 (NIV): You have rebuked the nations and destroyed the wicked; You have blotted out their name for ever and ever.

John 9:5 (NLT): "But while I am here in the world, I am the light of the world."

Matthew 9:5 (ESV): "For which is easier, to say, 'Your sins are forgiven you,' or to say, 'Arise and walk?'"

Hosea 9:5 (NLT): What then will you do on festival days? How will you observe the Lord's festivals?

 PRAYER

Dear Heavenly Father, El HaNe'eman (The God Who Is Faithful),

I come before You with a heart full of trust and gratitude. Psalm 9:5 reminds me that You have rebuked the nations and judged the wicked. I thank You for Your justice and fairness. Help me to trust in Your righteous judgments and to seek Your guidance in my own life. In John 9:5, Jesus says that He is the light of the world. I pray for Your light to shine brightly in my life, guiding me through any darkness and helping me to see clearly. Please help me to follow Your light and to reflect Your truth in all I do. Matthew 9:5 shows Jesus asking if it is easier to forgive sins or to heal a man. I am grateful for the forgiveness and healing You offer. I pray for Your healing touch in my life, both physically and spiritually. Help me to experience Your grace and to extend that grace to others. Hosea 9:5 speaks of the rejoicing and feasting of God's people. I ask for Your joy and peace to fill my heart. Help me to celebrate Your blessings and to find joy in Your presence, even in the midst of life's challenges. Thank You, Lord, for Your justice, light, forgiveness, and joy. I place my trust in You and seek to follow You faithfully each day.

In Jesus' trusting name I pray, Amen

SEPTEMBER 6

I HAVE GOOD JUDGMENT FROM THE LORD

Isaiah 9:6 (ESV): For to us a child is born; to us a son is given; and the government shall be upon his shoulder, and his name shall be called Wonderful Counselor, Mighty God, Everlasting Father, Prince of Peace.

Amos 9:6 (NLT): The LORD's home reaches up to the heavens, while its foundation is on the earth. He draws up water from the oceans and pours it down as rain on the land. The LORD is his name.

Leviticus 9:6 (NLT): And Moses said, "This is what the LORD has commanded you to do so that the glory of the LORD may appear to you."

Proverbs 9:6 (NLT): Leave your simple ways behind, and begin to live; learn to use good judgment.

Jermiah 9:6 (NLT): They pile lie upon lie and utterly refuse to acknowledge me," says the LORD.

PRAYER

Dear Heavenly Father, El Yerushalem (God of Jerusalem),

I come before You with a heart full of hope and faith. Isaiah 9:6 reminds us that You have given us a Wonderful Counselor, Mighty God, Everlasting Father, and Prince of Peace in Jesus. I thank You for this incredible gift and ask for Your peace to reign in my heart and life. Help me to seek Your counsel in all things and to experience Your mighty presence each day. In Amos 9:6, we see Your authority over creation and the building of the heavens and the earth. I am in awe of Your power and sovereignty. I trust in Your ability to guide and support me through every situation, knowing that You are in control of all things. Leviticus 9:6 describes the offerings and sacrifices that were made to You. I pray that my life may be a living offering to You, pleasing in Your sight. Help me to live in a way that honors You and reflects Your love and grace. Proverbs 9:6 speaks of wisdom calling us to leave our simple ways and find understanding. I ask for Your wisdom to guide me in my decisions and actions. Help me to grow in understanding and to walk in Your truth, leaving behind anything that does not align with Your will. Jeremiah 9:6 tells us that we are surrounded by deceit and unfaithfulness. I ask for Your protection and guidance in navigating through life's challenges. Help me to stay true to You and to live with integrity, trusting in Your truth amidst a world of confusion.

In Jesus' pleasing name I pray, Amen

I HAVE A JOYFUL, MERRY HEART

Isaiah 9:7 NIV): Of the greatness of his government and peace there will be no end.

Psalm 9:7 (NLT): But the LORD reigns forever, executing judgment from His throne.

Mark 9:7 (KJV): And a cloud overshadowed them, and a voice came out of the cloud, saying, "This is my beloved Son. Hear him!"

Genesis 9:7 (NLT): Now be fruitful and multiply, and repopulate the earth.

Ecclesiastes 9:7 (NKJV): Go, eat your bread with joy, and drink your wine with a merry heart; for God has already accepted your works.

PRAYER

Dear Heavenly Father, Elohay Selichot (The God Who Is Ready to Forgive),

I come before You with a heart full of gratitude and trust. Isaiah 9:7 speaks of the increase of Your government and peace with no end. I thank You for the promise of Your eternal reign and ask that Your peace would fill my life, helping me to experience Your calm and stability in every situation. In Psalm 9:7, we are reminded that You reign forever and have established Your throne for judgment. I am grateful for Your justice and sovereignty. Help me to trust in Your righteous rule and to find comfort in knowing that You are in control of all things. Mark 9:7 recounts how Your voice from the cloud affirmed Jesus as Your beloved Son. I ask for Your reassurance and guidance as I follow Jesus. Help me to listen to His teachings and to grow closer to Him each day. Genesis 9:7 includes Your command to be fruitful and multiply, blessing us with life and growth. I pray for Your blessings upon my endeavors and relationships. Help me to grow in Your grace and to make a positive impact in the world around me. Ecclesiastes 9:7 encourages us to enjoy life and the good gifts You provide. I thank You for the blessings in my life and ask that You help me to appreciate and make the most of each day. Fill my heart with joy and gratitude for the life You have given me. Thank You, Lord, for Your eternal peace, justice, and guidance. I place my trust in You and seek to follow Your will faithfully each day.

In Jesus' forgiving name I pray, Amen

SEPTEMBER 8

God provides for me generously

Ecclesiastes 9:8 (ESV): Let your garments be always white. Let not oil be lacking on your head.

Psalm 9:8 (NLT): He will judge the world with justice and rule the nation with fairness.

Proverbs 9:8 (NLT): So don't bother correcting mockers; they will only hate you. But correct the wise, and they will love you.

2 Corinthians 9:8 (NLT): And God will generously provide all you need. Then you will always have everything you need and plenty left over to share with others.

PRAYER

Dear Heavenly Father, Elohim Ahavah (The God Who Loves),

I come before You with a heart open to Your guidance and grace. Ecclesiastes 9:8 tells us to let our garments always be white and to keep our hearts joyful. I ask for Your help in living a life that reflects Your purity and joy. Fill me with Your peace and help me to maintain a heart of joy and gratitude. In Psalm 9:8, we are reminded that You will judge the world with righteousness and fairness. I trust in Your justice and ask for Your wisdom to guide me in my decisions and actions. Help me to act with integrity and to seek justice in all I do. Proverbs 9:8 advises us not to rebuke a mocker, as they will hate us, but to instruct the wise and they will love us. I pray for wisdom in how I interact with others. Help me to share Your truth with love and to seek to build up those who are open to Your guidance. 2 Corinthians 9:8 promises that You will provide us with all we need and more, so that we can be generous in every way. I am grateful for Your provision and ask for Your help to be generous and kind in my interactions with others. Knowing I will never be in need. Use me as a vessel of Your blessings to make a positive impact in the world. Thank You, Lord, for Your righteousness, provision, and guidance. I trust in Your promises and seek to follow You faithfully each day.

In Jesus' generous name I pray, Amen

GOD IS MY SHELTER

Proverbs 9:9 (NRSV): Give instruction to the wise, and they will become wiser still, teach the righteous and they will gain in learning.

Psalm 9:9 (NLT): The LORD is a shelter for the oppressed, and refuge in times of trouble.

Mark 9:9 (NKJV): Now as they came down from the mountain, He commanded them that they should tell no one the things they had seen, till the Son of Man had risen from the dead.

Genesis 9:9 (NLT): I hereby confirm my covenant with you and your descendants.

Daniel 9:9 (NIV): But the Lord our God is merciful and forgiving, even though we have rebelled against him.

PRAYER

Dear Heavenly Father, Georgos (The Gardener),

I come before You with a heart open to Your wisdom and guidance. Proverbs 9:9 encourages us to give instruction to the wise, and they will become wiser. I ask for Your guidance in seeking and sharing wisdom. Help me to grow in understanding and to be a source of wisdom and encouragement to others. In Psalm 9:9, it is written that You are a refuge for the oppressed and a stronghold in times of trouble. I thank You for being my refuge and ask for Your protection and support in any difficulties I face. Help me to find comfort and strength in Your presence. Mark 9:9 recounts the transfiguration of Jesus and the command to keep it quiet until the right time. I pray for the discernment to know when to speak and when to remain silent. Guide me in how I share Your truth and in how I listen to Your voice. Genesis 9:9 speaks of Your covenant with Noah and his descendants. I am grateful for Your promises and ask for Your guidance in my life. Help me to trust in Your covenant and to live in a way that honors You and reflects Your faithfulness. Daniel 9:9 shows that You are merciful and forgiving, even when we have sinned. I ask for Your forgiveness and mercy in my life. Help me to walk in Your ways and to experience the depth of Your grace and compassion. Thank You, Lord, for Your wisdom, protection, guidance, and mercy.

In Jesus' shielding name I pray, Amen

SEPTEMBER 10

Psalm 9:10 (NLT): Those who know your name trust in you, for you, O LORD, do not abandon those who search for you.

Proverbs 9:10 (NIV): The fear of the LORD is the beginning of wisdom, and knowledge of the Holy One is understanding.

Ecclesiastes 9:10 (NKJV): Whatever your hand finds to do, do it with your might; for there is no work or device or knowledge or wisdom in the grave where you are going.

Job 9:10 (NKJV): He does great things past finding out, yes, wonders without numbers.

PRAYER

Dear Heavenly Father, Akal Esh (Consuming Fire),

I come to You with a heart full of faith and gratitude. Psalm 9:10 tells us that those who know You trust in You because You have never forsaken those who seek You. I thank You for Your constant presence and faithfulness. Help me to deepen my trust in You and to experience Your unwavering support in all areas of my life. In Proverbs 9:10, we are reminded that the fear of the Lord is the beginning of wisdom, and knowledge of the Holy One is understanding. I pray for Your wisdom to guide me. Help me to understand and respect Your ways and to grow in my relationship with You and Holy Spirit. Ecclesiastes 9:10 encourages us to do whatever we do with all our might, knowing that our time on earth is limited. I ask for Your strength and motivation to do everything with excellence and dedication. Help me to make the most of the opportunities You give me and to honor You in all my efforts. Job 9:10 speaks of Your great wonders, which are beyond understanding. I am in awe of Your greatness and power. Help me to trust in Your wisdom and to recognize Your mighty works in my life. Even when I do not understand everything, may I find peace in knowing that You are in control. Thank You, Lord, for Your faithfulness, wisdom, strength, and greatness. I place my trust in You and seek to follow Your will faithfully each day.

In Jesus' wondrous name I pray, Amen

SEPTEMBER 11

I sing praises to God

Proverbs 9:11 (NLT): Wisdom will multiply your days and add years to your life.

Psalm 9:11 (NLT): Sing praises to the LORD who reigns in Jerusalem. Tell the world about his unforgettable deeds.

Romans 9:11 (KJV): For the children being not yet born, neither having done any good or evil, that the purpose of God according to election might stand, not of works, but of him that calleth.

2 Corinthians 9:11 (NLT): Yes, you will be enriched in every way so that you can always be generous. And when we take your gifts to those who need them, they will thank God.

PRAYER

Dear Heavenly Father, Jehovah Uzzi (The LORD My Strength),

I come before You with a heart full of faith and gratitude. Proverbs 9:11 says that wisdom will add length of days to us and give us years of life. I pray for Your wisdom to guide me each day, that I may live a life that honors You and is filled with purpose and longevity. In Psalm 9:11, we are encouraged to sing praises to You and to proclaim Your deeds among the nations. I thank You for Your blessings and ask for the courage to share Your goodness with others. Help me to be a witness of Your love and faithfulness in all that I do. Romans 9:11 speaks of how Your choices and plans are made before we even act, showing Your sovereign will. I trust in Your perfect plan for my life and ask for Your guidance in understanding and following Your will. Help me to rely on Your timing and trust in Your decisions. 2 Corinthians 9:11 promises that You will enrich us in every way so that we can be generous on every occasion. I am grateful for Your provision and ask for Your help to be generous and giving. Let my life reflect Your generosity and may I use the resources You provide to bless others. Thank You, Lord, for Your wisdom, guidance, and provision. I place my trust in You and seek to follow Your will faithfully each day.

In the praiseful name of Jesus I pray, Amen

I AM BECOMING WISE

Genesis 9:12 (NLT): Then God said, "I am giving you a sign of my covenant with you and with all living creatures, for all generations to come."

Proverbs 9:12 (NLT): If you become wise, you will be the one to benefit. If you scorn wisdom, you will be the one to suffer.

Matthew 9:12 (NLT): When Jesus heard this, he said, "Healthy people don't need a doctor—sick people do."

Ecclesiastes 9:12 (NKJV): For man also does not know his time: like fish taken in a cruel net, like birds caught in a snare. So the sons of men are snared in an evil time, when it falls suddenly upon them.

PRAYER

Dear Heavenly Father, Immanuel (God With Us),

I come before You with a heart full of gratitude and faith. Genesis 9:12 speaks of Your covenant with Noah and all living creatures, a sign of Your everlasting promise. I thank You for Your unending faithfulness and ask that You remind me of Your promises and keep me steadfast in my trust in You. Proverbs 9:12 tells us that if we are wise, we will benefit ourselves, and if we are mockers, we will suffer. I pray for Your wisdom to guide my actions and decisions. Help me to live wisely and to make choices that reflect Your teachings, benefiting myself and others. Matthew 9:12 shows Jesus saying that He came to call not the righteous, but sinners. I am grateful for Your grace and forgiveness. Help me to recognize my need for Your mercy and to extend that grace to others, living a life that reflects Your love and compassion. Ecclesiastes 9:12 reminds us that we do not know what will happen tomorrow, but we can trust in Your plan. I ask for Your guidance in navigating each day, knowing that I can rely on Your wisdom and timing. Help me to embrace each moment with faith and confidence in Your care. Thank You, Lord, for Your covenant, wisdom, grace, and guidance. I place my trust in You and seek to follow Your will faithfully each day.

In Jesus' name I pray, Amen

SEPTEMBER 13

Genesis 9:13 (NIV): I have set my rainbow in the clouds, and it will be the sign of the covenant between me and the earth.

Matthew 9:13 (NKJV): "But go and learn what this means: 'I desire mercy and not sacrifice.' For I did not come to call the righteous, but sinners, to repentance."

Psalm 9:13 (NLT): LORD, have mercy on me. See how my enemies torment me. Snatch me back from the jaws of death.

Proverbs 9:13 (AMP): The foolish woman is restless and noisy; she is naïve and easily misled and thoughtless, and knows nothing at all [of eternal value].

PRAYER

Dear Heavenly Father, Basilei ton Aionon (King Eternal),

I come before You with a heart full of gratitude and trust. Genesis 9:13 speaks of Your rainbow as a sign of Your covenant with the earth, a symbol of Your promise and faithfulness. I thank You for Your unchanging promises and ask that You remind me of Your commitment to us, especially during challenging times. In Matthew 9:13, Jesus tells us that He came to call sinners, not the righteous. I am grateful for Your grace and mercy. Help me to recognize my own need for forgiveness and to extend that same grace to others. Let my life reflect Your compassion and love. Psalm 9:13 says that You see our troubles and lift us from the gates of death. I ask for Your comfort and support in times of distress. Please lift me up and guide me through any difficulties I face, giving me strength and hope. Proverbs 9:13 warns us about the folly of the woman who is loud and undisciplined. I pray for wisdom and self-control in my own life. Help me to be wise in my speech and actions, and to seek Your guidance in living a disciplined and respectful life. Thank You, Lord, for Your covenant, grace, comfort, and wisdom. I trust in Your care and seek to follow Your will faithfully each day.

In Jesus' graceful name I pray, Amen

SEPTEMBER 14

I PREACH THE GOOD NEWS

Hebrews 9:14 (ESV): How much more will the blood of Christ, who through the eternal Spirit offered himself without blemish to God, purify our conscience from dead works to serve the living God.

Acts 9:14 (ESV): And here he has authority from the chief priests to bind all who call on Your name.

Romans 9:14 (NKJV): What shall we say then? Is there unrighteousness with God? Certainly not!

1 Corinthians 9:14 (NLT): In the same way, the Lord ordered that those who preach the Good News should be supported by those who benefit from it.

PRAYER

Dear Heavenly Father, Migdol Oz (Strong Tower),

I come before You with a heart full of gratitude and trust. In Hebrews 9:14, we learn about the cleansing power of Christ's sacrifice, which purifies our conscience from dead works to serve the living God. I am grateful for the forgiveness and new life You offer through Jesus. Help me to live a life that reflects Your grace and serves You faithfully. Acts 9:14 recounts how Saul (later Paul) was known to be a persecutor of the church but was transformed by Your grace. I am reminded of Your power to change hearts and lives. I pray for Your transformative work in my own life and in the lives of those around me. Romans 9:14 addresses the idea of God's justice and mercy. I trust in Your righteous judgments and ask for Your guidance to understand and follow Your will. Help me to recognize Your fairness and to respond with gratitude and obedience. 1 Corinthians 9:14 speaks of the Lord's command that those who preach the gospel should receive their living from the gospel. I pray for those who are serving You through ministry and ask that You provide for their needs. Help me to support and encourage those who are devoted to spreading Your message.

In the Good News of Jesus' name I pray, Amen

SEPTEMBER 15

I AM FREE

Genesis 9:15 (NIV): I will remember my covenant between me and you and all living creatures of every kind. Never again will the waters become a flood to destroy all life.

Ecclesiastes 9:15 (NLT): A poor, wise man knew how to save the town, and so it was rescued. But afterward no one thought to thank him.

Mark 9:15 (NKJV): Immediately, when they saw [Jesus], all the people were greatly amazed, and running to Him, greeted Him.

Hebrews 9:15 (NIV): For this reason Christ is the mediator of a new covenant, that those who are called may receive the promise eternal inheritance—now that he has died as a ransom to set them free from the sins committed under the first covenant.

PRAYER

Dear Heavenly Father, Shaphat (Judge),

I come before You with a grateful and open heart. Genesis 9:15 speaks of Your promise to never again destroy the earth with a flood. I thank You for Your faithfulness and for the assurance of Your unending covenant. Help me to trust in Your promises and find peace in Your constant presence. Ecclesiastes 9:15 tells of a wise man who saved a city through his wisdom, even though he was poor and unknown. I ask for Your wisdom in my own life, so that I can make a positive impact on those around me. Help me to use the gifts You've given me to serve others and to act wisely in all circumstances. Mark 9:15 describes how people were amazed when they saw Jesus with His disciples. I pray that my life may reflect Your grace and power in such a way that others are drawn to You. Help me to live in a manner that shows Your love and draws people closer to Your truth. Hebrews 9:15 speaks of Jesus being the mediator of a new covenant, bringing redemption and forgiveness. I am grateful for the new covenant You offer through Christ. Help me to fully embrace the grace and forgiveness You provide, and to live in the freedom of Your salvation. Thank You, Lord, for Your promises, wisdom, grace, and the new covenant through Jesus. I place my trust in You and seek to follow Your will faithfully each day.

In the free name of Jesus I pray, Amen

Psalm 9:16 (NIV): The LORD is known by his acts of justice: the wicked are ensnared by the work of their hands.

Romans 9:16 (NIV): It does not, therefore, depend on human desire of effort, but on God's mercy.

Exodus 9:16 (NIV): But I have raised you up for this very purpose, that I might show you my power and that my name might be proclaimed in all the earth.

Genesis 9:16 (NIV): Whenever the rainbow appears in the clouds, I will see it and remember the everlasting covenant between God and all living creatures of every kind on the earth.

PRAYER

Dear Heavenly Father, YAH (Self-Existent, I AM),

I come before You with a heart full of faith and gratitude. Psalm 9:16 reminds us that You are known by the judgments You make and that You are a just and righteous God. I thank You for Your fairness and ask that You help me to trust in Your just ways against the wicked, knowing that You are always right and true. Romans 9:16 tells us that it does not depend on human will or effort, but on Your mercy. I am grateful for Your grace and mercy in my life. Help me to rely on Your kindness rather than my own strength, and to recognize that all good things come from Your love. Exodus 9:16 speaks of You raising up Pharaoh to show Your power and declare Your name throughout the earth. I pray that Your power be evident in my life, and that I may honor Your name through my actions and words. Help me to be a witness of Your greatness and to reflect Your glory. Genesis 9:16 talks about the rainbow being a sign of Your covenant with all living creatures, a reminder of Your promise and faithfulness. I am thankful for this sign of Your enduring commitment. Help me to remember Your promises and to trust in Your unchanging love. Thank You, Lord, for Your justice, mercy, power, and faithfulness. I place my trust in You and seek to follow Your will each day, reflecting Your love and grace in my life.

In Jesus' purposeful name I pray, Amen

SEPTEMBER 17

I AM GOD'S SERVANT

Psalm 9:17 (NLT): The wicked will go down to the grave. This is the fate of all the nations who ignore God.

Genesis 9:17 (NIV): So God said to Noah, "This is the sign of the covenant I have established between me and all life on earth."

Daniel 9:17 (NLT): O our God, hear your servant's prayer! Listen as I plead. For your own sake, Lord, smile again on your desolate sanctuary.

Ecclesiastes 9:17 (NLT): Better to hear the quiet words of a wise person than the shout of a foolish king.

1 Corinthians 9:17 (NIV): If I preach voluntarily, I have a reward; If not voluntarily, I am simply discharging the trust committed to me.

PRAYER

Dear Heavenly Father, Elohay Selichot (The God Who Is Ready to Forgive),

I come before You with a heart full of faith and gratitude. Psalm 9:17 reminds us that the wicked will return to the grave, but You reign forever. I am thankful for Your eternal sovereignty and ask for Your strength to stay righteous and steadfast in a world that can be challenging. Genesis 9:17 speaks of the rainbow as a sign of Your covenant with all living creatures. I am grateful for this reminder of Your promises and faithfulness. Help me to remember Your enduring commitment to us and to trust in Your plans for my life. Daniel 9:17 is a prayer of Daniel asking for God's mercy and favor upon the desolate sanctuary. I, too, seek Your mercy and favor in my life. Please guide me, protect me, and bless me with Your grace as I navigate through the challenges I face. Ecclesiastes 9:17 speaks of the quiet words of the wise being more effective than the shouts of a ruler among fools. I pray for wisdom in my speech and actions. Help me to communicate with humility and insight, valuing quiet wisdom over hasty or loud responses. 1 Corinthians 9:17 talks about Paul being entrusted with the stewardship of the gospel. I ask for Your guidance and strength as I preach voluntarily according to Your will. Help me to be a faithful steward of the gifts and responsibilities You've given me and that I will be rewarded for.

In Jesus' speaking name I pray, Amen

SEPTEMBER 18

Acts 9:18 (NIV): Immediately, something like scales fell from Saul's eyes, and he could see again. He got up and was baptized.

Psalm 9:18 (ESV): For the needy shall not always be forgotten, and the hope of the poor shall not perish forever.

Isaiah 9:18 (NLT): This wickedness is like a brushfire. It burns not only briers and thorns but also sets the forests ablaze. Its burning sends up clouds of smoke.

Ecclesiastes 9:18 (KJV): Wisdom is better than weapons of war; but one sinner destroyeth much good.

Romans 9:18 (NLT): So you see, God chooses to show mercy to some, and he chooses to harden the hearts of others so they refuse to listen.

PRAYER

Dear Heavenly Father, Jehovah Gibbor Milchamah (The LORD Mighty in Battle),

I come before You with a heart full of trust and gratitude. Acts 9:18 describes how scales fell from Saul's eyes, and he regained his sight. I thank You for the transformative power of Your healing and restoration. I ask that You open my eyes to see Your truth clearly and to experience Your healing in every area of my life. In Psalm 9:18, we are reminded that the needy will not always be forgotten, and the hope of the afflicted will not perish. I am grateful for Your promise to remember and care for those who are struggling. Please provide comfort, support, and hope to those who are in need, and help me to be a fountain of resources and help to others. Isaiah 9:18 speaks of wickedness spreading like a fire, consuming thorns and briers. I pray for Your protection from the influences of evil in my life. Help me to stay strong in Your Word and to resist temptation, so that I may remain faithful and pure in Your sight. Ecclesiastes 9:18 tells us that wisdom is better than weapons of war, but one sinner destroys much good. I pray for Your wisdom to guide my decisions and actions. Help me to use the wisdom You give me to build up rather than tear down, and to live a life that honors You. Romans 9:18 shows that You have mercy on whom You choose and harden whom You choose. I trust in Your sovereign will and ask for Your mercy in my life. Help me to accept and embrace Your plans, even when I do not fully understand them.

In Jesus' seeing name I pray, Amen

I FIGHT IN THE LORD'S ARMY

Psalm 9:19 (NIV): Arise, LORD, do not let mortal triumph: let the nations be judged in your presence.

Genesis 9:19 (KJV): These are the three sons of Noah: and of them was the whole earth overspread.

Deuteronomy 9:19 (NLT): I feared that the furious anger of the LORD, which turned him against you, would drive him to destroy you. But again he listened to me.

PRAYER

Dear Heavenly Father, Jehovah-Go'el (The LORD My Redeemer),

I come before You with a heart full of trust and gratitude. Psalm 9:19 says that You will not forsake those who seek You. I am thankful for Your promise to be with us and to never abandon us. Please remind me of Your constant presence, especially when I face challenges or feel alone. Genesis 9:19 mentions the descendants of Noah, who spread out across the earth. I am grateful for the diversity and richness of the world You created. Help me to embrace and appreciate the different cultures and people around me, and to build bridges of understanding and kindness. Deuteronomy 9:19 recounts how Moses prayed for Your anger to turn away from the people, recognizing their sins. I thank You for Your mercy and forgiveness. Please help me to seek Your forgiveness when I fall short and to extend grace to others, just as You have extended grace to me. Thank You, Lord, for Your faithful presence, the beauty of Your creation, and Your mercy. I place my trust in You and seek to follow Your will in all aspects of my life.

In Jesus' beautiful name I pray, Amen

SEPTEMBER 20

I AM FREE

Psalm 9:20 (NIV): Strike them with terror, LORD; let the nations know they are only mortal.

Hebrews 9:20 (NIV): [Moses] said, "This is the blood of the covenant, which God has commanded you to keep."

Luke 9:20 (NLT): Then [Jesus] asked the [disciples], "But who do you say I am?" Peter replied, "You are the Messiah sent from God!"

Genesis 9:20 (NLT): After the flood, Noah began to cultivate the ground, and he planted a vineyard.

PRAYER

Dear Heavenly Father, Jehovah-Makkeh (The LORD Who Strikes/Disciplines You),

I come before You with a humble and grateful heart. In Psalm 9:20, we are reminded that God will judge the nations and that we can find refuge in You. I thank You for being our righteous Judge and protector. Help me to find peace and security in Your justice and to trust in Your plans for the world and for my life. Hebrews 9:20 speaks of the covenant sealed by the blood of Christ, showing the seriousness of our commitment to You. I am grateful for the new covenant through Jesus, which brings redemption and grace. Help me to live in the light of this covenant, embracing the forgiveness and new life You offer. Luke 9:20 recounts how Peter declared that Jesus is the Messiah. I am thankful for this truth and acknowledge Jesus as my Savior and Lord. Strengthen my faith and help me to proclaim this truth in my daily life, reflecting Your love and grace to those around me. Genesis 9:20 describes Noah planting a vineyard and enjoying its fruit. I thank You for the blessings and provisions You give us. Help me to appreciate and make good use of the blessings in my life, and to be thankful for the simple joys You provide. Thank You, Lord, for Your compassion, justice, covenant, truth, and blessings. I place my trust in You and seek to follow Your will each day.

In Jesus' fruitful name I pray, Amen

SEPTEMBER 21

Revelation 9:21 (NKJV): And they did not repent of their murders or their sorceries or their sexual immorality or their thefts.

Matthew 9:21 (NLT): For she thought, "If I can just touch his robe, I will be healed."

Nehemiah 9:21 (NLT): For forty years you sustained them in the wilderness, and they lacked nothing. Their clothes did not wear out, and their feet did not swell.

―――――――――――――――― **PRAYER** ――――――――――――――――

Dear Heavenly Father, Sar Shalom (Prince of Peace),

I come before You with a heart open to Your guidance and grace. Revelation 9:21 mentions that despite many signs, people did not repent of their evil deeds. I pray for Your mercy and strength to turn away from any wrongs in my life and to follow Your path faithfully. Help me to recognize and correct any areas where I need to change and to live in a way that honors You. Matthew 9:21 recounts the faith of a woman who believed that touching Jesus' cloak would heal her. I thank You for the power of faith and Your ability to bring healing and transformation. Please strengthen my faith and help me to trust in Your ability to bring about miracles and changes in my life. Nehemiah 9:21 speaks of Your faithfulness in providing for the Israelites during their time in the desert. I am grateful for Your provision and care in every season of life. Please continue to provide for my needs and guide me through any challenges I face. Help me to trust in Your ongoing faithfulness, knowing I will never lack anything while in Your presence. Thank You, Lord, for Your guidance, healing, and provision. I place my trust in You and seek to follow Your will each day. Strengthen my faith and help me to live a life that reflects Your love and grace.

In Jesus' peaceful name I pray, Amen

SEPTEMBER 22

My faith has healed me

Acts 9:22 (ESV): But Saul increased all the more in strength, and confounded the Jews who lived in Damascus by proving that Jesus was the Christ.

Job 9:22 (KJV): It is all one thing; Therefore I say, "He destroys the blameless and the wicked."

Romans 9:22 (NIV): What if God, although choosing to show his wrath and make his power known, bore with great patience the objects of his wrath—prepared for destruction?

Matthew 9:22 (NIV): Jesus turned and saw her. "Take heart, daughter," He said. "Your faith has healed you." And the woman was healed at the moment.

 **PRAYER**

Dear Heavenly Father, Jehovah-Nissi (The LORD My Banner),

I come before You with a heart full of faith and gratitude. Acts 9:22 describes how Saul (Paul) grew more powerful in preaching about Jesus, confounding the Jews. I pray that You strengthen me in my own spiritual journey, helping me to grow in understanding and to be bold in sharing Your truth. Job 9:22 speaks of the profound truth that God is greater than we can understand, and that our ways are in Your hands. I am humbled by Your greatness and seek Your wisdom. Help me to trust in Your plan, even when I do not fully understand Your ways. Romans 9:22 talks about how God's patience endures with those who are prepared for destruction. I am thankful for Your patience and mercy in my life. Help me to be patient with others and to extend the same grace and forgiveness that You have shown me. Matthew 9:22 recounts the story of a woman who touched Jesus' cloak in faith and was healed instantly. I am inspired by her faith and ask for Your healing and transformation in my life. Strengthen my faith and help me to trust in Your power to bring about change and healing, not only to myself but to others. Thank You, Lord, for Your strength, patience, and healing power. I place my trust in You and seek to follow Your will faithfully each day, growing in Your grace and wisdom.

In Jesus' healing name I pray, Amen

SEPTEMBER 23

I AM PRECIOUS TO GOD

Mark 9:23 (NKJV): Jesus said to him, "If you can believe, all things are possible to him who believes."

Romans 9:23 (NIV): What if he did this to make the riches of his glory known to the object of his mercy.

Daniel 9:23 (NLT): The moment you began praying, a command was given. And now I am here to tell you what it was, for you are very precious of God. Listen carefully to the meaning of your vision.

Nehemiah 9:23 (NLT): You made their descendants as numerous as the stars in the sky and brought them into the land. You had promised to their ancestors.

Luke 9:23 (NLT): Then Jesus said to the crowd, "If any of you wants to be my follower, you must give up your own way, take up your cross daily, and follow me."

PRAYER

Dear Heavenly Father, Jehovah-Raah (The LORD Is My Shepherd),

I come before You with a heart full of faith and trust in Your power and promises. Mark 9:23 reminds us that everything is possible for one who believes. I ask for Your help in strengthening my faith. Romans 9:23 speaks of Your purpose to make known the riches of Your glory to those whom You have called. I am grateful for the privilege of being called by You. Please reveal more of Your glory and purpose in my life and help me to live in a way that reflects Your greatness and grace. Daniel 9:23 tells of how Daniel was greatly loved and received understanding because of his prayers. I pray that You grant me understanding and wisdom as I seek You in prayer. Help me to grow closer to You and to gain insight into Your will for my life. Nehemiah 9:23 recounts how You provided for the Israelites, guiding and caring for them. I thank You for Your ongoing care and guidance in my life. Lord, I thank You for Your faithfulness across all generations. Please continue to lead me, provide for my needs, and protect me as I walk with You. Luke 9:23 encourages us to take up our cross daily and follow You. I ask for the strength to live a life that honors You, embracing the challenges and sacrifices that come with following Christ.

In Jesus' precious name I pray, Amen

SEPTEMBER 24

I boast about the Lord

Mark 9:24 (NLT): The father instantly cried out, "I do believe, but help me overcome my unbelief!"

Romans 9:24 (NIV): Even us, whom he also called, not only from the Jews but also from the Gentiles?

Luke 9:24 (NLT): "If you try to hang on to your life, you will lose it. But if you give up your life for my sake, you will save it."

Jeremiah 9:24 (NIV): "But let the one who boasts boast about this: That they have the understanding to know me, that I am the Lord, who exercises kindness, justice and righteousness on earth, for in these I delight," declares the Lord.

PRAYER

Dear Heavenly Father, Jehovah-Rapha (The Lord Who Heals),

I come before You with a heart full of trust and humility. Mark 9:24 tells us about a father who cried out, "I do believe; help me overcome my unbelief!" I, too, ask for Your help in overcoming any doubts I may have. Strengthen my faith and help me to trust in You more fully, even when I struggle. Romans 9:24 speaks of how You have called us from among the Gentiles, showing Your grace and mercy to all. I am thankful for Your inclusive love and the opportunity to be part of Your family. Help me to embrace this grace and to live in a way that reflects Your love and mercy. Luke 9:24 says that whoever wants to save their life will lose it, but whoever loses their life for Your sake will save it. I pray for the strength to follow You wholeheartedly, even when it requires sacrifice. Help me to let go of my own desires and to seek Your will above all else. Jeremiah 9:24 highlights that You are the Lord who exercises kindness, justice, and righteousness on earth. I thank You for Your perfect attributes and ask that You help me to reflect Your kindness, justice, and righteousness in my daily life. Guide me to act with integrity and compassion in all that I do. Thank You, Lord, for Your grace and inclusion, Your guidance in living sacrificially, Your perfect attributes, and for Your help in overcoming doubts. I place my trust in You and seek to follow Your will faithfully each day.

In Jesus' believable name I pray, Amen

I WAS BLIND, BUT NOW I SEE

1 Corinthians 9:25 (NLT): All athletes are disciplined in their training. They do it to win a prize that will fade away, but we do it for an eternal prize.

Luke 9:25 (KJV): "For what is a man advantaged, if he gain the whole world, and lose himself, or be cast away?"

Mark 9:25 (NIV): When Jesus saw that a crowd was running to the scene, he rebuked the impure spirits. "You deaf and mute spirit," he said, "I command you, come out of him and never enter him again."

John 9:25 (NIV): He replied, "Whether he is a sinner or not, I don't know. One thing I do know. I was blind but now I see."

PRAYER

Dear Heavenly Father, Jehovah-Shammah (The LORD Is There),

I come before You with a heart full of trust and devotion. 1 Corinthians 9:25 speaks of the need for discipline to win a prize, reminding us that we must strive for self-control and perseverance. Help me to be disciplined in my spiritual life, focusing on the eternal rewards instead of the perishable rewards given on earth. In Luke 9:25, Jesus asks what good it is to gain the whole world but lose one's soul. I pray that You help me to prioritize my spiritual well-being above worldly gains. Guide me to seek what truly matters and to align my life with Your will, valuing eternal treasures over temporary successes. Mark 9:25 describes how Jesus rebuked an unclean spirit and brought healing. I ask for Your power to overcome any spiritual or personal struggles in my life. Please bring healing and restoration where it is needed and help me to experience Your deliverance and strength in every challenge I face. John 9:25 recounts a man who was healed of his blindness and boldly testified that "One thing I do know: I was blind but now I see." I am grateful for the ways You have worked in my life and pray for the courage to share my testimony of Your goodness. Help me to be a witness of Your transformative power and to proclaim Your works with boldness. Thank You, Lord, for Your guidance, healing, and the opportunity to live a disciplined life for You.

In Jesus' present name I pray, Amen

SEPTEMBER 26

I AM NOT ASHAMED

Luke 9:26 (NIV): "Whoever is ashamed of me and my words, the Son of Man will be ashamed of them when he comes in his glory and in the glory of Father and of holy angels."

Hebrews 9:26 (NLT): If that had been necessary, Christ would have had to die again and again, ever since the world began. But now, once for all time, he has appeared at the end of the age to remove sin by his own death as a sacrifice.

1 Corinthians 9:26 (NLT): So I run with purpose in every step. I am not just shadowboxing.

PRAYER

Dear Heavenly Father, Jehovah-Sabaoth (The LORD of Hosts),

I come before You with a heart open to Your guidance and grace. Luke 9:26 warns us that if we are ashamed of Jesus and His words, He will be ashamed of us before the Father. I pray for the courage to stand firm in my faith and to boldly live out and share Your truth to the nations. Help me to be unashamed of my relationship with You and to honor You in all aspects of my life. Hebrews 9:26 speaks of Jesus appearing once for all at the end of the ages to do away with sin by His sacrifice. I am deeply grateful for the gift of salvation and the forgiveness You have provided through Christ's sacrifice. Help me to live in the freedom and grace that His sacrifice has secured and to continually grow in my relationship with You. By the blood of Jesus we are set free. 1 Corinthians 9:26 talks about running the race with purpose, not aimlessly. I ask for Your guidance to run my spiritual race with clear purpose and focus. Help me to stay disciplined and committed to the path You have set before me, striving toward the goal of living a life that is pleasing to You. Thank You, Lord, for Your grace, salvation, and guidance. I place my trust in You and seek to follow Your will each day, running my spiritual race with purpose and dedication.

In Jesus' undeniable name I pray, Amen

SEPTEMBER 27

Job 9:27 (KJV): If I say, I will forget my complaint, I will leave off my heaviness, and comfort myself.

Mark 9:27 (NIV): But Jesus took him by the hand and helped him to his feet, and he stood up.

1 Corinthians 9:27 (KJV): But I keep under my body, and bring it into subjection: lest, when I have preached to others, I myself should be a castaway.

PRAYER

Dear Heavenly Father, Jehovah-Tzidkenu (The LORD Our Righteousness),

I come before You with a heart seeking Your guidance and strength. Job 9:27 speaks of Job wanting to forget his troubles and find peace. I, too, ask for Your peace in my life. Please help me to find comfort and rest, even in the midst of life's tragic challenges. Guide me to focus on Your promises and to find tranquility in Your presence. Mark 9:27 recounts how Jesus took the hand of a boy and lifted him up, and he was healed. I am grateful for Your miraculous healing power and ask that You extend Your hand to lift me up in times of weakness. Help me to trust in Your power to restore and renew me, both physically and spiritually. 1 Corinthians 9:27 talks about the need to discipline our bodies and keep them under control to avoid being disqualified from the race. I pray for the strength to practice self-discipline in my life. Help me to make choices that honor You and to stay focused on the path You have set before me. Thank You, Lord, for Your peace, healing, and the strength to live a disciplined life. I place my trust in You and seek to follow Your will faithfully each day.

In Jesus' helping name I pray, Amen

SEPTEMBER 28

Yes, Lord. Yes, Lord. Yes, yes, Lord!

Hebrews 9:28 (NKJV): So Christ was offered once to bear the sins of many. To those who eagerly wait for Him He will appear a second time, apart from sin, for salvation.

Acts 9:28 (NIV): So Saul [Paul] stayed with them and moved about freely in Jerusalem, speaking boldly in the name of the Lord.

Matthew 9:28 (NKJV): And when He had come into the house, the blind man came to Him. And Jesus said to them, "Do you believe that I am able to do this?" They said to Him, "Yes, Lord."

PRAYER

Dear Heavenly Father, Hode (Majesty),

I come before You with a heart full of faith and gratitude. Hebrews 9:28 reminds us that Christ was offered once to bear the sins of many and will appear a second time to bring salvation. I am grateful for the sacrifice of Jesus and the promise of His return. Help me to live in the hope of His second coming, eagerly awaiting the full realization of Your salvation. Acts 9:28 describes how Paul moved about freely in Jerusalem, preaching boldly about You. I pray for the courage and boldness to share Your message and to live out my faith with confidence. Please give me the strength to speak Your truth and to be a witness of Your love and grace in all areas of my life, no matter if I'm coming or going. Matthew 9:28 recounts the story of two blind men who came to Jesus in faith, and He healed them. I am thankful for Your power to heal and restore. Lord, you don't just heal one but two at once, or as many as Your will desires. I ask for Your healing touch in my own life and in the lives of those I care about. Help me to have faith in Your ability to bring about change and healing, both physically and spiritually. Thank You, Lord, for the sacrifice of Jesus, the opportunity to boldly proclaim Your truth, and Your healing power. I place my trust in You and seek to follow Your will each day, living with hope and faith in Your promises.

In Jesus' bold name I pray, Amen

I RAISE MY ARMS TO THE LORD

Matthew 9:29 (NIV): Then Jesus touched their eyes and said, "According to your faith let it be done to you."

Luke 9:29 (NKJV): As [Jesus] prayed, the appearance of His face was altered, and His robe became white and glistening.

Mark 9:29 (KJV): And Jesus said unto them, "This kind can come forth by nothing, but by prayer and fasting."

PRAYER

Dear Heavenly Father, Ner (Lamp),

I come before You with a heart full of faith and trust in Your power. Matthew 9:29 tells us that Jesus touched the eyes of the blind men and said, "According to your faith let it be done to you." I ask that You increase my faith and trust in Your ability to work in my life. Help me to believe deeply in Your promises and to see Your power at work. Even just the touch of Your hand can heal the blind. In Luke 9:29, we read about how Jesus was transformed, and His appearance became radiant. I pray for Your transforming power to work in my life, making me more like Christ each day. Let Your light shine through me, reflecting Your love and grace to those around me. Mark 9:29 recounts how Jesus said that some kinds of evil can only be driven out by prayer and fasting. I seek Your guidance and strength in my prayers and in controlling my flesh while fasting, especially when facing difficulties or challenges. Help me to rely on prayer and Your power to overcome obstacles and to grow in my spiritual life. Thank You, Lord, for Your transforming power, the strength You provide in prayer, and the increase of faith You offer. I place my trust in You and seek to follow Your will faithfully each day.

In Jesus' glistening name I pray, Amen

SEPTEMBER 30

Romans 9:30 (KJV): What shall we say then? That the Gentiles, which followed not after righteousness, have attained to righteousness, even the righteousness which is of faith.

John 9:30 (NIV): The man answered, "Now that is remarkable! You don't know where he comes from, yet he opened my eyes."

Matthew 9:30 (NKJV): And their eyes were opened. And Jesus sternly warned them, saying, "See that no one knows it."

PRAYER

Dear Heavenly Father, Maon (Dwelling Place),

I come before You with a heart full of gratitude and a desire to understand Your will. Romans 9:30 speaks of how Gentiles, who did not pursue righteousness, attained it by faith. I am grateful for Your grace that makes righteousness accessible to everyone through faith in Jesus. Help me to embrace this gift and to live according to Your righteousness. John 9:30 tells of a man who was healed of blindness and boldly testified that Jesus must be from God. I thank You for the many ways You have worked in my life and in the lives of those around me. Help me to see all the remarkable miracles that surround me each day, and to give God the glory for them. Matthew 9:30 describes how Jesus healed the blind men, and their eyes were opened. I pray for Your healing touch in my life, both physically and spiritually. Open my eyes to see Your truth more clearly and to recognize Your work in my life and the lives of all those around me. Thank You, Lord, for Your grace, the opportunity to share my testimony, and Your healing power. I place my trust in You and seek to follow Your will faithfully each day.

In Jesus' remarkable name I pray, Amen

OCTOBER 1

Matthew 10:1 (NIV): Jesus called his twelve disciples to him and gave them authority to drive out impure spirits and to heal every disease and sickness.

Proverbs 10:1 (NIV): The proverbs of Solomon: A wise son brings joy to his father, but a foolish son brings grief to his mother.

1 Corinthians 10:1 (NLT): I don't want you to forget, dear brothers and sisters, about our ancestors in the wilderness long ago. All of them were guided by a cloud that moved ahead of them and all of them walked through the sea on dry ground.

PRAYER

Dear Heavenly Father, Di Ou Ta Panta (My Everything),

I come before You with a heart full of gratitude and a desire to follow Your guidance. Matthew 10:1 says, "Jesus called his twelve disciples to him and gave them authority to drive out impure spirits and to heal every disease and sickness." Lord, I ask for Your authority and strength to overcome the challenges in my life and to be a source of healing and hope to those around me. Proverbs 10:1 teaches, "A wise son brings joy to his father, but a foolish son brings grief to his mother." Help me to live wisely and to make choices that bring joy to You, my Heavenly Father, and to those who care about me. Guide me in all that I do to be a reflection of Your love and wisdom. 1 Corinthians 10:1 reminds us, "For I do not want you to be ignorant of the fact, brothers and sisters, that our ancestors were all under the cloud and that they all passed through the sea" (NIV). Lord, help me to remember the faithfulness You showed to those who came before me. May their stories inspire me to trust in Your guidance and provision. Thank You for Your constant presence and guidance in my life. Help me to live according to Your will and to tell the coming generations of Your love.

In Jesus' all-encompassing name I pray, Amen

OCTOBER 2

I AM A WORKER IN THE HARVEST FIELD

Ecclesiastes 10:2 (NIV): The heart of the wise inclines to the right but the heart of the fool to the left.

Proverbs 10:2 (NLT): Tainted wealth has no lasting value, but right living can save your life.

2 Corinthians 10:2 (NIV): I beg you that when I come I may not have to be as bold as I expect to be toward some people who think that we live by the standards of this world.

John 10:2 (NIV): "The one who enters by the gate is the shepherd of the sheep."

Luke 10:2 (NIV): [Jesus] told them, "The harvest is plentiful, but the workers are few. Ask the Lord of the harvest, therefore, to send out workers into his harvest field."

PRAYER

Dear Heavenly Father, Gabahh (Transcendent),

I come to You with a heart seeking Your guidance and wisdom. As I reflect on Your Word, I ask for Your help in my life. Ecclesiastes 10:2 says, "The heart of the wise inclines to the right, but the heart of the fool to the left." Guide my heart to follow Your wisdom and lead me in the right direction. Help me to make choices that honor You. Proverbs 10:2 teaches, "Ill-gotten treasures have no lasting value, but righteousness delivers from death" (NIV). Help me to seek righteousness and to value the things that matter to You, rather than pursuing temporary gains. 2 Corinthians 10:2 says, "I beg you that when I come I may not have to be as bold as I expect to be toward some people who think that we live by the standards of this world." Give me the strength to stand firm in Your truth and to live according to Your standards, even when it is challenging. John 10:2 says, "The one who enters by the gate is the shepherd of the sheep." Jesus, You are the Good Shepherd. Lead me through the right path and protect me from the dangers around me. Luke 10:2 says, "He told them, 'The harvest is plentiful, but the workers are few. Ask the Lord of the harvest, therefore, to send out workers into his harvest field.'" Lord, I ask You to guide me in serving others and helping to spread Your love and truth. Thank You for Your guidance, wisdom, and protection. Help me to live according to Your will and to trust in Your care.

In Jesus' seeking name I pray, Amen

OCTOBER 3

2 Corinthians 10:3 (NIV): For though we live in the world, we do not wage war as the world does.

Proverbs 10:3 (NKJV): The LORD will not allow the righteous soul to famish, but He casts away the desire of the wicked.

Luke 10:3 (NIV): "Go! I am sending you out like lambs among wolves."

Daniel 10:3 (KJV): I ate no pleasant bread, neither came flesh nor wine in my mouth, neither did I anoint myself at all, till three whole weeks were fulfilled.

PRAYER

Dear Heavenly Father, Miqweh Yisrael (Hope of Israel),

I come to You with a humble heart, seeking Your guidance and strength. 2 Corinthians 10:3 says, "For though we live in the world, we do not wage war as the world does." Help me to remember that my struggles are spiritual and grant me the strength to fight with the weapons You provide, not those of this world. Proverbs 10:3 teaches, "The LORD does not let the righteous go hungry, but he thwarts the craving of the wicked" (NIV). Thank You for Your provision and protection. Help me to trust in Your promises and to rely on Your faithfulness to meet my needs. Luke 10:3 says, "Go! I am sending you out like lambs among wolves." As I go about my daily life, protect me from harm and guide me in the path You have set before me. Help me to be wise and courageous in all situations. Daniel 10:3 says, "I ate no choice food; no meat or wine touched my lips; and I used no lotions at all until the three weeks were over" (NIV). Help me to seek You with all my heart, to make sacrifices if necessary, and to remain focused on Your will. Thank You for Your guidance, protection, and provision. Help me to live according to Your will and to trust in Your strength and care.

In Jesus' hopeful name I pray, Amen

2 Corinthians 10:4 (NKJV): For the weapons of our warfare are not carnal but mighty through God to the pulling down of strongholds.

Romans 10:4 (NIV): Christ is the culmination of the law so that there may be righteousness for everyone who believes.

Proverbs 10:4 (NKJV): He who has a slack hand becomes poor, but the hand of the diligent makes rich.

Psalm 10:4 (NIV): In his pride the wicked man does not seek him; in all his thoughts there is no room for God.

John 10:4 (NIV): "When he has brought out all his own, he goes on ahead of them, and his sheep follow him because they know his voice."

PRAYER

Dear Heavenly Father, Theos Monos Sophos (The Only Wise God),

I come before You with a heart seeking Your strength and guidance. As I reflect on Your Word, I ask for Your help and support in my life. 2 Corinthians 10:4 says, "The weapons we fight with are not the weapons of the world. On the contrary, they have divine power to demolish strongholds" (NIV). Lord, equip me with Your divine strength to overcome the challenges I face and to break down any barriers that stand in the way of Your will. Romans 10:4 teaches of the righteousness we receive through Jesus Christ. Help me to live in a way that reflects this righteousness and to trust in Your grace. Proverbs 10:4 says not to be lazy or else you'll be poor. Instead work diligently in all that you do, so the Lord can bless you. Psalm 10:4 teaches, "In his pride the wicked man does not seek him; in all his thoughts there is no room for God." Keep me humble and always seeking You, Lord. Help me to guard against pride and to make space for You in all my thoughts and actions. John 10:4 says, we should try to hear your voice clearly and follow You. Lead me on the path You have prepared for me and help me to trust in Your guidance. Thank You for Your strength, Your righteousness, and Your guidance. Help me to live according to Your will and to follow You faithfully.

In Jesus' wise name I pray, Amen

OCTOBER 5

2 Corinthians 10:5 (NLT): We destroy every proud obstacle that keeps people from knowing God. We capture their rebellious thoughts and teach them to obey Christ.

Job 10:5 (NKJV): Are your days like the days of the mortal man? Are your years like the days of a mighty man?

Proverbs 10:5 (NIV): He who gathers crops in summer is a prudent son, but he who sleeps during harvest is a disgraceful son.

Luke 10:5 (NIV): "When you enter a house, first say, 'Peace be to this house.'"

PRAYER

Dear Heavenly Father, Theos Pas Paraklesis (The God of All Comfort),

I come to You seeking Your guidance and strength. As I reflect on Your Word, I ask for Your help in my life. 2 Corinthians 10:5 says, "We demolish arguments and every pretension that sets itself up against the knowledge of God, and we take captive every thought to make it obedient to Christ" (NIV). Help me to guard my mind and heart, taking every thought captive and making sure it aligns with Your truth. Job 10:5 teaches, "Are your days like those of a mortal or your years like those of a strong man?" (NIV). Remind me of the brevity of life and the importance of living each day in accordance with Your will. Help me to use my time wisely and to focus on what truly matters. Proverbs 10:5 says, "He who gathers crops in summer is a prudent son, but he who sleeps during harvest is a disgraceful son." Grant me the diligence and wisdom to work effectively and to make the most of the opportunities You give me. Luke 10:5 teaches, "When you enter a house, first say, 'Peace to this house.'" Help me to bring peace into every situation I encounter, reflecting Your love and grace in all my interactions. Thank You for Your guidance, wisdom, and the strength You provide. Help me to live in alignment with Your will and to be a source of peace and blessing to others.

In the teaching name of Jesus I pray, Amen

OCTOBER 6

Proverbs 10:6 (NKJV): Blessings are on the head of the righteous, but violence covers the mouth of the wicked.

Mark 10:6 (NIV): "But at the beginning of creation God 'made them male and female.'"

Jeremiah 10:6 (NIV): No one is like you, Lord; You are great, and your name is mighty in power.

1 Samuel 10:6 (NIV): The Spirit of the Lord will come powerfully upon you, and you will prophesy with them; And you will be changed into a different person.

1 Corinthians 10:6 (NIV): Now these things occurred as examples to keep us from setting our hearts on evil things as they did.

PRAYER

Dear Heavenly Father, Pneuma (Spirit),

I come before You with a heart open to Your wisdom and guidance. As I reflect on Your Word, I seek Your help and blessings. Proverbs 10:6 reminds me that blessings are for the righteous, I ask for Your blessings in my life and the strength to live righteously, so that Your favor might rest upon me. Mark 10:6 teaches, that the Lord our God created male and female. Help me to honor Your design and purpose for relationships and to reflect Your love and truth in my interactions with others. Jeremiah 10:6 says, "No one is like You, Lord; You are great, and Your name is mighty in power." I praise You for Your greatness and power. Help me to trust in Your sovereignty and to recognize Your mighty work in my life. 1 Samuel 10:6 teaches, "The Spirit of the Lord will come powerfully upon you, and you will prophesy with them; and you will be changed into a different person." Fill me with Your Spirit and transform me to be more like Christ. Guide me to live according to Your will and to fulfill Your purpose for my life. 1 Corinthians 10:6 informs me to learn from the examples in Your Word and to avoid the pitfalls of setting my heart on things that are contrary to Your will. Thank You for Your guidance, Your power, and the blessings You provide. Help me to live righteously, to honor Your design, and to follow Your Spirit.

In King Jesus' name I pray, Amen

OCTOBER 7

I AM A KINGDOM BUILDER

Psalm 10:7 (NIV): His mouth is full of lies and threats; trouble and evil are under his tongue.

Matthew 10:7 (NKJV): "And as you go, preach, saying, 'The kingdom of heaven is at hand.'"

Mark 10:7 (NIV): "For this reason a man will leave his father and mother and be united to his wife."

Proverbs 10:7 (NIV): The name of the righteous is used in blessings, but the name of the wicked will rot.

———————————————— **PRAYER** ————————————————

Dear Heavenly Father, Melekh Hagoyim (King of Nations),

I come before You seeking Your wisdom and guidance. As I reflect on Your Word, I ask for Your help in my life. Psalm 10:7 says, "His mouth is full of lies and threats; trouble and evil are under his tongue." Help me to discern truth from deception and to speak words that build others up rather than causing harm. Guard my mouth and heart from falsehoods. Matthew 10:7 teaches, "As you go, proclaim this message: The kingdom of heaven has come near" (NIV). Inspire me to share Your message of love and grace with others. Help me to be a faithful witness of Your kingdom and to live out the Good News in my daily life. Mark 10:7 says, "'For this reason a man will leave his father and mother and be united to his wife,'" and Proverbs 10:7 teaches, "The memory of the righteous is a blessing, but the name of the wicked will rot" (ESV). Help me to build relationships that honor You and to leave a legacy of righteousness through my actions and choices. Thank You for Your guidance and for the wisdom found in Your Word. Help me to live in truth, to share Your message, and to build relationships that reflect Your love.

In Jesus' discerning name I pray, Amen

Romans 10:8 (NIV): But what does it say? "The word is near you; it is in your mouth and in your heart," that is, the message concerning faith that we proclaim.

Matthew 10:8 (NKJV): "Heal the sick, cleanse the lepers, raise the dead, cast out demons. Freely you have received, freely give."

Joshua 10:8 (NIV): The LORD said to Joshua, "Do not be afraid of them; I have given them into your hand. Not one of them will be able to withstand you."

Proverbs 10:8 (NIV): The wise in heart accepts commands, but a chattering fool comes to ruin.

PRAYER

Dear Heavenly Father, Yahweh-Channun (LORD of Grace/Undeserved Favor,)

I come before You with a heart full of gratitude and a desire for Your guidance in my life. As I meditate on Your Word, I seek Your help and blessings. Romans 10:8 says, "But what does it say? 'The word is near you; it is in your mouth and in your heart,' that is, the message concerning faith that we proclaim." Thank You for bringing Your Word close to me, filling my heart and mouth with faith. Help me to keep Your message close and to live out my faith daily. Matthew 10:8 teaches, "Heal the sick, raise the dead, cleanse those who have leprosy, drive out demons. Freely you have received; freely give" (NIV). Help me to use the gifts and blessings You have given me to help others, sharing Your love and compassion freely with those in need. Joshua 10:8 says, "The LORD said to Joshua, 'Do not be afraid of them; I have given them into your hand. Not one of them will be able to withstand you.'" I trust in Your promise of victory and protection. Help me to face my challenges with courage, knowing that You are with me and will provide the strength I need. Proverbs 10:8 teaches, "The wise in heart accept commands, but a chattering fool comes to ruin." Grant me wisdom and the ability to listen to Your guidance. Help me to act wisely and to avoid the pitfalls of foolishness. Thank You for Your guidance, protection, and blessings. Help me to use Your gifts to serve others and to follow Your commands with a wise and faithful heart.

In the freedom of Jesus' name I pray, Amen

Romans 10:9 (NKJV): If you confess with your mouth Jesus as Lord, and believe in your heart that God raised him from the dead, you will be saved.

John 10:9 (NKJV): "I am the door. If anyone enters by Me, he will be saved, and will go in and out and find pasture."

1 Corinthians 10:9 (NLT): Nor should we put Christ to the test, as some of them did and then died from snakebites.

Daniel 10:9 (NIV): Then I heard him speaking, and as I listened to him, I fell into deep sleep, my face to the ground.

Mark 10:9 (NIV): "Therefore what God has joined together, let no one separate."

Proverbs 10:9 (NIV): Whoever walks in integrity walks securely, but whoever takes crooked paths will be found out.

PRAYER

Dear Heavenly Father, Alpha and Omega (The First and the Last),

I come before You with a heart full of gratitude, seeking Your guidance. Romans 10:9 teaches I must confess with my words to have salvation. I declare out loud with my words that Jesus is my Lord and I believe in His resurrection. John 10:9 teaches to trust in Jesus as the gate to abundant life and salvation. Help me to enter through Him and find the spiritual nourishment and safety You provide. 1 Corinthians 10:9 commands me to trust in You fully and not to test Your patience or grace. Help me to learn from the past and remain steadfast in faith. Daniel 10:9 speaks of having a posture of reverence. When I hear Your Word, may it bring me into a deeper understanding and a more profound experience of Your presence. Mark 10:9 testifies of God's unity of two people. Guide me in all my relationships and commitments, ensuring that I honor the unity and love that You desire for us. Help me to respect and nurture the bonds You have established. Proverbs 10:9 asserts how important it is to walk in integrity. Lord, grant me the strength to walk in humility and an honest character. I trust that Your way is the path to true security and understand my crooked paths will always be brought to light. Thank You for Your guidance.

In Jesus' truthful name I pray, Amen

OCTOBER 10

I NEED NOTHING BUT AM RICH IN THE LORD

John 10:10 (NLT): "The thief's purpose is to steal and kill and destroy. My purpose is to give them a rich and satisfying life."

Romans 10:10 (NIV): For it is with your heart that you believe and you are justified, and it is with your mouth that you profess your faith and are saved.

Jeremiah 10:10 (NIV): But the LORD is the true God; he is the living God, and the eternal King. When he is angry, the earth trembles; the nations cannot endure his wrath.

Matthew 10:10 (NIV): "No bag for the journey or extra shirt or sandals or a staff, for the worker is worth his keep."

PRAYER

Dear Heavenly Father, Jehovah-Jireh (The Lord Will Provide),

Thank You for the guidance and promises found in Your Word. As I reflect on these Scriptures, I seek Your help and assurance in my life. John 10:10 reveals the enemy is here on earth to steal, kill and destroy our lives. But God brings us abundant life through Jesus. Help me to embrace the fullness of life that You offer, free from the enemy's schemes. Romans 10:10 teaches that my heart must be pure and justified. Lord, let my spoken words reflect the belief that leads to salvation. Jeremiah 10:10 says, "But the LORD is the true God; he is the living God, the eternal King. When he is angry, the earth trembles; the nations cannot endure his wrath." I acknowledge You as the true and living God. Help me to remember Your power and to trust in Your control, even when the earth trembles. In Matthew 10:10, Jesus teaches, "No bag for the journey or extra shirt or sandals or a staff; for the worker is worth his keep." Remind me to trust in Your provision and to focus on the work You have set before me, knowing that You will provide for all my needs. Thank You for the abundant life You offer, for the assurance of salvation, and for Your eternal presence. Help me to trust in Your provision and to live fully in Your grace.

In the life-giving name of Jesus I pray, Amen

OCTOBER 11

SHAME HAS NO HOLD ON ME

John 10:11 (NIV): "I am the good shepherd. The good shepherd lays down his life for the sheep."

Revelation 10:11 (NIV): Then I was told, "You must prophesy again about many people, nations, languages and kings.

Proverbs 10:11 (NIV): The mouth of the righteous is a fountain of life, but the mouth of the wicked conceals violence.

Romans 10:11 (NIV): As Scripture says, "Anyone who believes in him will never be put to shame."

PRAYER

Dear Heavenly Father, El Gibbor (Mighty God),

Thank You for Your guidance and the reassurance found in Your Word. As I meditate on these Scriptures, I seek Your comfort and direction in my life. John 10:11 testifies Jesus is the Good Shepherd who cares for me deeply. Help me to trust in Your guidance and protection, knowing that You lay down Your life for my sake. In Revelation 10:11 John sees a mighty angel. He is told to speak to the nations. Lord, guide me in the responsibilities You have given me as you did John. Help me to be a witness of Your truth and to share Your message with nations as You lead me. Proverbs 10:11 says, "The mouth of the righteous is a fountain of life, but the mouth of the wicked conceals violence." Help me to speak words that bring life and encouragement to those around me. Guard my speech and let my words reflect Your love and righteousness. Romans 10:11 teaches, "As Scripture says, 'Anyone who believes in him will never be put to shame.'" I place my trust in You, knowing that I will not be put to shame for believing in Your promises. Strengthen my faith and help me to stand firm in Your truth. Thank You for being my Shepherd, for guiding me, and for the assurance found in Your Word. Help me to live according to Your teachings and to share Your love with others.

In Jesus' firm name I pray, Amen

OCTOBER 12

Job 10:12 (NIV): You gave me life and showed me kindness, and in Your providence watched over my spirit.

Romans 10:12 (NKJV): There is no distinction between Jew and Greek, for the same Lord over all is rich to all who call upon Him.

Psalm 10:12 (NIV): Arise, LORD! Lift up your hand, O God. Do not forget the helpless.

Ecclesiastes 10:12 (NIV): Words from the mouth of the wise are gracious, but fools are consumed by their own lips.

Zechariah 10:12 (NIV): "I will strengthen them in the LORD and in his name they will love sincerely," declares the LORD.

PRAYER

Dear Heavenly Father, Bara (Creator),

Thank You for Your constant presence and the comfort found in Your Word. Job 10:12 declares that the Lord grants me life and favor. I am grateful for the life You've given me and for Your kindness. Help me to feel Your presence in all circumstances and to trust in Your watchful care over my life. Romans 10:12 teaches that the Lord loves Jews and Gentiles the same, and the He richly blesses all who call upon Him. Lord, I praise You for being a generous and inclusive God. I call on You now, asking for Your blessings and provision in my life. Psalm 10:12 says, "Arise, LORD!" God, I bring before You my struggles and the struggles of others. Please arise and help us, especially those who are helpless and in need. Show Your mercy and bring relief and support. Ecclesiastes 10:12 teaches, "Words from the mouth of the wise are gracious, but fools are consumed by their own lips." Grant me wisdom in my speech and interactions. Help me to speak with grace and to avoid the pitfalls of foolish words. Zechariah 10:12 says, "'I will strengthen them in the LORD and in his name they will love sincerely' declares the LORD." I take comfort in knowing that Your strength is with me. Help me to trust in Your divine counsel and to face each day without fear, knowing that You are with me. Thank You for Your kindness, blessings, and guidance.

In Jesus' favoring name I pray, Amen

OCTOBER 13

I CALL ON THE NAME OF THE LORD

Romans 10:13 (NLT): For, "Everyone who calls on the name of the LORD will be saved."

1 Corinthians 10:13 (NIV): No temptation has overtaken you except what is common to mankind. And God is faithful; he will not let you be tempted beyond what you can bear. But when you are tempted, he will also provide a way out so that you can endure it.

Deuteronomy 10:13 (NIV): Observe the LORD's commands and decrees that I am giving you today for your own good.

Psalm 10:13 (NLT): Why do the wicked get away with despising God? They think, "God will never call us to account."

Judges 10:13 (NIV): But you have forsaken me and serve other gods, so I will no longer save you.

PRAYER

Dear Heavenly Father, Maqowr Chay Mayim (Fountain of Living Waters),

Thank You for Your love and the promises You give through Your Word. I come to You with a heart full of trust and need, guided by these Scriptures. Romans 10:13 tells me to call upon You now, asking for Your help and salvation in my life. Please rescue me from my struggles and guide me in Your ways. 1 Corinthians 10:13 teaches that no temptation will take over me, there's always a way out with You, Lord. Thank You for Your faithfulness and for not allowing me to face more than I can handle. Help me to rely on Your strength to overcome the temptations and challenges I face. Deuteronomy 10:13 instructs me in following Your commands and living according to Your will. Help me to see the good in Your instructions and to trust that they are for my benefit. Psalm 10:13 asks "Why do the wicked get away with despising God?" Lord why, I do not understand, but with that uncertainty lead me when I feel overwhelmed by injustice and wickedness. Remind me that You see all things and that Your justice will prevail in Your perfect timing. Judges 10:13 instructs me to stay faithful and focused on You, avoiding distractions and false gods. Help me to seek Your wisdom in all my decisions and interactions.

In the saving name of Jesus I pray, Amen

OCTOBER 14

GOD IS MY HELPER

Romans 10:14 (NIV): How, then, can they call on the one they have not believed in? And how can they believe in the one of whom they have not heard? And how can they hear without someone preaching to them?

1 Corinthians 10:14 (NLT): So, my dear friends, flee from the worship of idols.

Psalm 10:14 (NIV): But you, God, see the trouble of the afflicted; you consider their grief and take it in hand. The victims commit themselves to you; you are the helper of the fatherless.

 PRAYER

Dear Heavenly Father, Malak Haggoel (Redeeming Angel),

Thank You for Your faithfulness and the guidance You offer through Your Word. As I reflect on Your Word, I seek wisdom and strength for my life. Romans 10:14 inspires me to share Your message of love and salvation with others. Help me to be a witness of Your grace and to spread Your truth. 1 Corinthians 10:14 says, "Therefore, my dear friends, flee from idolatry" (NIV). Guide me to keep my focus on You and not be distracted by anything that takes Your place in my heart. Help me to worship You alone and to remove any distractions that draw me away from Your will. Psalm 10:14 teaches, "But you, God, see the trouble of the afflicted; you consider their grief and take it in hand." I bring before You my concerns and struggles, trusting that You see my pain and are with me in every situation. Comfort me and help me to find peace in Your presence. Thank You for Your protection, guidance, and the promise of Your presence in my life. Help me to remain steadfast in my faith, to share Your message, and to keep You as the center of my heart.

In Jesus' helping name I pray, Amen

OCTOBER 15

I am wealthy in God's love

John 10:15 (NIV): "Just as the Father knows me and I know the father—and I lay down my life for the sheep."

Ecclesiastes 10:15 (NLT): Fools are so exhausted by a little work that they can't even find their way home.

Proverbs 10:15 (ESV): A rich man's wealth is his strong city; the poverty of the poor is their ruin.

Jeremiah 10:15 (NLT): Idols are worthless; They are ridiculous lies! On the day of reckoning they will all be destroyed.

1 Corinthians 10:15 (NLT): You are reasonable people. Decide for yourselves if what I am saying is true.

PRAYER

Dear Heavenly Father, El Shaddai (God Almighty),

Thank You for Your guidance and the wisdom You provide through Your Word. John 10:15 says that Jesus lays down his life for me. I am grateful for the deep relationship You have with us and the sacrificial love of Jesus. Help me to reflect this love and commitment in my own life, trusting in Your guidance and protection. Ecclesiastes 10:15 teaches me discernment and understanding, so that my efforts are directed wisely and I am not burdened by unnecessary struggles. Proverbs 10:15 says, "The wealth of the rich is their fortified city, but poverty is the ruin of the poor" (NIV). Help me to find contentment and security not in material wealth but in Your provision and love. Teach me to rely on You for my needs and to use my resources wisely. Jeremiah 10:15 teaches, not to trust in false idols. Lord protect me from placing my trust in things that are fleeting and unreliable. Help me to focus on what is eternal and true, finding my worth and purpose in You alone. 1 Corinthians 10:15 is a challenge and an invitation. Heavenly Father, grant me wisdom and understanding as I seek to apply Your Word to my life. Help me to make decisions that honor You and reflect Your truth.

In the loving name of Jesus I pray, Amen

OCTOBER 16

Mark 10:16 (NLT): Then [Jesus] took the children in his arms and placed his hands on their heads and blessed them.

Deuteronomy 10:16 (NIV): Circumcise your hearts, therefore, and do not be stiff-necked any longer.

Hebrews 10:16 (NLT): "This is the new [promise] I will make with my people on that day, says the LORD; I will put my laws in their hearts, and I will write them on their minds."

Matthew 10:16 (NIV): "I am sending you out like sheep among wolves. So be as shrewd as snakes and innocent as doves."

PRAYER

Dear Heavenly Father, El Baruch (God Is Blessed),

Thank You for Your constant love and guidance in my life. I come to You with a heart open to hear Your teachings. Mark 10:16 teaches, "And he took the children in his arms, placed his hands on their head and blessed them" (NIV). I am thankful for Your blessings and love. Please hold me in Your arms, bless my life, and guide me in all I do. Matthew 10:16 says You're sending me out like a sheep among wolves, I must be as shrewd as a snake and as innocent as a dove. Grant me wisdom and discernment as I navigate the challenges of life and help me to maintain purity and integrity in all my interactions. Deuteronomy 10:16 teaches that I must change my heart and stop being stubborn. Father God, please help me to transform my heart to be soft and receptive to Your will, and remove any stubbornness that keeps me from fully following You. Hebrews 10:16 says, "This is the covenant I will make with them after that time, says the Lord. I will put my laws in their hearts, and I will write them in their minds" (NIV). I pray for Your laws to be deeply embedded in my heart and mind, guiding my actions and thoughts according to Your will.

In the blessed name of Jesus I pray, Amen

Romans 10:17 (ESV): So faith comes from hearing, and hearing through the word of Christ.

Proverbs 10:17 (NLT): People who accept discipline are on the pathway to life, but those who ignore correction will go astray.

Isaiah 10:17 (NIV): The Light of Israel will become a fire, their Holy One a flame; in a single day it will burn and consume his thorns and briers.

Hebrews 10:17 (NIV): Then he adds: "Their sins and lawless acts I will remember no more."

Psalm 10:17 (NIV): You, LORD, hear the desire of the afflicted; you encourage them, and you listen to their cry.

PRAYER

Dear Heavenly Father, 'Or Yisrael (Light of Israel),

I seek Your wisdom and support as I reflect on Your Scriptures. Romans 10:17 says, "So faith comes from hearing, and hearing through the word of Christ." I ask that You increase my faith as I read and meditate on Your Word. Help me to listen to Your voice and to grow in my trust and belief in You. Proverbs 10:17 teaches, "Whoever heeds discipline shows the way to life, but whoever ignores correction leads others astray" (NIV). Guide me to embrace Your discipline and correction with a humble heart. Help me to follow Your path and to live a life that reflects Your truth. Isaiah 10:17 says, "The Light of Israel will become a fire, their Holy One a flame; in a single day it will burn and consume his thorns and briers." I pray for Your light to shine brightly in my life, illuminating the path before me and consuming any obstacles or troubles that stand in the way of Your will. Hebrews 10:17 declares I can break the power of sin and iniquity in my life through the blood of Jesus. Thank You, Lord, for the forgiveness You offer through Jesus. Help me to let go of past mistakes and to live confidently in the freedom You have provided. Psalm 10:17 shows me that God hears my desire, He encourages me, and He listens to my cries. I bring before You my worries and desires, trusting that You hear and care for me.

In the light of Jesus' name I pray, Amen

OCTOBER 18

Luke 10:18 (KJV): And he said unto them, "I beheld Satan as lightning fall from heaven."

Mark 10:18 (NLT): "Why do you call me good?" Jesus asked, "Only God is truly good."

Proverbs 10:18 (NLT): Hiding hatred makes you a liar; slandering others makes you a fool.

Matthew 10:18 (NLT): "You will stand trial before governors and kings because you are my followers. But this will be your opportunity to tell the rulers and other unbelievers about me."

Deuteronomy 10:18 (NLT): He ensures that orphans and widows receive justice. He shows love to the foreigners living among you and gives them food and clothing.

PRAYER

Dear Heavenly Father, El Qadosh (The Holy God),

As I come before You today, I am reminded of Your power and sovereignty, just as Jesus spoke in Luke 10:18, saying, "I saw Satan fall like lightning from heaven" (NIV). Lord, I trust in Your victory over darkness and evil, knowing that You are the ultimate source of light and truth in my life. In Mark 10:18, Jesus said, "No one is good—except God alone" (NIV). I acknowledge Your perfect goodness and holiness, and I ask that You help me reflect Your goodness in all that I do. Guide my actions, thoughts, and words so they may honor You and bring glory to Your name. Proverbs 10:18 teaches that "Whoever conceals hatred with lying lips and spreads slander is a fool" (NIV). Lord, cleanse my heart of any bitterness, anger, or deceit. May I speak with honesty and love, avoiding any words that would cause harm or division. As I face challenges and trials, as mentioned in Matthew 10:18, where Jesus warned of being brought before governors and kings for His sake, grant me the courage and wisdom to stand firm in my faith. Let my testimony be a light to others, even in difficult situations, and may Your Spirit empower me to be a faithful witness. Finally, I thank You, Lord, for Your compassion and justice as declared in Deuteronomy 10:18: "He defends the cause of the fatherless and the widow, and loves the foreigner residing among you, giving them food and clothing" (NIV). Help me to embody Your love and justice in my interactions with others. May I be a source of comfort and support to all.

In Jesus' mighty name I pray, Amen

OCTOBER 19

Luke 10:19 (NIV): "I have given you authority to trample on snakes and scorpions, and to overcome all the power of the enemy; nothing will harm you."

Hebrews 10:19 (NIV): "Therefore, brothers and sisters, since we have confidence to enter the Most Holy Place by the blood of Jesus."

Daniel 10:19 (ESV): "Oh man greatly loved, fear not, peace be with you; be strong and of good courage." When he spoke to me, I was strengthened and said, "Speak, my lord, since you have given me strength."

Proverbs 10:19 (NLT): Too much talk leads to sin. Be sensible and keep your mouth shut.

Joshua 10:19 (NLT): The rest of you continue chasing the enemy and cut them down from the rear. Don't give them a chance to get back to their towns, for the LORD your God has given you victory over them.

PRAYER

Dear Heavenly Father, Malak Haggoel (Redeeming Angel),

Thank You for Your presence and guidance in my life. Luke 10:19 says I have authority to tread upon serpents and scorpions. I am grateful for the protection and authority You have granted me over challenges and adversities. Help me to stand firm in Your strength and not be afraid. Hebrews 10:19 teaches I have boldness to enter into the presence of God through the blood of Christ. Help me to approach You with faith and reverence, trusting in the grace You have provided. Daniel 10:19 teaches me that I have Your peace and strength in my life. Help me to remain steadfast and encouraged, knowing that You are with me in every situation. Proverbs 10:19 says, "Sin is not ended by multiplying words, but the prudent hold their tongues" (NIV). Grant me wisdom in my speech and the ability to listen more than I speak. Help me to use my words wisely and to reflect Your love and truth. Joshua 10:19 teaches me not to stop chasing the enemy and cutting them down; to never give them a chance to come back, for the Lord my God has given me victory over them. Guide me to pursue Your goals with determination and not to be passive or apathetic.

In Jesus' strong name I pray, Amen

OCTOBER 20

The Holy Spirit speaks through me

1 Corinthians 10:20 (NIV): No, but the sacrifices of pagans are offered to demons, not to God, and I do nit want you to be participants with demons.

Romans 10:20 (NIV): And Isaiah boldly says, "I was found by those who did not seek me; I revealed myself to those who did not ask for me".

Luke 10:20 (NLT): "But don't rejoice because evil spirits obey you; rejoice because your names are registered in heaven."

Matthew 10:20 (NLT): "For it is not you who will be speaking—it will be the Spirit of your Father speaking through you."

PRAYER

Dear Heavenly Father, Yated Aman Maqom (Nail in a Firm Place),

Thank You for Your guidance and protection in my life. I seek Your wisdom and strength as I reflect on Your Word. 1 Corinthians 10:20 testifies that I break off any fellowship with devils through sin, the flesh, or sacrifice in the name of Jesus. Lord, Help me to stay away from anything that leads me away from You and to remain committed to serving You alone. Protect me from influences that might draw me away from Your truth. Romans 10:20 teaches, "And Isaiah boldly says, 'I was found by those who did not seek me; I revealed myself to those who did not ask for me.'" I am grateful for Your grace and revelation in my life, even when I did not actively seek You. Help me to recognize Your presence and to respond with gratitude and faithfulness. Luke 10:20 says, "However, do not rejoice that the spirits submit to you, but rejoice that your names are written in heaven" (NIV). I am thankful for Your salvation and the assurance of my place in Your kingdom. Help me to find joy in my relationship with You rather than in any personal achievements or power. Matthew 10:20 instructs me to rely on the Holy Spirit to guide me in my words and actions. Help me to be a vessel for Your message and to speak and act with Your wisdom and love. Thank You for Your protection, grace, and the Holy Spirit.

Rejoicing in Jesus' name I pray, Amen

1 Corinthians 10:21 (NIV): You cannot drink the cup of the Lord and the cup of demons too; you cannot have a part in both the Lord's table and the table of demons.

Mark 10:21 (NLT): Looking at the man, Jesus felt genuine love for him. "There is still one thing you haven't done," he told him. "Go and sell all your possessions and give the money to the poor, and you will have treasures in heaven. Then come, follow me."

Jeremiah 10:21 (NLT): The shepherds of my people have lost their senses. They no longer seek wisdom from the LORD. Therefore, they fail completely, and their flocks are scattered.

 **PRAYER**

Dear Heavenly Father, 'O Yisrael (Light of Israel),

Thank You for Your guidance and love. I seek Your wisdom and strength as I reflect on Your Word and apply it to my life. 1 Corinthians 10:21 says I can not be in two places at once. I must choose: The Lord or demons? Who do I choose to eat and drink with? Father God, help me to remain fully devoted to You and not be divided in my loyalty. Strengthen me to choose Your path and live a life that honors You. Mark 10:21 teaches that I may have to give up all earthly possessions to gain heavenly treasures. Father God, I pray for the courage to follow Your call, even if it means making sacrifices. Help me to prioritize Your kingdom and be generous with what You have given me. Jeremiah 10:21 says, "The shepherds are senseless and do not inquire of the LORD; so they do not prosper and all their flock is scattered" (NIV). Guide me to seek Your wisdom and direction in all that I do. Help me to make decisions that are aligned with Your will and to lead a life that reflects Your truth and care. Thank You for Your unwavering love and for the clarity found in Your Word. Help me to stay faithful, to follow Your guidance, and to seek Your wisdom in every aspect of my life.

In Jesus' wise name I pray, Amen

OCTOBER 22

Proverbs 10:22 (NIV): The blessing of the LORD brings wealth, without painful toil for it.

Hebrews 10:22 (NIV): Let us draw near to God with a sincere heart and with the full assurance that faith brings, having our hearts sprinkled to cleanse us from guilty conscience and having our bodies washed with pure water.

Matthew 10:22 (NLT): "And all nations will hate you because you are my followers. But everyone who endures to the end will be saved."

Luke 10:22 (NLT): "My father has entrusted everything to me. No one truly knows the Son except the Father, and no one truly knows the Father except the Son and those who the Son chooses to reveal to him."

1 Corinthians 10:22: What? Do we dare to rouse the Lord's jealousy? Do you think we are stronger than he is?

PRAYER

Dear Heavenly Father, El Chaiyai (God of My Life),

I seek Your blessings, strength, and understanding as I reflect on Your Word. Proverbs 10:22 says I am rich in the Lord. I ask for Your blessings in my life, trusting that You will provide what I need without the burdens of unnecessary stress. Help me to recognize and be grateful for Your provision. Hebrews 10:22 teaches me to draw near to God, let my heart be sprinkled and purified by the blood of Jesus from an evil conscience. Lord, draw me closer to You, and cleanse my heart and mind. Help me to come to You with sincerity and faith, knowing that You offer forgiveness and renewal. Matthew 10:22 says I will be hated for my love for Jesus. But because I keep my love alive I will be saved. Heavenly Father, grant me the strength and courage to remain steadfast in my faith, even in the face of challenges and opposition. Luke 10:22 shows me that You reveal Yourself to me through Your Son, Jesus. Help me to understand and embrace the depth of our relationship and Your divine revelation. 1 Corinthians 10:22 reminds me of Your supreme power and authority. Help me to accept Your ways over my own.

In Jesus' powerful name I pray, Amen

MY EYES ARE BLESSED TO SEE

Luke 10:23 (NIV): Then He turned to His disciples and said privately, "Blessed are the eyes that see what you see."

Mark 10:23 (NIV): Jesus looked around and said to his disciples, "How hard is it for the rich to enter the kingdom of God!"

Jeremiah 10:23 (NLT): I know, LORD, that our lives are not our own. We are not able to plan our own courses.

Proverbs 10:23 (NLT): Doing wrong is fun for a fool, but living wisely brings pleasure to the sensible.

PRAYER

Dear Heavenly Father, Elohim Qarob (God Is Near),

Thank You for Your wisdom and the guidance You offer through Your Word. I come before You seeking clarity and direction in my life. Luke 10:23 says my eyes are blessed to see as the Lord sees. I am grateful for the spiritual insights and blessings You have revealed to me. Help me to recognize and appreciate the ways You are at work in my life and in the world around me. Mark 10:23 teaches of earthly wealth and heaven. Lord, guide me to place my trust and values in You rather than in material wealth. Help me to seek Your kingdom first and to live with a heart focused on eternal things. Jeremiah 10:23 says, "I know, LORD, that our lives are not our own. We are not able to plan our own course." I trust in Your plan for my life, knowing that You are in control. Help me to surrender my own plans to You and to follow the path You have set before me. Proverbs 10:23 teaches, "A fool finds pleasure in wicked schemes, but a person of understanding delights in wisdom" (NIV). Grant me wisdom and understanding and help me to find joy in living according to Your truth rather than being swayed by foolishness. Thank You for Your guidance, insight, and the wisdom found in Your Word. Help me to recognize Your blessings, trust in Your plan, and seek wisdom in all that I do.

In Jesus' close name I pray, Amen

OCTOBER 24

1 Corinthians 10:24 (NIV): No one should seek their own good, but the good of others.

Hebrews 10:24 (NLT): Let us think of ways to motivate one another to acts of love and good works.

Luke 10:24 (NLT): "I tell you, many prophets and kings longed to see who you see, but they didn't see it. And they longed to hear what you hear, what you hear, but they didn't hear it."

Proverbs 10:24 (KJV): The fear of the wicked, it shall come upon him: but the desire of the righteous shall be granted.

Jeremiah 10:24 (NKJV): O LORD, correct me, but with justice; not in your anger, lest You bring me to nothing.

PRAYER

Dear Heavenly Father, Qeren Yesha' (Horn of My Salvation),

Thank You for Your guidance and love in my life. I come to You seeking wisdom and encouragement. 1 Corinthians 10:24 instructs me to live with a selfless heart, always considering the needs and well-being of others. Guide me to act in ways that uplift and benefit those around me. Hebrews 10:24 teaches me to be a source of motivation and love, prompting good deeds and growth in faith among my community. Luke 10:24 says I see and hear more than prophets and kings. Lord, thank You for the privilege of experiencing Your truth and grace. Help me to appreciate the blessings I have and to live in a way that honors the revelation You have given me. Proverbs 10:24 teaches, "What the wicked dread will overtake them; what the righteous desire will be granted" (NIV). I pray for Your protection and favor, trusting that as I seek righteousness, You will fulfill the desires that align with Your will. Help me to focus on what is good and right, knowing that You will provide for my needs. Jeremiah 10:24 says, "Discipline me, LORD, but only in due measure—not in Your anger, or You will reduce me to nothing" (NIV). I ask for Your guidance and discipline in my life, but also for Your mercy and grace. Help me to grow in Your wisdom and to be shaped by Your love.

In the good name of Jesus I pray, Amen

OCTOBER 25

Hebrews 10:25 (NLT): And let us not neglect our meeting together, as some people do, but encourage one another, especially now that the day of the return is drawing near.

Proverbs 10:25 (NIV): When the storm has swept by, the wicked are gone, but the righteous stand firm forever.

John 10:25 (NLT): Jesus replied, "I have already told you, and you don't believe me. The proof is the work I do in my Father's name."

Mark 10:25 (NLT): "In fact, it is easier for a camel to go through the eye of a needle than for a rich person to enter the kingdom of God."

PRAYER

Dear Heavenly Father, El (God),

Thank You for Your presence and guidance in my life. I come to You seeking Your strength and reassurance. Hebrews 10:25 says, "Not giving up meeting together, as some are in the habit of doing, but encouraging one another—and all the more as you see the Day approaching" (NIV). Help me to remain faithful in gathering with fellow believers and to encourage others in their faith. Strengthen my commitment to fellowship and community. Proverbs 10:25 teaches, "When the storm has swept by, the wicked are gone, but the righteous stand firm forever." Thank You for being my refuge in times of trouble. Help me to remain steadfast and righteous, trusting that You will keep me secure even when life's storms arise. John 10:25 says, "Jesus answered, 'I did tell you, but you do not believe. The works I do in my Father's name testify about me'" (NIV). Strengthen my faith to believe in Your works and the truth of Your Word. Help me to see Your hand at work in my life and to trust in Your promises. Mark 10:25 teaches, "It is easier for a camel to go through the eye of a needle than for someone who is rich to enter the kingdom of God" (NIV). Guide me to place my trust and value in You above all material things. Help me to live with a heart focused on Your kingdom and not be swayed by worldly possessions.

In Jesus' guiding name I pray, Amen

OCTOBER 26

1 Corinthians 10:26 (NLT): For, "the Earth is the LORD's, and everything in it."

Hebrews 10:26 (NKJV): For if we sin willfully after we have received the knowledge of the truth, there no longer remains a sacrifice for sins.

John 10:26 (NLT): "But you don't believe me because you are not my sheep."

Proverbs 10:26 (NLT): Lazy people irritate their employers, like vinegar to the teeth or smoke in the eyes.

Matthew 10:26 (NLT): "But don't be afraid of those who threaten you. For the time is coming when everything that is covered will be revealed, and all that is secret will be made known to all."

PRAYER

Dear Heavenly Father, El Elohe Yisrael (God of Israel),

Thank You for Your guidance and care in my life. I come to You today seeking Your protection, faith, and assurance. 1 Corinthians 10:26 says all the earth is God's. I trust in Your sovereignty over all things. Help me to remember that everything in my life is under Your control and care. Guide me to live with the assurance that You are in charge of all aspects of my life. Hebrews 10:26 teaches me not to deliberately sin once the truth has been revealed. Lord, help me to live according to Your truth and to avoid the pitfalls of deliberate sin. Strengthen my resolve to follow Your path and seek Your forgiveness and grace daily. John 10:26 says, I must believe, or I am not of God. I pray for Your help in strengthening my faith and trust in You. Open my heart and mind to Your Word and help me to truly follow You as Your beloved sheep. Proverbs 10:26 guides me to be diligent and hardworking in all that I do. Help me to avoid laziness and to be a reliable and productive servant in Your kingdom. Matthew 10:26 says nothing is hidden, God knows all, and He will let all the secrets be known. I pray for courage and trust in Your protection, knowing that You will reveal and handle all things in Your time. Help me to face my fears with faith and to rely on Your wisdom.

In the leading name of Jesus I pray, Amen

OCTOBER 27

Luke 10:27(NLT): The man answered, "You must love the LORD your God with all your heart, all your soul, all your strength, and all your mind" and, "Love your neighbor as yourself."

Isaiah 10:27 (NLT): In the day the LORD will end the bondage of his people. He will break the yoke of slavery and lift it from their shoulders.

Mark 10:27 (NLT): Jesus looked at them intently and said, "Humanly speaking, it is impossible. But not with God. Everything is possible with God."

Proverbs 10:27 (NKJV): The fear of the LORD prolongs days, but the years of the wicked will be shortened.

 **PRAYER**

Dear Heavenly Father, Jehovah Qadash (The LORD Who Sanctifies),

Thank You for Your guidance and love in my life. I come to You today seeking Your strength and wisdom. Luke 10:27 screams love. Lord, Help me to love You completely, with all my heart, soul, strength, and mind. Teach me to love those around me with the same depth and sincerity. Isaiah 10:27 teaches me to break the burdens and yokes that weigh me down. Grant me relief and strength to overcome the challenges I face. Mark 10:27 reveals nothing is impossible. Help me to remember that with You, all things are possible. Strengthen my faith and trust in Your ability to do what seems impossible in my life. Proverbs 10:27 teaches, "The fear of the LORD adds length to life, but the years of the wicked are cut short." Guide me to live in reverence of You, so that my life may be blessed and fruitful. Help me to seek Your wisdom and to honor You in all I do. The Lord is my Rock, and I know that Your guidance is always true and faithful.

In Jesus' perfect name I pray, Amen

OCTOBER 28

My soul is God's

John 10:28 (NKJV): "And I give them eternal life, and they shall never perish, neither shall anyone snatch them out of my hand."

Matthew 10:28 (NLT): "Don't be afraid of those who want to kill your body; they cannot touch your soul. Fear only God, who can destroy both soul and body in hell."

Proverbs 10:28 (NKJV): The hope of the righteous will be gladness, but the expectation of the wicked will perish.

 **PRAYER**

Dear Heavenly Father, Tsur Yisrael (Rock of Israel),

Thank You for Your unfailing love and care in my life. I come before You today seeking Your assurance and protection. In John 10:28, Jesus says, "I give them eternal life, and they shall never perish; no one will snatch them out of my hand" (NIV). Thank You for the promise of eternal life and the security that comes from being held in Your hand. Help me to trust fully in Your promise and to feel assured of Your protection and love. Jesus teaches us in Matthew 10:28, "Do not be afraid of those who kill the body but cannot kill the soul. Rather, be afraid of the One who can destroy both soul and body in hell." Give me the courage to face life's challenges without fear, knowing that my ultimate security is found in You. Help me to live with a heart focused on You rather than being overwhelmed by worldly fears. Proverbs 10:28 says, "The hope of the righteous brings joy, but the expectation of the wicked will perish." Fill me with hope and joy as I trust in Your righteousness. Let my hope in You bring a deep and abiding joy and guide me to live in a way that reflects Your goodness. Thank You for Your assurance, protection, and the hope that sustains me. Help me to live courageously, trust in Your promises, and find joy in Your righteousness.

In Jesus' courageous name I pray, Amen

THE WAY OF THE LORD IS MY STRONGHOLD

Proverbs 10:29 (NLT): The way of the LORD is a stronghold to those with integrity, but it destroys the wicked.

John 10:29 (NIV): "My father, who has given them to me, is greater than all; no one can snatch them out of my Father's hand."

Hebrews 10:29 (NIV): How much more severely do you think someone deserves to be punished who has trampled the Son of God underfoot, who has treated as an unholy thing the blood of the covenant that sanctified them, and who has insulted the Spirit of grace?

Matthew 10:29 (NLT): What is the price of two sparrows—one copper coin? But not a single sparrow can fall to the ground without your Father knowing it.

PRAYER

Dear Heavenly Father, Abir Jacob (The Mighty One of Jacob),

Thank You for Your steadfast love and faithfulness in my life. I come to You today seeking Your protection and strength. Proverbs 10:29 says, "The way of the LORD is a refuge for the blameless, but it is the ruin of those who do evil" (NIV). Help me to follow Your ways and find refuge in You. Protect me from harm and guide me to live a life that reflects Your righteousness. John 10:29 shows me the security and protection that comes from being in Your care. Help me to trust in Your strength and to know that I am safe in Your hands. Hebrews 10:29 says I must honor the sacrifice of Jesus and live in a way that reflects my gratitude for Your grace. Guide me to understand the seriousness of Your covenant and to live with reverence. Matthew 10:29 teaches me how much the Lord loves me. Thank You for Your care and concern for even the smallest details of my life. Help me to trust in Your providence and to know that You are aware of and concerned for all aspects of my life. Thank You for Your protection, strength, and care. Help me to follow Your ways, trust in Your security, honor Your grace, and believe in Your loving care.

In Jesus' strong name I pray, Amen

Justice is not mine, but God's

Hebrews 10:30 (NIV): For we know him who said, "It is mine to avenge; I will repay," and again, "The Lord will judge his people."

Matthew 10:30 (NIV): "And even the very hairs of your head are all numbered."

Proverbs 10:30 (NIV): The righteous will never be uprooted, but the wicked will not remain in the land.

John 10:30 (NIV): "I and the Father are one."

--- **PRAYER** ---

Dear Heavenly Abba (Father),

Thank You for Your constant presence and love in my life. I come before You today seeking Your guidance and reassurance. Hebrews 10:30 says, "For we know him who said, 'It is mine to avenge; I will repay,' and again, 'The Lord will judge his people.'" Help me to trust in Your justice and timing. Remind me that You are in control and that You will handle all matters of fairness and retribution. Matthew 10:30 teaches, "And even the very hairs of your head are all numbered." Thank You for Your intimate care and attention to every detail of my life. Help me to trust in Your provision and protection, knowing that You are mindful of all aspects of my existence. Proverbs 10:30 says, "The righteous will never be uprooted, but the wicked will not remain in the land." Guide me to live righteously and firmly rooted in Your ways. Help me to remain steadfast and unwavering in my faith, trusting that You will establish my path. In John 10:30, Jesus teaches, "I and the Father are one." Thank You for the unity and connection we have through You. Help me to experience and reflect this unity in my relationships, striving to align my life with Your will and to live in harmony with others. Thank You for Your guidance, care, and unity in my life. Help me to trust in Your justice, rely on Your intimate care, stay steadfast in righteousness, and reflect Your unity in all I do.

In Jesus' forgiving name I pray, Amen

OCTOBER 31

I GIVE GOD ALL THE GLORY

1 Corinthians 10:31 (NIV): So whether you eat or drink or whatever you do, do it all for the glory of God.

Proverbs 10:31 (NIV): From the mouth of the righteous comes the fruit of wisdom, but a perverse tongue will be silenced.

Matthew 10:31 (NIV): "So do not be afraid; You are worth more than many sparrows."

Mark 10:31 (NIV): "But many who are first will be last, and the last first."

PRAYER

Dear Heavenly Father, Jehovah Kabodhi (The LORD My Glory),

Thank You for Your unfailing love and guidance in my life. I come before You with a heart full of gratitude, seeking Your wisdom and strength. 1 Corinthians 10:31 says to live each day with the intention of glorifying You in everything I do. May my actions, words, and thoughts reflect Your love and purpose. Proverbs 10:31 teaches me to speak with wisdom and kindness and let my words be life giving rather than destructive. Help me to use my speech to honor You and reflect Your righteousness. Matthew 10:31 reminds me of my worth in Your eyes. Help me to trust in Your care and provision, knowing that I am valuable and loved by You. Mark 10:31 teaches, "But many who are first will be last, and the last first." Help me to embrace humility and service in my life. Let me seek to put others before myself and follow Your example of selflessness and love. Guide me to live with strength and honor, reflecting Your values in all that I do. Thank You for Your guidance and the wisdom found in Your Word. Help me to live for Your glory, speak with wisdom, trust in my worth, and embrace humility.

In Jesus' name I pray, Amen

NOVEMBER 1

I am God's warrior

Hebrews 11:1 (ESV): Now faith is the assurance of things hoped for, the conviction of things not seen.

Isaiah 11:1 (NIV): A shoot will come up from the stump of Jesse, from his roots a Branch will bear fruit.

Proverbs 11:1 (NIV): The LORD detests dishonest scales, but accurate weights find favor with him.

Genesis 11:1 (NIV): Now the whole world had one language and a common speech.

Ecclesiastes 11:1 (NLT): Send your grain across the seas, and in time, profits will flow back to you.

PRAYER

Dear Heavenly Father, Adonai (Lord),

Thank You for Your love and faithfulness. I come before You seeking Your strength and guidance in my life. Hebrews 11:1 speaks of how faith is our confidence, it may be unseen with our natural eyes, but this faith is real in the unseen realm. Biblical hope is not wishful thinking, it's confident expectation based on God's unchanging character. Lord, help me to have strong faith, trusting in Your promises even when I cannot see the outcome. Isaiah 11:1 describes a shoot, a stump, roots and a branch that bears fruit. Thank You for the hope and promise of new beginnings and growth in our lives. Abba, as I come to You help me to stay deeply rooted in You and to produce fruit in my lifetime. Proverbs 11:1 testifies how the Lord detests dishonesty, but favor comes when we deal with others in truth. Guide me to live with integrity and honesty in all that I do. I will act fairly and justly, seeking Your favor through my actions. Genesis 11:1 explains language and speech in history as all being one. Faithful One, lead me to work toward unity and understanding with those around me, striving to communicate with love and respect. Help me to build bridges rather than walls and to seek harmony in my relationships. Ecclesiastes 11:1 teaches, "Ship your grain across the sea; after many days you may receive a return." Guide me to invest my efforts and resources wisely, trusting that You will bring about fruitful results in Your timing.

In Jesus' victorious name I pray, Amen

NOVEMBER 2

Proverbs 11:2 (NIV): When pride comes, then comes disgrace, but with humility comes wisdom.

Ecclesiastes 11:2 (NLT): But divide your investments among many places, for you do not know what risks might lie ahead.

Isaiah 11:2 (TPT): The Spirit of YAHWEH will rest upon him, the Spirit of Extraordinary Wisdom, the Spirit of Perfect Understanding, the Spirit of Wise Strategy, the Spirit of Mighty Power, the Spirit of Revelation, and the Spirit of the Fear of YAHWEH.

Luke 11:2 (NLT): Jesus said, "This is how you should pray: 'Father, may your name be kept holy. May your kingdom come soon.'"

 **PRAYER**

Dear Heavenly Father, Adonai Tov (The Lord Is Good),

Thank You for Your guidance and love. I come before You today seeking Your wisdom and strength. Proverbs 11:2 affirms that pride and disgrace go hand in hand, as well as humility and wisdom. Father Adonai, help me to remain humble in all things and to seek wisdom through Your guidance. Protect me from the pitfalls of pride and grant me a heart that values humility and seeks Your understanding over my own. Ecclesiastes 11:2 teaches us to invest and diversify because life is uncertain. Guide me to be diligent and wise in my endeavors. Help me to plan and invest wisely, but also to trust in Your provision and protection regardless of the uncertainties of life. According to Isaiah 11:2, fill me with Your Spirit of wisdom and understanding. Guide me with Your counsel and strength and help me to grow in the knowledge and reverence of You. In Luke 11:2, Jesus teaches, "When you pray, say: 'Father, hallowed be your name, your kingdom come'" (NIV). Help me to approach You with reverence and to seek Your kingdom above all else. Let Your will be done in my life and guide me to honor Your name in everything I do. Thank You for Your guidance and the wisdom found in Your Word. Help me to live with humility, to make wise decisions, to seek Your Spirit, and to honor Your name.

In Jesus' name I pray, Amen

Proverbs 11:3 (NIV): The integrity of the upright guides them, but the unfaithful are destroyed by their duplicity.

Hebrews 11:3 (NKJV): By faith we understand that the worlds were framed by the word of God, so that the things which are seen were not made of things which are visible.

Isaiah 11:3 (TPT): He will find delight in living by the Spirit of the Fear of the Lord. He will neither judge by appearances nor make his decisions based on rumors.

Matthew 11:3 (NLT): Are you the Messiah we've been expecting, or should we keep looking for someone else?

Luke 11:3 (NLT): "Give us each day the food we need."

PRAYER

Dear Heavenly Father, El Tsuri (The Rock),

Thank You for Your endless love and guidance in my life. I come before You seeking Your wisdom and strength for the journey ahead. Proverbs 11:3 teaches us to live with integrity and honesty. Help me to make choices that reflect Your truth and righteousness, avoiding any deceitfulness or duplicity. Hebrews 11:3 challenges us to trust God's Word even when we can't see the outcome. It reminds believers that faith aligns us with God's creative power. Increase my faith to trust in Your power and sovereignty. Help me to believe in the unseen and trust that You are working in ways beyond my understanding. As Isaiah 11:3 teaches, help me to rely on Your wisdom and discernment rather than my own limited perspective. Guide me to make decisions based on Your truth and not solely on external appearances. Matthew 11:3 says, "Are you the one who is to come, or should we expect someone else?" (NIV). Help me to have clarity and certainty in my faith. Let me trust in Your promises and not be swayed by doubts or confusion. Luke 11:3 teaches me that You provide for my needs each day. Help me to trust in Your provision. Teach me to be content and grateful for what You supply. Thank You for Your guidance, wisdom, and provision.

In Jesus' name I pray, Amen

NOVEMBER 4

I WILL PROPHESY LOUDLY AND CLEARLY

Luke 11:4 (ESV): "And forgive us of our sins, for we ourselves forgive everyone who is indebted to us. And lead us not into temptation."

Proverbs 11:4 (ESV): Riches do not profit in the day of wrath, but righteousness delivers from death.

Ecclesiastes 11:4 (NIV): Whoever watches the wind will not plant; whoever looks at the clouds will not reap.

Ezekiel 11:4 (NLT): Therefore, son of man, prophecy against them loudly and clearly.

Psalm 11:4 (NLT): But the LORD is in his holy Temple; the LORD still rules from heaven. He watches everyone closely, examining every person on earth.

PRAYER

Dear Heavenly Father, El Chai (The Living God),

Thank You for Your love and the many ways You guide and bless my life. Luke 11:4 acknowledges human imperfection and our need for ongoing forgiveness. Help me to seek Your forgiveness for my shortcomings and to extend forgiveness to others just as You have forgiven me. Guide me away from temptation and protect me from the snares of the enemy. Proverbs 11:4 teaches, "Wealth is worthless in the day of wrath, but righteousness delivers from death" (NIV). Help me to focus on living a righteous life rather than seeking material wealth. May my actions reflect Your goodness and lead me to eternal life. Ecclesiastes 11:4 instructs me to act with faith and not to be paralyzed by uncertainty. Help me to take action in accordance with Your will, trusting that You will guide and bless my efforts. Ezekiel 11:4 reveals if God leads me the way He lead Ezekiel, then I must publicly confront and expose the sins of leaders. Lord, guide me to speak truth and stand up for what is right, even when it is difficult. Give me the courage to be a voice for justice and righteousness in my community. Psalm 11:4 says, I am comforted knowing that You see and understand all things. Help me to live in a way that is pleasing to You, knowing that You are always watching over me. Thank You for Your continuous guidance, wisdom, and love.

In the living name of Jesus I pray, Amen

Hebrews 11:5 (NIV): By faith Enoch was taken from this life, so that he did not experience death: "He could not be found, because God had taken him away." For before he was taken, he was commended as one who pleased God.

Proverbs 11:5 (NLT): The godly are directed by honesty; the wicked fall beneath their load of sin.

Ecclesiastes 11:5 (NKJV): As you do not know what is the way of the wind, or how the bones grow in the womb of her who is with child, so you do not know the works of God who makes everything.

Psalm 11:5 (NLT): The LORD examines both the righteous and the wicked. He hates those who love violence.

PRAYER

Dear Heavenly Father, Metzudah (Fortress),

Thank You for Your love and the guidance You provide in my life. I come before You seeking Your wisdom and strength. Hebrews 11:5 shows me to have faith like Enoch's, living in a way that pleases You. Guide me to trust in Your plan and to seek Your approval in all I do. I know You see what's hidden and will bring accountability. Proverbs 11:5 teaches me to live righteously and walk in Your ways, trusting that Your guidance will make my path clear. Protect me from wickedness and help me to stay on the path of integrity. Ecclesiastes 11:5 acknowledges that Your ways are not my ways and beyond my understanding. Help me to trust in the mystery of Your work in the world, particularly Your creative and sovereign power. Psalm 11:5 reveals that the Lord examines all of us—good or bad. Father, search my heart and examine my ways. Help me to live righteously and to avoid any actions that are contrary to Your will. Guide me to love what is good and to pursue justice. Thank You for Your guidance, wisdom, and the assurance of Your presence in my life.

In Jesus' honest name I pray, Amen

I HAVE BEEN GIVEN GRACE

Hebrews 11:6 (NIV): And it is impossible to please God without faith. Anyone who wants to come to him must believe that God exists and that he rewards those who sincerely seek him.

Proverbs 11:6 (NLT): The godliness of good people rescues them; the ambition of treacherous people traps them.

Romans 11:6 (NLT): And since it is through God's kindness, then it is not by their good works. For in that case, God's grace would not be what it really is—free and undeserved.

Ecclesiastes 11:6 (NLT): Plant your seed in the morning and keep busy all afternoon, for you don't know if profit will come from one activity or another—or maybe both.

PRAYER

Dear Heavenly Father, El Yalad (The God Who Gave You Birth),

Thank You for Your constant love and guidance. I come before You seeking Your strength and wisdom. Hebrews 11:6 says, "And without faith it is impossible to please God, because anyone who comes to him must believe that he exists and that he rewards those who earnestly seek him" (NIV). I ask for a strong faith that pleases You. Help me to earnestly seek You and trust that You will reward my efforts always. Proverbs 11:6 teaches, "The righteousness of the upright delivers them, but the unfaithful are trapped by evil desires" (NIV). Guide me to live a righteous life that reflects Your love and grace. Protect me from being trapped by unfaithful desires and keep my heart aligned with Your true will. Romans 11:6 says, "And if by grace, then it cannot be based on works; if it were, grace would no longer be grace" (NIV). I am grateful for Your grace, which is a gift and not something I can earn. Help me to fully accept Your grace and to extend grace to others as You have extended it to me. Ecclesiastes 11:6 teaches, "Sow your seed in the morning, and at evening let not your hands be idle, for you do not know which will succeed, whether this or that, or whether both will do equally well" (NIV). Help me to diligently work and invest my efforts, trusting that You will bring about success in Your timing. Let me be productive and not idle, while leaving the outcome in Your hands.

In Jesus' graceful name I pray, Amen

I PREACH THE GOOD NEWS

Hebrews 11:7 (NLT): It was by faith that Noah built a large boat to save his family from the flood. He obeyed God, who warned him about things that had never happened before. By his faith Noah condemned the rest of the world, and he received the righteousness that comes by faith.

Psalm 11:7 (NLT): For the righteous LORD loves justice. The virtuous will see his face.

Deuteronomy 11:7 (NLT): You have seen the LORD perform all these mighty deeds with your own eyes!

2 Corinthians 11:7 (NLT): Was I wrong when I humbled myself and honored you by preaching God's Good News to you without expecting anything in return?

— PRAYER —

Dear Heavenly Father, El Elyon (God Most High),

Thank You for Your guidance and care in my life. I seek Your wisdom and protection as I walk each day in Your presence. Hebrews 11:7 describes unexplainable faith. Noah built a boat in anticipation of a flood when it had never even rained before. Lord, help me to have faith like Noah, trusting in Your guidance even when I don't fully understand what lies ahead. Strengthen my faith to act on Your promises and live according to Your will. Psalm 11:7 expresses Your righteousness and love for justice. Help me to live a life that reflects Your justice and righteousness, and to seek Your face in all I do. Deuteronomy 11:7 says, "But it was your own eyes that saw all these great things the LORD has done" (NIV). Thank You for the many ways You have worked in my life. Help me to remember and be grateful for Your past blessings and to trust in Your continued goodness. 2 Corinthians 11:7 teaches, "Was it a sin for me to lower myself in order to elevate you by preaching the gospel of God to you free of charge?" (NIV). Guide me to serve others selflessly and to be generous with my time, money, and resources. Help me to follow Your example in caring for others without ever seeking anything in return.

In the providing name of Jesus I pray, Amen

NOVEMBER 8

Hebrews 11:8 (NLT): It was by faith that Abraham obeyed when God called him to leave home and go to another land that God would give him as his inheritance. He went without knowing where he was going.

Proverbs 11:8 (NLT): The godly are rescued from trouble, and it falls on the wicked instead.

1 Corinthians 11:8 (KJV): For the man is not of the woman; But the woman of the man.

PRAYER

Dear Heavenly Father, El Hakkavod (The God of Glory),

Thank You for Your love and guidance in my life. I come before You seeking Your wisdom and strength. Hebrews 11:8 teaches, "By faith Abraham, when called to go to a place he would later receive as his inheritance, obeyed and went, even though he did not know where he was going" (NIV). Help me to trust in Your plan for my life, even when the path is unclear. Grant me the faith to follow You obediently, just as Abraham did. Proverbs 11:8 says, "The righteous person is rescued from trouble, and it falls on the wicked instead" (NIV). I ask for Your protection and deliverance from troubles. Help me to live righteously and trust in Your protection from harm. 1 Corinthians 11:8 teaches, "For man did not come from woman, but woman from man" (NIV). Help me to understand and appreciate the roles and relationships You have designed for Your created sons and daughters. Guide me to respect and honor others in accordance with Your wisdom. Thank You for Your guidance and the promises in Your Word. Help me to have faith, trust in Your protection, respect the roles You have designed, and live a life of obedience and grace.

In Jesus' glorious name I pray, Amen

NOVEMBER 9

I ASK ALOUD AND HE ANSWERS

Proverbs 11:9 (NLT): With their words, the godless destroyed their friends, but knowledge will rescue the righteous.

Luke 11:9 (NIV): "So I say to you: Ask and it will be given to you; seek and you will find; knock and the door will be opened to you."

John 11:9 (KJV): Jesus answered, "Are there not twelve hours in the day? If any man walk in the day, he stumbleth not, because he seeth the light of this world."

PRAYER

Dear Heavenly Father, El Nathan Neqamah (The God Who Avenges Me),

Thank You for Your endless love and guidance in my life. I seek Your presence and wisdom as I navigate each day. Proverbs 11:9 says, "With their mouths the godless destroy their neighbors, but through knowledge the righteous escape" (NIV). Guide me to speak words that are life giving, rather than harmful words. Help me to use my knowledge and understanding to positively impact those around me. In Luke 11:9, Jesus teaches, "So I say to you: Ask and it will be given to you; seek and you will find; knock and the door will be opened to you." I ask for Your guidance and wisdom in my life. Help me to trust in Your promises and to seek Jesus morning, noon, and night, knowing that You will respond to my needs. John 11:9 teaches, "Jesus answered, 'Are there not twelve hours of daylight? Anyone who walks in the daytime will not stumble, for they see by this world's light'" (NIV). Help me to walk in the light of Your truth and guidance. Let Your light shine on my path so that I may avoid stumbling and follow Your way. Thank You for Your guidance and the light You provide. Help me to live in Your peace, trust in Your promises, speak with wisdom, and walk in Your light.

In Jesus' seeking name I pray, Amen

NOVEMBER 10

I LIVE IN GOD'S KINGDOM AND AM BLESSED

Mark 11:10 (ESV): Blessed is the coming kingdom of our father David! Hosanna in the highest!

Proverbs 11:10 (NLT): The whole city celebrates when the godly succeed; then shout for joy when the wicked die.

Ecclesiastes 11:10 (NLT): So refuse to worry, and keep your body healthy. But remember that youth, with a whole life before you, is meaningless.

Luke 11:10 (NIV): "For everyone who asks receives; the one who seeks finds; and to the one who knocks, the door will be opened."

Matthew 11:10 (NLT): "John is the man to whom the Scriptures refer when they say, 'Look, I am sending my messenger ahead of you, and he will prepare your way before you.'"

PRAYER

Dear Heavenly Father, El Olam (The Everlasting God, the Eternal God),

Thank You for Your love and guidance in my life. Mark 11:10 says I live in the kingdom of the blessed. I rejoice in the coming of Your kingdom and Your promises. Help me to live in the light of Your kingdom and to be a faithful follower of Christ. Proverbs 11:10 teaches, "When the righteous prosper, the city rejoices; when the wicked perish, there are shouts of joy" (NIV). I ask for Your blessings upon my life, that through Your guidance and grace, I may bring joy and positivity to those around me. Help me to live righteously so that my actions bring glory to Your name. Ecclesiastes 11:10 instructs me to trust You with my worries and to find peace in Your presence. Guide me to focus on what truly matters and to rely on Your strength rather than my own. Luke 11:10 teaches, "For everyone who asks receives; the one who seeks finds; and to the one who knocks, the door will be opened." Thank You for Your promise to hear and answer my prayers. Help me to seek You diligently and to trust that You will provide what I need. Matthew 11:10 speaks of the messengers You send into my life who guide and encourage me. Help me to be open to the Holy Spirit's wisdom and to follow the path You have set before me.

In Jesus' eternal name I pray, Amen

NOVEMBER 11

I believe God keeps His promises

Hebrews 11:11 (NLT): It was by faith that even Sarah was able to have a child, though she was barren and was too old. She believed that God would keep his promise.

Proverbs 11:11 (NIV): Through the blessing of the upright a city is exalted, but by the mouth of the wicked it is destroyed.

Luke 11:11 (NLT): "You fathers—if your children ask for a fish, do you give them a snake instead?"

Job 11:11 (NLT): For he knows those who are false, and he takes note of all their sins.

1 Corinthians 11:11 (NLT): But among the Lord's people, women are not independent of men, and men are not independent of women.

 PRAYER

Dear Heavenly Father, El Racham (The Compassionate God),

Thank You for Your unwavering love and guidance in my life. I come to You with a heart open to Your wisdom and grace. Hebrews 11:11 says my faith in God's promises will bring me blessings. Help me to trust in Your promises, even when circumstances seem impossible. Strengthen my faith to believe in Your miraculous power and faithfulness. Proverbs 11:11 teaches me to live a life that uplifts and blesses those around me. Let my actions and words contribute positively to my community and not bring harm. Luke 11:11 says, "Which of you fathers, if your son asks for a fish, will give him a snake instead?" (NIV). Thank You for being a good and loving Father who provides for my needs. Help me to trust in Your provision and to believe that You give what is good and perfect. Job 11:11 teaches me discernment to recognize what is true and right. Help me to avoid deceit and to act with integrity in all situations. 1 Corinthians 11:11 shows that both man and woman are interconnected and equally valuable. Lord, help me to value and respect the relationships and interdependence You have created. Let me live in harmony with others, appreciating our mutual roles and contributions.

In the promising name of Jesus I pray, Amen

NOVEMBER 12

I KNOW WHEN TO SPEAK

Hebrews 11:12 (NIV): And so from this one man [Abraham], and he as good as dead, came descendants as numerous as the stars in the sky and as countless as the sand on the seashore.

Proverbs 11:12 (NLT): It is foolish to belittle one's neighbor; a sensible person keeps quiet.

Deuteronomy 11:12 (NLT): A land that the LORD your God cares for. He watches over it through each season of the year!

Luke 11:12 (NLT): "Or if [your child] asks for an egg, do you give them a scorpion, of course not!"

Revelation 11:12 (NLT): Then a loud voice from Heaven called to the two prophets, "Come up here!" And they rose to heaven on a cloud as their enemies watched.

PRAYER

Dear Heavenly Father, Elohim Yare (God Most Awesome),

Hebrews 11:12 shows me the example of faith and the blessings that come from trusting in You. Help me to have faith like Abraham, believing in Your promises. Proverbs 11:12 teaches me the wisdom to speak with kindness and understanding. Help me to avoid belittling others and to be thoughtful in my words and actions. Deuteronomy 11:12 reveals Your constant care and attention to every detail of my life. Help me to trust in Your ongoing provision and care throughout every season of each year. Luke 11:12 teaches, "Or if he asks for an egg, will give him a scorpion?" Help me to trust in knowing that You give good gifts to Your children. Teach me to rely on Your love and faithfulness in every aspect of my life. Revelation 11:12 says, "Then a loud voice from heaven called to the two prophets, 'Come up here!' And they rose to heaven on a cloud as their enemies watched." Lord, let Your Spirit overshadow me like a cloud. Guide me, cover me, and carry me. And may my life testify of Your power, that others would see and believe that You alone are God. Help me to have faith like Abraham, speak with understanding, trust in Your care, rely on Your goodness, and stand firm in the power You've given me.

In Jesus' faithful name I pray, Amen

NOVEMBER 13

I AM TRUSTWORTHY AND KEEP CONFIDENCES

Proverbs 11:13 (NIV): A gossip betrays a confidence, but a trustworthy person keeps a secret.

Luke 11:13 (NLT): "If you sinful people know how to give good gifts to your children, how much more will your heavenly father give the Holy Spirit to those who ask him."

Isaiah 11:13 (NLT): Then at last the jealousy between Israel and Judah will end. They will not be rivals anymore.

Deuteronomy 11:13 (NLT): If you carefully obey the commands I am Giving you today, and if you love the LORD your God and serve him with all your heart and soul.

Hebrews 11:13 (NIV): All these people were still living by faith when they died. They did not receive the things promised; they only saw them and welcomed them from a distance, admitting that they were foreigners and strangers on earth.

PRAYER

Dear Heavenly Father, Gelah Raz (Revealer of Mysteries),

Proverbs 11:13 teaches how we should not gossip because it betrays the confidence of others and only trustworthy people can keep a secret. Lord let me be someone who is reliable and discreet in my interactions. Luke 11:13 says I've been given the gift of the Holy Spirit. Fill me, Holy Spirit, and guide me to steward this gift purposefully. Isaiah 11:13 instructs me to overcome any feelings of jealousy or hostility in all my relationships with You. Teach me to live in harmony and unity with others. Deuteronomy 11:13 tells me to faithfully obey Your commands and to love You with all my heart and soul. Guide me in serving You wholeheartedly. Hebrews 11:13 teaches, "All these people were still living by faith when they died. They did not receive the things promised; they only saw them and welcomed them from a distance, admitting that they were foreigners and strangers on earth." Strengthen my faith and help me to trust in Your promises, even when I do not see their fulfillment yet. Thank You for Your guidance and the strength You provide. Help me to discern truth, be trustworthy, embrace the Holy Spirit, live in harmony, obey Your commands, and maintain faith in Your promises.

In Jesus' revealing name I pray, Amen

NOVEMBER 14

I leave iniquity behind me

2 Corinthians 11:14 (NIV): And no wonder, for Satan himself masquerades as an angel of light.

Proverbs 11:14 (NLT): Without wise leadership, a nation falls; there is safety in having many advisors.

Luke 11:14 (NIV): Jesus was driving out a demon that was mute. When the demon left, the man who had been mute spoke, and the crowd was amazed.

Ezekiel 11:14 (NIV): The word of the LORD came to me.

Job 11:14 (NIV): If you put away the sin that is in your hand and allow no evil to dwell in your tent.

PRAYER

Dear Heavenly Father, Rum Rosh (The One Who Lifts My Head),

Second Corinthians 11:14 asserts I must be vigilant and discerning, recognizing and resisting any false angels that might come my way. I bind and rebuke in the mighty name of Jesus those disguised as an angel of light. Proverbs 11:14 advises me to seek and heed wise advice in all areas of my life. Lord, I pray You guard our nation with many God-fearing advisors. Luke 11:14 speaks of the power of Jesus to bring healing and transformation. I ask for Your power to work in my life, so that I can bring healing to those around me. Ezekiel 11:14 teaches, "The word of the LORD came to me." Speak to me, Lord, through Your Word and Your Spirit. Help me to listen and respond to Your guidance, and to be attentive to what You are saying to me. Job 11:14 says, "If you put away the sin that is in your hand and allow no evil to dwell in your tent." Help me to remove sin and evil from my life. Cleanse my heart and renew my mind and guide me to live in a way that is pleasing to You. Thank You for Your wisdom and guidance. Help me to discern truth, seek wise counsel, experience Your power, listen to Your voice, and live a life free from the open doors of sin. My flesh does not dominate me.

In Jesus' uplifting name I pray, Amen

NOVEMBER 15

THE HOLY SPIRIT IS IN ME

Acts 11:15 (NIV): As I began to speak, the Holy Spirit came on them as he had come on us at the beginning.

Job 11:15 (NIV): Then, free of fault, you will lift up your face; you will stand firm and without fear.

Proverbs 11:15 (NLT): There's danger in putting up security for a stranger's debt; it's safer not to guarantee another person's debt.

Matthew 11:15 (NLT): "Anyone with ears to hear should listen and understand!"

PRAYER

Dear Heavenly Father, El Nahsah (Forgiving God),

I'm here to be saturated in Your presence. Acts 11:15 explains the gift of the Holy Spirit. Heavenly Father, fill me with the Holy Spirit's wisdom and revelation in the knowledge of Jesus. Let my flesh melt off spiritually and Holy Spirit fill in the empty spaces. Job 11:15 teaches, "Then, free of fault, you will lift up your face; you will stand firm and without fear." Help me to face each day with confidence and courage, knowing that You are with me. Remove any fear or shame and grant me the strength to stand firm in my faith. Proverbs 11:15 says, "Whoever puts up security for a stranger will surely suffer, but whoever refuses to shake hands in pledge is safe" (NIV). Give me wisdom in my decisions and relationships. I will make choices that are prudent and will avoid unnecessary risks. Matthew 11:15 teaches, "Whoever has ears, let them hear" (NIV). Open my ears to hear Your voice clearly. Guide me to understand Your Word and to follow Your direction faithfully. I live in Your kingdom, avoid distractions, embrace the Holy Spirit, stand firm in faith, make wise choices, and hear Your voice.

In Jesus' forgiving name I pray, Amen

NOVEMBER 16

MY HEART IS NOT DECEIVED

Proverbs 11:16 (NIV): A kindhearted woman gains honor, but ruthless men gain only wealth.

Luke 11:16 (NIV): Others tested [Jesus] by asking for a sign from heaven.

Acts 11:16 (ESV): And I remembered the word of the Lord, how [Jesus] said, "John indeed baptized with water, but you shall be baptized with the Holy Spirit."

Deuteronomy 11:16 (NLT): Be careful! Do not let your heart be deceived so that you turn away from the LORD and serve and worship other gods.

Hebrews 11:16 (NLT): But they were looking for a better place, a heavenly homeland. That is why God is not ashamed to be called their God, for he has prepared a city for them.

PRAYER

Dear Heavenly Father, Jehovah Shalom (The LORD is Peace),

Proverbs 11:16 says, "A gracious woman gains honor, but ruthless men gain only wealth." Help me to embody grace and kindness in my interactions. Let my actions reflect Your love and honor, rather than seeking wealth or power. Luke 11:16 teaches, "Others tested him by asking for a sign from heaven." Help me to trust in Your presence and power without constantly seeking signs. Strengthen my faith and help me to rely on Your Word and promises. Acts 11:16 says, "Then I remembered what the Lord had said: 'John baptized with water, but you will be baptized with the Holy Spirit'" (NIV). Thank You for the gift of the Holy Spirit. Help me to embrace the Spirit's work in my life and to live according to His guidance. Lord, release Your glorious power upon me. Deuteronomy 11:16 teaches, "Be careful, or you will be enticed to turn away and worship other gods and bow down to them" (NIV). Guard my heart from being led astray by distractions or false teachings. Keep me focused on Your truth. Hebrews 11:16 says, "Instead, they were longing for a better country—a heavenly one. Therefore God is not ashamed to be called their God, for he has prepared a city for them" (NIV). Help me to keep my focus on the eternal promises You have made. Let my longing be for Your heavenly kingdom and Your promises, not the things of this world.

In Jesus' peaceful name I pray, Amen

NOVEMBER 17

MY KINDNESS REWARDS ME

Proverbs 11:17 (NLT): Your kindness will reward you, but your cruelty will destroy you.

Luke 11:17 (NIV): Jesus knew their thoughts and said to them: "Any kingdom divided against itself will be ruined, and a house divided against itself will fall."

Acts 11:17 (NLT): God gave these Gentiles the same gift he gave [the Jews] when [they] believed in the Lord Jesus Christ.

Revelation 11:17 (NIV): We give you thanks, O Lord God Almighty, the One who is and who was and who is to come, because you have taken your great power and have begun to reign.

Job 11:17 (NLT): Your life will be brighter than the noonday. Even darkness will be as bright as morning.

 PRAYER

Dear Heavenly Father, Logos (The Word),

Proverbs 11:17 expresses I must be kind and compassionate in all my interactions. Guide me to act with love and to benefit from the kindness I extend to others. Luke 11:17 teaches that Jesus knows our thoughts and He's warning us that unity is essential. Lord, I ask You to guide me to work toward reconciliation and understanding rather than division. Acts 11:17 says to recognize and celebrate the gifts and grace You give to others. Teach me to embrace Your work in all people and to support Your plan without hesitation. Revelation 11:17 is a song of worship and gratitude to the sovereign God who rules over all. He has come and is actively reigning. I trust in Your kingship and give thanks for Your mighty acts in my life and in the world. Job 11:17 says, "Life will be brighter than noonday, and darkness will become like morning" (NIV). Guide me through dark times and help me to see the light and hope You provide. Strengthen my faith and brighten my path with Your presence.

In Jesus' kind name I pray, Amen

NOVEMBER 18

I AM COMMITTED WHOLEHEARTEDLY TO GOD'S WORD

Proverbs 11:18 (NIV): A wicked person earns deceptive wages, but the one who sows righteousness reaps a sure reward.

Jeremiah 11:18 (ESV): The LORD made it known to me and I knew; then you showed me their deeds.

Deuteronomy 11:18 (NLT): So commit yourselves wholeheartedly to these words of mine. Tie them to your hands and wear them on your forehead as reminders.

Romans 11:18 (NLT): But you must not brag about being grafted in to replace the branches that were broken off. You are just a branch, not the root.

PRAYER

Dear Heavenly Father, Jehovah-Palat (The LORD My Deliverer),

Proverbs 11:18 instructs me to live righteously and to make choices that reflect Your truth. The enemy often promises quick rewards, but they come with hidden consequences. May I be diligent in sowing goodness and integrity, trusting that You will bring about a reward. Jeremiah 11:18 says God shows us the plans of the enemy. Help me to be aware of Your guidance and to trust in Your ability to reveal what is hidden. Deuteronomy 11:18 says, "Fix these words of mine in your hearts and minds; tie them as symbols on your hands and bind them on your foreheads" (NIV). Help me to keep Your Word central in my life. Let Your teachings guide my thoughts and actions, and let me remember them always as I walk in Your ways. Romans 11:18 teaches I am grafted into the spiritual family of God. Keep me humble and remind me that I am supported by Your grace and the faith of those who came before me. Help me to remain grounded in humility and gratitude. Thank You for Your wisdom and the strength You provide. Help me to live righteously, discern Your truth, keep Your Word close to my heart, and stay humble in Your grace.

In Jesus' committed name I pray, Amen

I AM RIGHTEOUS IN TRUTH

Leviticus 11:19 (ESV): The stork, the heron of any kind, the hoopoe, and the bat.

Proverbs 11:19 (NIV): Truly the righteous attain life, but whoever pursues evil finds death.

Revelation 11:19 (NLT): Then, in heaven, the Temple of God was opened and the Ark of his covenant could be seen inside the Temple. Lightning flashed, thunder crashed and roared, and there was an earthquake and a terrible hailstorm.

Ezekiel 11:19 (NIV): I will give them an undivided heart and put a new spirit in them; I will remove from them their heart of stone and give them a heart a flesh.

 **PRAYER**

Dear Heavenly Father, Qadosh Yisrael (The Holy One of Israel),

Leviticus 11:19 while this verse lists unclean animals and spirits, it reminds me of Your commands regarding purity. Help me to keep my life pure and to follow Your guidance in all things. I bind, rebuke, and cast out all unclean spirits. Proverbs 11:19 teaches, "Truly the righteous attain life, but whoever pursues evil finds death." Guide me to live a life of righteousness and to avoid the enemy's path of evil. Help me to seek what is good and to live in a way that leads to life and blessing. In Revelation 11:19 we see the heavenly unveiling. This verse signifies direct access to God's presence: His promise, His faithfulness, His divine power and judgment. God is near to us and unchanging. Ezekiel 11:19 teaches, "I will give them an undivided heart and put a new spirit in them; I will remove from them their heart of stone and give them a heart of flesh." Transform my heart, Lord, and renew my spirit. Remove any hardness and replace it with a heart that is tender and responsive to Your will. Let my heart feel what You feel Lord. I thank You for Your guidance and the work You are doing in my heart. Help me to live a pure and righteous life, to honor Your greatness, and to embrace the new heart and spirit You offer.

In Jesus' great name I pray, Amen

NOVEMBER 20

Proverbs 11:20 (NLT): The LORD detests people with crooked hearts, but he delights in those with integrity.

Luke 11:20 (NLT): "But if I am casting out demons by the power of God, then the Kingdom of God has arrived among you."

Romans 11:20 (NLT): Yes, but remember—those branches were broken off because they didn't believe in Christ, and you are there because you do believe. So don't think highly of yourself, but fear what could happen.

Deuteronomy 11:20 (ESV): You shall write the [LORD's commandments] on the doorposts of your house and on your gates.

PRAYER

Dear Heavenly Father, El Moshaah (The God Who Saves),

Thank You for Your guidance and care in my life. I seek Your help to live with integrity and faith. Proverbs 11:20 says, "The LORD detests those whose hearts are perverse, but he delights in those whose ways are blameless" (NIV). Help me to live a life of integrity and purity. Guide me to align my heart and actions with Your Word, and to avoid anything that is contrary to Jesus. Luke 11:20 teaches, "But if I drive out demons by the finger of God, then the kingdom of God has come upon you" (NIV). I acknowledge Your power and authority in my life. Help me to recognize and welcome Your kingdom in all aspects of my life and to trust in Your power to overcome all demons in my life. Romans 11:20 says, "Granted. But they were broken off because of unbelief, and you stand by faith. Do not be arrogant, but tremble" (NIV). Help me to stand firm in my faith and avoid arrogance. Keep me humble and reliant on Your grace, knowing that my standing before You is by faith alone. Deuteronomy 11:20 teaches, "Write them on the doorframes of your houses and on your gates" (NIV). Help me to keep Your Word close to my heart and to make it a central part of my life. Let Your teachings be evident in my daily actions and decisions. Thank You for Your guidance and the strength You provide.

In Jesus' heartfelt name I pray, Amen

I FLOURISH IN THE LAND GOD HAS GIVEN ME

Proverbs 11:21 (NLT): Evil people will surely be punished, but the children of the godly will go free.

Acts 11:21 (NLT): The power of the Lord was with them, and a large number of these Gentiles believed and turned to the Lord.

Deuteronomy 11:21 (NLT): So that as long as the sky remains above the earth, you and your children may flourish in the land the LORD swore to give your ancestors.

Ezekiel 11:21 (NLT): But as for those who long for vile images and detestable idols, I will repay them fully for their sins. I, the sovereign LORD, have spoken!

PRAYER

Dear Heavenly Father, El Shamayim (The God of Heaven),

Proverbs 11:21 says, "The wicked will not go unpunished, but those who are righteous will go free" (NIV). Help me to live righteously and to trust in Your justice. Guide me to make choices that honor You and avoid the ways of wickedness. I want to keep all doors to sin closed in my life. Acts 11:21 teaches, "The Lord's hand was with them, and a great number of people believed and turned to the Lord" (NIV). I ask for Your hand to be with me and to guide my efforts. Help me to be a witness to Your love and to bring others to faith in Jesus. Deuteronomy 11:21 says, "So that your days and the days of your children may be many in the land the LORD swore to give your ancestors, as many as the days that the heavens are above the earth" (NIV). Bless me with long life and prosperity as I follow Your commands. Help me to live in a way that honors Your promises and shower blessings over my family. Ezekiel 11:21 teaches, "But as for those whose hearts are devoted to their vile images and abominable idols, I will bring down on their own heads what they have done, declares the Sovereign LORD" (NIV). Help me to keep my heart focused on You and to avoid anything that takes me away from Your path. Guide me to remain devoted to You and to live a life that is obedient to You. Thank You for Your guidance and faithfulness. Help me to live righteously, be a witness to Your love, and keep my heart devoted to You.

In Jesus' powerful name I pray, Amen

NOVEMBER 22

I HAVE FAITH IN GOD

Mark 11:22 (NKJV): So Jesus answered and said to them, "Have faith in God."

Proverbs 11:22 (NLT): A beautiful woman who lacks discretion is like a gold ring in a pig's snout.

Deuteronomy 11:22 (NLT): Be careful to obey all these commands I am giving you. Show love to the LORD your God by walking in his ways and holding tightly to him.

Romans 11:22 (NLT): Notice how God is both kind and severe. He is severe towards those who disobeyed, but kind to you if you continue to trust in his kindness. But if you stop trusting, you also will be cut off.

PRAYER

Dear Heavenly Father, Jehovah-Machsi (The LORD My Refuge),

In Mark 11:22, Jesus teaches, "Have faith in God." Strengthen my faith and help me to trust in You completely. When faced with difficulties, remind me to lean on Your promises and rely on Your strength. Proverbs 11:22 says, "Like a gold ring in a pig's snout is a beautiful woman who shows no discretion" (NIV). Help me to live with wisdom and discretion, valuing inner beauty and character over external appearances. Guide me to make choices that reflect Your wisdom and honor. Deuteronomy 11:22 says, "If you carefully observe all these commands I am giving you to follow—to love the LORD your God, to walk in obedience to him and to hold fast to him" (NIV). Help me to follow Your commands with a heart full of love and obedience. Guide me to walk in Your ways and remain faithful to You. Romans 11:22 teaches, "Consider therefore the kindness and sternness of God: sternness to those who fell, but kindness to you, provided that you continue in his kindness. Otherwise, you also will be cut off" (NIV). Help me to understand and appreciate Your kindness and sternness. Teach me to remain steadfast in Your kindness and to live in a way that reflects Your grace. Thank You for Your faithfulness and the strength You provide.

In the refuge name of Jesus I pray, Amen

NOVEMBER 23

My faith is released through my word

Mark 11:23 (ESV): "Truly, I say to you, whoever says to this mountain, 'Be taken up and thrown into the sea,' and does not doubt in his heart, but believes that what he says will come to pass, it will be done for him."

Proverbs 11:23 (NLT): The godly can look forward to a reward, while the wicked can expect only judgment.

Luke 11:23 (NLT): "Anyone who isn't with me opposes me, and anyone who isn't working with me is actually working against me."

Acts 11:23 (NIV): When he arrived and saw what the grace of God had done, he was glad and encouraged them all to remain true to the Lord with all their hearts.

PRESENT

Dear Heavenly Father, Jehovah-Magen (The Lord My Shield),

Thank You for Your love and guidance in my life. In Mark 11:23 Jesus taught us that our faith is released through our words. Help me to have faith as strong as this, trusting in Your power to move obstacles and fulfill Your promises. Teach me to believe wholeheartedly in Your ability to move mountains in my life. Proverbs 11:23 teaches, "The desire of the righteous ends only in good, but the hope of the wicked only in wrath" (NIV). Guide me to align my desires with Your will, so that my hopes and actions lead to goodness and reflect Your righteousness. My reward is forever in eternity. Luke 11:23 says, "Whoever is not with me is against me, and whoever does not gather with me scatters" (NIV). Help me to stand firmly with You, aligning my life and actions with Your Spirit. Strengthen my commitment to follow You and to work together with others to build Your kingdom. Acts 11:23 reminds us, "When he arrived and saw what the grace of God had done, he was glad and encouraged them all to remain true to the Lord with all their hearts." Help me to see Your grace at work in my life and the lives of those around me. Encourage me to remain steadfast in my faith and to stay true to You with all my heart. Thank You for Your guidance and the strength You provide.

In Jesus' desirable name I pray, Amen

NOVEMBER 24

Mark 11:24 (NKJV): Therefore I say to you, whatever things you ask when you pray, believe that you receive them, and you will have them.

Proverbs 11:24 (NLT): Give freely and become more wealthy; Be stingy and lose everything.

Acts 11:24 (NIV): He was a good man, full of the Holy [Ghost] and faith, and a great number of people were brought to the Lord.

1 Corinthians 11:24 (NIV): And when [Jesus] had given thanks, he broke it and said, "This is my body, which is for you; do this in remembrance of me."

PRAYER

Dear Heavenly Father, YHWH (I AM),

Thank You for Your unending love and faithfulness. I come to You seeking Your help to strengthen my faith and cultivate a heart of gratitude. Mark 11:24 says, "Therefore I tell you, whatever you ask for in prayer, believe that you have received it, and it will be yours" (NIV). Help me to have faith in Your promises and to trust that You hear my prayers. Strengthen my belief that You are working for my good, even when I cannot see it. Proverbs 11:24 teaches, "One person gives freely, yet gains even more; another withholds unduly, but comes to poverty" (NIV). Help me to be generous and open-handed, trusting that as I give, I will also receive blessings. Guide me to share with others and to be a reflection of Your generosity. Acts 11:24 says, "He was a good man, full of the Holy Spirit and faith, and a great number of people were brought to the Lord." Fill me with Your Holy Spirit and strengthen my faith. Help me to live as a witness to Your goodness, drawing others to know and follow You. 1 Corinthians 11:24 teaches, "And when He had given thanks, He broke it and said, 'This is my body, which is for you; do this in remembrance of me.'" Help me to remember Jesus' sacrifice with gratitude and to live a life that honors His gift. May I continually give thanks for the grace and love You have shown me. Thank You for Your guidance and for the strength You provide. Help me to pray with faith, give generously, live by the Spirit, and remember Jesus with gratitude.

In Jesus' giving name I pray, Amen

Proverbs 11:25 (NLT): The generous will prosper; those who refresh others will themselves be refreshed.

Mark 11:25 (NLT): "But when you are praying, first forgive anyone you are holding a grudge against, so that your Father in heaven will forgive your sins, too."

Matthew 11:25 (NIV): At that time Jesus said, "I praise you, Father, Lord of heaven and earth, because you have hidden these things from the wise and learned, and revealed them to little children."

John 11:25 (NIV): Jesus said to her, "I am the resurrection and the life. The one who believes in me will live, even though they die."

PRAYER

Dear Heavenly Father, Entunchano (The God Who Intercedes),

Thank You for Your constant presence and guidance. I come to You seeking Your help to live a life of generosity and faith. Proverbs 11:25 says, "A generous person will prosper; whoever refreshes others will be refreshed" (NIV). Help me to be generous in my actions and spirit. May I refresh others with kindness and support, trusting that You will also refresh and bless me in return. Mark 11:25 teaches me to forgive others as You have forgiven me. Remove any bitterness or resentment from my heart and fill me with a spirit of grace and reconciliation. Matthew 11:25 says, "At that time Jesus said, 'I praise you, Father, Lord of heaven and earth, because you have hidden these things from the wise and learned, and revealed them to little children.'" Thank You for revealing Your wisdom and truths to us. Help me to approach You with the humility and openness of a child, trusting in Your guidance and understanding. John 11:25 reminds me to strengthen my faith in Jesus as the source of eternal life. Help me to live each day with the hope and assurance that comes from knowing Jesus is the resurrection and the life. Thank You for Your love and for the guidance You provide. Help me to live generously, forgive freely, approach You with humility, and trust in the promise of eternal life through Jesus.

In Jesus' unending name I pray, Amen

I CHOOSE BLESSINGS IN MY LIFE

Deuteronomy 11:26 (NIV): See, I am setting before you today a blessing and a curse.

Matthew 11:26 (NIV): "Yes, Father, for this is what you were pleased to do."

John 11:26 (NLT): "Everyone who lives in me and believes in me will never ever die. Do you believe this?"

PRAYER

Dear Heavenly Father, Sane (The God Who Hates Sin),

Deuteronomy 11:26 reminds me to choose blessing instead of cursing and life instead of death. Guide me to choose blessings by following Your commands and living according to Your will. Help me to discern Your path and to make choices that lead to Your blessings. Matthew 11:26 leads me to trust in Your divine plan and to accept that Your ways are perfect, even when I do not fully understand them. Thank You for the wisdom and guidance You provide. John 11:26 reminds us, "And whoever lives by believing in me will never die. Do you believe this?" (NIV). Strengthen my faith in Jesus and the promise of eternal life through Him. Help me to live with this belief at the forefront of my heart and mind, finding peace in Your promise of everlasting life. Thank You for Your faithfulness and the guidance You provide. Help me to stay strong in faith, make wise choices, trust in Your plan, and live with a firm belief in the promise of eternal life.

In the blessed name of Jesus I pray, Amen

I OBEY THE LORD'S COMMANDS

Deuteronomy 11:27 (NLT): You will be blessed if you obey the commands of the LORD your God that I am giving you today.

Proverbs 11:27 (NLT): If you search for good, you will find favor; but if you search for evil, it will find you!

John 11:27 (NLT): "Yes, Lord," she told [Jesus]. "I have always believed you are the Messiah, the Son of God, the one who has come into the world from God."

Matthew 11:27 (NLT): "My father has entrusted everything to me."

PRAYER

Dear Heavenly Father, Ori (My Light),

Thank You for Your constant presence and guidance. I seek Your blessings and understanding in my life today. Deuteronomy 11:27 says, "The blessing if you obey the commands of the LORD your God that I am giving you today" (NIV). Help me to follow Your commands and live in obedience to You. May Your blessings be evident in my life as I strive to honor Your Word. Proverbs 11:27 teaches, "Whoever seeks good finds favor, but evil comes to one who searches for it" (NIV). Guide me to seek goodness in all I do and to make choices that align with Your will. Help me to find favor in Your sight and avoid paths that lead to harm. John 11:27 says, "Yes, Lord," she replied, "I believe that you are the Messiah, the Son of God, who is to come into the world" (NIV). Strengthen my faith and belief in Jesus as the Messiah. Help me to trust in His promises and to recognize Him as the Savior and Lord of my life. In Matthew 11:27, Jesus reminds us, "All things have been committed to me by my Father. No one knows the Son except the Father, and no one knows the Father except the Son and those to whom the Son chooses to reveal him" (NIV). Thank You for revealing Yourself to us through Jesus. Help me to grow in my understanding of You and to deepen my relationship with both You and Your Son. Thank You for Your faithfulness and guidance. Help me to obey Your commands, seek goodness, strengthen my faith, trust in Your justice, and grow in my understanding of You.

In Jesus' favored name I pray, Amen

NOVEMBER 28

I rest in the Lord

Matthew 11:28 (NIV): "Come to me, all you who are weary and burdened, and I will give you rest."

Proverbs 11:28 (NLT): Trust in your money and down you go! But the godly flourish like leaves in spring.

Luke 11:28 (NLT): Jesus replied, "But even more blessed are all who hear the word of God and put it into practice."

1 Corinthians 11:28 (NLT): That is why you should examine yourself before eating the bread and drinking the cup.

 **PRAYER**

Dear Heavenly Father, Jehovah Shalom (The LORD Is Peace),

Thank You for Your endless love and grace. I come to You seeking rest and renewal. In Matthew 11:28, Jesus says, "Come to me, all you who are weary and burdened, and I will give you rest." Lord, I bring my burdens and worries to You. Please give me rest and peace and help me to find comfort in Your presence. Proverbs 11:28 says, "Those who trust in their riches will fall, but the righteous will thrive like a green leaf" (NIV). Help me to place my trust in You rather than in material wealth. Guide me to live righteously and to rely on Your provision and care. Luke 11:28 reminds us, "He replied, 'Blessed rather are those who hear the word of God and obey it'" (NIV). Help me to listen to Your Word and to follow Your guidance. Fill me with the desire to obey Your commands and to live according to Your will. 1 Corinthians 11:28 says, "Everyone ought to examine themselves before they eat of the bread and drink from the cup" (NIV). As I come before You, help me to examine my heart and to approach You with sincerity and reverence. Guide me in making things right and seeking Your forgiveness where needed. Thank You for Your faithfulness and for the rest You provide. Help me to trust in You, live righteously, obey Your Word, and approach You with a truthful heart.

In the Good News of Jesus' name I pray, Amen

Romans 11:29 (NLT): For God's gifts and His call can never be withdrawn.

Proverbs 11:29 (NLT): Those who bring trouble on their families inherit the wind. The fool will be a servant to the wise.

Matthew 11:29 (NLT): "Take my yoke upon you. Let me teach you, because I am humble, and you will find rest for your souls."

PRAYER

Dear Heavenly Father, Tsaddik (Righteous),

Romans 11:29 says, "For the gifts and the calling of God are irrevocable" (NIV). Thank You for the unique gifts and calling You have given me. Help me to use these gifts faithfully and to trust in Your unchanging plan for my life. Proverbs 11:29 teaches, "Whoever brings ruin on their family will inherit only wind, and the fool will be servant to the wise" (NIV). Help me to build my family and relationships with wisdom and love. Guide me to make choices that support and uplift those around me, avoiding actions that lead to ruin. Matthew 11:29 says, "Take my yoke upon you and learn from me, for I am gentle and humble in heart, and you will find rest for your souls" (NIV). I come to You with my burdens and seek rest in Your gentle and humble presence. Teach me to learn from You and to find peace in Your guidance. Thank You for Your faithfulness and the promises You give. Help me to use my gifts wisely, support my loved ones, find rest in You, have faith in Your guidance, and live according to Your will.

In Jesus' hopeful name I pray, Amen

NOVEMBER 30

I AM A WISE PERSON

Proverbs 11:30 (NLT): The seeds of good deeds become a tree of life; a wise person wins friends.

Matthew 11:30 (NLT): "For my yoke is easy to bear, and the burden I give you is light."

2 Corinthians 11:30 (NLT): If I must boast, I would rather boast about the things that show how weak I am.

PRAYER

Dear Heavenly Father, Or Goyim (Light of the Nations),

Thank You for Your steadfast love and guidance. I come to You seeking Your wisdom and peace in my life. Proverbs 11:30 says, "The fruit of the righteous is a tree of life, and the one who is wise saves lives" (NIV). Help me to bear good fruit through my actions and decisions, and to use my wisdom to positively impact the lives of others. Matthew 11:30 teaches, "For my yoke is easy and my burden is light" (NIV). Thank You for offering me rest and ease in the midst of life's challenges. Help me to trust in Your promises and to find comfort in knowing that You carry my burdens with me. 2 Corinthians 11:30 says, "If I must boast, I will boast of the things that show my weakness" (NIV). Help me to embrace my weaknesses and rely on Your strength. Teach me to find glory in how Your power is made perfect in my weaknesses. Thank You for Your faithfulness and the strength You provide. Help me to bear good fruit, trust in Your light burden, embrace my weaknesses, find refuge in You, and follow Your guidance.

In Jesus' embracive name I pray, Amen

DECEMBER 1

2 Corinthians 12:1 (NIV): I must go on boasting. Although there is nothing to be gained by it, I will go on to visions and revelations of the Lord.

Hebrews 12:1 (GNT): As for us, we have this large crowd of witnesses around us. So then, let us rid ourselves of everything that gets in the way, and of the sin which holds onto us so tightly, and let us run with determination the race that lies before us.

Romans 12:1 (NIV): Therefore, I urge you, brothers and sisters, in view of God's mercy, to offer your bodies as a living sacrifice, holy and pleasing to God—this is your true and proper worship.

Proverbs 12:1 (NKJV): Whoever loves instruction loves knowledge, but he who hates correction is stupid.

PRAYER

Dear Heavenly Father, Parakletos (Advocate),

Thank You for Your love and guidance in my life. I come to You today seeking strength and dedication in following Your path. 2 Corinthians 12:1 affirms that I receive visions and revelations of the Lord. Help me to focus on Your revelations and the wisdom You give knowing God's power works through my weakness. Hebrews 12:1 teaches I have the strength to let go of anything that holds me back and to run with perseverance in the race You have set before me. Help me to realize that if it's not helping me run, it's holding me back. Romans 12:1 urges us to understand we serve God not to earn mercy, but because we received it. Help me to offer my life to You as a living sacrifice, set apart, pleasing, and wholly Yours. Proverbs 12:1 is blunt and incredibly powerful. Help me to embrace discipline and correction with a humble heart, understanding that growth mindedness is correction mindedness. Help me to love discipline and not despise correction. I choose growth over comfort. I embrace Your revelations, run my race with perseverance, offer my life as a living sacrifice, and value discipline.

In Jesus' sacrificial name I pray, Amen

DECEMBER 2

I AM A NEW PERSON WITH GOD

Romans 12:2 (NLT): Don't copy the behavior and customs of this world, but let God transform you into a new person by changing the way you think. Then you will learn to know God's will for you, which is good and pleasing and perfect.

Proverbs 12:2 (NLT): The LORD approves of those who are good, but he condemns those who plan wickedness.

Hebrews 12:2 (NKJV): Looking unto Jesus, the author and finisher of our faith, who for the joy that was set before Him endured the cross, despising the shame, and has sat down at the right hand of the throne of God.

Luke 12:2 (NKJV): "For there is nothing covered that will not be revealed, nor hidden that will not be known."

PRAYER

Dear Heavenly Father, El Yeshuati (The God of My Salvation),

Thank You for Your guidance and the wisdom found in Your Word. I come to You seeking transformation and direction in my life. Romans 12:2 says God's people are called to be different, set apart, not blending in. Help me to renew my mind and to avoid the patterns of this world that lead me away from You. Transform me so I can understand and follow Your will for my life. Proverbs 12:2 teaches me to live a life that is pleasing to You, filled with goodness and integrity. Help me to seek Your favor by making choices that reflect Your righteousness and wisdom. Hebrews 12:2 says to keep my focus on Jesus, who is the perfect example of faith. Strengthen me to endure challenges and to find joy in following Him. Luke 12:2 reminds us God is a God of truth and light—He uncovers what man tries to hide. Help me to live with honesty and integrity, knowing that all things are ultimately revealed before You. Guide me to be transparent and true in my actions and thoughts. Thank You for Your faithfulness and for the transformation You bring into our lives. Help me to renew my mind, seek Your favor, fix my eyes on Jesus, and live with honesty.

In Jesus' transparent name I pray, Amen

DECEMBER 3

I am blessed through Jesus

Genesis 12:3 (NIV): I will bless those who bless you, and whoever curses you I will curse and all peoples on earth will be blessed through you.

John 12:3 (NKJV): Then Mary took a pound of a very costly oil of spikenard, anointed the feet of Jesus, and wiped His feet with her hair. And the house was filled with the fragrance of the oil.

Hebrews 12:3 (ESV): Consider him who endured from sinners such hostility against himself, so that you may not grow weary or fainthearted.

1 Corinthians 12:3 (NKJV): Therefore I make known to you that no one speaking by the Spirit of God calls Jesus accursed, and no one can say that Jesus is Lord except by the Holy Spirit.

PRAYER

Dear Heavenly Father, Alethinos Theos (True God),

Thank You for Your promises and guidance. I come to You seeking Your blessings and help to stay focused on Your path. Genesis 12:3 says my family is blessed through Jesus. Thank You for Your promise to bless those who follow You and for the blessings You have in store for me. Help me to be a source of blessing to others and to reflect Your love and grace in all I do. John 12:3 reminds us to offer our best to You, as Mary did, and to worship You with a heart full of love and devotion. May my life be a sweet fragrance of Your grace and mercy. Hebrews 12:3 says, when I face difficulties and opposition, to keep my focus on Jesus and His endurance. Give me strength to persevere and not lose heart in the face of challenges. 1 Corinthians 12:3 teaches me to be guided by Your Spirit and to affirm Jesus as Lord in my life. Fill me with Your Spirit and empower me to speak and act in a way that honors You. Thank You for Your faithfulness and for the guidance You provide. Help me to be a blessing, to offer my best to You, to stay focused on Jesus, and be guided by Your Spirit.

In the enduring name of Jesus I pray, Amen

DECEMBER 4

I PRAISE THE LORD

Hebrews 12:4 (NIV): In your struggle against sin, you have not yet resisted to the point of shedding your blood.

1 Corinthians 12:4 (NKJV): There are diversities of gifts, but the same Spirit.

Proverbs 12:4 (NLT): A worthy wife is a crown for her husband, but a disgraceful woman is like cancer in his bones.

Psalm 12:4 (NLT): They say, "We will lie to our hearts' content. Our lips are our own—who can stop us?"

Isaiah 12:4 (NIV): In that day you will say: "Give praise to the LORD, proclaim his name; make known among the nations what he has done, and proclaim that his name is exalted."

—————————————————— PRAYER ——————————————————

Dear Heavenly Father, Basileus Basileon (King of Kings),

Thank You for Your constant care and guidance. I seek Your help to understand and live according to Your Word. Hebrews 12:4 says to remain steadfast in my fight against sin. Give me the strength to resist temptation and to stay committed to living a life that honors You. 1 Corinthians 12:4 teaches there are diverse gifts You have given me and others. Help me to use my gifts for Your glory and to work together with others in unity, recognizing that all gifts come from You. Proverbs 12:4 says I'm to strive for noble character and to be a source of strength and honor in my relationships. Guide me to live with integrity and to support those around me with love and respect. Psalm 12:4 reminds me the Lord protects me from the pitfalls of flattery and boastfulness. Help me to speak with sincerity and to seek Your truth, rather than being swayed by false praise or empty words. Isaiah 12:4 tells me to give praise and proclaim the Lord. Fill my heart with gratitude and boldness to share Your goodness with others. Help me to proclaim Your name and to tell of Your wonderful deeds to everyone I encounter. Thank You for Your faithfulness and for the strength and wisdom You provide. Help me to resist sin, use my gifts well, live with noble character, speak sincerely, and share Your praises with the world.

In King Jesus' name I pray, Amen

339

I AM A MEMBER OF CHRIST

Proverbs 12:5 (NKJV): The thoughts of the righteous are right, but the counsels of the wicked are deceitful.

Acts 12:5 (NIV): So Peter was kept in prison, but the church was earnestly praying to God for him.

Romans 12:5 (NKJV): So we, being many, are one body in Christ, and every one members one of another.

Hebrews 12:5: And have you forgotten the encouraging words God spoke to you as his children? He said, "My child, don't make light of the LORD's discipline, and don't give up when he corrects you."

Isaiah 12:5 (AMP): Sing praises to the Lord, for He has done excellent and glorious things; let this be known throughout the earth.

PRAYER

Dear Heavenly Father, Hashem (The Name),

My eyes and ears are here to soak You up. Proverbs 12:5 teaches that my thoughts and decisions must be aligned with Your will. Help me to seek wisdom and avoid deceitful advice. Acts 12:5 tells us to remember the power of prayer in times of trouble. Teach me to pray earnestly and trust in Your ability to intervene and bring about Your will. Romans 12:5 reminds us to understand and embrace the unity of the body of Christ. Guide me to work together with others in love and to value each person's contribution in Your church. Hebrews 12:5 says to accept Your discipline with a humble heart, understanding it as a sign of Your love and guidance. Isaiah 12:5 says to sing praises to my glorious Lord, telling everyone of Your excellence in my life. I want to be where You are Lord. Thank You for Your faithfulness and for the guidance You provide. Help me to care for the needy, seek wisdom, pray earnestly, embrace unity, accept Your discipline, and praise You for Your glorious deeds.

In my brother Jesus' name I pray, Amen

Proverbs 12:6 (NLT): The words of the wicked are like a murderous ambush, but the words of the godly save lives.

Hosea 12:6 (NLT): So now, come back to your God. Act with love and justice, and always depend on him.

Romans 12:6 (NKJV): Having then gifts differing according to the grace that is given to us, let us use them: if prophecy, let us prophesy in proportion to our faith.

Hebrews 12:6 (NIV): Because the Lord disciplines the one he loves, and he chastens everyone he accepts as his son.

Psalm 12:6 (NLT): The LORD's promises are pure, like silver refined in a furnace, purified seven times over.

PRAYER

Dear Heavenly Father, Lo Shanah (Unchanging),

I come to You with adoration. Proverbs 12:6 teaches me to speak words of truth and kindness that build up and protect others, rather than causing harm or conflict. Hosea 12:6 says to return to You with a heart full of love and justice. Teach me to be patient and to trust in Your timing and plans for my life. Romans 12:6 reminds me of the unique gifts You have given me. Help me to use them according to Your will and to serve others faithfully with the grace You have provided. Hebrews 12:6 says to accept Your discipline with gratitude, knowing that it is a sign of Your love and a way to grow in righteousness. Psalm 12:6 reminds us to trust in the perfection of Your Word. I am like silver being refined in the fire until the reflection of God in me is seen. Help me to rely on Your truth and to let Your words guide and shape my life. Thank You for Your faithfulness and for the strength and wisdom You provide. Help me to be a light, speak truth, live with love and justice, use my gifts well, accept Your discipline, and trust in the perfection of Your Word.

In Jesus' unchanging name I pray, Amen

DECEMBER 7

Luke 12:7 (NLT): "And the very hairs on your head are all numbered. So don't be afraid; you are more valuable to God than a whole flock of sparrows."

1 Corinthians 12:7 (NKJV): But the manifestation of the Spirit is given to each one for the profit of all.

Proverbs 12:7(NIV): The wicked are overthrown and are no more, but the house of the righteous stands firm.

Psalm 12:7 (NLT): Therefore, LORD, we know you will protect the oppressed, preserving them forever from this lying generation.

Romans 12:7 (NLT): If your gift is serving others, serve them well. If you are a teacher, teach well.

PRAYER

Dear Heavenly Father, Yotzerenu (Potter),

In Luke 12:7, Jesus says, "Indeed, the very hairs of your head are all numbered. Don't be afraid; you are worth more than many sparrows" (NIV). Help me to remember that You care deeply for me, even in the smallest details of my life. Give me peace and assurance in Your constant care. 1 Corinthians 12:7 teaches, "Now to each one the manifestation of the Spirit is given for the common good" (NIV). Thank You for the gifts and abilities You have given me. Help me to use them to serve others and to contribute to the well-being of the community around me. Proverbs 12:7 says I must live righteously and build a life that stands firm on Your truth. Protect me from evil and help me to remain steadfast in my faith. Psalm 12:7 reminds me to trust in Your protection and care, knowing that You will keep me safe from harm and provide for my needs. Romans 12:7 tells me to fulfill my calling with dedication, whether it is serving, teaching, or in any other way. Guide me to use my gifts effectively to honor You and bless others.

In the righteous name of Jesus I pray, Amen

DECEMBER 8

2 Corinthians 12:8 (NIV): Three times I pleaded with the Lord to take it away from me.

1 Corinthians 12:8 (NLT): To one person the Spirit gives the ability to give wise advice; to another the same Spirit gives a message of special knowledge.

Proverbs 12:8 (NLT): A sensible person wins admiration, but a warped mind is despised.

--- **PRAYER** ---

Dear Heavenly Father, Elohim (Mighty Creator),

Thank You for Your wisdom and strength. I come to You seeking guidance in my life with Your Word. In 2 Corinthians 12:8, Paul says, "Three times I pleaded with the Lord to take it away from me." I bring my struggles and challenges before You, asking for Your help and intervention. Even when answers are not immediate, grant me patience and faith as I trust in Your plan. I believe all things are possible with faith in my Heavenly Father. 1 Corinthians 12:8 teaches, "To one there is given through the Spirit a message of wisdom, to another a message of knowledge by means of the same Spirit" (NIV). I ask for Your wisdom and understanding in all areas of my life. Guide me with Your knowledge and help me to use the gifts You've given me to serve others and honor You. I will seek out my gifts and use them for Your purpose. Proverbs 12:8 reminds us, "A person is praised according to their prudence, and one with a warped mind is despised" (NIV). Help me to act with prudence and integrity. Guide my thoughts and actions so that I may be wise and receive praise for the good I do, avoiding anything that could lead to misunderstanding or dishonor. Glory to glory, I honor You, Lord. Thank You for Your faithfulness and for the wisdom You provide. Help me to trust in Your timing, seek Your guidance, and act with prudence in all I do.

In Jesus' mighty name I pray, Amen

DECEMBER 9

I HATE ALL THAT IS EVIL

Daniel 12:9 (NIV): He replied, "Go your way, Daniel, because the words are rolled up and sealed until the time of the end."

Romans 12:9 (NIV): Love must be sincere. Hate what is evil, cling to what is good.

Revelation 12:9 (NIV): The great dragon was hurled down—that ancient serpent called the devil, or Satan, who leads the whole world astray. He was hurled to the earth, and his angels with him.

2 Corinthians 12:9 (TPT): But he answered me, "My grace is always more than enough for you, and my power finds its full expression through your weakness." So I will celebrate my weaknesses, for when I'm weak I sense more deeply the mighty power of Christ living in me.

PRAYER

Dear Heavenly Father, El Kanna (Jealous God),

Thank You for Your guidance and the wisdom found in Your Word. I come to You today seeking Your help and grace in my life. Daniel 12:9 says, "He replied, 'Go your way, Daniel, because the words are rolled up and sealed until the time of the end.'" Help me to trust in Your timing and understand that some things are revealed when You choose. Give me patience and faith as I wait for Your answers and guidance. Romans 12:9 advises, "Love must be sincere. Hate what is evil; cling to what is good." Teach me to love others with sincerity and to hold fast to what is good. Help me to avoid evil and to pursue goodness in all aspects of my life. Revelation 12:9 reminds us, "The great dragon was hurled down—that ancient serpent called the devil, or Satan, who leads the whole world astray. He was hurled to the earth, and his angels with him." I thank You for Your victory over evil. Help me to resist temptation and stay firm in my faith, knowing that You have defeated the enemy. 2 Corinthians 12:9 says, "But He said to me, 'My grace is sufficient for you, for My power is made perfect in weakness.' Therefore I will boast all the more gladly about my weaknesses, so that Christ's power may rest on me" (NIV). Help me to embrace my weaknesses and rely on Your grace. Teach me to find strength in Your power and to trust that Your grace is enough for all my needs. Thank You for Your faithfulness and the strength You provide. Help me to trust in Your timing, love sincerely, resist evil, and rely on Your grace.

In Jesus' graceful name I pray, Amen

DECEMBER 10

Romans 12:10 (NIV): Be devoted to one another in love, honor one another above yourselves.

Revelation 12:10 (ESV): And I heard a loud voice in heaven saying, "Now the salvation and the power and the kingdom of our God and the authority of his Christ have come, for the accuser of our brothers has been thrown down, who accuses them day and night before our God."

Matthew 12:10 (NLT): And a man was there with a withered hand. And they asked him, "Is it lawful to heal on the Sabbath?" So that they might accuse him.

2 Corinthians 12:10 (TPT): So I'm not defeated by my weakness, but delighted! For when I feel my weakness and endure mistreatment—when I'm surrounded with troubles on every side and face persecution because of my love for Christ—I am made yet stronger. For my weakness becomes a portal to God's power!

PRAYER

Dear Heavenly Father, Atik Yomin (Ancient of Days),

I'm here to be guided by Your Scriptures. Romans 12:10 tells me to show genuine love and respect to others, putting their needs before my own and fostering strong, supportive relationships. Revelation 12:10 reminds us of John's vision of the cosmic battle. Heaven is proclaiming that Jesus' authority is now and forever reigning. I rejoice in the salvation and power You bring. By Your blood the enemy's accusations no longer stand in the courts of heaven. Matthew 12:10 tells us to focus on the good You bring and to respond with compassion rather than criticism. Religious legalism can, at times, overlook human needs. Lord, help me to act with love and to seek to do good, even when faced with opposition. 2 Corinthians 12:10 says to find strength in my weaknesses and to rely on Your power during difficult times. Teach me to embrace challenges with faith, knowing that Your strength is made perfect in my weakness. Thank You for Your faithfulness and for the strength You provide. Help me to love others, trust in Your authority, act with compassion, and find strength in Your grace.

In the devoted name of Jesus I pray, Amen

DECEMBER 11

Revelation 12:11 (NKJV): And they overcame him by the blood of the lamb and by the word of their testimony, and they did not love their lives to the death.

Proverbs 12:11 (NIV): Those who work their land will have abundant food, but those who chase fantasies have no sense.

Romans 12:11 (NLT): Never be lazy, but work hard and serve the Lord enthusiastically.

Numbers 12:11 (NLT): He cried out to Moses, "Oh my master! Please don't punish us for this sin we have so foolishly committed."

Hebrews 12:11 (ESV): For the moment all discipline seems painful rather than pleasant, but later it yields the peaceful fruit of righteousness to those who have been trained by it.

PRAYER

Dear Heavenly Father, Shub Nephesh (Renewer of Life),

Thank You for Your guidance and the wisdom found in Your Word. I come to You today seeking Your help to overcome challenges and grow in strength. Revelation 12:11 says we have victory through Jesus' sacrifice. Help me to live boldly and faithfully, sharing my testimony and trusting in Your strength to overcome any temptation of the enemy. Proverbs 12:11 reminds us to focus on diligent work and practical steps rather than being distracted by fantasies. Help me to be productive and to use the gifts You've given me wisely. Romans 12:11 instructs me to be filled with Your zeal and passion for Your work. Keep my spirit fervent as I serve You and others, never losing enthusiasm for the calling You have placed on my life. Numbers 12:11 tells me to acknowledge my mistakes and seek Your forgiveness, trusting in Your mercy and grace to cleanse and restore me. Hebrews 12:11 reminds me to endure through discipline and challenges, trusting that You are using them to grow me in righteousness and peace.

In the fruitful name of Jesus I pray, Amen

DECEMBER 12

Romans 12:12 (NKJV): Rejoice in Hope, be patient in tribulation, continuing steadfastly in prayer.

Proverbs 12:12 (NLT): Thieves are jealous of each other's loot, but the godly are well rooted and bear their own fruit.

Luke 12:12 (NLT): "For the Holy Spirit will teach you at that time what needs to be said."

Job 12:12 (KJV): With the ancient is wisdom; and in the length of days understanding.

PRAYER

Dear Heavenly Father, El Haggadol (The Great God),

Thank You for Your guidance and the wisdom found in Your Word. I come to You today seeking Your help to live faithfully and wisely. Romans 12:12 instructs me to hold on to hope with joy, to be patient during difficult times, and to remain devoted in prayer. Strengthen my faith and help me to trust You fully. Proverbs 12:12 says to focus on being rooted in righteousness rather than being swayed by the desires of the wicked. Strengthen my foundation in You so that I may endure challenges. Luke 12:12 tells me Your Holy Spirit will guide me in all situations, giving me the right words and wisdom when I need them. Help me to rely on Your Spirit's guidance and to trust in Your timing. Job 12:12 reminds us, "Is not wisdom found among the aged? Does not a long life bring understanding?" (NIV). Grant me wisdom and understanding as I grow and help me to seek counsel from those who have experience and insight. Thank You for Your faithfulness and for the wisdom You provide. Help me to live with hope, patience, and trust in Your guidance.

In the counseling name of Jesus I pray, Amen

I HAVE WISDOM AND POWER THROUGH GOD

Proverbs 12:13 (NIV): The wicked are trapped by their own words, but the godly escape such trouble.

Ecclesiastes 12:13 (NIV): Now all has been heard; here is the conclusion of the matter: Fear God and keep his commandments, for this is the duty of all mankind.

Matthew 12:13 (NKJV): Then [Jesus] said to the man, "Stretch out your hand." And he stretched it out, and it was restored as whole as the other.

Hebrews 12:13 (NLT): Make out a straight path for your feet so that those who are weak and lame will not fall but become strong.

Job 12:13 (NLT): But true wisdom and power are found in God; Council and understanding are His.

PRAYER

Dear Heavenly Father, El Qadosh (The Holy God),

Thank You for Your wisdom and guidance. I come before You, seeking Your help to live according to Your Word and to grow in Your strength. Proverbs 12:13 says to guard my words and avoid deceit. Guide me to speak truthfully and righteously, avoiding any traps that come from dishonesty. Ecclesiastes 12:13 reminds me to respect and honor You in all things, following Your commandments faithfully as the foundation of my life. Fear of God from love is a healthy fear. Matthew 12:13 tells us to trust in Your power to restore and heal. Whatever I face, may I turn to You, believing in Your ability to bring wholeness and restoration. Hebrews 12:13 says to walk in a way that supports and encourages those around me. Job 12:13 acknowledges that all wisdom and strength come from You. Help me to seek Your counsel in every decision and to rely on Your understanding in all circumstances. Thank You for Your faithfulness and for the wisdom You provide. Help me to live according to Your Word, to seek Your guidance, and to walk in Your strength.

In Jesus' powerful name I pray, Amen

I AM A HARD WORKER

Hebrews 12:14 (NKJV): Pursue peace with all people, and holiness, without which no one will see the Lord.

Proverbs 12:14 (NLT): Wise words bring many benefits, and hard work brings rewards.

Ecclesiastes 12:14 (NIV): For God will bring every deed into judgment, including every hidden thing, whether it is good or evil.

Romans 12:14 (NLT): Bless those who persecute you. Don't curse them; pray that God will bless them.

1 Corinthians 12:14 (NKJV): For in fact the body is not one member but many.

PRAYER

Dear Heavenly Father, Jehovah-Jireh (The LORD My Provider,)

Thank You for Your guidance and the wisdom found in Your Word. I seek Your help to live according to Your teachings and to grow in peace and unity. Hebrews 12:14 says to strive for peace in all my relationships and to live a life that is pleasing to You, reflecting Your holiness in my actions. Proverbs 12:14 tells me to speak words that are uplifting and to work diligently, trusting that my efforts will bear fruit and be a blessing to others. Ecclesiastes 12:14 reminds me to live with integrity, knowing that all my actions are seen by You. Teach me to act righteously in all things, both in public and in private. Romans 12:14 advises me to respond with love and blessing, even to those who may treat me poorly. Teach me to show Your love and grace in every situation. 1 Corinthians 12:14 says to understand and appreciate my role within the body of Christ. Guide me to work together with others, recognizing that each person has a valuable part to play in Your kingdom. Thank You for Your faithfulness and for the wisdom You provide. Help me to live in peace, speak with kindness, act with integrity, and embrace my role in Your body.

In Jesus' rewarding name I pray, Amen

DECEMBER 15

Hebrews 12:15 (ESV): See to it that no one fails to obtain the grace of God; that no "root of bitterness" springs up and causes trouble, and by it many become defiled.

Proverbs 12:15 (NLT): Fools think their own way is right, but the wise listen to others.

Matthew 12:15 (NKJV): But when Jesus knew it, He withdrew from there. And great multitudes followed Him, and He healed them all.

Romans 12:15 (ESV): Rejoice with those who rejoice, and weep with those who weep.

1 Samuel 12:15 (NLT): But if you rebel against the LORD's commands and refuse to listen to him, then his hand will be as heavy upon you as it was upon your ancestors.

PRAYER

Dear Heavenly Father, Elohim Shama (The God Who Hears),

Thank You for Your love and guidance. I come to You seeking Your help in living out Your teachings with grace and compassion. In Hebrews 12:15, Your Word says to extend Your grace to others and to guard against any bitterness in my heart. Teach me to handle conflicts with love and forgiveness. Proverbs 12:15 reminds me to seek wisdom and listen to Your advice rather than relying solely on my own understanding. Help me to be open to Your guidance and the counsel of those You place in my life. Matthew 12:15 tells us to follow Your example, showing compassion and offering healing to those in need, whether through my actions or words. Romans 12:15 advises me to share in the joys and sorrows of others, offering support and empathy in all circumstances. 1 Samuel 12:15 says to obey Your commands and to stay close to You, seeking Your will in all things and avoiding rebellion. Thank You for Your faithfulness and for the wisdom You provide. Help me to live with grace, compassion, and a heart that seeks to follow Your will.

In Jesus' worshiped name I pray, Amen

DECEMBER 16

I AM WISE AND CALM

Proverbs 12:16 (NLT): A fool is quick-tempered, but a wise person stays calm when insulted.

Romans 12:16 (NLT): Live in harmony with each other. Don't be too proud to enjoy the company of ordinary people. And don't think you know it all!

1 Samuel 12:16 (NLT): Now stand here and see the great thing the LORD is about to do.

Job 12:16 (NLT): Yes, strength and wisdom are His; deceivers and deceived are both in His power.

PRAYER

Dear Heavenly Father, El Sela (God My Rock),

Thank You for Your wisdom and guidance. I seek Your help today to live in accordance with Your Word and to grow in humility and understanding. In Proverbs 12:16, it says to be wise and patient, choosing to overlook offenses and respond with grace rather than reacting in anger. Romans 12:16 advises me to live in harmony with others, to remain humble, and to value all people equally, regardless of their status. 1 Samuel 12:16 says to stand still and witness Your work in my life and in the world around me. Strengthen my faith to trust in Your plans and timing. Job 12:16 declares that I rely on Your strength and insight, recognizing that You are in control of all things. Thank You for Your faithfulness and for the wisdom You provide. Guide me to live with humility, seek harmony, and trust in Your great work.

In Jesus' great name I pray, Amen

DECEMBER 17

I AM AN HONEST WITNESS

Job 12:17 (NIV): He leads counselors away stripped and makes fools of judges.

Proverbs 12:17 (NLT): An honest witness tells the truth; a false witness tells lies.

Romans 12:17 (NKJV): Repay no one evil for evil. Have regard for good things in the sight of all men.

Ezekiel 12:17 (NLT): Then this message came to me from the LORD.

PRAYER

Dear Heavenly Father, El Roi (The God Who Sees Me),

Thank You for Your guidance and the wisdom found in Your Word. I seek Your help today in living according to Your teachings. In Job 12:17, Your Word says even the wisest of human minds are nothing without God's guidance. I ask for Your protection and wisdom in my decisions and those I rely on for guidance. Help me to seek Your counsel above all. Proverbs 12:17 reminds me to be truthful in all I say and do, reflecting Your honesty and integrity. Romans 12:17 advises me to respond to others with kindness and goodness, not seeking revenge but striving to do what is right. Ezekiel 12:17 says to approach every aspect of my life with reverence and trust in You, not with fear or anxiety, but with faith in Your provision and care. Thank You for Your faithfulness and for guiding me through Your Word. Help me to live with truth, integrity, and faith in Your care.

In Jesus' truthful name I pray, Amen

DECEMBER 18

Proverbs 12:18 (NKJV): There is one who speaks like the piercings of a sword, but the tongue of the wise promotes health.

Romans 12:18 (NKJV): If it is possible, as much as depends on you, live peaceably with all men.

1 Corinthians 12:18 (NIV): But in fact God has placed the parts in the body, every one of them, just as he wanted them to be.

PRAYER

Dear Heavenly Father, El Shaddai (The All-Sufficient One, God Almighty),

Thank You for Your guidance and wisdom. I come to You today seeking Your help to live according to Your Word. Proverbs 12:18 says to use my words wisely and kindly, offering healing and encouragement rather than causing harm. Romans 12:18 advises me to do my part in promoting peace and harmony in my relationships, striving to live peacefully with others. 1 Corinthians 12:18 reminds me my role is not random, its assigned by divine design. Thank You for placing me where You want me and for giving me a role in Your plans. Help me to understand and embrace my role, working together with others to fulfill Your purpose. Thank You for Your faithfulness and for guiding me through Your Word. Help me to speak wisely, seek peace, embrace my role in Your plan, and remain humble.

In Jesus' peaceful name I pray, Amen

Job 12:19 (NIV): He leads priests away stripped and overthrows officials long established.

Proverbs 12:19 (NLT): Truthful words stand the test of time, but lies are soon exposed.

Romans 12:19 (NIV): Do not take revenge, my dear friends, but leave room for God's wrath, for it is written: "It is mine to avenge; I will repay," says the Lord.

----------------------------------- **PRAYER** -----------------------------------

Dear Heavenly Father, Jehovah Ezrah (The LORD My Helper),

Thank You for Your guidance and the wisdom found in Your Word. I seek Your help in living out Your teachings in my life. In Job 12:19, Your Word says God can expose spiritual pride or false holiness. I ask for Your protection and strength to remain steadfast in faith. Strip away anything in me that stands against Your truth. Proverbs 12:19 teaches me to speak the truth always and to uphold honesty in all my interactions. May my words be a reflection of Your truth and integrity. Romans 12:19 advises me to trust in Your justice and to refrain from seeking revenge. Help me to leave matters in Your hands and to respond to others with grace and forgiveness. Thank You for Your faithfulness and for guiding me with Your Word. Help me to live with integrity, trust in Your justice, and honor Your name in everything.

In Jesus' helping name I pray, Amen

Proverbs 12:20 (NLT): Deceit fills hearts that are plotting evil; joy fills hearts that are planning peace!

Romans 12:20 (NIV): "If your enemy is hungry, feed him; if he is thirsty, give him something to drink. I'm doing this, you will heap burning coals on his head."

Job 12:20 (NIV): He silences the lips of trusted advisors and takes away the discernment of elders.

———————————— **PRAYER** ————————————

Dear Heavenly Father, El Yeshuati (The God of My Salvation),

Thank You for Your guidance and the wisdom found in Your Word. I come to You today seeking Your help in living according to Your teachings. Proverbs 12:20 teaches me to pursue peace and to be honest in all my dealings. Fill my heart with Your joy as I work to promote harmony and understanding. Romans 12:20 advises me to show kindness even to those who oppose me, reflecting Your love and grace in every situation. Remind me compassion is a weapon of light in a dark world. Job 12:20 says to ask for Your wisdom and guidance in my decisions. No one is too wise or influential to be humbled. Age and position do not guarantee wisdom, God alone gives true understanding. Lord, help me to seek Your understanding and to rely on Your insight rather than my own. Thank You for Your faithfulness and for the wisdom You provide. Help me to live with compassion, seek peace, and rely on Your understanding.

In the saving name of Jesus I pray, Amen

DECEMBER 21

I OVERCOME EVIL WITH GOOD

Proverbs 12:21 (NLT): No harm comes to the godly, but the wicked have their fill of trouble.

Romans 12:21 (NIV): Do not be overcome by evil, but overcome evil with good.

Matthew 12:21 (NLT): And His name will be the hope of all the world.

Luke 12:21 (NKJV): "So is he who lays up treasure for himself, and is not rich toward God."

1 Corinthians 12:21 (NLT): The eye can never say to the hand, "I don't need you." The head cannot say to the feet, "I don't need you."

PRAYER

Dear Heavenly Father, El HaNe'eman (The God Who Is Faithful),

Thank You for Your guidance and the wisdom of Your Word. I come to You seeking Your help to live out Your teachings each day. Proverbs 12:21 says to trust in Your protection and guidance, knowing that You are with me through every challenge. Help me to stay righteous and faithful, trusting in Your care. Romans 12:21 advises me to respond to negativity and challenges with kindness and goodness. Help me to reflect Your love in all my interactions and to be a light in dark situations. Matthew 12:21 tells me to place my hope in You, Lord, and ask that You help me to live in a way that brings honor to Your name and inspires hope in others. In Luke 12:21, Jesus reminds me to focus on being rich in my relationship with You rather than just accumulating material things. Teach me to invest in what truly matters over what the world highlights. 1 Corinthians 12:21 reminds us to recognize the value of every person and every role in Your body, understanding that we all have important parts to play in Your work. Thank You for Your love and for guiding me through Your Word. Help me to live with Your wisdom, to overcome evil with good, and to be a faithful part of Your community.

In Jesus' caring name I pray, Amen

DECEMBER 22

GOD WILL NOT ABANDON ME

1 Corinthians 12:22 (NLT): In fact, some parts of the body that seem weakest and least important are actually the most necessary.

Matthew 12:22 (ESV): Then a demon-oppressed man who was blind and mute was brought to him, and he healed him, so that the man spoke and saw.

Proverbs 12:22 (NLT): The LORD detests lying lips, but he delights in those who tell the truth.

Job 12:22 (NLT): He uncovers mysteries hidden in darkness; he brings light to the deepest gloom.

Luke 12:22 (NLT): Turning to his disciples, Jesus said, "That is why I tell you not to worry about everyday life—whether you have enough food to eat or enough clothes to wear."

1 Samuel 12:22 (NLT): The LORD will not abandon his people, because that would dishonor his great name. For it has pleased the LORD to make you his very own people.

PRAYER

Dear Heavenly Father, Elah Yerushalem (God of Jerusalem),

Thank You for Your guidance and the wisdom found in Your Word. I seek Your help and strength today. 1 Corinthians 12:22 tells me to understand the value of every part of Your body, including myself, and to use my unique gifts to serve others and contribute to Your work. Lord, I know You see value in the hidden and humble. In Matthew 12:22, Your kingdom shows miraculous deliverance. I want to have unexplainable faith knowing You could deliver me as well. Proverbs 12:22 says to be honest and trustworthy in all my dealings, reflecting Your truth in my words and actions. Job 12:22 reminds me Your light shines on all areas of my life that need illumination, and You help me to walk in Your light, away from the shadows. Luke 12:22 advises me to trust in Your provision and to not be anxious about my needs, knowing that You care for me deeply. 1 Samuel 12:22 promises Your love is not based on our performance, but Your promises. Thank You for choosing me and not rejecting me. Help me to live in a way that honors You and reflects Your love and grace. Thank You for Your faithfulness and guidance. Help me to live with integrity, trust in Your provision, and serve others with love.

In Jesus' honorable name I pray, Amen

DECEMBER 23

John 12:23 (NKJV): But Jesus answered them, saying, "The hour has come that the Son and Man should be glorified."

Proverbs 12:23 (NLT): The wise don't make a show of their knowledge, but fools broadcast their foolishness.

Luke 12:23 (NLT): "For life is more than food, and your body more than clothing."

PRAYER

Dear Heavenly Father, Elohay Selichot (The God Who Is Ready to Forgive),

Thank You for Your guidance and wisdom. I come to You today seeking Your help and understanding. In John 12:23, Jesus says to recognize and embrace the important moments in my life when You are at work. Guide me to follow Your example and seek Your glory in all that I do. Proverbs 12:23 reminds us, "The prudent keep their knowledge to themselves, but a fool's heart blurts out folly" (NIV). Grant me the wisdom to be thoughtful and careful with my words and actions, and to seek Your guidance in making wise decisions. In Luke 12:23, Jesus teaches us, to focus on what truly matters—my relationship with You and living according to Your will—rather than being overly concerned with material things. Our purpose is greater than our physical needs. I am not what I eat or wear, my value is spiritual and eternal. Thank You for Your love and guidance. Help me to live in a way that honors You and to grow in wisdom and faith.

In Jesus' committed name I pray, Amen

DECEMBER 24

I know God's Word and His power

Luke 12:24 (NLT): "Look at the ravens. They don't plant or harvest or store food in barns, for God feeds them. And you are more valuable to him than any bird!"

Proverbs 12:24 (NLT): Work hard and become a leader; be lazy and become a slave.

Mark 12:24 (NLT): Jesus replied, "Your mistake is that you don't know the Scriptures, and you don't know the power of God."

John 12:24 (NLT): "I tell you the truth, unless a kernel of wheat is planted in the soil and dies, it remains alone. But its death will produce many new kernels—a plentiful harvest of new lives."

PRAYER

Dear Heavenly Father, Elohim Ahavah (The God Who Loves),

Thank You for Your guidance and wisdom. I come to You today seeking Your help in understanding and living out Your Word. In Luke 12:24, Jesus tells me to trust in Your provision and to remember that You care for me deeply, even more than You care for the birds. Proverbs 12:24 reminds us, "Diligent hands will rule, but laziness ends in forced labor" (NIV). Give me the strength and determination to work diligently in all that I do, using the gifts and opportunities You've given me to serve You and others. In Mark 12:24, Jesus calls out it's a mistake to not know Scripture and the power of God. Lord, help me to deepen my understanding of Your Word and to recognize Your power in my life. Guide me to study Your Scriptures and to apply them in my daily walk, to memorize them and take them with me everywhere I go. In John 12:24, Jesus is telling us to pay close attention—this is very important. He is prophesying His own death, which is necessary for the salvation of the world. Lord, teach me to embrace a surrendered life, laying down what I hold dear so You can bear fruit through me. I trust that nothing surrendered to You is wasted. Use my life to multiply Your love. Thank You for Your faithful presence and for the wisdom You provide. Help me to trust in You, work diligently, and grow in faith.

In Jesus' loving name I pray, Amen

DECEMBER 25

I HAVE ETERNAL LIFE

Proverbs 12:25 (ESV): Anxiety in a man's heart weighs him down, but a good word makes him glad.

John 12:25 (NKJV): "He who loves his life will lose it, and he who hates his life in this world will keep it for eternal life."

Matthew 12:25 (NIV): Jesus knew their thoughts and said to them, "Every kingdom divided against itself will be ruined, and every city or household divided against itself will not stand."

Luke 12:25 (NLT): "Can all your worries add a single moment to your life?"

PRAYER

Dear Heavenly Father, Georgos (The Gardener),

Thank You for Your love and guidance. I come before You today asking for Your peace and wisdom. In Proverbs 12:25, Your Word says, "Anxiety weighs down the heart, but a kind word cheers it up" (NIV). Lord, help me to release my anxieties and worries to You. In Jesus name, I tell all unclean spirits of anxiety to leave my body and go to the pit. Fill my body back up with the Holy Spirit, Lord. In John 12:25, Jesus tells us, "Anyone who loves their life will lose it, while anyone who hates their life in this world will keep it for eternal life" (NIV). Help me to focus on eternal values rather than temporary concerns. Teach me to live for You and to find joy in serving others and following Your ways. In Matthew 12:25, Jesus says, "Every kingdom divided against itself will be ruined, and every city or household divided against itself will not stand." Guide me in maintaining unity in my relationships and in my community. Help me to work toward harmony and understanding in all areas of my life. In Luke 12:25, Jesus asks, "Who of you by worrying can add a single hour to your life?" (NIV). Remind me that worrying does not change my circumstances or extend my life. Worry does nothing but steal peace. Teach me to rest in You quietly instead of trying to control what only You can handle. I trust in Your plan and will focus on living each day with faith and gratitude. Thank You for Your constant presence and for the comfort Your Word brings. Help me to find peace in You and to live with purpose and unity.

In Jesus' planted name I pray, Amen

DECEMBER 26

John 12:26 (NLT): "Anyone who wants to serve me must follow me, because my servants must be where I am. And my Father will honor anyone who serves me."

Proverbs 12:26 (NLT): The godly give good advice to their friends, the wicked lead them astray.

Luke 12:26 (NKJV): "If you then are not able to do the least, why are you anxious for the rest?"

PRAYER

Dear Heavenly Father, Akal Esh (Consuming Fire),

Thank You for Your love and for guiding us through Your Word. I come before You today seeking Your wisdom and direction in my life. In John 12:26, Jesus reminds us that true service requires total surrender. Closeness to Him is the reward of faithfulness. Heaven takes notice of the humble and faithful servant. I will walk in obedience knowing You are with me. Proverbs 12:26 reminds me to choose friends and relationships that uplift and support my walk with You. This fellowship will give me good advice. I will stay away from those who are wicked and lead me astray. In Luke 12:26, Jesus asks me to trust You with all my worries and to focus on Your promises rather than being anxious about things beyond my control. Thank You for Your faithfulness and for guiding me through Your Word. Help me to follow You, trust You, and make wise choices in my life.

In Jesus' consuming name I pray, Amen

Proverbs 12:27 (NIV): The lazy do not roast any game, but the diligent feed on the riches of the hunt.

John 12:27 (NLT): "Now my soul is deeply troubled. Should I pray, 'Father, save me from this hour'? But this is the very reason I came."

Luke 12:27 (NLT): "Look at the lilies and how they grow. They don't work or make their clothing, yet Solomon in all his glory was not dressed as beautifully as they are."

1 Corinthians 12:27 (NLT): All of you together our Christ's body, and each of you is a part of it.

PRAYER

Dear Heavenly Father, Jehovah Uzzi (The LORD My Strength),

Thank You for Your guidance and for the wisdom found in Your Word. I seek Your help in living according to Your teachings. First, I reflect on Proverbs 12:27, which says to be diligent and hardworking, using the gifts and opportunities You've given me to the fullest. I will not be lazy. In John 12:27, Jesus didn't come to escape suffering but instead overcome it for us. He chooses the cross willingly. He chooses purpose over comfort. Lord help me not to run from the hour You've called me to, instead I will walk in faith. In Luke 12:27, Jesus speaks about the beauty of the lilies, saying, "Consider how the wild flowers grow. They do not labor or spin. Yet I tell you, not even Solomon in all his splendor was dressed like one of these" (NIV). Remind me to trust in Your provision and to focus on Your kingdom, knowing that You care for all of creation. I can see that Your creation surpasses the best of any human achievement. 1 Corinthians 12:27 says to recognize my role in Your church and to use my gifts to serve others and build up the body of Christ. Lord, use me to build up the church and reflect Your love. Thank You for Your faithfulness and for the guidance of Your Word. Help me to live diligently, trust in Your plan, and be a faithful part of Your community.

In Jesus' present name I pray, Amen

DECEMBER 28

I HAVE LIFE IN GOD

Mark 12:28 (NIV): One of the teachers of the law came and heard them debating. Noticing that Jesus had given them a good answer, he asked him, "Of all the commandments, which is the most important?"

Proverbs 12:28 (NLT): The way of the godly leads to life; that path does not lead to death.

Deuteronomy 12:28 (NKJV): Observe and obey all these words which I command you, that it may go well with you and your children after you forever, when you do what is good and right in the sight of the LORD your God.

Hebrews 12:28 (NLT): Since we are receiving a Kingdom that is unshakable, let us be thankful and please God by worshiping him with holy fear and awe.

 PRAYER

Dear Heavenly Father, Immanuel (God With Us),

Thank You for Your guidance and wisdom. Your Word provides me with truth and encouragement, and I seek to live by it each day. First, I remember the answer Jesus gave to this question in Mark 12:28, where He tells us that loving You with all our heart, soul, mind, and strength is the most important commandment. Help me to love You fully and to put You first in everything I do. In Proverbs 12:28, it says to walk in righteousness and to make choices that reflect Your values, knowing that this path leads to life and fulfillment. Deuteronomy 12:28 advises me to follow Your commands and live according to Your Word, so that my life and the lives of those I love may be blessed and prosperous. Hebrews 12:28 reminds us, "Since we are receiving a kingdom that cannot be shaken, let us be thankful, and so worship God acceptably with reverence and awe" (NIV). I thank You for the unshakable kingdom You've given us and ask for Your help in worshiping You with true reverence and gratitude. Thank You for Your faithfulness and for guiding me each day. May my life reflect Your love and truth in all that I do.

In Jesus' leading name I pray, Amen

DECEMBER 29

I am not worried, I am a child of God

Mark 12:29 (NLT): Jesus replied, "The most important commandment is this: 'Listen, O Israel: The Lord our God is the one and only Lord.'"

Hebrews 12:29 (NLT): For our God is a devouring fire.

Luke 12:29 (NLT): "And don't be concerned about what to eat or what to drink. Do not worry about such things."

1 Corinthians 12:29 (NLT): Are we all apostles? Are we all prophets? Are we all teachers? Do we all have the power to do miracles?

 **PRAYER**

Dear Heavenly Lord, Basilei ton Aionon (King Eternal),

Thank You for Your constant presence and guidance in my life. Your Word teaches me important truths, and I want to align my heart with them. Remembering what Jesus said in Mark 12:29, "The Lord our God, the Lord is one" (NIV), help me to keep You at the center of my life, knowing that You alone are God and worthy of all my trust and devotion. In Hebrews 12:29, Your Word tells me, "Our God is a consuming fire" (NIV). May Your presence be a powerful force in my life, refining me and burning away anything that does not honor You. Luke 12:29 encourages me to focus on You rather than on material concerns, trusting that You will provide for all my needs. 1 Corinthians 12:29 asks, "Are all apostles? Are all prophets? Are all teachers?" (NIV). Help me to recognize and embrace the unique role and gifts You have given me, and to use them to serve others and build up Your church—inside and outside a building. Thank You for being my guide and provider. Help me to live in a way that honors You and reflects Your love to those around me.

In Jesus' miraculous name I pray, Amen

DECEMBER 30

Mark 12:30 (NIV): "Love the Lord your God with all your heart and with all your soul and with all your mind and with all your strength."

Matthew 12:30 (NLT): "Anyone who isn't with me opposes me, and anyone who isn't working with me is actually working against me."

Luke 12:30 (NLT): "These things dominate the thoughts of unbelievers all over the world, but your Father already knows your needs."

1 Corinthians 12:30 (NIV): Do all have gifts of healing? Do all speak with tongues? Do all interpret?

PRAYER

Dear Heavenly Father, Migdol Oz (Strong Tower),

Thank You for Your endless love and guidance. Your Word reminds me of how important it is to love You with all that I am. As Jesus teaches me in Mark 12:30, "Love the Lord your God with all your heart and with all your soul and with all your mind and with all your strength." Help me to dedicate every part of my being to loving You fully and wholeheartedly. In Matthew 12:30, You tell me, "Whoever is not with me is against me, and whoever does not gather with me scatters" (NIV). Help me to stay close to You, fully committed to Your ways, and to work alongside You in all that I do. Luke 12:30 encourages me, "For the pagan world runs after all such things, and your Father knows that you need them" (NIV). Teach me to trust in Your provision and to focus on seeking Your kingdom first, knowing that You will take care of all my needs. 1 Corinthians 12:30 reminds me, "Do all have gifts of healing? Do all speak in tongues? Do all interpret?" Help me to recognize and use the gifts You've given me to serve others and to honor You. Guide me to understand and appreciate the unique ways in which You have equipped me to contribute to Your work in the world. Thank You for Your faithfulness and for guiding me in every step of my journey. May my love for You grow deeper each day, and may I always seek Your will in all things.

In King Jesus' name I pray, Amen

DECEMBER 31

I seek the Kingdom above all else

Mark 12:31 (NIV): "The second is this: 'Love your neighbor as yourself.' There is no commandment greater than these."

Matthew 12:31 (ESV): "Therefore I tell you, every sin and blasphemy will be forgiven people, but the blasphemy against the Spirit will not be forgiven."

Luke 12:31 (NLT): "Seek the Kingdom of God above all else, and He will give you everything you need."

PRAYER

Dear God, Elohim (Mighty Creator),

Thank You for Your incredible love and guidance. Your Word teaches me that loving people is not optional, it is essential. Real love considers the needs of others as equal to our own. As Jesus said in Mark 12:31, "Love your neighbor as yourself." Help me to live out this command each day, showing kindness and compassion to everyone I meet. This command of love will be my lifestyle. In Matthew 12:31, I am reminded of the words of Jesus, who said that every sin and blasphemy can be forgiven, but the blasphemy against the Holy Spirit will not be forgiven. Lord, I ask You to search my heart and cleanse me of anything that grieves Your Spirit. I acknowledge my need for Your forgiveness and healing in every area of my life. I will keep my heart soft, my ears open, and allow the Holy Spirit to control my life. In Luke 12:31, You encourage us to "Seek His kingdom, and these things will be given to you as well" (NIV). Guide me to prioritize Your kingdom in my life, trusting that You will provide for all my needs. Lord, help me to live with love in my heart and to seek Your kingdom above all else, knowing that You are always with me.

In Jesus' never-ending name I pray, Amen

ACKNOWLEDGEMENTS

~God - my Father, my friend, my most trusted confidant. Who has never left me alone.

~Angel - my loving husband, who no matter what comes our way, he stays in the fight with me. Let the floodgates of heaven be opened over our marriage for as long as we live.

~My children - Lexi, Dominic, Diego, and Zeke, words can not express the love I have for the four of you. You come alongside me in all I do. You show up stronger than could ever be expected. Let the Lord's fire always be on your tongues to preach and prophesy!

~Jacob and Josiah - my precious grandsons who are hearers of God. When they enter a room they will change the atmosphere.

~Pastor Kim - your voice and boldness to prophesy over me is truly inspiring. Thank you for speaking this book into existence.

~Grandpa Luke, Grandma Francis, and Grandma Ruth - you three never ceased to pray for me. I know you stood in the gap and ushered me into the legacy I have today: Each of you was the definition of honorable, kind, and loving. I know you are dancing in heaven!

~Daniele, Karyn, Laura, and Reyna - you four are my fighting-words sisters. Each of you brings something unique and special to my life each day! Never do life alone! Mine would be so incredibly boring without these women who show up for me each day of my life.

~Shurvone - my God-given (literally) from a parking lot first meetup mentor! Who took a chance on me being a good student! Who ushered in her new business at the drop of a dime for my sake. Who trusted in God each step of the way through the journey of creating this book! I can't say thank you enough. La' Bosspreneur Academy of Creative Solutions: Self-Publishing Coaching Course.

~Annamay - for always being bold and networking the world together! You're the mostest of all gatherers. Without the gathering I would have never met Shurvone! Check out her SoGod podcast.

~Johanna - your logo making is beyond what a normal business would do! You're inspired by the Lord which takes your work to another level! @theredletterco

~My Salon Vitor family, est. 2006 - whose encouraging words and love each day keep me moving forward, always excited about what's next!

~Secret Sisters, est. 2016 and Fire Starters sisters, est. 2023 - These two groups of women have fallen down on their knees with me and warred until we had the strength to get back up. They have held my arms up in the dark warring places and have celebrated with me as the light of the Lord filled my closets! Joyful praise is what we do daily and they are a cup full of unexplainable blessings! Get yourself some supernatural sisters and go light fires together for Jesus!

~ To my publisher, Arilia and my editor, Roberta (Joyful-One-Editing.com) – thank you. God positioned you both in ways you may never fully realize. You didn't just help me finish a book—you helped me carry through a calling. Your obedience, even in your own personal storms, helped bring to life the vision my Creator gave me. You are both answers to prayers I didn't even know how to pray. It truly takes the body of Christ–many members with different gifts, working together in unity to reveal His glory.

~ To El Elyon, God Most High – this book is yours. Every word, every page, every word spoken aloud belongs to You. May it point hearts back to the One who formed them, called them, and named them with purpose. You are the Author of life, the Redeemer of stories, and the only One worthy of all glory. May Your name be magnified in every celebration, every heart, and every generation that touches this book.

This book is a testimony to God's perfect timing. When I felt like things were falling apart, God was actually aligning hearts, gifts, and timing with His divine will. Every delay was mercy. Every detour, His grace. And when I felt disappointment, it was truly God making room for something better than I, myself, could imagine.

"Just as the body, though one has many parts, but all its many parts form one body, so it is with Christ" (1 Corinthians 12:12 NIV).

"The Lord will perfect that which concerns me; Your mercy, O Lord, endures forever; Do not forsake the work of your hands" (Psalm 138:8 NKJV).

Hallelujah—all praise to YHWH.

ABOUT THE AUTHOR

Trina Angeles is passionate about her heavenly Father. She is a devoted wife, loving mother, and Nana to her two grandsons. With her heart to serve others, she has spent years behind the chair as a skilled hairstylist and successful salon co-owner. As she serves her clients in their hair needs she also serves the Lord spiritually by speaking life into them.

Beyond her professional expertise, Trina Angeles lives in California, she's a dedicated evangelist, giver, and invited speaker. She uses her platform to share the transformative truth of God's love. Her undeniable faith and commitment to spreading the Gospel of Jesus has touched countless lives; within her community and beyond.

As a first-time author, Trina Angeles combines her life experiences and spiritual insights to inspire and uplift others in their identity through Christ Jesus. Exemplifying the unique calling God has placed not only on her life but on all those she encounters.